# DECADENCE AND CATHOLICISM

# Decadence
# and
# Catholicism

Ellis Hanson

HARVARD UNIVERSITY PRESS

Cambridge, Massachusetts
London, England
1997

*Publication of this book was aided by the Hull Memorial Publication Fund
of Cornell University.*

**Library of Congress Cataloging-in-Publication Data**
Hanson, Ellis, 1965–
Decadence and Catholicism / Ellis Hanson.
p.  cm.
Includes bibliographical references and index.
ISBN 0-674-19444-6 (alk. paper). — ISBN 0-674-19446-2 (pbk. : alk. paper)
1. Decadence (Literary movement)  2. Literature, Modern—19th century—History and
criticism.  3. Religion and literature.  4. Catholics in literature.  I. Title.
PN56.D45H36  1997
840.9'11—dc21      97-20127

*To d.*
*"Chantons ses louanges."*

—Paul Verlaine

# ACKNOWLEDGMENTS

I would like to thank those friends who have read individual chapters of this book in manuscript form and offered their comments or recommendations, namely Diana Fuss, Eve Kosofsky Sedgwick, Jonathan Arac, Lindsay Waters, Charles Bernheimer, Michael Cadden, Deborah Nord, and Lawrence Danson. I am especially grateful to U. C. Knoepflmacher and Elaine Showalter for their friendship and their critical attention to my prose throughout the writing of this book.

I would also like to acknowledge the assistance of the National Library of Scotland, the Victoria and Albert Museum, the Armand Hammer Museum of Art, the Staatliche Kunsthalle (Karlsruhe), the Wellcome Centre for Medical Science, the Hull Memorial Publication Fund of Cornell University, and research funding offered by the Princeton University Department of English.

# CONTENTS

# Contents

# ILLUSTRATIONS

# Introduction

The divine world is contagious and its contagion is dangerous.

Georges Bataille

To know one's god as in itself it really is has been justly said to be the true aim of religion; and in religious criticism the first step toward seeing one's god as it really is is to know one's own impression as it really is, to discriminate it, to realize it distinctly. *Decadence and Catholicism* is a study of such religious impressions among the so-called decadent or symbolist writers of the late nineteenth century. In particular, this book examines the intersections of Christian, aesthetic, and erotic discourses in the works of J.-K. Huysmans, Walter Pater, and Oscar Wilde, among others. But what is meant by the term *decadence*? In what way is Catholicism decadent or decadent writing Catholic? Are not the religious, the aesthetic, and the erotic three entirely distinct categories of experience that should not be confused?

Many attempts have been made by critics of art and poetry to define *decadence* in the abstract, to express it in the most general terms, to find some universal formula for it. The value of these critical efforts has most often been in the suggestive and penetrating things said by the way. As we might suspect, given the sense of uncertainty and imminent collapse that is associated with the word, the task of defining it may well be doomed from the start. Nevertheless, I find that the word has considerable force and value, despite its vagueness and historical shortcomings. I do not wish to dispose of such a resonant term, as Richard Gilman would have us do in his book on the subject. "For 'decadence,' the word," he writes, "is an epithet, neither more nor less, and this should alert us at least to the possibility that there is nothing to which it actually and legitimately applies."[1] Unfortunately, the same

1

may be said of a great many literary-historical terms. Words like "Victorian" or "modernist" or "impressionist" have not always been spoken with great kindness, and all such terms, whether they are epithets or not, are categorical conveniences that wince under close inspection. Nevertheless, in a literary context, the word *decadence* is wonderfully suggestive of the fin de siècle fascination with cultural degeneration, the persistent and highly influential myth that religion, sexuality, art, even language itself, had fallen at last into an inevitable decay. The word conjures, if not a coherent movement, then a few choice books whose thematic and stylistic preoccupations are strikingly similar: Charles Baudelaire's *Les Fleurs du Mal,* J.-K. Huysmans' *A Rebours,* Rachilde's *Monsieur Vénus,* the conclusion to Walter Pater's book on the Renaissance, Oscar Wilde's *Salomé* and *The Picture of Dorian Gray,* George Moore's *Confessions of a Young Man*—there are many others. Of course, not everything these particular writers produced would qualify as decadent. Huysmans' early work, for example, is naturalistic after the fashion of his mentor, Emile Zola, as are a number of Moore's novels. Some of the writers who typified the decadent style, such as Paul Verlaine and Huysmans, resisted the label, especially when they recognized the vulgarity of their imitators.

The literary category of decadence is somewhat vague and heterogeneous. It overlaps both stylistically and historically with naturalism, romanticism, aestheticism, Pre-Raphaelitism, symbolism, impressionism, and modernism.[2] I define decadence as a late-romantic movement in art and literature that raised the aesthetic dictum of "art for art's sake" to the status of a cult, especially in the final decades of the nineteenth century. Decadent style is characterized by an elaborate, highly artificial, highly ornamented, often tortuous style; it delights in strange and obscure words, sumptuous exoticism, exquisite sensations, and improbable juxtapositions; it is fraught with disruption, fragmentation, and paradox; it has a tendency to vague and mystical language, a longing to wring from words an enigmatic symbolism or a perverse irony. Decadent writing is also commonly defined by its thematic preoccupation with art—not only literature and painting, but also masquerade, cosmetics, and the sartorial and epigrammatic flamboyance of the dandy. Even nature itself is exposed as a work of art, as in Wilde's brilliant contention that London fogs were invented by Turner.

Most notoriously, the decadents cultivated a fascination with all that was commonly perceived as unnatural or degenerate, with sexual perversity, nervous illness, crime, and disease, all presented in a highly aestheticized context calculated to subvert or, at any rate, to shock conventional morality. Both stylistically and thematically, decadence is an aesthetic in which failure and decay are regarded as seductive, mystical, or beautiful. Decadent art, as typified by the work of Gustave Moreau, Félicien Rops, Odilon Redon, and Aubrey Beardsley, is usually elegant, dreamlike, and bizarre, and it is more often than not an illustration for a decadent book. As for decadent music, there is Wagner, or more precisely the cult of Wagner, a widespread enthusiasm for his great romantic arias of shame and expiation, myth and the twilight of the gods. Decadent poetry, at its most perfect in Baudelaire and Verlaine, is often a maudlin affair that traces the more esoteric sensations of art, desire, and mysticism. The decadent novel is more likely to resemble a volume of art criticism or a book of sketches, since it usually eschews anything like a plot, wandering off into aesthetic meditations or clever conversations. The typical decadent hero is, with a few exceptions, an upper-class, overly educated, impeccably dressed aesthete, a man whose masculinity is confounded by his tendency to androgyny, homosexuality, masochism, mysticism, or neurosis. Whether it be Huysmans' jaded aristocrat Des Esseintes or Pater's epicurean Marius or Wilde's dandy Lord Henry, this decadent hero is a scholar of wondrous obscurities, a collector of objets d'art, and a connoisseur of brilliant sensations.

Baudelaire wrote one of the earliest and most imaginative definitions of decadent literature in one of his essays on Edgar Allan Poe, who merits a peculiar place of his own in the decadent canon. Baudelaire's definition is not only thematically but also stylistically decadent:

The phrase "literature of decadence" implies there is a scale of literatures, a literature in infancy, a literature in childhood, in adolescence, etc. I mean that the term supposes a fatal and providential process, like some inescapable decree; and it is altogether unjust to reproach us for accomplishing the mysterious law . . . That sun which, a few hours ago, was crushing everything beneath the weight of its vertical white light will soon be flooding the occidental horizon with varied colors. In the tricks of this dying sun, certain poetic minds will find new joys; they will discover dazzling colonnades, cascades of molten metal, a paradise of fire, a sad splendor, a rapture of regret, all the magic of dreams, all the memories of opium. And the sunset will then appear to them as the marvelous allegory of a soul charged with life, going down beyond the horizon with a magnificent wealth of thoughts and dreams.[3]

All the stigmata of the decadents are here: a twilight world languidly degenerating toward evening, a senescence enervated by the opiate of its own imagination, the splendor of empires in decline; and perhaps most curious amid this magnificent furniture of dream and decay is the "marvelous allegory of a soul"—we might even say the marvelous allegory that is the soul—a discordant note of spirituality. In the course of the essay, Baudelaire draws out this strange note, developing it into a motif, discovering in the perversity of Poe a spiritual aspiration that resounds through the prose of the decadents:

Our unquenchable thirst for all that lies beyond, and that life reveals, is the liveliest proof of our immortality. It is both by poetry and *through* poetry, by music and *through* music, that the soul glimpses the splendors beyond the tomb; and when an exquisite poem brings tears to our eyes, those tears are not the proof of an excess of bliss; they bear witness rather to an aggravated melancholy, an appeal from our nerves, our nature exiled in imperfection, which desires to enter into immediate possession, while still on this earth, of a revealed paradise. (334)

Desires to enter, of course, but probably never does. The decadent is addicted to his own longing, his desire to desire without respite. Baudelaire found this particular passage to be so fine an expression of his own spiritualized aestheticism that he repeated it word for word in his essay on the great theorist of "art for art's sake" Théophile Gautier. In decadent writing, as in certain romantic poets, melancholy acquires a mystical significance that should be familiar to us from the rhetoric of the Church. The splendors beyond the tomb acquire an aura of spiritual grandeur only when likened to the sort of aristocratic opulence that was becoming increasingly anachronistic in the nineteenth century. Beauty and belief were endowed with the aura of the elect, but that aura was nevertheless in decline on the Western horizon.

Roman Catholicism is central to both the stylistic peculiarities and the thematic preoccupations of the decadents. When they defined their own styles, whether they spoke of aestheticism, symbolism, euphuism, or mystical realism, the decadents often emphasized Christianity and the spiritual quality of language. In the preface to *A Rebours,* the novel that was referred to by Arthur Symons as the "breviary of decadence," Huysmans defines his conversion to decadence as an essentially Roman Catholic revolt against the materialism of the age. Furthermore, in the opening chapter of *Là-Bas,* he finds in Grünewald's painting of the Crucifixion an occasion to define his own style, and he coins a brilliant oxymoron, "spiritual naturalism," to describe how he has rendered visionary the psychological realism of Zola. Huysmans and Pater both returned to the peculiarities of the so-called Latin decadence—not only Petronius and Apuleius, but also early Christians such as Tertullian and Saint Cyprian—as a mirror for modern decadence. In *De Profundis,* Oscar Wilde finds in Christ the very ideal of the romantic artist, a sexually ambiguous individualist and aesthete much like himself.

One of the earliest and most influential efforts at defining decadence was Arthur Symons's essay "The Decadent Movement in Literature." Although later critics would trivialize or dismiss the Catholicism of the decadents, Symons finds in their work a genuinely religious symbolism. For example, in Villiers de L'Isle-Adam he sees the Church as a "symbol of austere intellectual beauty," while in Verlaine he observes "the love of God is not merely a rapture, it is a thanksgiving for forgiveness." Glancing over the entire movement, he remarks that "after the world has starved its soul long enough in the contemplation and the rearrangement of material things, comes the turn of the soul; and with it comes the literature of which I write in this volume, a literature in which the visible world is no longer a reality, and the unseen world no longer a dream."[4]

This mystical dimension has always been an element of romantic literature, though the decadents introduced a taste for all that is sumptuous, brutal, and bizarre in Christian traditions. It has been said that romanticism is a spilt religion. For this phrase to have any force, we have to imagine a religion that is immutably placid and upright, self-contained and categorically pure—and this is a commonplace illusion that I no longer feel obliged to accept. In decadence, we might find art as a spilt religion, but we also discover a far more intriguing possibility: religion as a spilt art. At any rate, we cannot read decadent writing on Catholicism without feeling a trifle *moist*. The categories of religion, art, and sexuality, so pure in the abstract, are in practice always already overturned, a little tipsy, forever spilling onto one another, and the decadents were never the sort to cover up a stain.

The Church is itself a beautiful and erotic work of art, a thing jeweled over like the tortoise that expires under the weight of its own gem-encrusted carapace in *A Rebours*. It is like a great museum in its solemn respect for art and its extraordinary accumulation of dead and beautiful things. It is a relic of itself, and like all saintly relics it commands devotion. The sheer excess of the Church—its archaic splendor, the weight of its history, the elaborate embroidery of its robes, the labyrinthine mysteries of its symbolism, the elephantine exquisiteness by which it performs its daily miracles—has always made it an aesthetic and fetishistic object of wonder. The decadents had much to say about the gothic and Byzantine architecture of the great cathedrals, not to mention the sumptuousness of church vestments, chalices, altars, even the symbolic grandeur of the Mass itself. Huysmans devoted an entire book to Notre-Dame de Chartres, while Pater admired the archaic charm of Notre-Dame d'Amiens. The sheer sensuality of its ritual, whether Anglo or Roman Catholic, exposed the Church to accusations of paganism, even hedonism, rendering it the ideal stage for the subversive gestures of the Catholic dandy.

The decadents were transfixed by the textual *bizarrerie* of Catholicism. Some of them were ardent scholars of Church history, and they reproduced in their own work the obscure debates of theologians, the sublime eroticism of the mystics, the very leap of faith that every Christian genre ultimately demands. Martyrdom and hagiography were cause for considerable speculation. Huysmans rendered Blessed Lydwina a religious grotesque, Pater admired Saint Cecilia as a new Demeter, and John Gray found in Saint Sebastian and Saint John of the Cross a homoerotic iconography to ornament his own journey to the priesthood.

Although the decadents spoke at length about Plato and Petronius, the Bible was the one "fatal book" that never ceased to fascinate them. The women of the Bible were especially popular as icons of religious paradox and perversity—not only Eve and the Blessed Virgin, but the countless Salomés of the fin de siècle, Mary Magdalene as she appears in Wilde's *De Profundis,* Esther as she is macerated in oils and rolled in powders in Huysmans' *En Rade.* But the very style of the Bible can, in some of its books, be described as decadent, especially the Canticles and Apocalypse, with their erotic spectacles, their strange profusion of symbols, their demonization of nature, and their mesmerizing repetitions. Even decadent satanism, when not simply laughable, belies a paradoxical piety, since it is a mystical indulgence in evil and abjection that would be sheer nonsense apart from the moral authority of the Church. T. S. Eliot, by no means a sympathetic reader of the decadents, made the point a long time ago when he remarked that the satanism of Baudelaire is an attempt to enter Christianity by the back door: "In the middle nineteenth century, . . . an age of bustle, programmes, platforms, scientific progress, humanitarianism and revolutions which improved nothing, an age of progressive degradation, Baudelaire perceived that what really matters is Sin and Redemption."[5]

Catholicism is itself an elaborate paradox. The decadents merely emphasized the point within their own aesthetic of paradox. The Church is at once modern and yet medieval, ascetic and yet sumptuous, spiritual and yet sensual, chaste and yet erotic, homophobic and yet homoerotic, suspicious of aestheticism and yet an elaborate work of art. For English decadents Christianity was the last hope of paganism in the modern world. In the Crucifixion they found the suffering of a great criminal and individualist. In the Catholic universe of Wagner's *Tannhäuser* and *Parsifal,* they found redemption reconfigured as an aria. They discovered grace in the depths of shame and sainthood in the heart of the sinner. In chastity and the priesthood they found a spiritualization of desire, a rebellion against nature and the instincts, and a polymorphous redistribution of pleasure in the body. In the elaborate stagecraft of ritualism they celebrated the effeminate effusions and subversions of the dandy. Under the cowl of monasticism was a cult of homoerotic community. In the ecstatic utterance of mysticism was an intensification of desire and a hysterical fragmentation of language. Within the industrial sprawl of modern Paris and London were gothic churches that stimulated the imagination with medieval dreams of a violent faith. Christianity presented itself as the primary source of modern morality, and yet for many, especially in England, Roman Catholicism was regarded as a scandal.

Throughout the fin de siècle, Catholicism and decadent literature were often condemned in much the same terms by a great many writers for a wide variety of reasons. At least since the Tudors, there had been a fierce and lively tradition of puritan anti-Catholicism in England. This prejudice was especially severe between 1850 and 1890, when the Roman Catholic Church was re-establishing its hierarchy in England. Victorian Evangelicals were outraged by the introduction of Roman rituals into the Anglican service. They regarded auricular confession as lascivious and elaborate vestments as effeminate, and they were wont to liken the Catholic Church itself to the whore of Babylon—an irony that delighted Wilde. Since the Enlightenment, there had also been a scientific condemnation of Christianity and every other religion as an assault on reason and a hindrance to human progress. During the Third Republic, French anticlericalism was especially vehement, for the Church was justly regarded as a reactionary threat to democracy and science. The pre-eminent French psychologist Jean-Martin Charcot diagnosed early modern mystics as hysterics. Karl Marx declared religion to be an insidious opiate of the masses, while Charles Darwin effectively replaced the biblical myth of human genesis with his own theory of evolution. Although Friedrich Nietzsche proclaimed that God is dead, it is evident from his own writing that God was in fact *undead,* an effete and aristocratic vampire, risen from the grave in a curious resurrection, a Catholic revival that was sweeping northern Europe. Nietzsche uses the word *décadent* over and over—in French, no less—to describe Christianity as the epitome of all that is weak, archaic, and irrational in modern civilization. "The Christian and the anarchist are both decadents," he writes in *The Antichrist;* "they are both incapable of acting in any other way than disintegratingly, poisonously and witheringly, like *blood-suckers . . .* Christianity was the vampire of the *imperium Romanum.*"[6]

In his influential book *Entartung* (swiftly translated into English as *Degeneration*), Max Nordau condemned virtually all the great writers of his time as neo-Catholic hysterics—including Wagner, Baudelaire, Verlaine, and Huysmans. Octave Mirbeau's libertine narratives and tortuous syntax have qualified him for the label of decadent, but he is also a master of anticlerical propaganda who railed against the cultural degeneration of the age. In his novel *Sébastien Roch,* for example, little Sébastien is abandoned to the care of a Jesuit school for upper-class boys, where he is seduced and abused by his rather mystical confessor, Father de Kern. In *L'Abbé Jules* Mirbeau seeks to confirm our worst fears of the Catholic priest as libertine. Jules is a parody of decadent Catholicism, a pure sensualist who finds in the Church a model for weakness and evil. The confessional is for him an incitement to obscenity, hagiography a disguise for masochism, the priesthood an opportunity to exercise sadistic authority over others. "On all sides," Mirbeau writes, "society is cracking, religion collapsing, everything falling apart. At the top, on the throne, lolls shameless orgy, orgy made law."[7]

On a similar note, in his novel *Rome,* another anticlerical tome, Emile Zola depicts Pope Leo XIII as an aging and ineffectual figurehead with an "emaciated face of old diaphanous ivory" who is overwhelmed by the sumptuous paganism of the Vatican.[8] Although he is not very good at it, Zola lapses into a decadent rhetoric of sensuality, offering an elaborate catalog of Greek statuary, Renaissance paintings, and rich ecclesiastical vestments: "Ah! that Pope, that old man strolling with his Divinity of grief, humility, and renunciation along the paths of those gardens of love, in the languid evenings of the hot summer days, beneath the caressing scents of pine and eucalyptus, ripe oranges, and tall, acrid box-shrubs! The whole atmosphere around him proclaimed the powers of the great god Pan" (311–312). Here, the Church is in decline, its religious gestures and genuflections have experienced a crisis in meaning. With its temporal power and authority seriously challenged, the language of the Church suffered a fall from a transcendent symbolism to something more like the symbolism of Maeterlinck and Mallarmé—uncertain, atmospheric, sensual, a bit neurotic. The hero of Zola's novel has an almost cosmic sensation of the Vatican's impending ruin, even amid a modern-day Catholic celebration: "But even in that hour of the papacy's triumph he already felt that the giant of gold and marble on which he stood was oscillating, even as totter all old and rotten societies" (372). In short, the decadents did not invent decadent Catholicism, they simply embraced it where they found it. They were the culmination and the ironic reversal of an already popular tradition that regarded the Church as a decaying empire. Instead of writing anticlerical tirades, they drew from the mysticism and archaic strangeness of the Church a romantic ideal.

At least since Chateaubriand, romantic writers of every stripe had found in Christianity a poetic cult of the imagination, the unseen captured in a dream of form, an assertion of the spiritual quality of beauty in an age of rationalism and vulgar materialism. The decadents are at once the climax and the exhaustion of this romantic tradition. In their lives, no less than in their art, they enacted the romance of faith as a tenuous possibility for modernity—a proposition at once beautiful and improbable. The mind of this modernity is, in decadent writing, cluttered with contradictory ideas, weighed down with a tangle of histories, sharpened and distracted by neurosis; and in this mind the Church is at once endangered and dangerous. It has a malady and is a malady at the same time. When not merely nostalgic, the decadent view of faith revealed the Church—and indeed the concept of beauty itself—as an empire in its decline, an archaic daydream of an effete aristocracy demystified by the forces of industrialization, socialism, democracy, evolutionary theory, psychology, anthropology, and comparative religion. "Je suis l'Empire à la fin de la décadence," Verlaine writes in his poem "Langueur," connecting his own poetic ennui with the Latin decadence; but he might also have been speaking of his faith, as he gave it form in *Sagesse* and his other religious volumes. Decadent Catholicism is the assertion of faith as a work of art in an age when one ought to know better. Catholicism is embraced even as it falls to pieces.

The decadents were at times enamored of Christ, but they were also enamored of his persistent twilight, his gem-like flame like a pane of stained glass, amethyst and cool as it died out, flickered with a wondrous luminescence, then died out again in the modern mind. Decadent writing is often a literature of Christian conversion, but a conversion that never ends, a continual flux of religious sensations and insights alternating with pangs of profanity and doubt. All the great works of decadent literature are conversion narratives. Verlaine's passage from *Romances sans Paroles* to *Sagesse* to *Parallèlement* to *Amour* follows his own conversions from the profane to the pious and back again, as does Huysmans' passage from *A Rebours* to *En Route*. *A Rebours* itself ends with the desperate prayer of Des Esseintes, in whose mystical idiosyncrasies Huysmans captured the first glimmerings of his own faith. *Là-Bas* is also a conversion narrative in that it contains an account of the repentance of the medieval satanist Gilles de Rais. Pater's *Marius the Epicurean* offers a series of conversions through a number of antique philosophies and culminates in a tenuous embrace of Christianity. Even Dorian Gray contemplates conversion during a somber celebration of the Mass—an uncanny premonition of Wilde's own deathbed drama of submission to the Church.

No other literary movement can claim so many converts to Rome. The most famous, and certainly the most influential, of decadent conversions was that of Huysmans. Having lost the faith of his childhood, he established his literary reputation as a naturalist and materialist. In the 1880s, however, he grew dissatisfied with what he saw as the mechanistic psychologism of Zola and Charcot, and he developed what came to be known as a decadent style in an effort to define the spiritual and mystical aspirations of literature. The perverse eroticism and hysterical mysticism of books like *A Rebours* and *Là-Bas* gave him a certain notoriety, and so his conversion in 1892 was greeted with considerable surprise. After his conversion, Huysmans wrote a string of autobiographical fictions, his so-called Catholic novels, that further trace the development of his religious opinions. Some of the Catholic novels actually sold more copies than *A Rebours,* and they apparently incited a number of conversions among his readers. Eventually, he became a Benedictine oblate, a person associated with a monastery but not bound by the same vows as the monks. Beginning with *En Route,* he replaces the explicit eroticism of his earlier work with an equally bizarre and violent mysticism. Although the style is somewhat more tame, it is still highly idiosyncratic and decadent. As Arthur Symons quipped, "His style is always the same, whether he writes of a butcher's shop or of a stained window."[9]

Huysmans' conversion may have come as a surprise to some, but he himself traced its beginnings to the publication of *A Rebours* and his conversion to decadent style. In fact, a few of the decadent or proto-decadent writers who merit distinction in Des Esseintes's library were also converts. Barbey d'Aurevilly, whose *Un Prêtre Marié* and *Les Diaboliques* garner praise from Des Esseintes, underwent two conversions to Catholicism, the first in 1846 and the second in 1855. He was also the outspoken editor of the *Revue du Monde Catholique* and a radical Catholic who was not afraid to challenge Church authorities.

The eroticism and occultism of his novels led many to question the orthodoxy of his faith, but he vociferously defended himself by declaring that Catholic literature need not be bloodless and ignorant of evil in order to be pious. Villiers de L'Isle-Adam, another proto-decadent figure championed by Huysmans, was also a convert late in life and, after 1885, even returned to his earlier work to censor some of its more occult and nihilistic passages. Paul Verlaine, lionized by Huysmans as the only great Catholic poet of his time, also underwent a conversion while serving a prison sentence for shooting his lover, Arthur Rimbaud, who was himself a deathbed convert. "I am Catholic," Verlaine told Symons, "but . . . a Catholic of the Middle Ages!"(98). Like Huysmans, he wrote of a profound longing for the mystical faith he found in medieval literature. He did indeed write some of the finest religious poetry in the French language, the best of it appearing in two volumes, *Sagesse* and *Amour.* Verlaine oscillated between extremes of shame and grace, sexual indulgence and extreme piety, re-enacting his conversion over and over again in a Christian narrative of sin and redemption.

Conversions were no less commonplace among the English decadents. Oscar Wilde's is perhaps the most famous and, for that matter, the least probable. He was inclined toward conversion a number of times during his life. His mother apparently had him baptized in the Church when he was a child, but Wilde also contemplated conversion at Oxford in the 1870s and again somewhat later. His most profound engagement with Christianity occurred during his prison term and during his exile on the Continent, where he became, as he put it, a violent papist. He finally converted on his deathbed, although by that time he is thought to have been virtually unconscious. Walter Pater is also the focus of this study, even though he never underwent a formal conversion. Many of his friends actually suspected he would convert, especially since he was fond of attending ritualistic services. Many of the figures in his books are converts—Montaigne, Pascal, and Ronsard, among them, and also Marius, after a fashion. George Moore also wrote about conversion but did not himself convert. For example, two of his novels, *Evelyn Innes* and *Sister Teresa,* document the conversion of a Wagnerian diva and her life as a nun.

Lionel Johnson was one of the more pious converts in Wilde's circle. His reputation as a repressed homosexual and alcoholic has overshadowed his Catholicism, but he wrote religious poetry and was an avid theological scholar. Like his French contemporaries, he was especially adept at the poetics of shame, and a number of his religious verses are tinged with the melancholy of sexual guilt. Johnson is also said to have instigated the conversion of Ernest Dowson, who also regarded Catholicism as an escape from desire, however unlikely the prospect. Aubrey Beardsley converted around the time of his death, while Lord Alfred Douglas, after years of flaunting his sins, converted in 1911. Douglas's life offers the best argument for conversion as a flight from decadence, since he spent the rest of his years publishing his regrets about the errors of his youth.

John Gray presents a rather different picture. He began his literary career as a disciple, possibly even a lover, of Oscar Wilde, and in 1893 he published *Silverpoints,* a famous though slight volume of decadent poetry. By this time he had already undergone a conversion to Catholicism, but he claimed to have entered upon a "course of sin" of the sort that recalls Verlaine, some of whose poems he translated. After what appears to be a nervous breakdown, he entered a seminary, the Scot's College at Rome, and he eventually became a Roman Catholic priest in Edinburgh. Although he lived a life of studied reserve as a priest, he was engaged for most of his life in a presumably chaste romantic friendship with a poet and theorist of sexual inversion, André Raffalovich, who also converted. In his book *Uranisme et Unisexualité,* Raffalovich defined his notion of "sublime" inversion, a highly sublimated, even saintly, homosexuality that he hoped would excite sympathy for people who were so inclined. John Gray clearly exploited this notion in the "spiritual poems" he published throughout the 1890s. These were mystical verses written in a decadent style—richly ornamented effusions about Saint Francis, Saint John of the Cross, Saint Sebastian, and other homoerotic Christian icons.

There were also decadent converts outside Wilde's immediate entourage. Frederick Rolfe, also known as Baron Corvo, converted to Catholicism and even attended the same seminary as John Gray in a failed effort to become a priest. John Francis Bloxam, publisher of *The Chameleon,* the homoerotic Oxford journal used against Wilde at his trials, was also a convert. His notoriously pederastic story "The Priest and the Acolyte" was apparently his last publication before he became an Anglo-Catholic priest. Montague Summers was a convert and a priest, though his biographers have been unable to authenticate his orders. Summers is best known for his critical studies on demonology, the gothic novel, and Restoration theater, but his first publication was a 1907 volume of homoerotic decadent poetry entitled *"Antinous" and Other Poems*. Other important literary converts included Ronald Firbank, E. F. Benson, and Evelyn Waugh, who carried the spirit of Wildean dandyism and aestheticism well into the twentieth century.

Katherine Bradley and her niece Edith Cooper wrote decadent poetry, Catholic poetry, and lesbian love poetry under the pseudonym Michael Field. With the guidance of John Gray, they converted to Catholicism upon the death of their beloved dog Whym Chow. Renée Vivien was a lesbian and a Catholic convert who wrote in the tradition of Swinburne and the French symbolists. She was divided between her love for the pagan Natalie Barney and her highly spiritualized devotion to another Catholic convert, Violet Shiletto. The spirit of Violet, the mystical "violet" that pervades Vivien's lesbian verses, appears to have got the upper hand in the end. The poet converted shortly before her death in 1909.

With this extraordinary migration of French and English decadents toward Rome, we might well wonder why literary criticism on the fin de siècle has never really addressed the phenomenon with any great seriousness, except in biographies of individual figures. Until recently, the decadents have not had many sympathetic critics, though they have had many avid readers. The mixture of elitism, homosexuality, misogyny, satanism, and "art for art's sake" proved, for the most part, lethal in academic circles, and decadence was declared shallow, adolescent, purple, and pathological—a failure rather than an aesthetic of failure. From this perspective, the satanism and occultism of the period made sense, but the decadent tendency to piety and conversion did not. Decadent faith, or the decadent critique of faith, is often trivialized as a mere trend, a cultural aberration, or bad theater. It is said to be a heretical or insincere "perversion" of Catholicism. There is also a redemptive tendency to regard conversion as an antidote to decadence, despite the evidence of decadent style and themes in the post-conversion work of writers such as Verlaine, Huysmans, Johnson, and Gray.

I could cite any number of instances of this critical tradition, but I shall limit myself to a single passage from Jean Pierrot's study *The Decadent Imagination:*

Caught between a diffuse nostalgia for the supernatural and a rejection of orthodox forms of worship, many writers of the time were led to express not so much a genuine religious belief as a sort of emotional and mythical reverie that produced what were often rather bizarre imaginative developments: search for new sensations derived from hitherto unknown mixtures of erotic elements with religious themes or "props"; stimulation of their sensuality by an awareness of doing evil; curiosity with regard to sexual aberrations . . . ; abandonment to mythicoreligious reveries in which, as in Flaubert's *Tentation,* all the heterodox religious speculations accumulated by western culture since Greco-Roman antiquity were regurgitated pell-mell in a great maelstrom of recapitulation.[10]

I think one could make a case for Pierrot's account with respect to writers like Joséphin Péladan or Aleister Crowley, with their comical and pornographic obsession with the occult. The problem with this passage, however, is that it fails to describe the texts or the lives of any of those writers we call decadent and still read. In fact, apart from his alarmingly lame appraisal of Flaubert's book on Saint Antony, he does not seem to be describing what he calls the "literature of the imagination" at all. Surely Flaubert's romances, not to mention Verlaine's *Sagesse* or Huysmans' *En Route,* are of an entirely different order. Few would have difficulty locating passages in the Catholic writings of the decadents that might suggest "genuine religious belief," not to mention a genuine engagement with issues that were central to religious debates of the time. In Pierrot's account, words like "bizarre" and "sensuality" and "reverie" are placed in dubious opposition to terms like "orthodox." He thus creates a theoretical impasse that places decadent Catholicism beyond the scope of his understanding. He seems to regard the Church as something pleasantly sentimental, bourgeois, and dull. Surely, one need only attend a service at the Vatican or the Brompton Oratory or glance through the writings of Saint Alphonsus or Saint Teresa to recognize that there is much in Roman Catholic orthodoxy—its ritual, its theological tradition, its mystical literature—that might reasonably be qualified by terms like *bizarre, sensuality,* and *reverie.*

This critical tendency is, I think, a suggestive one, since it is symptomatic of a high modernist rejection of decadence from which we are only just recovering. For example, T. S. Eliot's appraisal of Walter

Pater reveals the depth of the modernist distaste for the "art for art's sake" sensibility of the preceding generation. Eliot writes that Pater is incapable of sustained reasoning, that his work has nothing to do with the so-called direct current of religious development, and that he confuses aesthetics with religion. An admirable yet questionable insistence upon theological orthodoxy, tradition, and cerebral rigor in religious experience undergirds his remarks. We see it also in Pierrot's reference to "orthodox forms of worship" and "heterodox religious speculations." The overriding concern with some putative orthodoxy posits an ideological center to Roman Catholic discourse, and anyone who writes on Roman Catholic themes but does not somehow acknowledge the essential importance of this center is deemed shallow, incorrect, or aberrant. When I read decadent literature, however, I find a genuine engagement with what I take to be orthodox aspects of Catholicism. I find both a celebration and a critique of Christianity that is insightful and challenging. Huysmans writes about conversion, sin, religious art, Christian mysticism, and monasticism. Pater writes about the nature of ritual, and Wilde about the personality of Christ. Sometimes their tone is pious, sometimes it is not. But if these are not orthodox concerns, what are? That the decadent conception of Catholicism is regarded as trivial leads me to question the concept of orthodoxy that is applied to them.

The view of Catholicism presented in this sort of criticism is highly intellectualized and Pauline. Nevertheless, the perils of the Pauline are many. I am certainly not the first to regard Saint Paul as a highly productive and influential neurotic; indeed, Bishop Spong has recently outed him as a repressed homosexual—a revelation that has caused no end of speculation and distress. It is precisely the neurotic sensibility of Saint Paul that makes him a genius from the point of view of art, if I may be permitted to invoke a fin de siècle connection between madness and creativity. Oscar Wilde was also seduced by Saint Paul, though he found his style unbearable. It is chiefly in the humility and modesty with which the saint mastered his own paradox that we uncover his true charm. He was profoundly offended by both sex and art, since one was merely lust and the other a clever refinement upon lust. His rebellion against nature was so extreme that it was even a rebellion against art. It is, however, in this gesture of asceticism that we glimpse the mark of the neurotic, since his rebellion against sex and art disguises a profound investment in both, an enjoyment of the body and a celebration of the word through a peculiar enactment of their many pleasures. The body and the word return to him in symptomatic form as a mystical reverie or a demonic plot.

A great many theologians enticed the decadents with this paradox. Saint Augustine, for example, tells us in *De Doctrina Christiana* that inflated and ornamental prose is an unforgivable form of sophism, and yet he praises a few passages of figurative language from the Bible that are voluptuous to the point of being silly. He delights in the Canticles, in which the Church is "being praised as a beautiful woman" whose pretty teeth are likened to flocks of particularly fruitful sheep. He claims that, "in a strange way," this flowery language allows him "to contemplate the saints more pleasantly."[11] I could not agree more, but the sentiment sounds in an even stranger way like Oscar Wilde. Augustine's own confessions are memorable precisely because they militate against his habit of rhetorical ascesis. For instance, his parable of the pear tree, with its subtle and homoerotic suggestiveness, renders those inedible pears more inviting in their way than the most nubile pomegranate. Saint Teresa is in the same predicament in her justly famous description of the arrow of God as it sears through her body like a divine phallus. As is Saint Antony, who conjures imaginary fleshpots to dance before his outraged eyes. Anyone who has learned about sexuality from the Bible or the lives of the saints must surely be in for a grave disappointment upon encountering the real thing. Like libertines, Christians must necessarily spice up their scenes of sin, no less than their flights of spiritual eros, lest we think their swooning anything but sublime. There is nothing more decadent than the sensuality of the chaste and the art of the artless.

Nevertheless, in the tradition that we call Pauline, we are asked to appreciate saintly *jouissance* without ever analyzing it. We are obliged to define the spiritual through a turning away from sex and a turning away from art. Any degree of erotic or aesthetic pleasure therefore immediately disqualifies a sensation as heterodox and irrelevant to any serious discussion of Catholicism. In the modernist rejection of decadence, we find this sort of Christian evasion painfully unanalyzed— one of the many ways that modernism failed to be modern. When Pierrot speaks of "hitherto unknown mixtures of erotic elements" or "curiosity with respect to sexual aberrations," the sexual politics of his distaste for decadent spirituality is abundantly clear. He seems to have in mind a sexual orthodoxy as well as a religious one. His language comes straight from modernist psychology that posits a normative heterosexuality and then pathologizes and devalues any deviation from it. Since decadent writing is all about aberrant aesthetics and aberrant sexuality, it logically follows in this argument that it must also be about aberrant religious experiences—and therefore have nothing important to say about orthodox art, orthodox sex, or orthodox religion. Karl Beckson demonstrates many of the same sexual and aesthetic presumptions in his anthology of English aesthetes and decadents. He includes biographical snippets about the various writers he has chosen for the book, and many of them say—with respect to John Gray or Lord Alfred Douglas, for example—that the subject was once a decadent but then became a Roman Catholic, or that he was once a homosexual but then became a Roman Catholic. Are we to assume that decadents and homosexuals are never Catholics?

Underlying these critical assertions is the presumption that aesthetic, erotic, and religious experiences are or ought to be mutually exclusive and categorically pure. One of the great accomplishments of decadent writing, however, was essentially to deconstruct that presumption—to question it, to subvert it, to rehearse its contradictions, even at times to ridicule it. The decadents found that the Church was, and had always been, as sensual as it was spiritual, as pagan as it was Christian, as textual as it was transcendent. They began with the one great conflict, the great paradox at the heart of Christianity, the always already transgressed boundary between spirit and flesh, the Word of God and the words of humankind. This highly improbable and unstable dichotomy is the engine behind the narrative of sin and redemption, a story without an end (not on earth, anyway). The literature of decadent Catholicism is the documentation of a border war that the Church has lost in modern times—that is, the battle to maintain the paradox as such, to maintain the distinction between the spirit and the flesh, the Word and mere words. Decadent writing exposes the sexual and aesthetic dimension of Catholicism, but never in the manner of an anticlerical tirade. It raises the possibility of a purely performative and textual foundation for faith, the possibility of religion as the most spiritualized form of aestheticism. By this remark I do not mean to suggest the critical cliché—and it is a cliché in dire need of retirement—of art as a substitute for religion, but rather art as an incitement to religion. There is a difference. The first is atheistic, and the second is usually not atheistic. Indeed, for many a decadent the fascination of aestheticism was no less spiritual than the fascination of the Church; and through the performative magic of conversion, this interpenetration of aestheticism, desire, and Catholicism was sublated into a genuine, if imperiled, vocation.

It is for this reason that I speak of art, eroticism, and religion as *discourses*. I speak of them as textual phenomena that can intersect, overlap, even become interdependent and indistinguishable. In speaking of religious discourses, I am drawing upon poststructural notions of textuality, of ideologies as heterogeneous texts—impure, unstable, constantly in flux according to the vagaries of social practice. Religious discourses function differently, they mean differently, in different contexts, according to the social and political and cultural purposes they serve. This much, I hope, is obvious. But this indeterminacy renders suspect, if not wholly untenable, the very concept of religious orthodoxy. The capacity of orthodoxy to say what it means and to mean what it says is placed in doubt.

Roman Catholic discourse generates important meanings far in excess of the conscious intentions of doctrinal authorities, who are themselves in a constant state of flux, of self-contradiction and political negotiation. To enter the morass of theological speculation as though awaiting some divine revelation of the truth is for the most part a distraction, though, like most distractions, it has its charms. Christianity has no essential content of its own. Theology does not reveal the meanings of Christianity: it produces them. The meanings of Christianity inhere in the social practices of people identified as Catholics, and the process of that identification is always fiercely political and uncertain. In the context of this book, a discursive approach to religion allows me to place my emphasis on decadent writing rather than on prevailing presumptions about Catholic orthodoxy that I, no less than the decadents themselves, am wont to find misleading or naive.

I also speak of discourses because I am primarily concerned with the language and the artistry of Roman Catholicism—by which I do not mean that faith and God are irrelevant, but quite the opposite. I am concerned in this study with what Kenneth Burke has called the "rhetoric of religion," the way Catholicism has functioned historically as language, as text or work of art. Burke begins his book on religious rhetoric with a chapter called "On Words and The Word," cutting straight to the key paradox. "Whether or not there is a realm of the 'supernatural,'" he writes, "there are *words* for it."[12] In the context of decadent literature, this sentence can only be read as a tragedy or a triumph. Baudelaire prefigured Burke's remark when he wrote in *Fusées* that even if God did not exist, religion would still be holy and divine. Where do we search for God's holiness, his divinity, if not in the poetry of religion, the very articulation of God as such? We are in terrestrial exile from a "supernatural" realm that is made available to us only through the symbol; indeed, there may be no difference at all between the Word and mere words.

In any case, we are left with language, which is notoriously slippery and arbitrary, not at any rate a reliable tool for grasping the ineffable, however subtle it may be in constructing it. The pope may well be infallible, but the words he uses are decidedly not. His words, our words, the words of the Bible where Jesus speaks in red—all are subject to interpretation, to different traditions of interpretation, to a dissemination of meanings that is difficult, if not impossible, to contain. As the decadents knew, civilization invites the piling up of traditions, of interpretations, in an often contradictory, incoherent, yet sublime mountain of doctrinal textuality that, as Freud points out in *The Future of an Illusion,* exercises a certain fascination and authority if only by virtue of its bulk. The flux of history, the vicissitudes of desire, and the metamorphoses of language and religious practice render this great mountain of words and gestures, this discourse of Roman Catholicism, unstable. In its search for orthodoxy amid this chaos, theology is ever lapsing into propaganda and poetry. We might well ask if God is possible without theology; but then we might well ask if God is possible with theology. There is a good reason why poststructural theorists have turned to decadent and symbolist literature, to Baudelaire, Mallarmé, or Wilde, in order to discuss the play of the signifier, the unlikelihood of transcendence, and the tendency of life to imitate art. As an aesthetic of failure, as a celebration of the decay of language itself, decadent writing can make us peculiarly sensitive to the failed idealism of Catholic discourse and the precariousness of its many efforts at weaving words into revelations and binding language into dogma. I have my doubts about whether the

Church, or any spiritual authority, is ever really capable of saying what it means or meaning what it says. Moreover, such authorities, despite their pretensions to the contrary, cannot help but to produce spirituality as a fleeting effect of style every time they ascend to the pulpit or apply the nib to the page.

The divine contagion that is religion is traceable in part to the viral quality of language itself, always in motion, corroding our every defense, and inevitably contaminating its putative referent with its peculiar and alien inflection. Oddly, the very word *inflection* seems to carry infection in its very utterance. The Church is always at the mercy of language in the sense that the word is the paradoxical precursor of the Word, whose very transcendence is a symptom of its contamination. How, after all, is the transcendent nature of God made known? How does the Church make its fascination palpable? Inevitably, the answer is through language, through the symbol, through the brilliant lie that is great art.

Sexuality, or more precisely the art of sexuality, is also part of the answer. Eroticism, however "perverse" or "aberrant," is what renders the decadent discourse of Catholicism extraordinary, not shallow. In juxtaposing the sexual and the Christian, one always risks appearing farcical and disrespectful, but this is by no means my intention. I do find, however, that this tendency to find religious eroticism comical or scandalous is instructive, for we are most eager to make a joke of those difficult truths that everyone knows but no one really wants to believe. Erotic mysticism—the masochist, for example, with a passion for the Blessed Virgin—is comical or scandalous not because it is heretical, but because it is not. The enormous popularity of Roman Catholic iconography among masochists and fetishists intrigues me because it demonstrates not only how sexuality exploits religion but also how religion exploits sexuality.

The writers in this study realized that no matter how much the Church might deny it, no matter how much good Christians might rebel against it, sexual pleasure is an important element of virtually every religious experience. After Freud, this point comes as no surprise to us, or at any rate it should not. But in the 1890s the psychology of religious experience was something radical and new. Even before it became commonplace to do so, the decadents explored with considerable daring the relationship between sexuality and religion. Roman

Сholicism has always been founded on a peculiar organization of sexuality, a certain deployment of sexual secrets and revelations, a system of repression, punishment, confession, sublimation, displacement, and fetishization. As we might infer from the myriad psychoanalytic examinations of mysticism, of the spectacle of virgin motherhood or Christ's passion or Saint Sebastian run through with arrows, this libidinal organization might well be described as perverse. To be a good Catholic, to submit oneself body and soul to the Church, is to have what in a more fashionable parlance would be described as an "alternative sexuality." The Catholic lifestyle, from the early Church fathers to the present day, has prided itself on its improbability, its blatant disregard for the demands of nature and common sense; and it is in part for this reason that Rome continues to exercise an extraordinary influence over people of genius.

To speak of Catholic sexuality, then, is by no means an oxymoron. I am reminded of Foucault's discussion of the "confessional mode" of modern sexology: society does not repress desire; rather, society exploits it—forces us to confess it, to put it into an appropriate discourse so that it can be managed, manipulated, and contained. His model for this process is, of course, auricular confession, one of the most powerful ideological tools the Church has for policing desire, for rendering it visible and meaningful in specifically Catholic terms. The Church, like the Victorian sexologist, has a categorical passion for talking about sex. It can speak of little else. To read seventeenth- or eighteenth-century casuists—to read Liguori or Sanchez or Dens—on the topic of sex or confession is like reading Krafft-Ebing as he enumerates and classifies all the perversions he has discovered. Indeed, many decadents read both, and Huysmans and Montague Summers were especially explicit in their opinions on the subject. They also read Saint Paul and Saint Teresa, Saint Augustine and Saint John of the Cross, as well as the spicier pages of Christian mysticism over which the Church has always been in a quandary. Admittedly, many decadents toyed with religion and merely burned their fingertips. For example, Rémy de Gourmont—a very Catholic atheist, though not a very subtle writer—sought to unseat rather than to appreciate the Christian tendency to sexual discipline, and indeed one of his books, *La Fantôme*, is little more than an extended pornographic meditation on the pleasures of incense and flagellation. In more sophisticated work, however—in Huysmans' novels or Baudelaire's troubling "flowers of evil"—the decadents captured the essential paradox of Roman Catholic sexuality: they remind us, in their way, that the Church excites and exploits the very desires it claims to disavow.

Decadent sexuality and Roman Catholic sexuality have much in common. When I read Baudelaire on lesbianism or Huysmans on sodomy, I find this point all too evident. They have difficulty construing sexual pleasure in any but Christian terms. There is no such thing as good sex in decadent literature; it is always attended by shame, remorse, disgust, and the occasional bout of syphilis. In fact, there is a very well kept secret about decadent eroticism: it exists, for the most part, only on paper. Verlaine and Wilde are notable exceptions, with their well-documented passion for prostitutes, but even they demanded a certain artistry from sexual experience. We might ask ourselves why so many decadents, like so many Christian mystics, wrote in a highly erotic and sensuous style and yet never described a truly satisfying orgasm. Huysmans, Rolfe, and Gray took vows of chastity, while others, like Pater, Beardsley, and Johnson, might as well have. George Moore even wrote a work of fiction with Catholic overtones called *Celibate Lives,* in which the main characters seek respite from sexuality altogether. In their cult of artifice, the decadents often eschewed sex for the more refined pleasure of writing about it—for the highly erotic pleasures of writing itself. Often, they wrote of the sexual act as a bore, a disappointment, or a disgrace. The more unnatural, the more grotesque, the more like a work of art it was, the better. The ecstasies of art and religion are infinitely superior to the physical spasm of sex because they are a spiritualization and an intensification of desire. Even Wilde would have agreed.

The tendency of the decadents to displace sexuality onto textuality rendered them susceptible to the allure of the Church, in which sexuality was more likely to find articulation in the stylistic excesses of gothic and baroque art than in any genital transgression. The decadent devotion to art was often virtually cenobitic in its sexual continence, no less than in its aesthetic sensibility. Furthermore, there is the question of desire. Many of the decadents, whether they acted upon it or not, were homosexual, and their sexual desire inevitably made a difference in their writing. In fact, decadence was virtually a synonym for sodomy—and I choose that word for all its religious reverberations.

More than any other literary movement, the decadents explored the powerful historical relationship between homoeroticism and Roman Catholicism.

Homophobia is another reason why the decadents have been dismissed and trivialized by generations of literary critics. When I look over the list of decadent converts, I am struck by how many of them were homosexual or bisexual: Verlaine, Pater, Wilde, Douglas, Johnson, Gray, Summers, Rolfe, Field, and Vivien, among others. And yet the question has rarely been asked—why, throughout history, have so many homosexuals been attracted to Christian institutions that vociferously condemn homosexuality? I am reminded of the title of Joanne Glasgow's essay on the Catholic conversion of Radclyffe Hall: "What's a Nice Lesbian Like You Doing in the Church of Torquemada?" Eve Kosofsky Sedgwick offers a very witty answer: "Christianity may be near-ubiquitous in modern European culture as a figure of phobic prohibition, but it makes a strange figure for that indeed. Catholicism in particular is famous for giving countless gay and proto-gay children the shock of the possibility of adults who don't marry, of men in dresses, of passionate theatre, of introspective investment, of lives filled with what could, ideally without diminution, be called the work of the fetish."[13] I might also add that, when those countless gay and proto-gay children grow up, some of them find in the Church what a great many others find there—namely, faith. Some of them also find a vocation, a disguise, a philosophy, a politics, an aesthetic style, or a sense of community. Some find solace and a powerful language through which to cope with guilt, shame, and sorrow—the particular birthright of all those gay and proto-gay children in a homophobic society. Not a few decadent writers made this discovery in the course of their lives. Oscar Wilde, for example, may be popularly regarded as an aesthetic clown, but in *De Profundis* he could be quite moving and eloquent on the subject of sorrow, the pain of homophobic violence, and the consolations of Christ.

It has been said that gay people turn to the Church to hide from their desire, but I suspect that they are searching for a suitable stage on which to perform it. Homosexuality is not essentially at odds with Christianity; rather, the sexual difference of homosexuality inevitably inflects the particular style of religious experience, occasionally to the distaste of the homophobic majority. I would further add that Catholicism, despite its homophobic pretensions, has exercised in certain historical periods a homosexualizing influence over culture. Sedgwick's remarks on introspection and men in dresses lead us in the direction of the all too familiar cultural constellation of spirituality, aestheticism, effeminacy, and male homosexuality, which had its brightest moments among the decadents. They regarded the Church as, among other things, a theater for the articulation of homosexual desire and identity through faith and through ritual. With Wilde and the Oxford movement, aestheticism joined hands with Roman Catholic ritualism to create an atmosphere of homoerotic exuberance unprecedented in the history of Christianity. Anglo-Catholicism, with its attention to ritual and vestments, acquired a certain gender-bending extravagance and exoticism within the context of Victorian puritanism. It was straight and queer, respectable and subversive, at the same time.

By the 1920s, the notion of Anglo and Roman Catholicism as a magnet for homosexuals had passed from a running joke to a simple fact. Radclyffe Hall, herself a lesbian and a convert to Rome, is positively solemn on the subject in her 1928 novel *The Well of Loneliness*. This book, the first great lesbian novel, is rich in Christian imagery, culminating in what appears to be a rhetorical question: "And what of that curious craving for religion which so often went hand in hand with inversion?"[14] In the following decade, in Evelyn Waugh's novel *Brideshead Revisited*, Charles Ryder is warned to stay away from Anglo-Catholics, since they are invariably sodomites.

Although Catholicism ceased to be fashionable among the post-Stonewall generation, the queer fascination for the Church is everywhere in evidence even today. Those who construe the relationship of homosexuality to Christianity entirely in terms of doctrinal denunciations seem to me to miss the point. Church rhetoric still leads a double life, though this duplicity has a habit of announcing itself. Some of these announcements appear to be unintentional. For example, there is not a single diocese in the United States that has not been rocked by a homosexuality or pederasty scandal among its pastoral ranks. Furthermore, given the statistics on AIDS in the priesthood, one would think it was an occupational hazard.

On a happier note, the movement for gay rights has fostered a further movement among gay Christians to resist the language of duplicity and the popular belief that sex between men and sex between women are incompatible with a religious life. Christian titles continue to be best-sellers in gay bookstores, although they do not on the whole compare to the flowers of evil that impassioned an earlier generation. Academic studies—such as the work of John Boswell, Uta Ranke-Heinemann, Judith Brown, David Hilliard, and Jeannine Gramick, to name a few—have sought to challenge the invisibility of homosexuals in Church history and to question the historical basis for the Church's condemnation of homosexuality. Gay Catholics, both men and women, have bravely risked excommunication to form support groups and congregations of their own. Gay priests and lesbian nuns are coming out of the closet and describing in their own words their devotion to the faith. The Roman Catholic Church may well be the world's most homophobic institution, but it also may well be the world's largest employer of lesbians and gay men.[15]

This book is a work of literary history that examines the cultural and historical significance of the connections the decadents drew between aestheticism, sexuality, and Catholicism. Like all discursive practices, Christianity presents a highly unstable field for sexual negotiation. I am concerned here with some of the historical forms of that negotiation among late-nineteenth-century aesthetes, many of them homosexual, who found in the Church a peculiar language for artistic and sexual expression. In decadent Catholicism we can glimpse the beginnings of a conception of religion that we might now regard as poststructural or postmodern in its valorization of perversity, paradox, textuality, and performativity. Catholicism was the odd disruption, the hysterical symptom, the mystical effusion, the medieval spectacle, the last hope of paganism, in an age of Victorian puritanism, Enlightenment rationalism, and bourgeois materialism. The decadents regarded faith, their own faith, as a beautiful possibility curiously out of place in a modern context, but no less beautiful for that. They found in the Church a volatile eroticism that was not necessarily an affront to Catholic belief. They exposed the textuality of Catholicism, its status as a work of art, as an impure discourse tainted with the maladies of language and desire.

# ONE

# The Dialectic of Shame and Grace

## Perfect Wagnerites

Richard Wagner, ostensibly the most triumphant creature alive; as a matter of fact, though, a cranky and desperate *décadent*, suddenly fell helpless and broken on his knees before the Christian cross.

Friedrich Nietzsche

Nietzsche's remarks about Wagner tell us less about the composer than about his own decadent sensibility. Only with copious qualifications can we define Wagner as either decadent or Christian. And yet there is a certain context, a peculiar perspective, from which Nietzsche's comment made sense at the end of the nineteenth century. As far as he was concerned, Wagner and Christianity were both cut from the same decadent brocade. Wagner was one of the great inspirations for fin de siècle aestheticism, even though he would have been appalled by the idea and, like many a decadent, was outspoken in his disgust for the degeneration of the race.

Wagner was also a great inspiration for decadent Catholicism, with its fragrant fascination with the liturgy, mysticism, ritual, symbolism, and music of the Church. Even in this passage by Nietzsche, the discerning eye will detect the outlines of Barbey d'Aurevilly's prophecy about Baudelaire and Huysmans: his belief that, having written the great satanic works of the age, they had no other options left in life but the pistol or the cross. As it happens, Barbey's formulation is as

Fig. 1. Aubrey Beardsley, *The Wagnerites* (courtesy of the Board of Trustees of the Victoria & Albert Museum, London).

far off the mark as Nietzsche's comment on Wagner, but the image of the great sinner rejecting suicide to prostrate himself at the foot of the cross will always resonate with a certain poetic truth that excites our forgiveness. Why should not Wagner be characterized in the same Christian pose as Baudelaire and Huysmans, given the extraordinary influence he exercised over their work? Certainly all three—and Barbey as well—propagated a public image of themselves as tortured Catholics, stimulated with mystical inspiration even as they were shaken with shame and desire. Wagner is a touchstone for the peculiar dialectic of shame and grace that is the foundation for decadent Catholicism. As Nietzsche makes clear, the desperate decadent and the penitent Christian have much in common. As is well known, the decadents were much seduced by the Christian discourse of sin, but they were also drawn to the more poetic flights of shame, remorse, and piety. For the decadents, the opposition between the depths of shame and the heights of grace was a tenuous one, always in danger of collapse within a discourse of mystical intensity.

Like Nietzsche, Baudelaire and Huysmans were two of the great interpreters of Wagner's decadence—the writers who were virtually responsible for bringing it into view, for impressing it upon the imagination of their time and, for that matter, our own. Walter Pater once wrote that all art aspires to the condition of music, and for the decadents that music was usually either Wagner or the plainchant. Indeed, I would argue that much of what is decadent about Wagner has less to do with his music, or even his life, than with the peculiar atmosphere of devotion he excited among those aesthetes who were his most articulate and enthusiastic audience. Just as the art of Moreau, Redon, and Rops came to be regarded as decadent primarily by virtue of Huysmans' appreciation of it in *A Rebours*, so Wagner's decadence is to be discovered for the most part not onstage at Bayreuth but in the piquant pages of certain literary admirers, the progenitors of art for art's sake, from Gautier and Baudelaire to Aubrey Beardsley and Arthur Symons (see Figure 1).

In the present day, Wagner is a relatively well-domesticated beast, such that the word "decadent" is unlikely to rise to the lips of anyone attending a Good Friday performance of *Parsifal*. The hysterical expressions of outrage that he elicited in his own time are now read as period curiosities. Nevertheless, there have been a number of critical attempts in recent times to define his music as decadent. In his book *Decadent Style,* for example, John R. Reed has claimed that "Wagner's style is Decadent in that it concentrates on atomistic motifs that, by their interlocking growth, create instead a new, more cerebral form that depends upon the audience's intellectual participation, for the full meaning is graspable only when the symbolism is understood."[1] While Reed has made an excellent point, he hardly does justice to Wagner's innovations in the field of music, nor does he capture the enthusiasm of his reception among decadents. The "participation" that Wagner excited surely extended well beyond the "intellectual," as anyone might have agreed who witnessed the spiritual prostration of the perfect Wagnerite at Bayreuth. Reed's attempt to define Wagner, Chopin, and Strauss as decadent stylists is the one dry chapter in an otherwise stimulating work of criticism.

Decadence is, after all, not only a style but a sensibility—in particular, a critical sensibility and an unusually worshipful mode of spectatorship. Decadents not only created art, they were also creative in appreciating it. The only reason I associate Chopin with decadence is because Gilbert is playing one of his nocturnes on the piano in Wilde's aesthetic dialogue "The Critic as Artist." Only by reading literary decadents do I recognize what they recognized of themselves in their favorite composers. The decadent Wagner is largely a French creation, a contagious emanation of the Parisian *Revue Wagnérienne,* which included Huysmans, Verlaine, Mallarmé, and Péladan among its contributors. It is with good reason that Huysmans reprinted his essay on Wagner in his book *Croquis Parisiens* and that Nietzsche slipped out of his mother tongue when he exclaimed, "Wagner est une névrose"[2]—for, despite his Teutonic charm, Wagner seems to have given many the impression that he had been translated into German from the original French.

We might, as did many French decadents, discover in Wagner himself a man who was as radical in his youth as he was reactionary in his old age. He was a dandy who impoverished himself by purchasing sumptuous clothing and palatial residences. He was a lothario, whose sexual morals still make for titillating reading. He seduced and courted the patronage of a homosexual prince who lavished money on him, not to mention a good many chivalrous love letters, most of them

violet in their rhetorical flourishes. He was arguably the greatest composer in a musical form notorious for its extravagance, aristocratic
pretensions, exoticism, and eroticism. His first production in Paris
degenerated from a scandal into a riot. He wrote legendary paeans to
the Church, even though he was for the most part an atheist. He was
a genius devoted to his genre, he spoke of music as though it were a
religion, he established Bayreuth as a site of pilgrimage, a temple to
his own personality and music. He was the most written about and
argued about artist of his time. In spite of himself, Wagner was better
at being a decadent than most decadents.

In the great themes of his operas, the decadents recognized their own
obsessions in spectacular form. First of all, Wagner is preoccupied with
feminine evil, the Eternal Woman who ceases somehow to be a cliché
in his rendering, and his various femmes fatales, his Kundrys and
Venuses, resonate well with the literary and pictorial Salomés of the
age. Many of his heroes are at once pious and perverse, great converts
and great sinners, who languish in the shadow of temptation and
hysteria no less fervently than in the beatific rays of redemption. Love
is not simply an emotion in Wagner but a metaphysical agony. It is by
his own description an endless yearning and an unquenchable hunger.
He has no interest in realism, but rather catapults the spectator into a
romantic dream, enlivened by myth and mysticism. Like few other
composers, he appeals to the cultural unconscious through bold emotional effects and a symbolism that impressed Baudelaire with its
primal antiquity no less than its startling originality and modernity.

Wagner's Catholicism is an important element of this appeal to the
unconscious. Like many a decadent, he celebrated a highly sensual and
ritualistic conception of the faith that was visionary in its temptations,
exquisite in its repentance, medieval in its intensity, and mystical in its
tone. It is not only Wagner's magnificent Venus who wends her way
through the decadent imagination, but also the hymn of praise the
pilgrims sing, the Magdalene hair of Kundry in her moment of pious
submission, and the barren rod whose blossom proclaims the essential
beauty of Tannhäuser's errant soul. Most important, from the point
of view of style, Wagner explored the peculiar resonances among
artistic genres and among modes of experience that were traditionally
held to be distinct. He allied opera with classical tragedy and Church

ritual. He blurred the conventional categorical distinctions between the religious, the erotic, and the aesthetic in a way that is typically decadent.

In his essay on Wagner, Baudelaire is moved to quote from his own poem "Correspondances," on the mystical convergence of sensations in nature and in the mind:

> Comme de longs échos qui de loin se confondent
> Dans une ténébreuse et profonde unité,
> Vaste comme la nuit et comme la clarté,
> Les parfums, les couleurs et les sons se répondent.[3]

Amid such mystical correspondences, where perfumes, colors, and sounds resonate with one another in a forest of symbols, religious experience is never fully distinguishable from the polyvalent voice that sings its praise. Wagner's Catholicism, as both an aesthetic and an erotic experience, proved a masterful appropriation of religion from the confines of dogma and churches where it was said to malinger. He erased an embattled distinction between Catholicism and opera, rendering certain Christian moods as arias—the paroxysms of grace no less than the spasms of shame. Wagner performed Catholicism anew on a stage typically reserved for art and entertainments of quite another sort. The perfumes, colors, and sounds of faith suffered a mysterious resurrection and fanned the ardor of a Catholic revival already aflame among the French and English literati. "Listening to the music of *Parsifal*," Max Nordau observed rather tartly, "has become the religious act of all those who wish to receive the Communion in musical form."[4]

To see the effect of Wagner on the Catholic sensibility of these literati, we might look at the status of the nun in decadent writing. The nun has always been a curiously eroticized figure in the literature of both England and France. Denis Diderot's *La Religieuse*, with its earnest heroine imprisoned in convents that are either sadistic or lesbian, might be taken as the touchstone for Western nun fantasies. Whether the nun appears in a Canterbury tale, a gothic novel, an anticlerical diatribe, or a cinematic farce, the failure of her sexual repression has always been a topic of perennial interest, not the least because the audience of nun stories is rarely nuns themselves. After

*Parsifal,* the nun, not to mention the Blessed Virgin and a select coterie of female saints, became for decadent Catholicism what Salomé had become for decadent paganism. More to the point, she became Kundry, the Eternal Woman turned convert with the voice of a soprano. "Either a nun or a monster! God's bosom or passions!" Rachilde writes in *Monsieur Vénus.* "It would, perhaps, be better to put her in a convent, as we put hysterical women in the Salpêtrière! She does not know vice, she invents it!"[5] In her reference to Charcot's asylum, the Salpêtrière, Rachilde recognizes the fin de siècle correspondence between hysteria, religious conversion, and the female voice.

Perhaps the most famous of these Wagnerian nuns is Villiers de L'Isle-Adam's Sara from *Axël,* his posthumously published drama of symbolist mysticism and *Parsifal* pastiche. Like Diderot's nun, she is railroaded into a convent, and throughout the preparations for her taking the veil, she is prodigiously silent. In the moment of her confirmation in her new vocation, she kneels on a carpet strewn with lilies, her necklace of mystic opals sparkling through the fumes of incense. Gently, she says, "No." But like the negation of a Catholic Antigone, her no has an explosive effect that sends the entire stage into an uproar of overexcited nuns and upset breviaries.

*Parsifal* was also the inspiration for John Davidson's poem "A Ballad of a Nun" (a companion piece to another poem, "A Ballad of Tannhäuser"), in which a bewimpled Kundry goes wild during Carnival, discovers she is sister to the sun and moon, and is still blessed by the Virgin Mother upon her return to the convent. In *Under the Hill,* Aubrey Beardsley's pornographic rewriting of *Tannhäuser,* Saint Rose of Lima makes an appearance rather improbably as a virgin coquette, swooning in a lesbian embrace with the Virgin Mother, who is known to have conversed with her through an icon that the pious girl adored to distraction (see Figure 2). In her love for the icon, magically come to life, she is one of the many Pygmalion figures of decadent literature, and in Beardsley's line drawing she is herself a work of art in long flowing robes, "some slim, sensitive plant, whose lightness, sweetness, and simplicity defy and trouble the most cunning pencil."[6] Beardsley is playing on the scandal that ensued when the Tractarians attempted to publish an English life of the saint, whose ascetic sensuality and hysterical self-lacerations struck not a few Victorians as the very embodiment of Catholic decadence. The great unread classic of this genre,

Fig. 2. Aubrey Beardsley, *The Ascension of Saint Rose of Lima*, from *Under the Hill* (1895).

however, must certainly be George Moore's *Evelyn Innes* and its sequel, *Sister Teresa*. Although his style is naturalistic, Moore tells the story of a woman who becomes a Wagnerian diva and then renounces the stage to become a nun. Her shame is scarcely distinguishable from her transcendence. The decadent aspect of the story is assured by a classic dandy named Sir Owen, who is an editor of *La Revue Wagnérienne* and given to wearing embroidered waistcoats, pearl studs, and butterfly bow ties. He is Evelyn's scented Svengali, and at the very beginning of their acquaintance he is able to seduce a shudder from her flesh by playing an air from *Tristan* on a harpsichord with "gnawing, creeping sensuality."[7] In each of these iconic nun images, we find the same dialectic of shame and grace. In her mystical intensity, the perverse diva of the opera house is never more than a step away from becoming the pious nun, and vice versa.

Although he insinuated himself into the best literary minds of the age, Wagner also had a great many critics. Nordau and Nietzsche were the best-known writers to condemn him. Ironically, however, their accusations of hysteria and decadence in Wagner are themselves hysterical and decadent. Nordau speaks of "Wagnerism" as a malady of spectatorship by no means endemic to Bayreuth since it had, in his view, contaminated the whole of modern art and criticism. He may have assumed a pious tone when he dismissed *Parsifal* as "at once a foolish and a frivolous caricature of Jesus Christ" (186), but it is clearly the work's mysticism and neo-Catholicism that he finds most offensive. According to Nordau, Wagner heads the pack of mystical degenerates that includes virtually every good writer of the period. At its best, however, his exaggerated condemnation offers us a stylistic whiff of Huysmans: "There are modest parasites and proud parasites. Their range extends from the insignificant lichen to the wondrous rafflesia, the flower of which, a yard in breadth, illumines the sombre forests of Sumatra with the wild magnificence of its blood-red colour. Wagner's poems have in them something of the carrion stench and uncanny beauty of this plant of rapine and corruption" (192). This from Nordau, who claims to find no charm in the many decadent "flowers of evil" that he abuses.

A great many critics of the age actually admired Wagner, and a surprising number of them were clergymen; but even in their efforts to sentimentalize Wagner's Christian sensibility, they often ran aground on the same paradox, the decadence of Catholicism. Their criticism suffers from a nagging ambivalence. They delight in his pious celebration of the Church, but they grimace at what appears to be an equally fervent celebration of sin and moral weakness. Thus, Edmund Gurney, writing in England in 1883, can exclaim, "It is a joy to remember as we follow the sublime story of *Parsifal*, that in one of his last published letters Wagner makes an earnest and unhesitating profession of allegiance to Christ"; but then he must also confess that, even in its finest moments, Wagner's music betrays "a faint flower of disease, something overripe in its lusciousness and febrile passion."[8]

This paradox is more self-conscious in Nietzsche, who had been a friend and admirer of Wagner. In the preface to *The Case of Wagner*, where we find the bulk of his fulminations against the great composer, Nietzsche writes: "I am just as much a child of my age as Wagner—*i.e.*, I am a decadent. The only difference is that I recognised the fact, that I struggled against it. The philosopher in me struggled against it" (xxix–xxx). Like all decadents, Nietzsche enjoyed a struggle that he was sure to lose. He writes with both shame and pleasure that "Wagner belongs only to my diseases." Nietzsche finds the Christian themes of Wagner's work especially repellent, and with disdain he dubs the entire oeuvre the "opera of salvation" (5). Christianity and decadence become synonymous in his general condemnation: "There is nothing exhausted, nothing effete, nothing dangerous to life, nothing that slanders the world in the realm of the spirit, which has not secretly found shelter in his art; he conceals the blackest obscurantism in the luminous orbs of the ideal. He flatters every nihilistic (Buddhistic) instinct and togs it out in music; he flatters every form of Christianity, every religious expression of decadence" (39).

Nietzsche is, however, a more astute reader of Wagner than was Nordau. He located one of the essential paradoxes that made Wagner's Catholicism, indeed the spiritual aspirations of all decadents, offensive to their age—namely, the ritual celebration of sin and shame as the distinguishing feature of the faith. Shame and guilt are given pride of place in Catholicism, especially through the sacrament of auricular confession, in which moral weakness acquires all the suspense and repetitiveness of a serial melodrama. Wagner's great converts, his gloriously repentant sinners, are distinguished as much by the splendor of their sins as the depth of their shame. Nietzsche is exceptionally ironic on this point: "If it were not for Wagner, who would teach us that innocence has a preference for saving interesting sinners? (the case in 'Tannhäuser') . . . Or that the venerable Almighty, after having compromised himself morally in all manner of ways, is at last delivered by a free spirit and an immoralist? (the case in the 'Ring')" (6). Wagner certainly has a preference for bestowing sainthood on the most unseemly of candidates, but the annals of hagiography bear him out on that point.

For Wagner, as for many decadents, from Baudelaire to Wilde, the Church was indispensable as the only institution that really appreciated the beauty and artistry of shame. I speak of shame in particular, rather than sin or guilt, because I want to emphasize the affective, performative, and social dimension of such terms. Shame has a certain immediacy, a physical language of downturned eyes and reddening face that is perceivable in a child long before moral laws or even language leave their mark. In this sense, shame precedes both guilt and sin. It is the gesture that brings sin into existence as such. Furthermore, sin and guilt involve failure with respect to a given law. Shame, however, is a failure with respect to other people within a social context. It is not a private sensation, nor does it succeed as an abstraction. Above all, it is a performance—one that the Church has thoroughly explored and exploited.

Roman Catholicism singled out shame from the drone of worldly experience and crowned it with the metaphysical note of sin, elaborating it into a recurrent motif and decking it out in the most theatrical of costumes. As a Catholic, one is made peculiarly aware of sin as a birthright, an inheritance from Eve acutely felt as though, through shame, it were imprinted in one's own flesh. One dare not partake in the celebration of the Mass without first submitting to confession, the closet re-enactment of shame through the ritualized language of sin. Even the saints confess. That is the beauty of original sin. Sin attains the status of shame, an originary affect as inevitable as desire. With the paradox of original sin, we all have something to be ashamed of even if, by a more reasonable standard of right and wrong, we are innocent. When we are a crime, we need not commit one. No one escapes sin except through the forgiveness of God—an indulgent gesture that, like every other art form, acquires its sublimest effects through frequent repetition. The rituals of shame in the Church have a language of their own, as breathtaking in its grandeur as it is mystical in its simplicity.

Through Wagner, we might recognize the crucial importance of shame to art no less than to religion. The sheer iterability of religious ritual signals the status of religion as art, as a performative possibility, such that the vulgar music hall need only repeat Christian litanies of shame to excite a pilgrimage. For the decadent convert, Wagner's accomplishment was twofold. First, he insisted upon the dialectical tension between shame and grace, their mutual dependence rather than their mutual exclusion. And second, he celebrated the status of religion as art. As Wagner knew, the Church will always owe an inexhaustible debt to its sinners; after *Tannhäuser* and *Parsifal*, the Church owed a considerable debt to opera. The decadents owe much the same debt. "What yonder lures is Rome, Rome's faith sung without words," Nietzsche writes of Wagner's operas,[9] capturing in an epigram that alluring vision of faith in a dream of pure form that the decadents sought in prose. In the strange underwater music of the overture to *Tannhäuser*, Huysmans saw precisely that vision, a landscape as unnatural as it was difficult to capture in words. In his essay on the same opera, Baudelaire would evoke and repeat what he saw as the archetypal Wagnerian gesture, the interminable shift from shame to grace and back again.

Wagner was their inspiration. We may hold him at least in part responsible for their fall, their precipitation into a mysticism of good and evil. *Parsifal* begins not with innocence but with an original sin or, more to the point, an originary shame, announcing itself through the spiritual hysteria of Kundry and the blackening gash in the leg of Amfortas. Their sins, as deeds, are never witnessed. Their sins are elsewhere—indeed, they are secondary; and what we see before us is the physical spectacle of shame, the enigmatic cries on the lips of the accursed woman, the degenerative ooze from the leg of the accursed man, always already in a state of aggravation when the curtain rises. All is perverse and out of joint from the start. In the same way, shame—not to mention the sin it enacts—is the founding gesture of decadent style, a gesture appropriated from an earlier art form that we might call Christian penitence.

Although it is unusually brief and seldom read anymore, "L'Ouverture de Tannhaeuser," which first appeared in *La Revue Wagnérienne* in 1885, is one of Huysmans' finest pieces of criticism. In his characteristically sumptuous and tortuous style, he makes evident both the quality of artifice and the quality of shame that he admired in Wagner. In his view the overture reveals an artistry that is not only beyond nature but also beyond many artists. At about this time, Huysmans was also publishing his influential essays on Grünewald, Redon, and Rops, artists he felt transcended the classical, representational aspect of painting with a highly subjective or spiritual element. In this essay he locates that same transcendent quality in Wagner. His appreciation of Wagner's style is so visual, so painterly, that we might at first suspect that he is talking about the staging of *Tannhäuser*, rather than the music:

> In a landscape such as nature would never create, in a landscape where the sun pales to the exquisite and superb dilution of golden yellow, in a sublime landscape where, under a morbidly luminous sky, the mountains above the bluish valleys render opalescent the crystallized whiteness of their peaks; in a landscape inaccessible to painters, since it is composed for the most part of visual chimeras, of silent frissons and moist tremblings of the air, a chant rises up, a singularly majestic chant, an august canticle launched from the soul of the pilgrims as they advance in a troop.[10]

With his sunlit mountains and valleys, Huysmans seems to effect a romantic shift of art in the direction of nature, but he is misleading. Long before we hear the chant, before we reach the putative subject of this pyrotechnical sentence, he treats us to a series of elaborate prepositional phrases, the repetitive "in a landscape" that checks the advance of the pilgrims so that we might contemplate the beauty of the art that produces them. His prose winds down to a pensive stillness, a still-life as it were, overwhelmed by its own sensations. He moves from art to nature and back to art again, which we discover he has never left. Music becomes a landscape, but it is one that "nature would never create" and even painters can rarely grasp because of its largely imaginative or spiritual, rather than realistic, effects. Nevertheless, Huysmans uses the blue, the golden yellow, the opalescent white of the paintbrush that he has supposedly disqualified. Nature is further perverted in typical decadent fashion into a psychosomatic malady of artifice, something morbid and pale, given to hysterical frissons and tremblings. The scene is not nature, but neither is it music. The landscape precedes and overburdens the chant. The landscape literally displaces the music on which it is based.

Throughout the essay, the orchestra does not play, it paints: "Then the tempest of roaring flesh, the electrifying flashes and glimmers that are bursting in the orchestra die down; the incomparable sound of the brass, which seems a transposition of blinding purples and sumptuous golds, subsides;—and a murmuring, tenuous and delicious, a caress almost divine of sounds adorably blue and heavenly rose, trembles in the nocturnal ether that is already brightening" (159). Wherein lies this roaring flesh? How can a murmur be delicious? How exactly does a sound become adorably blue or heavenly rose? We also learn of a musical scene that exhales unknown scents in which "the biblical mustiness of myrrh is mingled with the voluptuously complicated perfumes of modern extracts" (156). The orchestra literally paints the figure of Tannhäuser, "sketching him in from head to toe with heraldic melody" (157). The experience of the music is physical and immediate, playing on the body, a confusion of genres that overwhelms every sense. This mystical connection between colors, caresses, aromas, flavors, and sounds, between the eroticized body and the music that causes it to convulse and to dream, is not merely a psychological peculiarity but also an aspect of the religious dimension of symbolist and decadent writing. This mystical confusion is presumed to be divine. Huysmans effects a Baudelairean correspondence between his faith, his words, his body, the painted scene, and the musical sound, much as Wagner discovered in opera an extraordinary convergence of the arts and their interpenetration with religion and myth.

It is important to Huysmans that Wagner's music should be not just heard but acutely felt as a sensation in the body. It is important to his religious beliefs as well as to his art. Huysmans was concerned with the spirituality, no less than the sensuality, of art. In his view Wagner is not about the triumph of good over evil, or the triumph of the spirit over the body, but their eternal struggle, the dialectical opposition by which one seems always to be disappearing into the other:

> In the distance hovers the hymn of intercession, the pilgrims' hymn of faith, cleansing the last wounds of the soul torn by the diabolical

struggle;—and, in an apotheosis of light, in the glory of Redemption, the Body and the Spirit are intermingled, Evil and Good are reconciled, Lust and Purity are knit together by the two motifs that wind around, mingling the rapid, exhausting kisses of the violins, the dazzling distressing caresses of the tense, fidgety strings, with the calm, majestic, expansive chorus, the melody of mediation, the hymn of the kneeling soul as it celebrates its final submission, its unshakable stability in the bosom of the Deity. (159–160)

At this point, however, far from "unshakable stability," Huysmans tells us that we leave the vulgar music hall trembling and entranced at "the confused greatness of the three-act drama" (160). This "melody of mediation" is distinguished by its failure to resolve anything. The pilgrims would offer us the stability of a serene piety, but the violins drown them out, leaving us wracked by temptation. In Huysmans' opinion, Catholicism cannot do without violins. At best, the kneeling soul discovers not perfect transcendence but an intermingling of Body and Spirit, a knitting together of Lust and Purity. In other words, our godly and diabolical possibilities cannot live with each other, nor can they live without each other. They remain locked in a violent embrace.

Huysmans had already addressed the same theme in *A Rebours*, though he focused on Barbey d'Aurevilly's novels rather than Wagner. *Un Prêtre Marié,* with its story of a delirious monk and demonic possession, sends Des Esseintes into a Catholic reverie that is virtually indistinguishable from Huysmans' commentary on Wagner:

This belief that man is an irresolute creature, a being torn between two forces of equal strength, alternately victorious and vanquished in the battle for his soul; this conviction that human life is nothing more than an uncertain combat waged between hell and heaven; this faith in two opposed entities, Satan and Christ, must fatally engender those internal discords where the soul, exalted by incessant battle, stimulated as it were by promises and threats, ends up by surrendering and prostituting itself to whichever of the two parties in the pursuit has been the more tenacious.[11]

The ambivalence of this final battle, the belief that humankind is a pawn caught in the middle of a battle among Christian titans, removes religious experience from the realm of mundane duty and moral choice and places it on the metaphysical plane of a glorious war in which the individual is not so much a soldier as a prize.

Huysmans had no taste for sentimental religion and bourgeois piety. He was always in search of a faith that he regarded as masculine and even brutal—and he described it as such in his essay on Wagner:

> And this chant, devoid of feminine effusions, devoid of all wheedling prayers that endeavor to obtain, through the hazardous antics of the modern conception of grace, that meeting with God which is reserved for a few, spreads out with that certainty of pardon, that conviction of atonement, that asserted itself among the humble souls of the Middle Ages.
>
> Worshipful and superb, manly and upright, it speaks of the appalling weariness of the sinner who has descended into the cavernous depths of his conscience. (155–156)

For the modern Church, with its feminine effusions and wheedling, Huysmans reserves a gendered jab. But he finds nothing whiny or effeminate in Wagner. The diabolical struggle is violent, difficult, mystical, and medieval, and Huysmans' "cavernous depths" are evidently a manly orifice. As for the face of God, it shows itself only to the elect.

A performance of *Tannhäuser* was an excellent occasion for Huysmans' depiction of this struggle, this back-and-forth commotion of the soul, since the allegiance of the hero himself is always in question from one moment to the next. One minute he has buried himself in the mons veneris, the next his staff is blossoming before the incredulous pope. Nor does the narrative resolve itself on the side of either the Body or the Soul. Venus is disavowed and the pope is made a fool of. Through the intervention of Elisabeth, Tannhäuser appears in the end to have the blessing of God, even as he returns to the Venusberg, the site of his shame. The music of the overture encapsulates this back-and-forth movement with its own thematic shifts between a motif of hedonistic revelry and one of spiritual repose. Huysmans endeavors to reproduce this motion in the structure of his essay. The chant that asserts itself in such a manly and upright way in the opening paragraphs soon "weakens and little by little fades away." The clouds and the sky take on rearing shapes like thighs and swelling breasts, cries of desire are heard, lascivious shouts, "outbursts from a carnal beyond" that shoot forth from the orchestra to hail the emergence of Venus amid an espalier of swooning nymphs (157).

Venus, like the more famous Salomé of *A Rebours,* may be the creation of another artist, but Huysmans affixes his signature to her nevertheless. His vision of feminine evil is all paradox. She is not a pagan goddess, the old Aphrodite, but rather a Christian Venus, "if the sin against nature of combining these words is indeed possible!" She is a woman of apparent oxymorons, at once beautiful and demonic as she crushes Christian souls in her "delicious and maleficent arms" (157). She is the embodiment of his own decadent style, a paradox of medieval mysticism and modern hysteria:

> But although in conception she recalls the allegorical entities of the Middle Ages, she brings to them a modern spice, and insinuates an intellectual current of refinement into this seething mass of wild delights; she adds, in some fashion, certain aggravated sensations to the naive canvas of ancient times, assuring at last with greater certainty, through this overstimulation of nervous acuity, the defeat of the hero, who has been suddenly initiated into the lascivious cerebral complexities of the exhausted age in which we live. (158)

He could be describing Wagner's Venus or, more likely, he could be describing himself as a decadent writer. Like his goddesses, Huysmans was a purveyor of immortal hysteria.

This dense and highly wrought passage complements the opening landscape in which we first hear the pilgrims' chant—in which we first glimpse medieval piety as decadent and operatic artifice. Just as the chant fades away, so too does the music of Venus dissolve in an orchestral roar. From the musical distance, the pilgrims' chant returns, not with a restoration of virtue but, as I have said, a recognition of eternal struggle. What Huysmans accomplishes is not an opposition between decadent hedonism and Christian redemption, but rather two distinct spiritual moods locked by decadent style in a strange embrace.

## Christianity as *Paradis Artificiel*

The veil of modesty torn, the shameful parts shown, I know—with
my cheeks aflame—the need to hide myself or die, but I believe by
facing and enduring this painful anxiety I shall, as a result of my
shamelessness, come to know a strange beauty.

Jean Genet

> We worship Love, adore him,
> Low in the dust before him
> We bow down, and implore him,
>      Give thanks for our sweet shame.

Montague Summers

Baudelaire, in his poetry as well as his own essay on Wagner, was a
master of the strange beauty of shame that Huysmans describes. In *A
Rebours*, Des Esseintes details his admiration for Baudelaire much as
Huysmans details his admiration for Wagner, examining the poet's
power to reveal the soul in its depths of shame and yet always remain
within the performative and fictive domain of art and the imagination.
Des Esseintes keeps Baudelaire's poetry in his library of Catholic literature. The paradox of Baudelaire's diabolical Christianity, his discovery of the soul through its destruction, was for many years the great
preoccupation of modernist criticism on the poet. At the risk of repeating those observations, I want once again to evoke and, I hope,
to complicate this paradox, especially with regard to his 1861 essay
"Richard Wagner et *Tannhäuser* à Paris."

If we look carefully at Des Esseintes's appreciation of Baudelaire,
we find more than the familiar appetite for evil. In the "morbid depravities and other-wordly aspirations" that Des Esseintes locates in
his favorite poet, the taste for evil is articulated in very Catholic terms.
Baudelaire is valued for his uncompromising depiction of the soul in
spiritual abjection—"he had descended to the bottom of the inexhaustible mine, had picked his way along abandoned and unexplored
galleries, and had reached those districts of the soul where the monstrous vegetations of the mind unfurl" (216). But Des Esseintes is a
notoriously cerebral character who takes only a meager pleasure in
the sins of the body; he prefers, rather, the sins of art and the imagination, the passive and morbid contemplation of sin, its exquisite

aggravation in the realm of the spirit—what the Church has called "morose delectation." So too, he appears to admire in Baudelaire a purely imaginary transgression, a sin rendered all the more beautiful precisely because it is never committed, except of course to paper. It is similar to Oscar Wilde's depiction of Lord Henry as a man who can never say a moral thing and never do a wrong one.

Baudelaire, as we know, said a great many immoral things and tried his best to do a fair number of wrong ones. But Des Esseintes does not dwell on the sordid details of the poet's life—his taste for whores, his opium use, his syphilis, and so on—since such details never quite live up to the horror expressed in the poetry. Not evil but "consciousness in Evil" is the aim of his poetry; therefore, Des Esseintes focuses on art and the imagination: "There, near those confines where reside the aberrations and maladies, the mystical tetanus, the burning fever of lust, the typhoids and nauseas of crime, he had found, spreading under the dismal knell of ennui, the frightening climacteric of sentiments and ideas" (216). He describes not the crime but its spiritual fever in the mind or the soul. Baudelaire is further framed by his status as aesthetic curio in Des Esseintes's library, a fatal book enclosed in a binding that is itself a work of art. The discussion of Baudelaire begins with the binding: "This edition, limited to a single exemplary copy in a shade of black that was velvety as China ink, had been dressed outside and lined inside with a mirific and authentic pigskin the color of flesh" (214), and so on for an entire paragraph. As in the opening reverie of his Wagner essay, Huysmans calls attention to the status of religious experience as art.

As Huysmans was clearly aware, Baudelaire's poetry offers us not only consciousness in evil but self-consciousness in evil. As in Huysmans' Wagner, the perennial theme appears to be the duality of the soul, the interminable struggle of good and evil, and we are always aware of this alternation between shame and grace as an intense sensation, highly wrought, highly artificial, eminently repeatable as one might reread a book or listen again to a favorite aria. His poetry performs the shame it ostensibly describes, producing sins of the mind with only the most tenuous reference to actual crimes beyond itself. His poetry aestheticizes shame, but it is not art as a vicarious experience, for it does not recognize the validity or the beauty of any experience, any crime, apart from itself. It is, in other words, superior to experience, as in his poem "L'Ame du Vin," in which it is not drunkenness but the poetry of drunkenness that will spring toward God like a rare flower.

Some of Baudelaire's finest poems touch upon the dialectic of shame and grace that Huysmans would admire in Wagner much later. In the depths of shame, Baudelaire discovers the face of God. In the final line of "Femmes Damnées: Delphine et Hippolyte," a pair of lovers, whose only crime appears to be their lesbianism, excite from their male voyeur a curious exclamation: "Et fuyez l'infini que vous portez en vous!" (1:155). The Baudelairean subject is always fleeing the infinite within himself, denying the God that, nevertheless, he carries in his own heart. Through the act of denial and negation, he professes to his belief in the deity he would disavow. In the preceding line, when he depicts the lesbians as disordered souls who design their own destiny— "Faites votre destin, âmes désordonnées"—we might recognize a rather Lacanian blurring of the distinction between destiny and design, not to mention disavowal and design. Through their disavowal they designate their destiny, and they acknowledge in spite of themselves the God whose disapproval they have in effect enacted.

A number of poems evince this sort of backhanded compliment to God. "Les Litanies de Satan" is ostensibly one of the more explicit examples of Baudelaire's satanism. Nevertheless, in its refrain "O Satan, prends pitié de ma longue misère!" (1:123–125)—O Satan, at long last take pity on my misery!—we hear a litany that sounds as though it were in fact a prayer to Christ, a plea for pity for those driven from Paradise by a wrathful God, for hope in a world where God has hidden himself, for comfort amid the torture of life. Satan in this poem offers a soft shoulder to cry on for those of us who, like most people in the world, are unworthy of heaven. "L'Imprévu," which begins as a typical Baudelairean paean to Satan, ends with an angel of redemption sounding a trumpet for all those who are willing to kiss the rod. "Hymne" is simple in its piety, with its repeated line "Salut en l'immortalité!" (1:162). Baudelaire depicted satanism and sexual transgression as spiritual horrors. At the same time, he wrote litanies of a more conventional piety.

"A une Madone" is, I would say, his most complicated and beautiful expression of shame, which is, after all, a recognition of the validity of Christian virtue despite one's own spiritual abjection. To regard this poem as a desecration of the Blessed Virgin or simply an autobiographical spasm of rage against an unnamed mistress would be to overlook the quality of its shame, its confessional intensity, and the subtlety of its emotional ambivalence. The speaker of the poem erects in the depths of his despair an altar for the Madonna or, at any rate, for a woman whom he likens to the Madonna—"Madone, ma maîtresse." He places her in an enameled niche of azure and gold in the darkest corner of his heart, far from worldly desire and mockery. From his verse he fashions for her a rhyme-encrystalled crown, and from his jealousy he offers her a coat of mail, embroidered with his tears in place of seed pearls. His devotional offerings become increasingly erotic as he enrobes her with his desire:

> Ta Robe, ce sera mon Désir, frémissant,
> Onduleux, mon Désir qui monte et qui descend,
> Aux pointes se balance, aux vallons se repose,
> Et revêt d'un baiser tout ton corps blanc et rose. (1:58)

The Madonna becomes the object of lust, of a sexual desecration, her white and rose flesh exciting in the speaker a dream of kisses; but she remains aloof, as yet unmoved. He has supposedly already placed her far from worldly desires, and so how are we to read the sexual imagery? Is this a purely spiritual desire and, if so, why is it articulated through carnal metaphors? Baudelaire seems to be speaking of the spirituality of sexual desire, the mysticism of lust, which I have already touched upon in Huysmans. He is describing not so much a physical pleasure as a spiritual or metaphysical one, a lust of the soul. He sublates sexuality into shame through a paradoxical alternation between physical and metaphysical language. The ritualized offerings continue, each crafted from the very material of spiritual abjection. He places a serpent beneath her foot to be crushed, presumably a serpent of guilt, since it gnaws at his entrails. His thoughts, like fiery eyes, act as tapers to light the altar, and his spirit, though stormy, rises to her snowy white summit, her "sommet blanc et neigeux," like the vapors of incense or perhaps a lover's caress (1:59).

Before this as yet impassive icon, he presents his spiritual failures, enacting his shame in a strikingly ritualized and aestheticized evocation of auricular confession. But his sins are not simply heard; they are worn by the Blessed Virgin—they are heaped upon her like so much filth. And yet, in her silence, we might recognize that his offerings are not a desecration. Rather, they are appropriate, just as, in the confessional, no sin is unspeakable. Although the fine white flesh of the Virgin has been revealed, she is no Venus unless she is what Huysmans called a Christian Venus. The Virgin is merely herself, immutable, her enamel skin familiar to us from thousands of Renaissance paintings. It is the poet who is exposed, not she. In his shame he has revealed himself as despicable—indeed, an artist of the despicable in himself—a role that the Church had already perfected in the sacrament of confession, with its dimly lit rituals of shame and self-laceration, its unburdening of filth into the ear of a priest.

The final stanza is extraordinary not only for its violence, but also for its shame. The Madonna, or the woman who has taken her place, has not yet fulfilled the role for which the Blessed Virgin is best known, that of Mater Dolorosa. "Enfin, pour compléter ton rôle de Marie," Baudelaire writes, and he proceeds to describe how he will sharpen the Seven Deadly Sins into blades and, like an unfeeling knife thrower at the circus—"un jongleur insensible"—thrust them into her panting, bleeding, streaming heart, "ton Coeur sanglotant, dans ton Coeur ruisselant!" Baudelaire may reveal in this poem a sadistic desire to torture Marie Daubrun, the mistress who is thought to be the target of this poem. He does, after all, refer to her as a "mortal Madonna," a name that is on the face of it an oxymoron since, if she were really to "complete her role as Mary," she would no longer be subject to death. This purely secular interpretation, however, explains only the mistress half of the phrase "Madone, ma maîtresse." Why associate her with Mary at all? And what completes the role? I gather that the role is only complete when the mistress suffers, when her heart bleeds, when she has taken upon herself the full violence of his shame. He lashes out at the Madonna, at God himself, and he takes aim at her love, brutally rejecting the proffered gift of divine love. But I presume that he speaks of the Madonna precisely because her love is not his to reject—because it is unconditional and inexhaustible. He stabs her. She bleeds, she suffers, she weeps in her heart—but that is what Blessed Virgins are for. Through her mystical sympathy, we all take a stab at Mary. To lash out at her is simply to justify her love.

The mistress of the poem is not simply a woman murdered; she is the divine Woman herself, Woman as the Church has constructed her in its more charitable moments, the very embodiment of pity and melancholic suffering. The knives of sin vanish into her bleeding heart as though into a storm-tossed ocean that is paradoxically, at its depths, as immovable and immortal as her faith. There is no horror we can bring to her that is not already accounted for in the sublime expansiveness of her pity. I would say that it is in part her love that excites his violence, which is paradoxically his celebration of his own impotence. He subverts his own sadism. In his wish to make the heart of the Madonna bleed, he discovers the intensity of the shame she inspires and the violence of his will to confess.

The circus imagery of the poem, so jarring amid the accoutrements of religious ritual, raises to my mind a further point. Why do we often encounter images of the theater in Baudelaire's religious and erotic poetry? Not only the so-called legitimate theater, but music hall actresses, a circus knife-thrower, the hanged man of a public execution—all find their metaphorical significance in his various paeans to shame. Such imagery is surely important in a poet who claimed, in *Mon Coeur Mis à Nu,* that as a child he aspired to be sometimes a pope and sometimes an actor. In "A une Madone," a woman resembling Marie Daubrun—who was, after all, an actress—is decked in an elaborate costume for her role as Madonna and mistress. The religious is theatrical.

One of Baudelaire's most operatic images of this sort occurs in the poem "L'Irréparable." In its final passage we suddenly find ourselves in a theater, where a fairy costumed in gold and gauze triumphs over a stagy Satan to the fiery accompaniment of an orchestra. The poet, grown weary in his remorse over an unnamed sin, finds himself waiting in vain for such a divine being to deliver him from evil:

> J'ai vu parfois au fond d'un théâtre banal
>
> Un être, qui n'était que lumière, or et gaze,
> > Terrasser l'énorme Satan;
> Mais mon coeur, que jamais ne visite l'extase,
> > Est un théâtre où l'on attend
> Toujours, toujours en vain, l'Etre aux ailes de gaze! (1:55)

The speaker's heart is a theater, so he says, and the same may be said of his poetry. Like Amfortas in *Parsifal,* his sin is but a memory, but his shame is spectacular. Like a stage, Baudelaire's confessions are eminently public, but are they not also self-consciously artificial, the studied performances of an actor?

As Jean-Paul Sartre once pointed out, Baudelaire's shame seems to precede his sin. The performance of shame seems indeed to produce the sin. In his drafts for a preface, the poet emphasizes the status of his art as a theater whose mechanisms are to remain a secret: "Do we invite the crowd into the workrooms of costume and scene designers; into the dressing room of the actress?" He compares his art to cosmetics, which achieve their deceptive effects simply through analogy and contrast—an art of difference and performance, not sincerity and authenticity. He is careful to distinguish between the man he is and the man he is perceived to be: "Being chaste as paper, sober as water, devout as a woman at communion, harmless as a sacrificial lamb, it would not displease me to be taken for a debauchee, a drunkard, an infidel and a murderer" (1:185). The likelihood that he was none of the former and some of the latter is immaterial. He eagerly invited upon himself the sensations of shame, guilt, remorse, hatred, and ennui in a self-conscious cultivation of abjection that had little if anything to do with actual crimes. Although his life was scandalous, he still exaggerated his crimes in an effort at provocation. So eager was he to invite calumny that he spread rumors that he was a pederast. *"Exasperated that people always believed what I said,"* he writes in a letter, "I let it be known that I had *killed* my father and *eaten* him, and also that I had been allowed to escape from France because of the services I was rendering the French police, AND THEY BELIEVED ME! *I have taken to disgrace like a duck to water.*"[12]

Baudelaire's evocations of shame, and all their attendant sins and sensations, are self-consciously theatrical, no more evidence of their author's true character than are the pious and shameful arias of *Parsifal* a biographical mirror of Wagner. Baudelaire takes great pride in the force of his lies. "I propose," he writes, "in order to prove again the excellence of my method, to apply it in the near future to celebrating the pleasures of devotion and the raptures of military glory, though I have never known either"(1:184). Are we to suppose, then, that *Les Fleurs du Mal* is evidence of his innocence?

In his book on Baudelaire, Sartre characterizes this strange passion for lying as a key to understanding the poet. He is especially astute at locating the paradoxes in Baudelaire's spirituality and his public persona. With considerable epigrammatic charm, he remarks upon the dialectic of Good and Evil and their mutual dependence, suggesting that in Baudelaire Evil "pays tribute to Good and by describing itself as wicked admits that it is relative and derivative, that without Good it would not exist."[13] In his admirable positing of Good as the ultimate origin, Sartre neglects the proposition, also evident in Baudelaire, that Good is relative and derivative, that without Evil it would not exist. He neglects still another proposition: in Baudelaire, Good and Evil are mutually constitutive possibilities with no objective existence of their own apart from the beautiful utterances of poetry. In this sense, Baudelaire aestheticizes morality. Sartre, however, offers us a Baudelaire who merely toys with morality, as though it were some transcendent flame at which the poet simply singes his fingers. He is offended by the insincerity of Baudelaire, whose dandyish gestures of shame and spirituality he regards as sterile. He is expertly sardonic in his revelation of the poet's various ruses, his lies, his curious need to lie. Baudelaire is revealed as someone who needed virtue so that he might have something to desecrate, who needed nature so that he might have something to transcend, and who needed stupidity so that he might have something to ridicule. All of this strikes me as true. In fact, virtue, nature, and stupidity have rarely been put to better use. At the heart of Baudelaire, however, underneath all the lies, Sartre discovers sterility, a profound emptiness, an infantile narcissism, a defensive and guilty fear of life, a poetry merely of form rather than a poetry of form and matter. Sartre likens him to a voyeur, a fetishist, a schizophrenic, a mythomaniac, a child who masturbates, and a disobedient sulky child who craves attention from his father. The modernist cult of sincerity and authenticity is all too evident here, as is the modernist tendency to Freudianize and otherwise pathologize every idiosyncrasy of a poet's character and art.

To the neurotic falsity of Baudelaire, Sartre opposes Rimbaud as a poet who *really* sought to crush virtue and who *really* sought to reject nature. The distinction is, I think, an instructive one, not only for what it tells us about Baudelaire but also because of what it tells us about some of his critics. Sartre says of Rimbaud: "He was not putting on an act; he really did set out to produce extraordinary thoughts and feelings. Baudelaire, on the other hand, stopped half-way. When faced with that total solitude where living and invention were identical, where his reflective lucidity was diluted into the reflective spontaneity, he became afraid" (158). We are to presume, then, that Rimbaud was about art and life and Baudelaire was just about art or, more to the point, bad faith.

I would argue, however, that Baudelaire is not a poet of bad faith, but rather a poet of the badness of faith—*badness* in the sense of evil, corruption, and falsity. Faith always presumes evil as one of its more seductive gestures, but it also maintains a curious corruption or falsity with respect to language itself. Faith invariably militates against the figurative on which it depends, and the decadents, in particular Baudelaire and Huysmans, were especially adept at inscribing the religious experience as a failure within language—a contradiction, a paradox, an assault on meaning. Insofar as truth is a linguistic proposition—and as subjects of the fall into language we can hardly experience it otherwise—the divine, one might even say the transcendent truth of the divine, is only readable as the most obscene lie. As a poet of "bad faith," Baudelaire enacted the divine as a corrupt trope, an obvious lie, one that does its most profound damage through frequent repetition. Baudelaire presented himself as an oracle for the lie and celebrated religious experience as a stylistic effect, a devotional posture that has little to do with what we might in our duller moments refer to as reality or life. In short, great religions, no less than great art, have no need of sincerity or authenticity, except of course as a pose.

Baudelaire's sufferings, or more to the point, their falsity, are especially distressing to Sartre, who regards them as "harassing ghosts, not realities; they were the creation not of events, but of the inner life" (93–94). Perhaps unintentionally, Sartre gives us a fine description of religious experience. Nevertheless, such distinctions between life and art, realities and ghosts, events and inner life, are perilous ones, especially in the context of Baudelaire, who sought to reveal the status of "life," "reality," and "events"—not to mention "good" and "evil"—as theater. What, after all, were the "realities" that Rimbaud rejected, if not the phantom realities that he and Baudelaire both summoned in their poems. The "I" that Rimbaud sought systematically to derange, the "I" that is *not* other, is surely one the most phantasmatic of his enemies. In effect, Sartre condemns Baudelaire for fighting against ghosts of his own invention, and then applauds Rimbaud for doing much the same.

When Sartre says that Baudelaire's poems have a dandyism of their own, he reveals a possibility he has no desire to entertain. Like the hero of *La Fanfarlo*, Baudelaire discovered a performative magic in human gestures, and like many a decadent he turned a favorite pose into satiric comedy: "A thoroughly honest man from birth and a bit of a rogue by pastime,—an actor by temperament,—he performed for his own enjoyment and in secret session some incomparable tragedies or, to be more precise, tragi-comedies. If he felt himself touched or tickled by gaiety he had to make a careful record of it, and our hero practiced roaring with laughter. If a tear were generated in the corner of his eye by some memory, he would go to the looking-glass and watch himself weep" (1:554). The emotion is not valuable in itself, but only insofar as it is repeatable in the gesture. We might suspect that the gaiety is distinct from the laugh, as a thing in itself is thought to be distinct from its articulation. Baudelaire allows for the possibility of a certain dumb and inert nature that is distinguishable from art, just as he allows for the possibility of a God that is distinguishable from God's law. But emotion only acquires beauty and significance when it is reproducible as a polished gesture, as art or performance. This passion for artistry and authorship is looked upon by Sartre as a neurotic need for self-consciousness and control. I would argue, rather, that such preoccupation with gesture is not a travesty of life or a fear of reality, but an insight into both—and the very basis of art. Sartre has far too much faith in reality; but, as Baudelaire demonstrated, reality requires a leap of faith.

Rimbaud's life is one of his more extraordinary poems. Baudelaire's life was just a life, a failed poem. Like Oscar Wilde, who once quipped that he could never live up to his blue china, Baudelaire never lives up to his own poetry and the porcelain quality of shame to which he aspired. His biographers have turned his life upside down in search of a crime that is equal to his guilt, a failing that is equal to his shame, an injustice that is equal to his rage. In vain, they search for that fatal moment when the young Baudelaire is gang-raped by sailors or sentenced to hard labor or abused by a parent, that precious moment that flatters our own vulgar sense of trauma as the origin of human suffering. In this sense, we are inferior artists of suffering. We cast ourselves as the naked slaves, impregnated with perfumes, who fan the poet's brow in "La Vie Antérieure" and wonder what secret grief has made him sad, what "secret douloureux qui me faisait languir" (1:17).

Baudelaire has a very Christian understanding of suffering as an art and as an inevitable spiritual condition. "The *spiritual* was Baudelaire's poetic reality," Sartre writes (173), and I would add that it is fruitless to look elsewhere for it than in poetry. Baudelaire's value as a Catholic poet is to be found not in some private habit of devotion or self-sacrifice, nor in his dutiful submission to the Church, for in his case there would be very little worth mentioning. He is what Susan Sontag once called a "fellow traveler" of the Church, a very Christian atheist, like a great many of the very finest Catholic poets. I would say, rather, that we value him simply for his evocation of original sin as an originary shame, a theatrical performance of mythic significance. For Baudelaire, the spiritual surely was no more than a poetic reality, no more than a function of style and certainly no less. Spirituality, not to mention its moral polarity of good and evil, is a *Paradis artificiel*— what Huysmans would call a *Thébaïd raffinée* in a witty gesture of respect for Flaubert's Saint Antony. Baudelaire's soul longs for a place "anywhere out of the world," and this "anywhere" is not reducible to an opium dream or an aesthetic reverie, nor is it ever fully distinguishable from them.

It is this spiritual reality, produced through a self-conscious stimulation of the imagination, that attracted Baudelaire to Wagner. His first letter to the great composer, a long hymn of praise dated 17 January 1859, is characterized by the same sensual effusion that we would expect of Wagner's greatest fan, Ludwig of Bavaria. The etherealized homoeroticism is certainly present, as when he writes of a performance of *Tannhäuser,* "I often experienced a feeling of a nature quite bizarre, it is the pride and bliss of understanding, of allowing myself to be penetrated, possessed, a truly sensual rapture similar to that of rising in the air or rolling upon the sea" (2:1452). Like Huysmans, Baudelaire emphasizes his fascination with artistry, especially in the elaborate comparisons of the music not to life but to pictorial art: "For example, to draw comparisons borrowed from painting, I imagine that I have before my eyes a vast expanse of a somber red. If this red represents passion, I see it appear gradually, through every gradation from red to rose, to the incandescence of the furnace," and so on. The effect of the music is also artificial in that it is like an opiate, conjuring up in the mind of the poet "those stimulants that accelerate the pulse of the imagination" (2:1453). This quickening of the pulse, this artificial stimulation that seeks an intensification of experience, is virtually indistinguishable from the religious sentiments the music inspires, "the supreme cry of the soul that has climbed to its paroxysm" and "the whole majesty of a life that is larger than ours" (2:1452). Baudelaire's language continually strives toward the spiritual, but the music acts upon him like a visual and narcotic seduction. In other words, it is religion with all the aesthetic and erotic wiles of the music hall.

Baudelaire's essay "Richard Wagner et *Tannhäuser* à Paris" evokes in an especially subtle and playful manner the aesthetic structure of this highly religious experience of Wagner's operas. Through his own rhetorical repetitions and the peculiar orchestral movements of his prose, Baudelaire seeks to foreground the function of iterability in Wagner's music. He seeks to reproduce Wagner's reproduction of religious experience, to appropriate his Christian appropriations in the domain of art. If Wagner reproduced Catholic sensations in the musical hall, so Baudelaire would reproduce them in critical prose. Both were composing arias of shame and grace, appropriating for the domain of art the repeatable gestures of Christianity.

Repetition is not only a stylistic idiosyncrasy of Baudelaire's essay, it is also a theme. The essay begins with the words "Remontons, s'il vous plaît, à treize mois en arrière" (2:779), thus beginning with a returning, reliving the first performance of *Tannhäuser* in Paris, but also setting in motion the theme of eternal return. Wagner is returning to Paris to pay another visit, while Baudelaire is returning to back issues of music criticism and returning to the views of Liszt and the program of the performance. Baudelaire recalls how Godfrey, Duke of Brabant, returns as a swan in *Lohengrin,* how the phantom ship of *The Flying Dutchman* returns to the shore once every seven years, and how Tannhäuser returns in despair to the Venusberg. The essay teems with repeated references to repeating, returning, remembering, re-enacting, re-emerging, re-establishing, recapturing, renewing, reuniting, reintroducing, reproducing, rediscovering, remodeling, redeeming, recurring, reviving, and reforming.

Baudelaire's passion for the music has the repetitive urge of an addiction, something of "the reverie, the vertiginous imaginings of opium," but his addiction and his reverie are also religious: "I had undergone (or so at least it appeared to me) a spiritual operation, a revelation. My rapture had been so strong and so terrible that I could not resist the desire to return to it over and over" (2:785). He works this eternal return into his very style of interrupting himself, thus necessitating the repeated "I repeat," the "But to return to my theme" or the "I have already referred to" or the "I come back now to," that mark the numerous back-and-forth shifts in the direction of his argument. Furthermore, he seeks to convince us of Wagner's originality, and yet Wagner's music and theoretical works remind him of a vast array of reputable precursors: he recalls Liszt, he recalls Beethoven, he recalls Diderot, Maturin, Hugo, Delacroix, Shakespeare, Greek tragedians, medieval mystery plays, the myths of Psyche and the Wandering Jew. The question arises, why is repetition so central to his conception of Wagner that scarcely a paragraph can pass without our being reminded of it?

Baudelaire discovers repetition, or the eternal return, at the very heart of Wagner's aesthetic. He is enigmatic about his discovery at first: "And yet the frequent repetitions of the same melodic phrases in pieces drawn from the same opera implied mysterious intentions and a method that was unfamiliar to me" (2:786). The function of repetition in this essay is, as we eventually learn, manifold. First of all, through a revival of what he regarded as a phenomenon peculiar to Ancient Greece, Wagner re-enacts a conception of theater as a civic forum and a religious experience. Furthermore, through a representation of myths, he effects an eternal return of experiences, especially religious ones, rendered not only universal but also repeatable and transferable through the medium of art. Finally, the repetition of musical motifs creates a philosophical argument that is elaborated through the operatic narrative. The constant repetition and resurgence of certain motifs, however, militates against any clear resolution, especially in *Tannhäuser*, with its eternal wandering and wavering between good and evil, grace and shame.

Baudelaire returns to Wagner's own theoretical works to learn the meaning of these repetitions in the words of the master himself. In the Athens of antiquity, Wagner found a dramatic tradition in which "the theater opened its precincts only for certain solemnities, when a religious festival was being held that was accompanied by the raptures of art" (quoted 2:790). In this theater, which combines the art of music and poetry, drama is virtually indistinguishable from religion. Baudelaire then repeats some of Wagner's other pronouncements about repetition, in particular the importance of myth and music to the religious theater: "The rhythmical arrangement and the (almost musical) adornment of the rhyme are for the poet the means of assuring to the line or to the phrase a power that captivates like a charm and governs feeling as it wills" (quoted 2:791). In other words, art and religion seduce us. They bypass consciousness for a more immediate connection with feeling, and they accomplish this magic through the repetitions of "rhythmical arrangement." But also through legend. Myths are eminently repeatable and yet, according to Wagner, they bear within them something immediately intelligible, something always already there, because they are in some essential way human. He offers us the paradox of something that is supposedly universal and yet for some reason requires articulation and even repetition. Like the exploitation of shame by the narrative of sin, myth renders experience self-conscious by giving it form and significance.

"Legend," Wagner writes, "no matter to what epoch or nation it belongs, has the advantage of understanding exclusively what is purely human in that epoch or that nation, and of presenting it in an original and very salient form, thus intelligible at first glance" (quoted 2:792). The legend is universal and yet particular, original and yet a repetition, launching the mind into a dream state of "perfect clairvoyance." Baudelaire fastens upon the power of music to generate this reverie of racial memory as "the sacred, the divine character of myth." In this sense, religion is an art form that seduces, that thrums with an uncanny rhythm on our various native sensitivities and produces in us a mystical experience of clarity and comprehension, then claims that sensation was already there in us all along, as yet inchoate, invisible, and unspoken. Emphasizing the notion of "mnemonic echo" or eternal return, Baudelaire proclaims that the same "scientific, poetic and artistic problems reproduce themselves without end throughout the ages, and Wagner does not make himself out to be an innovator but rather he simply confirms an ancient idea that will doubtless more than once again be by turns vanquished and victorious" (2:788).

But Baudelaire is not content to let myth remain so static. The art of the Wagnerian legend lies in its modernity, its peculiar remodeling in the present day. Using a plethora of words that begin with *re,* Wagner writes, "The myth is the primitive and anonymous poetry of the people, and we rediscover its reprise in every epoch, remodeled over and over into something new by the great poets of cultivated ages" (quoted 2:792), and so Baudelaire can claim that "phenomena and ideas that come back periodically through the ages always borrow at every resurrection the complementary character of the variant and the circumstance" (2:790).

Thus, the modernity of myths, we may suppose, lies in their refashioning of old material, not in an originality so much as in a rewriting. Baudelaire finds in Wagner an all important iterability, a power of misreading and appropriation. Through the perils of repetition, legend acquires the peculiar dissonance that marks it as modern, perhaps even decadent. I say decadent, for what is this modern quality in Wagner, this attribute that emerges sui generis in all its exquisite originality? "What above all appears to me to mark in an unforgettable manner the music of the master is nervous intensity, violence in passion and in will." This passionate excess that makes Wagner "the most genuine representative of the modern nature" is notably similar to the nervous brutality, at once hysterical and medieval, that was one of the more distinctive traits of the decadent persona (2:806). In other words, through the sheer iterability of Christian legend, Wagner's operas refigure Christian mysticism—indeed, the whole narrative of transgression and penitence, shame and grace—as a decadent aria self-consciously aware of its status as art.

As Huysmans would do more than twenty years later, Baudelaire focuses our attention on the overture to *Tannhäuser* and the dialectic of shame and grace. The theme of repetition also plays a role in defining the modern temperament as peculiarly erratic and uncertain with regard to religion. We see the first outlines of Huysmans' essay in Baudelaire's lines: "Every well-ordered brain bears within it two infinities, heaven and hell, and in any image of one of these it suddenly recognizes the moiety of itself" (2:795). It is through repetition that both Wagner and Baudelaire place these two mystical possibilities in terminal conflict.

I have already referred to Wagner's repetition of certain musical motifs, his alternating between moods of shame and grace. Baudelaire not only attempts to repeat these movements in the structure of the essay, he repeats his repetition: "I have already spoken of certain melodic phrases, whose persistent return in different passages drawn from the same work had intrigued my ear in a lively way during the first concert presented by Wagner at the Salle des Italiens. We have observed that in *Tannhäuser* the recurrence of the two primary themes, the religious motive and the hymn to pleasure, served to awaken the attention of the public and to reproduce in them a state of mind analogous to the actual situation" (2:801). Phrases like "already spoken," "persistent return," "recurrence," and "reproduce" are essential to an aesthetic that seeks to seduce us through repetition, to bypass our consciousness with a music that makes "our nerves vibrate in unison" (2:795). We learn of "incessant returns to bliss" (2:794), then the religious theme "reconquers little by little its empire," then lust is reawakened, then the religious theme "little by little re-establishes order and regains the ascendancy" (2:795). The same ineffable experience is "reproduced" later when, escaping from Venus, the hero "rediscovers" the pious life.

To underscore the contrast, which begins to look more like a comparison, Baudelaire repeats the movement again, noting that first we were in the depths of the earth, then at last we are above ground where humanity is "reunited" to its homeland. In the same manner, Baudelaire has a tendency to extended reveries in this essay, reveries that are by turns pious and demonic. In order to make a point of the universality of certain experiences, he quotes three long passages describing the effect of Wagner's music—one from Liszt, one from the program of a performance, and one his own. Each one details the mystical flights of music in ethereal and religious terms—a moment of ecstasy strangely encapsulated like an aria within the otherwise sober critical prose.

He lapses again into oddly ripe and imaginative language when describing the demonic spirituality of Venus: "She no longer inhabits Olympus nor the shores of a perfumed archipelago. She has retired to the depths of a cavern, albeit a truly magnificent one, illumined by fires other than those of the kindly Phoebus" (2:790). A few pages later, he waxes passionate again: "First come the satanic titillations of a vague love soon followed by enticements, swoonings, cries of victory, groans of gratitude, then by howls of ferocity, the reproaches of victims and the impious hosannas of the sacrifice" (2:795), and so on, back and forth between shame and grace, without hope of resolution. He signals only that the battle has reached a febrile pitch of nervous intensity. In the jarring purpleness of his prose, a richness of imagery and expression that swoops down on us without warning, Baudelaire seeks to vibrate our senses with a literary music that is no less than Wagnerian. Like decadents at the opera, we drift along on some mundane melody, when suddenly we recognize certain familiar and potent strains, and we tilt our heads to capture the sound of a favorite aria.

## Verlaine's Amour

> He had already begun, in following *Sagesse* with *Jadis et Naguère,* to inaugurate that system based on the famous *homo duplex.* The "sinful" volumes in question were entitled *Parallèlement.*
>
> Paul Verlaine

If Wagner's Tannhäuser had been attracted to men as well as women, he would have been a lot like Paul Verlaine. I am reminded of Oscar Wilde's dictum that life imitates art when I read the myriad biographical accounts of Verlaine and his interminable meandering between spirit and flesh. Baudelaire and Huysmans could write about Tannhäuser with great insight, but Verlaine lived the part. He had two lives, one as a saint and the other as a sinner, *parallèlement,* as he put it—side by side, without any real effort at reconciliation. As he wrote in "Le Bon Disciple" even before his conversion, "Je suis élu, je suis damné!"—"I am the elect, I am the damned!"[14] In *Les Hommes d'Aujourd'hui* (1885–1892), from which his *homo duplex* comment is drawn, Verlaine attempted to articulate this religious struggle in aesthetic terms as an irresolvable paradox, a juxtaposition of the sacred and the profane that resists any real synthesis. While Pater and Wilde, among other decadents, sought to cure the soul with the senses and the senses with the soul, Verlaine left both in melancholic estrangement, one yearning hopelessly for the other. As Stefan Zweig has pointed out, this paradox of a soul alienated from itself, desiring grace and abjection at the same time, is central not only to Verlaine's poetry but to Christianity itself: "There was the great antithesis between flesh and spirit, between body and soul; contempt for the sensual and continual fall into sin—the immanent conflict of childish and animal feeling which flooded forever wildly through Verlaine's years of manhood. This also has been for centuries the symbol of the Catholic Church."[15]

The dual nature of the soul was even in the poet's own time a philosophical cliché, and yet few of his admirers are ever quite willing to forgive him for repeating it with such freshness and audacity in his poetry. To read a complete edition of his poems is to pass from the Venusberg to the Vatican many times, from carefree erotica to what many have called the most beautiful Christian verse in the French language. From the melancholy eroticism of *Romances sans Paroles* (1874), to the spiritual simplicity of *Sagesse* (1881), to the profane preciosity of *Jadis et Naguère* (1884), to the sublimated musings of *Amour* (1888), to the pagan sensuality of *Parallèlement* (1889) and *Femmes* (1891), to the Christian *Bonheur* (1891), to the eroticism of *Chansons pour Elle* (1891), to the church music of *Liturgies Intimes* (1892), to the pornographic wit of *Odes en Son Honneur* (1893), *Chair* (1896) and *Hombres* (1903)—Verlaine's oeuvre is a roller coaster veering radically downward and upward from the work of a satyr to the work of a monk and back again. When we further note that some of his best Catholic lyrics were composed at about the same time as some of his most adventurous sexual lyrics, we may well be baffled. We may doubt his sincerity and scrutinize his credentials as a Catholic—and as a pagan.

Verlaine's sincerity, however, is the crowning paradox of his achievement. Unlike Baudelaire, he rarely had the intellectual coolness or critical distance from his subject matter to be truly ironic or to play a role he did not genuinely feel. He even prays for simplicity and sincerity. He has the peculiar talent of being always hopelessly himself, and leaving it to others of a more philosophical frame of mind to sort out his numerous contradictions. As Wilde once observed, the wise contradict themselves. In Verlaine's career as *homo duplex,* in his tendency to self-contradiction and paradox, we can glimpse the essential wisdom of the author of *Sagesse*. Mathilde Mauté, who was Verlaine's wife until the time of his imprisonment, puts the matter bluntly when she says: "He was always a man of periodic repentances. He spent half of his life doing wrong and the other half repenting it. He had a double nature."[16] Stefan Zweig sums up this double nature in far more Wagnerian terms when he writes: "In Verlaine . . . there was always a cleft: now he is pure pilgrim of yearning, now roué; now priest, now gamin. He has wrought the most beautiful religious poems of Catholicism, and at the same time has won the crown of all pornographic works with perverse and indecent poems."[17]

For those perverse and indecent poems, Zweig is unable to forgive the poet, but that is the typical gesture of all Verlaine criticism—a singular lack of forgiveness for the sin of sincere faith no less than the sins of the flesh. Verlaine had neither a great critical intelligence nor any great mastery of prose, but he did make a few valiant attempts at disarming the attacks on his sincerity as a Christian poet. These critical moments, however, read more like a shrug of the shoulders than a carefully argued defense: "I believe, and I am a good Christian at one moment; I believe, and I am a bad Christian an instant later."[18] In other words, through shame and repentance the sinner remains a Christian, but even in his shamelessness he is still a bad Christian, which is not the same as being an atheist. Even when he is in a state of rebellion or doubt, his Catholic faith determines the moral significance of his thoughts and actions. Blasphemy and doubt ironically bear within themselves the mark of faith, such that decadent Catholicism, as it was espoused by Baudelaire, Huysmans, and Verlaine, feels strangely inescapable. All roads lead to Rome. In decadent writing, especially in Verlaine, sin is not a rejection of the faith, but rather a moment, a peculiar mood, in a parable the faithful tell about themselves. One is never worse than the prodigal son, an "enfant prodigue avec des gestes de satyre," as Verlaine phrases it in *Sagesse*. His narrative of childlike rebellion always leads to humble reconciliation and paternal indulgence—followed by a renewed course of sin.

Verlaine made this Christian duality perfectly explicit in "Birds in the Night," a pre-conversion love poem to his wife that was published in *Romances sans Paroles*. He confesses that at times he dies the death of a sinner. At other times, he experiences the red ecstasy of an early Christian martyr who, motionless, appeals to Jesus as he is devoured by the lions. I am reminded of Venus in the opening scene of *Tannhäuser* as she turns to her lover amid the paradisical pleasures of the Venusberg and asks where his mind is straying. Verlaine's mind was always straying to precisely what was absent from the present moment. His was a melancholic wandering that raised the absence of the beloved or the absence of God to a persistent romantic pang. The characteristic plaintive mood of so much of his poetry attests to an aggravated desire, an interminable longing, for either the abjection of the flesh or the mystical flights of the spirit. Even amid utter dissipation he lapsed into ennui, and he longed for an anywhere out of the present world. He is like Tannhäuser, longing for a lost experience of grace, telling Venus of the dreamlike and uncanny pealing of bells that he hears, at once foreign to his ear and strangely familiar, like a song from childhood. The bafflement and impatience of Venus in this scene resonates well with the frustration of many of Verlaine's critics, who wish to this day that he had contented himself with being either a great saint or a great sinner.

Until he met Rimbaud, however, he was not much of a sinner, and he was certainly not saintly until his conversion in prison. Because much of what is distinctly Catholic about Verlaine was written after he was sentenced to prison, I am obliged to focus on the later work, much of which has been judged all too harshly. The prison "conversion" has become something of a pun in Verlaine criticism, since it marks not only a sudden thematic interest in Christianity but also an aesthetic change, a shift from the cool and highly artificial style of his early works, like *Fêtes Galantes* (1869), to a more perverse, emotional, and mystical quality that many have seen as a turn for the worst. Although late in life Verlaine wrote an enormous amount of verse that lacked the musicality and atmospheric power of his earlier efforts, some of his best work appears in *Sagesse, Amour,* and *Parallèlement,* the later books that were in fact most admired by his contemporaries. In these books he established his signature gesture of the double parallel movement toward the spirit and the flesh. In order to put these books in biographical perspective, I first need to sketch in the events of Verlaine's life that led up to his conversion.

Although Verlaine was attracted to boys and to other men from an early age, he was also attracted to women, and he married Mathilde Mauté in 1870. His affection for her is attested to by the love poetry of *La Bonne Chanson* (1870), and she soon gave birth to a son named Georges. For a time the Verlaines lived a life of tenuous bourgeois respectability, insofar as such a life was possible in the midst of a civil war. Their domestic happiness was disrupted, however, by two forces that Verlaine was powerless to repress, his temper and his love for another man. Rimbaud was only sixteen when, with a letter and some poems, he sought the friendship of Verlaine, the only living poet he could bear. The boy was talented, rebellious, arrogant, and also extremely handsome in a gamin-like way. For a time, Rimbaud dominated Verlaine's life, making a mockery of the older man's efforts at connubial bliss and leading him in a life of utter dissipation. There have been many accounts of this period in Verlaine's life, all of them ripe with anecdotes about his penniless wandering, his bizarre letters to Mathilde, his suicidal threats, his taste for absinthe, his sexual euphoria, and Rimbaud's malevolent imagination.

The romance finally came to a close when, in a drunken altercation, Rimbaud threatened to leave and the frustrated and incoherent Verlaine shot at him with a pistol. This act of violence was more theater than homicidal wrath. He shot twice, in fact—one bullet grazed Rimbaud's hand and the other was directed ineffectually at the floor—and a remorseful Verlaine then begged to be shot himself. Rimbaud ran for a train, and Verlaine pursued, the pistol in his pocket. He was eventually arrested when Rimbaud sought the aid of a policeman. The authorities were made aware of Verlaine's homosexuality and were therefore apparently inclined to severity. He spent sixteen months in prison, from the summer of 1873 to January 1875.

Nevertheless, Verlaine warmed to his incarceration at Mons and often wrote of it with sentimental affection, as in his prose memoir *Mes Prisons* (1893) and in poems like "Ecrit en 1875" (published in *Amour*), which opens with a comparison of his prison to the finest of castles in the countryside. This good humor and resignation is largely attributable to his conversion and the profound sense of spiritual contentment that he discovered while in prison. Whatever doubts he might have excited about his sincerity, no one denies any longer that Verlaine's conversion was a genuine one. He referred to it as "my private happiness, the belated flower of my soul."[19] Like most decadents, he embraced the Church rather suddenly in a moment of emotional desperation, and his faith was mystical rather than philosophical or doctrinal. He set the tone for a number of other decadent conversions, especially those of Huysmans and John Gray, in which grace was experienced passively as an overwhelming and mysterious sensation of peacefulness that follows a period of great dissipation or perturbation of mind.

The catalyst for Verlaine's conversion was indeed an emotional one: the news that Mathilde had obtained an order of legal separation. He learned that he had lost, along with virtually everything else, his wife and child. He threw himself on his bed in a fit of tears and, without knowing why, he eventually found himself prostrate before a crucifix and a lithograph of the Sacred Heart that were in his cell. He sent for the prison chaplain, and by the next morning Verlaine was already in spirit a Catholic. His confession to the chaplain was a spasm of self-revelation, lengthy and lurid in its detail, and not long afterward he received absolution. From this moment, Catholicism became a central theme in his work, as well as the only moral point of reference in his life.

From his prison conversion sprang the inspiration for *Sagesse,* the first of his four major volumes of religious verse. *Sagesse* helped to establish Verlaine's literary reputation as both a Catholic and a decadent. He was extolled by Huysmans, Rémy de Gourmont, Jules Lemaître, George Moore, and a host of other contemporaries as the great Catholic poet of the age, and yet he is also listed among the profane writers in Des Esseintes's library in *A Rebours,* where an entire paragraph is devoted to the fulsome delights of *Sagesse* in particular. If we first examine what is Catholic about *Sagesse,* we might also better understand what is decadent about it. Verlaine developed a new simplicity of style, and most of the volume is couched in a devotional and penitential idiom familiar to any Christian. He adopts a consistent tone of humility and piety as he enumerates his sins and elaborates on his remorse. He is at once mystical, penitential, humble, and childlike.

Perhaps his most successful poem in the volume, and certainly the best known, is the sonnet sequence "Mon Dieu m'a dit," a passionate conversation between Christ and the poet. The year before *Parsifal* was first performed at Bayreuth, Verlaine published his own tribute to Christian love and remorse. Christ commands the poet to love him, pointing out the wounds in his own side, his arms straining under the weight of the other's sins, and his feet bathed by the tears of Mary Magdalene:

> Mon Dieu m'a dit: Mon fils, il faut m'aimer. Tu vois
> Mon flanc percé, mon coeur qui rayonne et qui saigne,
> Et mes pieds offensés que Madeleine baigne
> De larmes, et mes bras douloureux sous le poids
>
> De tes péchés, et mes mains! (268)

The form is pious and traditional, yet dramatic and even incantatory with its repetitive and alliterative exclamations. Verlaine meditates on each part of Christ's body as though it were a symbol in a precious allegory. His tone is one of perfect honesty and simplicity, speaking "franchement et simplement" as, in a later sonnet in the same sequence, he seats himself before the banquet his God has laid for him. It is difficult to doubt his sincerity when he writes of Christ's invitation to the feast, which is also a summons to humility, honesty, confession, and repentance:

> Approche-toi de mon oreille. Epanches-y
> L'humiliation d'une brave franchise.
> Dis-moi tout sans un mot d'orgueil ou de reprise
> Et m'offre le bouquet d'un repentir choisi. (271)

*Sagesse* brings to Catholic poetry an unusual literary virtuosity without ever sacrificing the seriousness and sincerity of its devotional pose. In fact, Verlaine was explicit in his distaste for false religion. As early as *Poèmes Saturniens* (1866), in a poem entitled "Jésuitisme," he described the suffering he endures when his martyr, his dream lying helpless and half-decayed on a funeral bier, is transformed into an amusing spectacle by some fatuous Tartuffe.

In emphasizing sincerity, however, I am not suggesting that *Sagesse* is not decadent or that it is a flight from the decadent style and sensibility for which Verlaine is best known. On the contrary, he proves the absurdity of the critical truism that Catholicism was an antidote to decadence rather than one of its peculiar symptoms. He committed the unpardonable faux pas of writing quintessentially decadent poetry before, during, and after his conversion. His religious idiom is to my mind decadent for a number of reasons, some of them obvious and others more subtle. Max Nordau quoted from *Sagesse* in *Degeneration* as an example of hysterical mysticism. *Le Décadent,* a journal well named, published a few poems from Verlaine's religious volume *Amour,* including the relentlessly pious "Prière du Matin." *La Plume,* another journal associated with the decadent movement, published a special issue on *Catholiques-mystiques* that singled out Verlaine for special praise and *Sagesse* as his most important work. John Gray translated "Mon Dieu m'a dit" as part of *Silverpoints,* his own archetypally decadent volume of poetry. *Sagesse* is most decadent when it is least distinguishable from the writings of medieval mystics— when it cultivates its own religious sensibility as an anachronistic reverie.

In *Sagesse,* there are poems devoted to Saint Antony and Saint Teresa, who were two of the many patron saints of the decadents. Verlaine also left behind a fragment of a religious drama with a familiar title, "La Tentation de Saint Antoine," presumably intended for *Sagesse.* He once wrote to his friend and biographer Edmond Lepelletier and asked him to send a copy of Flaubert's *Tentation* at "my present Thebaid."[20] For many decadents, Saint Antony represented a dreamlike correspondence between religion, art, and sexuality. With the publication of Flaubert's *Tentation,* Antony became the perfect decadent Catholic, a veritable portrait of the artist as a delirious eremite, so imaginative and seductive were his temptations. In the hands of Verlaine, Antony was a genius of religious panic who warded off desire in a desert of white stones. Like Des Esseintes, Verlaine sought a more refined Thebaid, and he found it in the prison at Mons, or more to the point, in his religious idealization of the life *cellulairement,* to use his own term. In his most Catholic book, Verlaine celebrated a key decadent trope, the disjunction of the body and soul and their eternal conflict in the life of Saint Antony:

> De près, de loin, le Sage aura sa Thébaïde
> Parmi le fade ennui qui monte de ceci,
> D'autant plus âpre et plus sanctifiante aussi
> Que deux parts de son âme y pleurent, dans ce vide! (286)

As Verlaine knew, the power of Catholic literature lies not so much in the quality of its grace as in the intensity of its temptations. Verlaine, like Barbey and Huysmans, longed for a religious intensity, at once sublime and delicate, that he associated with the early Church and the Middle Ages—what he called *le Moyen Age énorme et délicat.*

This mystical quality is also captured in Verlaine's recurrent image of the child. When George Moore remarked that Verlaine abandoned himself to the Church as a child to a fairy tale, he was simply repeating what was even then a critical truism, that Verlaine's faith was childlike. It is customary, in every biography of Verlaine, to claim that everything about the man was childlike—his mind, his temper, his sexuality, his faith—as if his entire success as a poet were an expression of arrested development. But Verlaine's identification with the child is an intentional, explicit, and profound one. As Harold Nicholson once observed, "He had always liked being 'even as a little child.' To his relief he discovered that in the Christian Church this was a positive advantage."[21] As Wilde would later discover, the childlike sensibility of Christianity is one of its greatest virtues.

With his constant use of the word *enfant,* Verlaine is of course invoking both the infant Jesus and the prodigal son. He is also capturing the sense of innocence, purity, helplessness, and parental love for which the child is often a symbol. Verlaine is fond of variations on words like *faiblesse,* in the sense of both innocent helplessness and moral weakness, and *bercer,* the rocking motion of the infant's crib that brings peace and unconsciousness. Psychoanalytic critics of Verlaine have pointed out his emotional attachment to his mother and discussed his conversion as a desperate cry for the intensity of love he lost when, in prison, he was separated from his wife, son, lover, and mother. The theory is well justified, but there is a further spiritual significance to the child image, in particular the sinner as child. Verlaine sought in mysticism a freedom from systems, laws, and rhetoric. Beneath his sentimental evocation of childhood is a mystical nihilism, a destruction of self and world that allows at last, in the silence of a dreamless sleep, the sensation of God's finger on the melancholy cradle that rocks the senses into a state of bliss:

> Un grand sommeil noir
> Tombe sur ma vie:
> Dormez, tout espoir,
> Dormez, toute envie!
>
> Je ne vois plus rien,
> Je perds la mémoire
> Du mal et du bien . . .
> O la triste histoire!
>
> Je suis un berceau
> Qu'une main balance
> Au creux d'un caveau:
> Silence, silence! (279)

I know of no other poem that captures the nihilism of an "obscure night of the soul" better than this one. Verlaine effects a regression to childhood, but one that is fraught with the profound sadness of Christ's passion, *la triste histoire*. Desire, whether it be the longing of hope or envy, the memory of good or evil, decomposes into a funereal sleep. His cradle is rocking peacefully, but with the delicate balance of a divine hand in the hollow of a tomb. His rebirth presumes a certain intimacy with the horror of death. The child of this cradle is no longer innocent, nor does he remain the sinner he has become. The sinner is not a monstrous figure in Verlaine's religious poetry, but a weak one, overwhelmed by the forces of good and evil, passive and pitiable as an infant, and in his sorrow he surrenders his will and his consciousness to God with the naive trustfulness that can only come through faith. Christ asked that we receive the kingdom of God like a little child, and Verlaine elaborated this blessing on the head of the *enfant* into a sublime mystical effect.

Perhaps the most overpowering temptation of all, whether we are reading a decadent writer or an early modern mystic, is the fascination for the word itself, the sumptuous rhetoric by which faith articulates itself. Not even Antony was able to forbear it. In *Sagesse* Verlaine has a tendency toward the sensual and precious imagery for which decadent verse is notorious. When, for example, he describes Christ as the new Adam who devours the old Adam, devours indeed our very Rome and our Paris, our Sparta and our Sodom, in one grim banquet, we know we have arrived in familiar fin de siècle territory. Verlaine then likens the love of Christ to a fire that burns the senseless flesh, evaporating it like a perfume:

> Mon amour est le feu qui dévore à jamais
> Toute chair insensée, et l'évapore comme
> Un parfum. (270)

Sublimation was never so divine. In a subtle sleight of hand, the language of an earlier Parnassian poem like "Cythère," with its line "L'odeur des roses, faible, grâce," is revived in a Catholic setting.

"Dévotions" from *Liturgies Intimes* is a seldom-read classic in the genre of fulsome worship, with its five-stanza sentence overflowing with what the poet calls the pure perfume of red and blue flowers that awakens the soul from its lethargy, hymns that burn with an intense theology, and amid the fiery Aves a chaste delirium and an excess of ecstasy. Even in his moments of greatest piety, Verlaine betrays a mystical sensuality that would be the envy of any decadent. In "Et Pour Récompenser ton Zèle" in *Sagesse,* he speaks of the zeal, the calm aspiration, and the love of poverty that distinguish the elect who have suffered in the name of Christ. At the same time, he describes the "ineffable delights" and "mystical evenings," "the perpetual ecstasy" and "lovely radiance," in which these same elect are likely to indulge. Like one of his earlier romances, this sonnet sips from an Eternal Chalice amid the glimmer of moonlight and the sound of the Angelus ringing, rose and black. The poet moves invisibly from the dutiful to the ecstatic:

> Et l'extase perpétuelle et la science,
> Et d'être en moi parmi l'aimable irradiance
> De tes souffrances,—enfin miennes,—que j'aimais! (272)

The intensity of mystical Catholicism—the horror of its suffering, the grand gestures of its humility, the sensuality of its delirium, the extravagance of its metaphors, and, above all, the obliteration of self in its supernatural *joie extraordinaire*—forms one of the defining sensations of decadent art, and beside it, the fabled sexual perversity of the movement is decidedly upstaged.

Like Baudelaire and Huysmans, Verlaine also at times drew attention to the self-conscious artistry of Catholicism in his own poetry. He was already widely admired for the painterly quality of his work, especially in poems like "Green" and "Spleen" in the "Aquarelles" section of *Romances sans Paroles,* verses that read like an impressionist still life. The most self-consciously artistic of his Catholic poems is "Un Crucifix," which appeared in *Amour* and was also translated by John Gray for *Silverpoints.* In a manner that is typically decadent, Verlaine does not just write about the Crucifixion, he writes a poem about a copy of a painting of the Crucifixion, thus redoubling the sense of aesthetic displacement. He emphasizes the aesthetic decisions of the painter, the colors used, even the painting's placement within a Gothic church where it is given a stained-glass kiss by the decline of a mystical day from "un long vitrail d'azur et d'or finement roux." In lines that prefigure the opening chapter of Huysmans' *Là-Bas,* the poet submits the horrible suffering of Christ to an aesthetic meditation. He ends by dedicating the poem to the friend who has copied the painting. The friend has intentionally left the copy behind because he noticed the poet's admiration. Verlaine describes him as "a good painter and a good Christian, and a good poet also,—the three go well together" (416). Faith is not an antidote for aestheticism, but a stimulant for it.

Perhaps the most compelling testament to *Sagesse* as a decadent icon is its appearance in *A Rebours*. Huysmans singles out one poem in particular, "J'avais Peiné de Sisyphe," which he praises for its representation of the Blessed Virgin as a Christian soldier of no mean military prowess. She descends in a storm cloud to rescue the beleaguered poet, who has placed himself at the mercy of the dreaded Gorgon, the *Monstre* we call sexual desire. In a tempest of rage and inhuman cries, she sends the Jabberwock galumphing off through the woods again, and in her victory she proclaims herself the heart of virtue, the soul of wisdom, the sweetness of redress, and so on.

Verlaine's poem is for Huysmans another evocation of the "Christian Venus" that he found in Wagner's *Tannhäuser*. In the Wagner essay he recalls the scene from the *Psychomachia* of Prudentius in which the allegorical figure of Christian modesty is a female soldier who clobbers a pitch-spitting Venus. In his description of Verlaine's Virgin in *A Rebours*, the line between Modesty and Venus is a fine one:

> Des Esseintes would often reread this book *Sagesse*, allowing the poems to inspire in him clandestine reveries, dreams of an occult love for a Byzantine Madonna who changed, at a certain moment, into a Cydalisa who had strayed into our own century, who was so mysterious and so troubling that it was impossible to know whether she aspired to depravities that, once accomplished, were irresistible; or whether she herself was soaring upward in an immaculate dream, in which the adoration of the soul would float about her in a state forever unconfessed, forever pure. (7:282–283)

This passage is one of those interminable and ambivalent sentences for which Huysmans is well known. It bears some of the hallmarks of decadent Catholicism: the easy slippage from depravity to piety, the fascination for the antique, the opium dream of Christian mysticism, the masculine woman as perverse icon, and the Byzantine cult of Mary. In true decadent fashion, Huysmans has rendered Verlaine's Lady even more terrifying and bizarre than she already is. Like Saint Antony in the throes of a vision, we scarcely know whether to sigh or groan. The decadent quality of *Sagesse* is apparent as much in its reception as in its inscription.

Especially after the publication of *A Rebours,* Verlaine became, almost by accident, a champion of the decadent movement. His followers delighted in his religious poems, but he was also inspired to write poems of a less ennobling kind. He was not long in returning to the Venusberg. At first, he accepted the scandalous epithet of *décadent* as a witty riposte, a way of thumbing his nose at the philistines. "I like the word *decadent,*" he told Ernest Raynaud, "all shimmering with purple and gold . . . It throws out the brilliance of flames and the gleam of precious stones. It is made of carnal spirit and unhappy flesh and of all the violent splendors of the Lower Empire."[22] Eventually, however, he tired of the role, but not before he had tempted the pallets of his followers with poems like "Langueur," which appeared in *Jadis et Naguère.* The poem is a touchstone of the decadent sensibility and evidence of how far its author had strayed from the Catholic themes of *Sagesse.* "I am the Empire at the end of the decadence," he begins, casting himself as a languid Nero, entertaining himself with "indolent acrostics in a golden style" even as the conquering barbarians gather at the gates:

> Je suis l'Empire à la fin de la décadence,
> Qui regarde passer les grands Barbares blancs
> En composant des acrostiches indolents
> D'un style d'or où la langueur du soleil danse. (370)

In the end, all is drunk, all is eaten, and nothing remains but ennui and a disobedient slave. The poem is infused with a sense of opulence and degeneration, satiety and inanition. Even the hint of irony in Verlaine's voice is decadent, like the note of self-parody in *A Rebours.* Rather than mining the language of medieval mysticism, Verlaine turns to the corruption of the Latin decadence and the gross debauchery that others would seek out in the likes of Messalina and Heliogabalus, Apuleius and Petronius.

The real scandal, however, was to be found in Verlaine's erotic verses, which complemented the decorative charm of "Langueur" with a sexual explicitness that sometimes defied publication. Many of these poems are about the various female prostitutes who excited his fondness in his later years, women like Eugénie Krantz and Esther Boudin who populate his *Chansons pour Elle, Odes en Son Honneur,* and *Chair.* In these books his tendency to mysticism is purely erotic, a worship of the body rather than the soul. His childlike simplicity wandered only in search of sexual pleasure, what he called in *Parallèlement* a "second childhood less morose," reigning instinctively "like a phallus" (516).

Although in *Mes Prisons* he would claim that he was only "feigning to be of the Devil's company" when he wrote *Parallèlement* (352), he could at times be forthright in his blasphemy. In "A la Princesse Roukhine," the poet counts himself at once the priest and the slave of a woman for whom he would be damned without remorse. In other poems Verlaine strikes a more Baudelairean pose of lost idealism and bitter pleasure. He is again the prodigal son, victim of his own *faiblesse.* In the opening poem of the "Lunes" section of *Parallèlement,* he calls himself a frightful Tiberius full of remorse, who longs to destroy the present day, to return to chaste loves and—the cradle theme again—rock to sleep his lust and shame:

> Je veux, pour te tuer, ô temps qui me dévastes,
> Remonter jusqu'aux jours bleus des amours chastes
> Et bercer ma luxure et ma honte au bruit doux
> De baisers sur Sa main et non plus dans Leurs cous. (503)

As *poète maudit,* Verlaine mastered the melancholic regret, the sensation seemingly as inevitable as original sin, by which he acknowledged his incapacity and unworthiness with respect to his own Catholic ideals.

In his two pornographic works *Femmes* and *Hombres,* Verlaine abandons religious concerns altogether, except for the occasional blasphemous suggestion. Here the descent into the Venusberg is complete, and there is even a suggestion of *Tannhäuser* in a poem suitably entitled "Ouverture," in which he speaks of the breasts of an otherwise unidentified woman as the "double mount of pride and lust." Buried in this mons veneris, the poet describes his whores as "the only true priestesses of the one true God," saving themselves only for the chosen in their "tabernacles of shamelessness":

> Et le toucher font des élus de vos dévots,
> Tabernacles et Saints des Saints de l'impudeur. (1388)

In the opening line of *Hombres*, Verlaine priggishly warns the poet not to blaspheme, but he is being facetious. He is merely telling the poet not to discount the buttocks of woman simply because he favors men. No less than in *Femmes*, Verlaine sometimes finds in sex between men an occasion for a bawdy remark about the Church. In the first part of "Balanide," for example, he muses on his lover's cock as it ejaculates inside him, and he compares it to a bishop, full of unction, whose benediction is heard the whole length of the nave, from the altar to the choir:

> Comme un évêque au choeur
> Il est plein d'onction.
> Sa bénédiction
> Va de l'autel au choeur. (1407)

He extends the metaphor to describe the swollen and purple glans of his lover's erection as the bishop's pastoral ring of amethyst and black gold that is worn only at night. In the daytime, his duty discharged, the bishop pulls up his pretty monastic hood. Throughout these two books, however, religion is for the most part ignored in favor of a rollicking and gleeful account of copulation.

The homoerotic poems that Verlaine wrote about Rimbaud are understandably some of his most powerful. The best of them appear in *Parallèlement*, the book that Verlaine explicitly intended as a profane counterpoint to *Sagesse* and *Amour*. These are the poems that have endeared him to modern gay readers in particular, since they rise to the defense of love between men in a manner unheard of among other Catholic poets. Soon after he left prison, Verlaine tried to resume a relationship with his former lover, but he failed. Redolent with the odor of sanctity he had acquired through his conversion, he wrote to Rimbaud with the improbable invitation, "Let us love one another in

Jesus Christ." Rimbaud agreed to see him, referring to him tartly as "Loyola." The facts about their meeting are difficult to ascertain, but apparently Verlaine's long-dormant desire for both drink and men was stimulated by a renewed acquaintance with his friend. In a justly famous interlude along the banks of the Neckar, the two men quarreled and became violent, and Verlaine was found the next morning lying unconscious by the river. They never saw each other again. As Rimbaud told Ernest Delahaye, Verlaine had come with a rosary in his hands but, three hours later, had denied his God "and made the ninety-eight wounds of our Blessed Lord bleed again."[23]

Despite this challenge to his piety, Verlaine idealized his relationship with Rimbaud in a handful of brilliant poems in which he captured the excitement of love and sexual liberation. They represent the finer moments in Verlaine's post-conversion project of celebrating the beauty of the flesh *parallèlement* alongside the beauty of religious devotion. In "Crimen Amoris" in *Jadis et Naguère*, Rimbaud is figured as a fallen angel or faun whose pride invites an apocalyptic destruction of his own hedonistic milieu. In Verlaine's fascinated ambivalence, Rimbaud is man, angel, and demon—"Mortel, ange ET démon" (601), as he writes in the poem "A Arthur Rimbaud" in *Dédicaces*. In *Parallèlement*, however, Verlaine wrote homoerotic poems about Rimbaud in which the Catholic ambivalence is left behind in favor of a strikingly modern defense of sexual adventure and love between men. In "Ces Passions" he discusses what he sees as the superiority of that love to marriage between a man and a woman. He says that these passions, "which they alone still call loves" (522), are loves indeed, tender and furious, with particular charms that everyday loves have not.

Verlaine's championing of homosexuality takes a form that became increasingly familiar in fin de siècle apologias on the subject: the idealization of homosexuality as a pure act of love, superior in its intensity, beauty, and pagan spirituality. He refers to sex between man and woman as gross, bestial, and, worst of all, normal, and he bemoans the tendency of women to get pregnant. Love between men, on the other hand, is depicted as a beautiful gambol, grand and gay. He remarks on the plenitude of their sexual pleasure, the richness of caresses that lead to the "final divine annihilation." He speaks of their "emancipation from heavy nature." In casting aside any thought of sexual reproduction, in making of their desire an adventure of pure love, Verlaine sees these passions as witnesses of the soul in the combat against base nature. They are a spiritualized and aestheticized desire *à rebours*. He does not sublimate, he simply idealizes. Sex between men is subjected to some truly charming euphemisms as the lovers trade positions, each taking his turn with the "supreme act," the "perfect ecstasy," now "cup or mouth," now "vase," rapturous as the night and fervent as the day:

> Et pour combler leurs voeux, chacun d'eux tour à tour
> Fait l'action suprême, a la parfaite extase,
> —Tantôt la coupe ou la bouche et tantôt le vase—
> Pâmé comme la nuit, fervent comme le jour. (522)

"Laeti et Errabundi," the poem that follows "Ces Passions," treats the same theme but is more explicitly autobiographical in its evocation of Verlaine's adventures with Rimbaud. The very title suggests the sheer pleasure that Verlaine associated with sex between men—the romantic wandering, the childlike lightness of heart, and the dissociation from the confines of a settled bourgeois respectability. He emphasizes freedom in the sense of erotic liberation but also freedom from heterosexuality, responsibility, and shame. His "ponsard" knows no limit, since sexual scruples are left behind for the monkish at heart—that is to say, for Verlaine himself in a different mood. The romance of man and man is rated above the model marriage, as the male lovers pride themselves on being "freer than the freest in the world." For Verlaine, sex with Rimbaud excited a violent and invigorating rejection of family life and Christian morals altogether. When at last he speaks of the memory of his lover burning in his blood and brain, religious scruples return only as an afterthought. When he speaks of him as "my grand and radiant sin" (525), he is not, for once, saddened by his remorse. Rather, he is playing the role of Tannhäuser, at peace in the Venusberg, if only for a time.

In reading *Parallèlement* or *Hombres,* we might suppose that Verlaine regarded the Catholic and the homoerotic as mutually exclusive categories. On the contrary, desire between men has a religious dimension in his work. In his profane writings Verlaine tossed discretion aside with considerable daring, speaking the relatively unspeakable.

In his religious writings, however, he was an accomplished hand at queering the Church without ever compromising his studied *odeur de sainteté*. His devotion was infused with homoeroticism. "Whoever thinks that my faith is not sincere," he told his friend W. G. C. Byvanck, "does not know the ecstasy of receiving the very flesh of the Lord into one's own body. For me, it's a dizzying happiness: a physical emotion."[24] After reading Verlaine's profane works, this dizzying happiness is certainly familiar, but in his tone and phrasing he takes advantage of a long history of Catholic homoeroticism that allows him to indulge his "physical emotion" with a degree of impunity. As Stefan Zweig has written, Verlaine "is a reverberating echo of the great seekers after God, of the church fathers, of St. Augustine and of the mystics, and he wrestles for an almost physical love of God."[25]

If Verlaine was an agile Tannhäuser, he was also a brilliant Parsifal—or perhaps I should say a brilliant Amfortas, given his groans of remorse. I hope that, this late in the *siècle,* I need not speak at great length about the blue smoke of homoeroticism wafting up from the censers in Wagner's most Christian opera. Others before me have recognized it, and I would argue that Verlaine was one of them. The effusive fondness of Ludwig of Bavaria for this opera and its composer is only the very earliest sign that *Parsifal* was a classic in the genre of chivalric homosexuality. Parsifal himself could have stepped straight out of a Freudian case study. Kundry's description of his childhood reads like Verlaine's own childhood to a degree, but also like the classic psychoanalytic account of homosexual etiology: the boy born fatherless to a mother who keeps him to herself to save him from the masculine world of battle, stoicism, military valor, and so on. The mother clasps the boy fiercely in her arms, and Kundry wonders, as we all wince, why he was not frightened at her kisses. He longs to be like the men but never measures up, and so he remains an effeminized fool. The temptations of the Eternal Woman are little more than a running joke. We are hardly surprised when Parsifal overcomes his desire for the flower maidens and Kundry herself. Like many homosexual adherents of the New Chivalry, as it came to be called in England, he could pride himself on his misogynistic transcendence of feminine evil, even though the likelihood of his temptation is moot. No woman has a chance of seducing the boylike Parsifal until Kundry comes up with the oedipal strategy of exploiting his mother love.

Klingsor fills a very different homosexual role. His sexual sin dares not speak its name. Even Klingsor knows it was awful, whatever it was, and so he castrates himself. Like Parsifal he is effeminized, but ignobly so, and thus it seems inevitable that he acquire a taste for the occult, a practice that was already popularly associated with the sodomite. Instead of a phallus, he has Kundry, the somnambulistic witch whose will he controls and through whom, in a classic triangulation of homoerotic desire, he seeks to seduce Parsifal. He also has the spear that pierced the side of Christ, another detachable phallus, which he acquired by seducing Amfortas with the help of a flower maiden. The clever spear-play is always the dead giveaway to the homoeroticism of *Parsifal*. Klingsor stabs Amfortas in the leg, thus ensuring in this profane homoerotic contact that the leg will forever ache and bleed in evidence of the phallic corruption of its owner. Amfortas can only be healed again with another touch of the spear by a foolish boy, pure at heart. Parsifal is his Christian knight in shining armor, the sublimation of a pederastic dream come true. His benevolent sexuality is drawn to a higher and higher spiritual plane in the temple of the Grail, enraptured by the voices in the dome, perfect in their boyish loveliness. Like Cornelius in Walter Pater's *Marius the Epicurean*, he inspires the other man to goodness through a homoerotic love in Christ.

Verlaine's religious poetry continually echoes the homoerotic chivalry of *Parsifal*. Christ himself became the object of this Wagnerian affection, as suggested by the palpitating wound imagery in the opening sonnet of "Mon Dieu m'a dit." With an incantatory moan, Verlaine repeatedly directs the attention of Christ to his own love wounds, singing, "O my God, you have wounded me with love, and the wound is throbbing still, O my God, you have wounded me with love." The opening poem of *Sagesse,* in which the masked knight of Misfortune pierces the poet's heart with a lance, is even more distinctly Wagnerian:

> Bon chevalier masqué qui chevauche en silence,
> Le Malheur a percé mon vieux coeur de sa lance. (240)

In this wonderfully plaintive and medieval allegory, Verlaine plays at being Amfortas, calling on his Parsifal, in the figure of Misfortune, to bring him to redemption through suffering. The knight, who is actually based on a prison guard at Mons, touches the poet with his gloved finger, entering like a flame into his wound, and speaks of the law in a hard voice. Through the icy contact of this finger of fire, so suggestive of Christ's own homoerotic interlude with the doubting Thomas, his heart is magically reborn to purity and bravery.

Verlaine met his real Parsifal, however, in Lucien Létinois, his other great love. In biographies of the poet, Létinois is easily upstaged by the more charismatic Rimbaud, but he plays an equally important role in Verlaine's later poetry. As a gaumless youth from the provinces, naive about sex and boyish in his piety, Létinois was the ideal object of Verlaine's chivalric affections. He was handsome and, like Rimbaud when he first appeared on Verlaine's doorstep years before, he was also still an adolescent. At the time, Verlaine was a teacher at the Collège Notre-Dame at Rethel, and he was trying so hard to be saintly that the students mocked him with the nickname "Jesus Christ." The boy responded perfectly to the older man's chivalric overtures, and for a while they tried their hand at farming together, though Verlaine clearly knew nothing about agriculture. The religious disposition of the boy and his unassailable earnestness were an inspiration to Verlaine in his own efforts at piety and Christian love. Whether the two ever had sex is unknown, though the highly ambiguous poem "O l'Odieuse Obscurité," which appears in the long sequence on Létinois in *Amour,* suggests that around Christmas in 1879 the boy had sex probably with a woman and possibly with Verlaine. Far from a consummation of their love, however, this transgression excited regret in the two men and appears not to have been repeated. They maintained a passionate friendship together until Létinois died of typhus at the tender age of twenty-three.

In the nineteenth century, an era steeped in the language of religious and Platonic eros, two men or—even less suspiciously—two women could sustain such a sexually ambiguous relationship with impunity. They might even regard the relationship as more intense because more pure, so to speak. Thus we find Edmond Lepelletier pointing to Létinois as evidence of Verlaine's elevated affection for other men, rather than of his homosexuality. He even tries to desexualize Verlaine's love for Rimbaud, but with no great persuasiveness. In his love for Létinois, Verlaine attempted to live out his belief in a romantic Christian desire between men. Modern biographers, however, are loath to believe that such a homosexual desire can exist happily, and this disbelief strikes me as homophobic. Even today, the figure of the homosexual is so saturated with sexuality in the popular imagination that the very possibility of religious faith or chaste devotion in gay men is held to be highly improbable. Like everyone else, homosexuals eroticize religion, eroticize fatherhood, eroticize friendship, and eroticize aesthetics, but only through the utmost discretion are they allowed to get away with it. Gay men as a rule are not permitted to sublimate.

Despite the lack of any evidence for lechery in his relationship with Létinois, Verlaine's critics will nevertheless find it under every bush. Joanna Richardson, for example, regards Verlaine's paternalism as hypocritical. His advice to the boy that he avoid sexual temptation is to her mind so much queer double-talk, even though Verlaine was at the time applying the same standards to himself. A. E. Carter's homophobia with regard to Verlaine and Létinois is especially vivid: "He was becoming an aging libertine, the sort of person who makes a nuisance of himself in parks and steam baths. When religion is added to this mixture we get something very smelly indeed: there is a stench of hypocrisy about his affection for Lucien from first to last. If he did not corrupt his pupil he would have liked to—though he never admitted the fact, not even to himself."[26] This passage reveals little more than its author's overstimulated imagination. Such critics can identify Verlaine's belief that the spiritual and the sensual exist *parallèlement* in the same person, but they cannot learn anything from it. I think the preferable model for understanding Verlaine's love for Létinois is not Tiberius, but Parsifal.

*Amour,* which was Verlaine's second volume of largely religious poetry, was dedicated to his son Georges, but it is dominated by the memory of Létinois, the boy that the poet regarded as his adopted son. The book is also haunted by the presence of Wagner's *Parsifal,* which drifts through it as a spiritual and sexual motif. The central text within the book is a sequence of poems entitled "Lucien Létinois," a moving tribute to the dead boy that is similar to Tennyson's *In Memoriam* in its form, its eulogizing tone, and its homoeroticism. It is no coincidence that this book also includes the sonnet "Parsifal," one of Verlaine's best poems. It was written for the same issue of *La Revue Wagnérienne* in which Huysmans' essay on *Tannhäuser* appeared. As a work of decadent Wagnerism, "Parsifal" is a highly sublimated performance; in the *Revue* version of the poem, this is suggested by the epigraph from Tennyson, which identifies "Sir Percivale" as the one whom "Arthur and his Knighthood call'd the Pure."

In recounting the plot of Wagner's opera, Verlaine celebrates a boy's resistance to the sexual temptation of women. In the first quatrain, Parsifal is praised for conquering *les Filles,* the seductive flower maidens who seek to woo him with their breasts and gentle babble. In the second quatrain he is praised for conquering the more subtle Kundry, *la Femme belle* herself, and Klingsor, referred to here as *l'Enfer,* or Hell. In the final line of the octet, Parsifal carries away the phallic spear, *un lourd trophée,* in his boyish arms. In the sextet the poet describes how Parsifal cured the king Amfortas, who is also the priest of the "very holy and essential Treasure," the Grail. Verlaine describes the boy in a golden robe and speaks of the resplendent Grail as the pure *vase,* using a term that in "Ces Passions" has a very different meaning indeed. The poem closes with a swooning evocation of the boy voices in the dome of the temple:

> En robe d'or il adore, gloire et symbole,
> Le vase pur où resplendit le Sang réel.
> —Et, ô ces voix d'enfants chantant dans la coupole! (427)

Given that he wrote this poem at the same time that he was memorializing Létinois, it is difficult not to see Verlaine in the role of Amfortas here, unworthy priest of the holy treasure, full of remorse, hoping to be made whole again through a boy's love, the touch of the spear in the arms of the saintly youth. Verlaine was certainly aware of the homoerotic chivalry in Wagner's relationship with Ludwig of Bavaria, since he wrote about it in the opening poem of *Hombres,* where he describes Ludwig as the "virgin king with the great heart that beat for men alone" (1405).

I am also struck by the wistfulness of Verlaine's tone in "Parsifal." As George Moore recalls, this poem was written years after Létinois's death, while Verlaine was in a hospital. He had clearly become a satyr once again, as evidenced by the rosy-faced butcher-boy that Moore met upon visiting him. The word *butcher-boy* was, like *telegraph-boy,* a euphemism for a male prostitute—Huysmans, for example, speaks suggestively of the butcher-boys in Les Halles—and in Moore's context the purpose of the boy in the poet's room is unmistakable. Verlaine was also suffering at the time from a serious debilitation of his leg, and Moore dreaded the likelihood that the poet, like Amfortas, would want to show off his wound. Wagnerian misogyny is also part of the scenario, as suggested by Moore's remark, "We refrained from expressing our doubts regarding the subject of the sonnet, for when he began to tell the subject, he turned to the butcher-boy and described women as trash."[27] The homoerotic connection between leg, boy, misogyny, and Wagner, seems to be lost on Moore. Unable to stand the company of Verlaine or the boy any longer, he fled from the scene, but when he read the poem he was amazed to encounter a work of beautiful religious sentiment. All the makings of an Amfortas were there in the hospital room, but clearly the butcher-boy was not the primary inspiration for the *garçon vierge* of Verlaine's poem. For that figure, we would have to search "Lucien Létinois," the extended work of mourning that Verlaine was composing at about the same time.

"Lucien Létinois" is rich in the language of homoerotic chivalry. In "Mon Fils Est Brave," for example, Verlaine depicts the boy he calls his adopted son as a Christian knight riding valiantly into battle on his *cheval de guerre,* avoiding all snares, wounded but victorious in the path of righteousness:

> Mon fils est brave: il va sur son cheval de guerre,
> Sans reproche et sans peur par la route du bien,
> Un dur chemin d'embûche et de piège où naguère
> Encore il fut blessé, mais vainquit en chrétien. (447)

In the next quatrain the knight overcomes the desire to delight in his youth and strength and take pleasure in the languid evening. He laughs at the sexual bait of vile temptations and aspires to duty alone:

> Mon fils est fier: en vain sa jeunesse et sa force
> L'invitent au plaisir par les langueurs du soir,
> Mon enfant se remet, rit de la vile amorce,
> Et, les yeux en avant, aspire au seul devoir. (447)

Verlaine goes on to speak of the beauty of his adopted son, how God surrounds him with light and love because he is pious and worthy of the Holy Crown, *la Sainte Couronne,* reserved for soldiers in the fight for Heaven. Létinois's role as Parsifal, the wise young fool who redeems the debauched older man, is further emphasized in the constant references to his innocence.

In "O Ses Lettres d'Alors!" (447), Verlaine rereads the letters from his dead friend, whom he characterizes as a kind of Parsifal turned naive poet. He is an "ignorant angel" and a "pure spirit robed in an innocent flesh." In his childlike phrases, "naive and chaste" in style, virtue walks in a manner I can only describe as Wagnerian, a sort of pomp of uncoiling incense and crystal cymbals. In the next poem, "Je Te Vois Encore à Cheval," the boy seems like a toy soldier marching to trumpets—presumably a reference to his brief military service. Although father-and-son role-playing is common enough among male couples, these poems sound as though Verlaine really did identify Létinois with his real son, Georges, who was only about seven years old when the two friends first met. Like Parsifal, Létinois became a much adored *enfant*.

The treatment of women in this sequence also has a Wagnerian quality. Verlaine interrupts his praise for his friend to throw in a few odd poems on the evils of women that most critics have regarded as bafflingly out of place. One of them, "O la Femme!" is usually thought to be yet another lash at Mathilde, of which Verlaine wrote many. In the context of this poem, he may have been expressing his anger at her for separating him from his son. But in the opening line, "O la Femme! Prudent, sage, calme ennemi" (444), we might detect a Wagnerian horror of Woman, the formidable and calculating enemy of men, especially since *la Femme* is precisely the term that Verlaine applies to Kundry in the *Parsifal* poem. As Kundry, rather than Mathilde, *la Femme* makes much more sense, since it is the temptation of Woman that both Parsifal and Létinois are called upon to resist, Christian knights that they are.

In "Tout en Suivant ton Blanc Convoi," Verlaine describes an escapade in which Létinois imperiled his soul with love for a woman. He describes how his heroic boy dallied with the redoubtable *Femme,* as she is again named, but then rejected her in disgust. He returns to noble and simple Virtue, where he flowers like a lily blown for an instant but more manly for having weathered the storm and suffered magnificently. Although the trite religious metaphors might sound a sour note with modern audiences, we can hardly doubt the sincerity of

Verlaine's tone. Many have cited this poem as evidence of his hypocrisy, and yet its grave concern about sexual temptation makes perfect sense, even beyond his evident jealousy, when we read it in the context of homoerotic chivalry. Through the misogynistic rejection of Woman, heterosexuality is characterized as bestial, and homosexuality as a valiant and transcendent form of Christian devotion. Even when a woman is praised, as in "Ma Cousine Elisa," she is valued as a spiritual "camarade" rather than a sexual temptation. Elisa becomes the saintly Elisabeth of *Tannhäuser.*

"Lucien Létinois" is, above all, an extraordinary poem of love between men. It is overshadowed by the more sexual poems in *Parallèlement* and *Hombres,* but its intensity of feeling nevertheless bespeaks a great romance. Even through the sublimating Wagnerian gestures, it is possible to recognize the many frissons of sexual desire. In one poem Verlaine even speaks metaphorically of a wedding between himself and Létinois with shades, I suppose, of *Lohengrin,* but God steps in to claim the boy for himself. When not characterizing him as a Knight of the Holy Grail, Verlaine could express candidly and beautifully the simpler pleasures of his everyday life with the boy. The poems in this sequence have been unjustly maligned, I think, and among the most moving are those in which Verlaine watches his friend ice-skate, when he meets him at the train station, when he dreams of holding the dying boy in his arms, and when he meditates on a portrait of the dead Lucien, a "pastel specter" in which he finds once again that bliss and hypnotic reverie, that "jouissance et transe" (456), for which he mourns.

The ice-skating poem, "Il Patinait Merveilleusement," retains the light and melancholy touch that marks the best of Verlaine's early work. In the eyes of his lover, Létinois skates with the grace of a girl, "une grande jeune fille." Sometimes he skates so swiftly toward some invisible and distant goal that he himself becomes invisible, leaving Verlaine with a strange premonition of the boy's death:

> Parfois il restait comme invisible,
> Vitesse en route vers une cible
> Si lointaine, elle-même invisible . . .

Invisible de même aujourd'hui.
Que sera-t-il advenu de lui?
Que sera-t-il advenu de lui? (450)

The poem moves with a swift rhythm, graceful as the skater himself, and it too disappears into a plaintive and repeated question that cannot be answered: "What will have become of him? What will have become of him?" The unusual grammatical construction looks to the past and to the future at once, searching as the poet does for an anywhere out of the present world, the here and now where he is left alone in his sadness and in his faith. Indeed, the question resonates through the many poignant and meditative elegies that have been written recently by gay poets who are losing their friends and lovers to AIDS. It is not through Rimbaud alone that we recognize ourselves in Verlaine's evocations of love. Although Létinois was evidently not a graceful creature, Verlaine leaves us with a profound sense of a youth who was handsome and elegant, who was loved, but who now is lost. That this love of one man for another inspired fine religious poetry should come as no surprise.

## In Praise of Shame

SIMONE: Nay, you are caught in such a cunning vice
    That nothing will avail you, and your life
    Narrowed into a single point of shame
    Ends with that shame and ends most shamefully.
GUIDO: Oh! let me have a priest before I die!

Oscar Wilde

In this very ironic line from his very bad dramatic fragment *A Florentine Tragedy* (1893), Oscar Wilde repeats the word *shame*, one of his favorite themes, like a nervous tic. Given his appalling imprisonment for acts of "gross indecency" with other men and the deathbed conversion to Catholicism that followed a few years later, the final line in particular resounds with a prophetic ring, his own courtroom performance degraded to a melodrama *avant la lettre*. The summoning of a priest, not to mention the Italian setting, lends to shame the peculiarly Catholic aura it maintained throughout Wilde's work. Nevertheless, while shame falls victim here to poor dramatic taste, Wilde often deploys the term in a manner that is subtle, disarming, and ironic, especially in his work after the trials, when his own experience of shame was most painful. He might serve as the ideal illustration for a recent critical announcement about shame by Eve Kosofsky Sedgwick: "I want to say that *at least* for certain ('queer') people, shame is simply the first, and remains a permanent, structuring fact of identity: one that has its own, powerfully productive and powerfully socially metamorphic possibilities."[28]

It is the contagious and metamorphic quality of shame that intrigues me in Wilde. For him shame is less an affect than a performative possibility, less a force of nature than an effect of language, less a moral predicament than an artistic opportunity for self-fashioning. Wilde renders Shame an allegorical figure. It is a place one resides, a pose one is assigned, a shape one acquires. No English aesthete played with the word as artfully and suggestively as Wilde. Like Douglas, he recognized in shame the potential for a reconfiguration of desire between men in his own terms, but he went beyond a simple transvaluation of the experience. Like Baudelaire, Huysmans, and Verlaine, he explored the peculiar dialectic of shame and grace, but in a manner that was far more astute in its critique of the hypocrisy of those who sought to condemn him.

For a handful of homosexual decadents in England in the 1890s, the word *shame* had become virtually a synonym for sexual acts between men. Some decadents, notably Lionel Johnson, wrote homoerotic Catholic poetry that was pitiless in its self-laceration, while others, notably Lord Alfred Douglas in his Oxford days, wielded the word *shame* with irony. I have devoted an entire chapter to Wilde, but I would like to examine this one particular theme in the context of his English and French contemporaries. Wilde was the most adept at deploying the concept of shame playfully, without ever sacrificing its power as an affect or as a religious concept. Unlike Johnson, he did not succumb entirely to the Christian discourse that execrated sexual acts between men as one the most egregious of mortal sins. Douglas was much closer to Wilde in this regard. In his youth, he was notoriously brazen in his sexual behavior, and in his poetry he effected a typically decadent transvaluation of the concept of shame, regarding the word as a pejorative sign of a transgressive pleasure. Later in his life, however, Douglas converted to Catholicism and, conforming to its official doctrines, became an accomplished homophobe. He became a proponent of the very discourse of shame he had once turned on its head. Wilde, however, stood in ironic relation to shame throughout his career, continually courting and subverting the Christian and legal discourses by which he was condemned.

The image of Lionel Johnson that we have inherited is one of an enigmatic and reclusive aesthete given to melancholia, loneliness, alcoholism, religious enthusiasm, and sexual shame. He was loath to express physically his desire for other men, and there is little evidence that he ever had sex with anyone, especially after his conversion. In his letters and in his poetry, whenever he indulges his love for other men, it is usually in the highly sublimated terms of religious enthusiasm, male chivalry, and passionate friendship. In a fashion not uncommon among the decadents, Johnson either extols love between men as spiritual, Platonic, and noble, or he execrates it as shameful. Johnson aspired to be like the Paul Verlaine of *Sagesse* and *Amour.* In fact, he aspired a little too hard. His religious poems often strain for sentimental piety and an absurdly idealized homoeroticism.

In his best work, however, Johnson wrestles with his sexual shame and guilt without fleeing desperately into a seraphic pose. If he communes with an angel at all in these poems, it is a dark angel. In "The Dark Angel" and "Vinum Daemonum," both written in 1893, he draws an implicit connection between his alcoholism, his desire for men, and his religious sense of shame. He begins "The Dark Angel" with an invocation to his demonic other:

> Dark Angel with thine aching lust
> To rid the world of penitence:
> Malicious Angel, who still dost
> My soul such subtile violence![29]

His wrestling with this Dark Angel is cast in what appear to be sexual terms, such as "aching lust," "sultry fire," "flames of evil ecstasy," "ardour of red flame," and "passionate powers" (65–66). Johnson uses the same imagery in "Vinum Daemonum," however, to describe the image and effects of wine: "ruby flame," "alluring," "pang of fire," "wanton in passion" (194). In a subtle merger of eroticism and alcoholism, the poet suggests that the wine increases the likelihood of sexual transgression, that his descent into drunkenness and desire are the tragic signs of his spiritual failure. The Dark Angel dissolves any attempt at sublimation:

> When music sounds, then changest thou
> Its silvery to a sultry fire:
> Nor will thine envious heart allow
> Delight untortured by desire. (66)

The struggle is a hopeless one, inevitable and interminable, not the least because desire is an attribute and a function of religious discipline and spiritual delight. But the inevitability of desire, like the inevitability of sin, spurs the poet to an even fiercer struggle. With all the shame and paranoid violence of homosexual panic, he lashes out against the Angel, the enemy of his own making, in suitably biblical terms, speaking of "Apples of ashes," a "banquet of foul delight," "dark Paraclete," and the eternal damnation of the "second Death, that never dies" (66–67).

Johnson's language is desperate and increasingly painful to read, especially since his battle of conscience—"I fight thee, in the Holy Name!"—is evidently in vain. The final lines are extraordinary, not only for their dramatic force, but also for their recognition of the sadness and the loneliness of the Victorian homosexual in his efforts at sublimation:

> Do what thou wilt, thou shalt not so,
> Dark Angel! triumph over me:
> *Lonely, unto the Lone I go;*
> *Divine, to the Divinity.* (67)

Renunciation has rarely been expressed in a more chilling tone. The poet's triumph, such as it is, sounds like bitterness and despair, and surely this is Johnson's bleakest poem. The final lines, though a quotation from Plotinus, appear in this context to be Christian in origin— an account of the disciple, in an almost eremitic solitude, identifying with the loneliness and suffering of Christ's passion. Lonely unto the Lone he goes, no less in desire than in death. Johnson's solitude and celibacy, often noted in his friends' memoirs, are defined here as aspects of a necessary loneliness, a cross to bear, in the irresolvable conflict with a sexual desire at once produced and exploited by his religious discipline.

Lord Alfred Douglas was not one to go lonely unto the lone until very late in his life. In his youth he was the golden boy of English decadence and an unusually daring singer of praises for desire between men. Lionel Johnson once wrote an embarrassingly homophobic poem attacking Wilde for robbing Douglas of his soul, but that soul was already in a perilous state of disarray long before his days as the beloved "Bosie." Having very little respect for the Church as an undergraduate, he treated the language of shame ironically. In "Two Loves" and "In Praise of Shame," Douglas presses images of Christ and Apollo beyond the familiar impasse of Christian and Platonic sublimation in order to represent sex between men as an unjustly execrated pleasure. In "Two Loves," the speaker is shown a vision of two beautiful men by a Virgilian guide, a naked youth who kisses him and feeds him grapes. The "love of comely girl and boy"[30] is represented by one of the two men singing to the music of an ivory lute. His mysterious comrade, however, is the very archetype of the decadent aesthete: melancholic, pale, red-lipped, and romantic. His clenching hands attest to his neurosis; his purple and gold robe with "the device of a great snake" suggests an occult mysticism whose insignia, like the green carnation, was a symbol of homosexuality. When he claims also to be Love, his happy comrade cries, "He lieth, for his name is Shame." The melancholy one surrenders, offering the line for which Douglas is best remembered: "I am the Love that dare not speak its name" (110).

In this poem Douglas engages the familiar Hellenic paraphernalia of flutes, lutes, grapes, and pretty youths in an allegory of homosexual oppression that is nevertheless wholly modern. *Shame* becomes the homophobic term of execration behind which a beautiful pleasure seeks to articulate itself. When the homosexual Love speaks through the mask of Shame, his language is enigmatic and indirect, melancholic and nervous. It is not that his love has no name. In fact, it had several names, thanks to the categorical abundance of late-Victorian sexology.

It is, rather, the name Love that it dares not speak. Only as Shame, not as Love, could homosexuality be permitted to have any emotional, ethical, or political content. Moreover, in the word *dare* we find the fear of retribution that renders the homosexual Love so circumspect in his speech.

In a poem entitled "Rejected," Douglas depicts homosexual desire as caught in an impasse between Apollo and Christ, one offering sublimation and the other repression. Both prospects seem to lead to shame and despair:

> And now I am lost in the mist
> Of the things that can never be,
> For I will have none of Christ
> And Apollo will none of me. (142)

In one of the best-turned phrases of the decade, Douglas sums up the inadequacy of both the Christian and the Hellenic conceptions of desire between men. Both were extremely influential in the gay apologetics of the day, whether we are reading John Addington Symonds, André Raffalovich, or Edward Carpenter, but in their relentless idealism and desexualization of homosexuality, they were hardly adequate as paradigms for a modern gay identity. In its pandering idealism and assimilationism, such an apologetics produces the very sense of shame it seeks to disavow, since it presumes that certain sexual acts between men are indeed inherently shameful. Both Christianity and Hellenism had their charms, but they could also contribute to the sense of shame and moral failure heaped upon late-Victorian men who sought to have sex with one another. As Douglas felt trapped between Christ and Apollo in "Rejected," he is trapped between Shame and Love in "Two Loves." Shame was not adequate, Love was not permitted. In other words, he would have none of Shame, but Love would have none of him.

In his poem "In Praise of Shame," Douglas exploits the negative connotations of the word *shame* by embracing them ironically, much as the sexual radicals of our own fin de siècle have redeployed the word *queer.* In "Two Loves," *shame* is the mark of oppression, but the word is emptied of its conventional connotations through the homosexual's disidentification with it. With "In Praise of Shame,"

Douglas strikes an even more ironic pose. In a typically decadent fashion, Douglas values shame as a pleasure in its own right, not the least for its capacity to shock. In this poem shame is articulated primarily in Christian and mystical terms. The speaker is visited by "Our lady of strange dreams" (22), spoken of as "Notre-Dame" in the French version, possibly a reference to such visions of the Blessed Virgin as had occurred recently at La Salette and Lourdes. Her visions are passionate, poured like fire from an urn. Douglas engages the language of ardent faith in a poem that appears to be about sexual desire, thus blurring the distinction between the pious visitation and the phantasmatic temptation. Are these strange dreams like the passionate visions of Saint John of the Cross or Saint Teresa, or are they more like the temptations that beset Flaubert's Saint Antony?

In an echo of "Two Loves," the vision of Shame declares itself to the poet:

> "I am Shame
> That walks with Love, I am most wise to turn
> Cold lips and limbs to fire; therefore discern
> And see my loveliness, and praise my name."

No doubt succumbing to Oscar Wilde's famous dictum "The only way to get rid of a temptation is to yield to it,"[31] the speaker wakes and sings, "Of all sweet passions Shame is loveliest." There is no explicit mention of homosexuality in this poem. Rather, the specific nature of the "Shame" is only apparent through the juxtaposition of this poem with "Two Loves," which was published in the same issue of *The Chameleon,* a single-issue Oxford journal with a notoriously homoerotic slant. Desire between men has in fact completely disappeared into a feminine allegorical figure of Shame, from which it derives its significance and apparently also much of its fire and beauty. Rather than disavowing the shame imposed on the Victorian homosexual, Douglas delights in it as a site of sexual abjection and intensity, the loveliest of strange dreams.

In his transvaluation of shame, Douglas may have taken his cues from Wilde, if not the French decadents. Even in his early poetry, Wilde explored much the same territory. In "Hélas!" (1881), the first poem in his first published book, he describes the same jarring oscillation between Apollo and Christ and between sublimation and shame that would later occupy Douglas in "Rejected." Wilde's poem is a classic of English decadence, opening with a Paterian sensation of drifting desire and drifting consciousness against a backdrop of classical austerity and masculine self-control:

> To drift with every passion till my soul
> Is a stringed lute on which all winds can play,
> Is it for this that I have given away
> Mine ancient wisdom, and austere control?
> Methinks my life is a twice-written scroll
> Scrawled over on some boyish holiday
> With idle songs for pipe and virelay,
> Which do but mar the secret of the whole. (709)

As Wilde continues, we find that his scroll is "twice-written" not only in the sense that Apollonian austerity is scribbled over with Dionysian dissipation, but also in the sense that Apollonian austerity is complemented with Christian renunciation. Christ and Apollo are both on the side of "austere control."

The entire volume of poetry is notable for its shifting allegiance, which is divided between the Christian and the Hellenic, but in "Hélas!" the speaker seems to suffer from both:

> Surely there was a time I might have trod
> The sunlit heights, and from life's dissonance
> Struck one clear chord to reach the ears of God:
> Is that time dead? lo! with a little rod
> I did but touch the honey of romance—
> And must I lose a soul's inheritance.

The rest of the sonnet draws on a biblical image that Wilde no doubt read with amusement in Pater's homoerotic essay on Winckelmann in *The Renaissance*. The line refers to Jonathan's remark to Saul, "I did but taste a little honey with the end of the rod that was in mine hand, and lo! I must die" (1 Sam. 14:43). Richard Ellmann, one of Wilde's more recent biographers, sees the poem as an allegory of aestheticism, and dismisses it as fatuous, so much "sighing in French."[32] What he misses, however, is the ironic suggestion of fellatio in this remark by

Jonathan, who, after all, admired David with a love "passing the love of women." David and Jonathan were a commonplace of homoerotic literature, and they figure along with Shakespeare and Michelangelo in Wilde's famous defense of "Two Loves" and the "Love that dare not speak its name" during his trial.

The title is indeed a sighing in French, and the all too precious despair surely suggests a want of seriousness in the face of philistinism and puritanical displeasure. But the poem is not a meaningless pose. To some degree, I think it wise to take Wilde at his word. The suggestion of an idyllic homoeroticism in the Bible presents an irony that he would evoke again and again in an effort to recontextualize the shame that homosexuality tended to excite in a violently homophobic society. This motive would culminate in the figure of Christ as a speaker of Greek, an aesthete, and a lover of sinners, in *De Profundis*. But in "Hélas!" we find, beyond the French sigh, a genuine distress at the fact that one taste of homoerotic romance, or even the romance of decadent style, can bring shame and damnation, whether the ethical model is Christ or Apollo. The moral outrage of which he speaks, the very likelihood of his losing "a soul's inheritance," according to the ethical standards of his day, was very real, as were the problems inherent in the Christian and Hellenic discourses in which many homosexuals and aesthetes were seeking refuge in the 1890s.

Beyond the familiar Greek and Christian dualism, there are two Wagnerian figures through whom Wilde manipulated the concept of shame—namely, Tannhäuser and the unnamed sinner of the Gospels whom Wilde and a great many others are wont to refer to as Mary Magdalene. In Wilde's hands they became beautiful sinners who understood the poetry of shame and remorse. Rather than reaffirming the more familiar Christian narrative of transgression, punishment, repentance, and salvation, Wilde uses Tannhäuser and Magdalene in particular to render ironic the Christian discourse of shame through an identification with the beautiful sinner. Shame is thus transferred to the ugliness of Victorian sexual hypocrisy and philistinism, while his own splendid sins bring him closer to beauty and salvation.

Wilde delighted in this paradox of sin: "What is termed Sin is an essential element of progress," he writes in "The Critic as Artist." "Through its intensified assertion of individualism it saves us from monotony of type. In its rejection of the current notions about morality, it is one of the higher ethics" (1023–1024). Sin, not to mention its attendant shame, was not a hindrance to Wilde's art, nor for that matter to his sexuality; rather, the Christian discourse of sin and shame was a text to be artistically transfigured. He tells of how we, as readers, wear Dante's own raiment when we meet the sinners of *The Divine Comedy* and are "fascinated by their shame" (1035), and how, in the stained raiment of Villon, we "put our shame into song" (1041). Wilde also admires the confessions of Rousseau and Cellini for their splendor and their shame. Especially after his trials, Wilde felt his shame acutely, and yet he never regarded shame as something to be ashamed of. As in the decadent cult of Wagner, in the great arias of abjection and expiation in *Parsifal* and *Tannhäuser*, shame and grace acquire an aesthetic significance above and beyond their religious or ethical one. For Wilde, shame is an eminently textual experience, though no less powerful for that. Moreover, in the perfection of its form, in the felicity of its expression, shame is potentially a work of art.

Mary Magdalene as beautiful sinner is a recurrent figure in Wilde's work from his earliest poems to his prison letters. His enthusiasm for her was no doubt enlivened by the final act of Wagner's *Parsifal*, in which the sinner Kundry, in the passionate throes of redemption, re-enacts the signature gesture of Mary Magdalene by laving her savior's feet and drying them with the seductive tresses of her hair. But even before the first performance of *Parsifal* at Bayreuth, Wilde defined his kinship with Mary Magdalene in a poem, "Quia Multum Amavi." The title, which means literally "because I have loved much," is a reference to the spirit of forgiveness with which Christ accepts the attentions of Mary Magdalene. When he enters the house of a Pharisee, she comes to him, washes his feet with tears, dries them with her hair, kisses them incessantly, and anoints them with oil from an alabaster vessel. The Pharisee doubts that Christ is a prophet because he allows himself to be touched by such a sinner. Christ responds: "Her sins, which are many, are forgiven; for she loved much" (Luke 7:47).

In Wilde's poem, the speaker compares his love for a woman to idolatry and, heretically, to a young priest's love for God in the Eucharist. Now that he feels remorse and sorrow treading on his heels, he is still glad to have loved much. In *The Duchess of Padua* (1883), Wilde enacts the scene once again, this time with an operatic melodrama that is more distinctly Wagnerian, with its echoes of *Tristan und Isolde.* In the final moment before the curtain falls, the Duchess, who regards herself as "guilty beyond all women," speculates on the possibility of her redemption:

> No, I have sinned, and yet
> Perchance my sin will be forgiven me.
> I have loved much. (645)

She kisses Guido and then suddenly leaps up in a dreadful spasm of death. Guido kills himself with her dagger. In the final tableau, she has the peaceful look of God's forgiveness on her face, and Guido has expired across her body in imitation of the *Pietà*. However stagy, Wilde's language is clear: love, no matter how sinful, is the beginning of salvation.

During his imprisonment, when the significance of sin and shame became a daily preoccupation for him, Wilde was much consoled by this notion of Christ as the god of love. He identified with Christ as a romantic artist who could recognize sin and suffering as "beautiful, holy things, modes of perfection."[33] Note the shift from a religious to an aesthetic register. Love, in Wilde's later letters, is most poetic when it is given freely to the unworthy. He speaks of this love in ritual terms as a sacrament to be taken while kneeling, the words *Domine, non sum dignus* on our lips. In his days of exile, he was comforted by the belief that, like the harlot, he was forgiven—"I know at any rate that Christ would not turn me out" (*Letters*, 600). He has loved much. Far too much, and loved a man—Lord Alfred Douglas, who was unworthy, who ruined him, who brought him to shame, and who, for that very reason, so he claimed, he loved all the more. Love is Wilde's final poetic bid for salvation.

In *De Profundis,* Wilde's elaborate and well-wrought letter to Douglas, Mary Magdalene gives her finest performance. Wilde's description of her is to Saint Luke what his Salomé was to Saint Matthew: a poetic elaboration that further aestheticizes the stories of the Gospels. He speaks of the romantic artistry of Christ's forgiveness: "Those whom he saved from their sins are saved simply for beautiful moments in their lives. Mary Magdalen, when she sees Christ, breaks the rich vase of alabaster that one of her seven lovers had given her and spills the odorous spices over his tired, dusty feet, and for that one moment's sake sits for ever with Ruth and Beatrice in the tresses of the snow-white Rose of Paradise" (486). Humility is rarely this divine! Despite her history as a sinner, one beautiful gesture renders Magdalene a saint. And it is the beauty of her performance that Wilde admires. The slippage from the Word to its poetry, from the Gospels to Dante, is a signature motif in Wilde, who was especially skillful at refiguring the Bible as an aesthetic icon. In the context of *De Profundis,* this fragrant Magdalene with her seven lovers is not only a work of art but a work of homoerotic iconography; her abundant capacity for love and penitence harmonizes perfectly with Wilde's own tragedy of love, ruin, and shame.

In the legend of Tannhäuser, Wilde again finds a beautiful sinner who loved much and is forgiven. Like Magdalene, Tannhäuser is looked upon as unworthy of forgiveness—even the Pope rejects him—and his redemption, symbolized by the flowering rod that blooms in the Pope's sight, is deemed a miracle, symbolic evidence of Christ's profound love for sinners. Although Pater and Beardsley made use of the tale as well, the principal inspiration for Wilde's use of the Tannhäuser legend is once again, of course, Wagner, whom he refers to as "Christlike" in "The Soul of Man under Socialism." Dorian Gray finds in the overture to *Tannhäuser* "a presentation of the tragedy of his own soul" (107). In "The Critic as Artist," Wilde's alter ego Gilbert describes the overture no less extravagantly than did Baudelaire and Huysmans. He evokes the "comely knight treading delicately on the flower-strewn grass" while listening for the call of Venus; Gilbert then drifts into a vague and mystical mood, noting that at other times the overture "speaks to me of a thousand different things, of myself, it may be, and my own life, or of the lives of others whom one has loved and grown weary of loving, or of the passions that man has known, or of the passions that man has not known, and so has sought for" (1029).

Tannhäuser becomes the ultimate decadent, ever searching for new pleasures, ever touched by ennui, always languishing in the sweetness of an *amour de l'impossible,* a pursuit of a fascinating glimmer perceived no less in God than in Venus. The most sustained revision of the tale by an English decadent is Beardsley's delightfully prurient story *Under the Hill,* which details, in both prose and his own line drawings, the descent of the hero into the carnal pleasures of the

Venusberg. No doubt Wilde was himself attracted to the sensuality of the legend, especially the image of the phallic staff as it bursts into bloom. Christian salvation is thereby associated with the sort of erotic plenitude and aesthetic beauty so often symbolized by roses or lilies in decadent art. Unlike Beardsley, however, Wilde was not merely concerned with the *ars erotica* of the hero's amorous adventures. He was far more interested in Tannhäuser's Christian transfiguration after he rejects Venus. The blossoming staff is one of Wilde's favorite motifs, not only because it is phallic but also because it is miraculous. Wilde thought this religious eroticism the supreme paradox of the tale. The sinner performs miracles, while the Pope, the Vicar of Christ, is fraught with doubt and requires divine edification.

The blossoming staff occurs in Wilde as early as his fairy tale "The Young King" (1888), where, despite the hypocrisy of the Bishop, a Christ-like aesthete is bedecked in rich spiritual raiment. "The dead staff blossomed," Wilde writes, "and bare lilies that were whiter than pearls. The dry thorn blossomed, and bare roses that were redder than rubies" (233). One of the most elaborate uses that Wilde makes of the blossoming staff is in his fairy tale "The Fisherman and His Soul" (1891), which is similar in theme to *Dorian Gray* and was published about the same time. In this tale the legend of Tannhäuser, like the biblical story of Mary Magdalene, is seen as a parable for the miraculous power of love. Wilde does not simply mean spiritual love but the sensual love of the sinner as well. For Wilde the satanic and the puritanical were equally regrettable extremes, the former all too often a sensuality without love and the latter all too often a spirituality without love. The two extremes are often reconciled only through sorrow and suffering. The "broken heart" is therefore a key trope in Wilde, not only in the fairy tales like "The Happy Prince" (1888) and "The Birthday of the Infanta" (1889), but also in *De Profundis* and "The Ballad of Reading Gaol" (1898), where a broken heart is the sign of the sinner's capacity for love and for identification with the suffering of Christ.

In "The Fisherman and His Soul," sensuality is represented by the Fisherman, who, like Tannhäuser, has sold his soul for the pleasure of love. Loveless piety is represented by the overly conscientious Priest, who, when the Fisherman confesses his love for the Mermaid, exclaims, "The love of the body is vile" (251). The conflict between the

Priest and the Sea-folk represents the familiar Victorian dichotomy between pagan sensuality and Christian asceticism. But the opposition is a false one in Wilde's view, and it is resolved through the Fisherman's re-enactment of the Tannhäuser legend. The Priest becomes the Pope who sends the sinner away or, for that matter, the Pharisee who supposes Magdalene unworthy of Christ's love. Even when the Fisherman has lost the Mermaid, when he mourns for her day and night and drowns with her dead body in his arms, the Priest still does not recognize the beauty of his love. The Fisherman's heart is broken and his alienated soul re-enters it—a suggestion that, as with Christ, the beauty of love is glimpsed only through suffering and sorrow. The Priest, however, requires a miracle. He orders that the Fisherman and the Mermaid be buried in the Field of the Fullers, a barren, unhallowed ground "where no sweet herbs grew." Nevertheless, like Tannhäuser's staff, the grave blooms with "strange flowers" of "curious beauty"—a tribute not only to love but to the Paterian language of aestheticism by which the flowers are distinguished. Overcome with the beauty of the flowers, the Priest ceases to speak of the God of wrath and speaks instead of the God whose name is Love. He even blesses the pagan sea and all the "wild things" that are in it—namely, the Wildean Fauns and the Wildean Sea-folk (271).

"The Fisherman and His Soul" is prophetic in light of Wilde's arrest and imprisonment. His love was put on trial, and the Priest of his tale had become the criminal-justice system. In "The Ballad of Reading Gaol," Wilde returns again to Tannhäuser to describe the roses that might bloom from the condemned man's grave were the righteous not cruel:

> Out of his mouth a red, red rose!
>     Out of his heart a white!
> For who can say by what strange way,
>     Christ brings His will to light,
> Since the barren staff the pilgrim bore
>     Bloomed in the great Pope's sight? (855)

Unfortunately, so loveless and inhumane is the punishment in Reading Gaol that no such miracle is possible. The grave does not flower, and the barren staff remains a barren staff. The poem itself becomes the "strange flower," the romantic gesture through which suffering is assigned an essentially Christian meaning as an incitement to love.

The blessing of forgiveness that the criminal can enjoy, his communion with Christ through suffering and repentance, is nothing short of miraculous for Wilde at this time in his life. In the letters he wrote after his imprisonment, he was wont to refer to himself as a martyr. He could write of a friend's visit as a "Pilgrimage to the Sinner" and a miracle of kindness "compared to which the blooming of the dry staff of the Pope when Tannhäuser knelt before him is, in my eyes, nothing" (*Letters*, 596). Nevertheless, Wilde's version of love was by no means widely acknowledged among Christians. Sex between men, whether loving or not, was still regarded as shameful, despite the efforts of a number of "uranian" apologists to reconcile it to Christianity. Although he contemplated conversion many times, Wilde was never altogether certain of his own miraculous capabilities. As he wrote to his friend Robert Ross, "I fear if I went before the Holy Father with a blossoming rod it would turn at once into an umbrella or something dreadful of that kind" (*Letters*, 819).

Despite his doubts, Wilde successfully sought the blessing of the pope no fewer than seven times during his exile to the Continent. By virtue of his degradation, his suffering, and his despair, Wilde pursued an identification with Christ in both his poetry and his letters. His prison experience lends an aura of immediacy and sincerity to the erotic and aesthetic celebration of Christian love that he articulated in his earlier poems and fairy tales. The suffering of his later works is his own. The broken heart, ever the fractured jewel, is his own. But the word *shame*, already closely associated in his mind with homosexuality, begins to burn on the page with increasing frequency. *Shame* is only the most polished gem in a constellation of synonyms, each with its own nuance—words like *degradation, humiliation, disgrace, blame, guilt, remorse, ruin, pariah, outcast.* Hardly a page goes by without reference to one of them. In "The Ballad of Reading Gaol," the prisoner lives in the "secret House of Shame" built with the very "bricks of shame." He is hanged with the "rope of shame," he dies a "death of shame," and his body is thrown into an unmarked grave that is the very "pit of shame."

In *De Profundis* shame is cast in similarly metaphorical terms. Wilde speaks of the "streets of shame" and, through the prison bars, he may be seen in a "shape of shame." This last phrase is especially interesting. How does one maintain the "shape of shame"? Shame is eminently performative. It is assigned, enacted, and rehearsed as an intense discipline and punishment of the body. It is a far more physical and concrete word than *sin,* since it refers to an affect. It presumes a burning sensation on the skin, a tremor in the voice, a casting downward of the eyes. It is the painful laceration of the self under the hot gaze of another. Perhaps the most vivid image of shame in Wilde's poem is the burning body of the hanged prisoner in the grave. The corpse is covered with "burning lime" that eats away at his flesh and bone. The lime is compared to the effects of shame:

> Deep down below a prison-yard,
> > Naked for greater shame,
> He lies, with fetters on each foot,
> > Wrapt in a sheet of flame! (855)

Wilde reserves a similar fate for Douglas. In *De Profundis* he wants dearly for the boy to share in his shame, if not his imprisonment: "Your pale face used to flush with wine or pleasure. If, as you read what is here written, it from time to time becomes scorched, as though by a furnace-blast, with shame, it will be all the better for you" (448).

As Wilde shifts the focus of his confession from himself to Douglas, shame is revealed to be a highly unstable performance. Furthermore, it is not a force of nature so much as a social frame of reference, and the frame gets wider and wider as we read. Shame becomes contagious. Clearly, Wilde does not consider himself innocent: "Of course there are many things of which I was convicted that I had not done, but then there are many things of which I was convicted that I had done, and a still greater number of things in my life for which I was never indicted at all" (470). With penitent phrases like "I admit" and "I confess" and "I give to myself shame and blame," Wilde seems eager to take upon himself the burdens of shame. Nevertheless, that shame is constantly getting reassigned to someone else. In the "Ballad" it is usually assigned to society in general, while in *De Profundis* it is usually assigned to Douglas in particular.

This widening of the frame of reference for shame takes place through Wilde's identification with Christ. The paradigm for love in his later work is the penitent sinner who identifies with the suffering of Christ, who in turn has taken on the burden of all sins. It is not enough, as he says, that the martyr in his "shirt of flame" (504) should see the face of God; the one who is piling the faggots on the fire must suffer as well. He repeatedly exhorts Douglas to empathy. He says that everything that happens to someone else happens also to oneself, an unlikely assertion that relies for its effect on the figure of Christ as he suffers for our sins. "For the secret of life is suffering," Wilde writes, adding that "love of some kind is the only possible explanation of the extraordinary amount of suffering that there is in the world" (473–474). He comes to value his imprisonment not because he deserved it, but rather because it was long enough to break his heart, to teach him through suffering the necessity of love. Shame becomes the failure to love, the failure to recognize this necessity of love. Its identification with homosexuality is exploded. Wilde was not in prison because he loved a man, but rather because he failed to love one. He lists a great many things for which we ought to feel shame, but homosexuality, the crime for which he was imprisoned, is not one of them. The only vices worthy of shame are shallowness, stupidity, hate, and philistinism, and these are the crimes that have caused his friendship with Douglas to go awry.

This tragic connection between suffering and love would seem to be the point of the assertion that "each man kills the thing he loves," the famous echoing line of "The Ballad of Reading Gaol." The line is a reference, of course, to the central figure, the man who, while drunk, murdered his wife and must now hang for his crime. But the sentiment is far from transparent, apart from its Christian context. Surely the man did not have to kill his wife, nor is it clear that the man even loved her. The line derives much of its force from the poet's association of the murderer with Christ, the Thief in Paradise: the long progress to his execution, his ignominy, his humble attire, his thirst, the crowing of the cock, and the hypocrisy and cruelty of those around him. Christ's name is repeatedly evoked, recasting the murderer's death as a kind of martyrdom. But for what? Wilde is not interested in his crime so much as his status as pariah.

"Each man kills the thing he loves" is ultimately a reference to Christ's crucifixion. Like the man in a drunken rage who kills his wife, the men who killed Christ knew not what they did. They killed the thing they loved or, rather, failed to love, even though he took upon himself the burden of their sins. The recognition of love comes only after the spectacle of suffering. The blood and wine on the murderer's hands are, in this sense, an ironic reference to the Mass, the miracle of transubstantiation in which the spectacle of murder and love is re-enacted through ritual. This poem speaks to a number of lovers, a number of killers: the murderer and his wife, the murderer and his executioners, Christ and his executioners, the murderer and Wilde, Christ and Wilde, Wilde and his long-suffering wife Constance, and, most important perhaps, Wilde and Douglas. The shame and guilt of the murder is universalized:

> Yet each man kills the thing he loves,
>     By each let this be heard,
> Some do it with a bitter look,
>     Some with a flattering word.
> The coward does it with a kiss
>     The brave man with a sword.
>
> Some kill their love when they are young,
>     And some when they are old;
> Some strangle with the hands of Lust,
>     Some with the hands of Gold:
> The kindest use a knife, because
>     The dead so soon grow cold. (844)

Evidently, Wilde was the sort who killed with kisses and flattering words, though knives also play an important role in the prison writings. Alongside the "Ballad," *De Profundis* becomes an ironic acknowledgment of love as it is recognized only through the painful spectacle of mutual crucifixion. Wilde sees the capacity for love in himself and even in Douglas, but through his suffering he has recognized his failure to love. When he writes to Douglas, "You must read this letter right through, though each word may become to you as the fire or knife of the surgeon that makes the delicate flesh burn or bleed" (*Letters*, 425), he means that the boy should recognize his own failure as well. In another scene Wilde describes Douglas in one of his fits of epileptic rage and imagines him with a pistol or a knife. The letter enacts the spectacle of murder through which the necessity of love is to be glimpsed. Like the knife of the surgeon, the knife that kills can also make us whole.

Another remarkable image in the "Ballad" is the "kiss of Caiaphas" (845) that the murderer feels upon his shuddering cheek. The reference to Caiaphas, a priest who condemned Christ, serves to identify once again the murderer's execution with the Crucifixion. But it is also one of Wilde's many revisions of the Bible. Nowhere in my Bible does Caiaphas kiss anyone, much less Christ, but the gesture, at once affectionate and hypocritical, is a suggestive one. Caiaphas has also killed the thing he loves. Indeed, whenever we scapegoat a man, he suffers for our sins. We give him the kiss of Caiaphas because through our violence we reveal his necessity. We love him, but only hypocritically. We love him because he allows us to hide from ourselves. Only through the spectacle of his suffering, through the recognition of our own capacity for hatred and cruelty, are we shamed into a love that is genuine and redemptive.

Through the kiss of Caiaphas, Wilde extends his sense of shame to the society that created Reading Gaol and passed the Criminal Law Amendment Act under which he was condemned. Here I mean not only the cruelty of the prison officials or the hypocrisy of the prison chaplains or the various other targets of Wilde's efforts at prison and legal reform. I am also thinking of a scene that Wilde describes with great vividness: when he was obliged to stand on a train platform in his prison uniform and suffer the mockery and spitting of a crowd who recognized him. It is the most theatrical demonstration of shaming—shame as a verb, as affect that is assigned and performed—that Wilde ever wrote. We recognize at last the grim necessity of his imprisonment. Through the kiss of Caiaphas, we may recognize how the ballad and the prison letter are not so much about the shame of homosexuality as about the shame of homophobia, the real crime for which Wilde was imprisoned. The enormous violence with which he was condemned and the journalistic glee with which he was shamed stand as ample historical illustration of his contention that each man kills the thing he loves.

In *De Profundis* we hear a great deal about feasting with panthers, but it is already apparent in Wilde's argument that homosexuality per se is not shameful in his eyes. Indeed, he repeats over and over in the letters he wrote after prison that he never subscribed to the popular

"British view that Messalina is better than Sporus" (*Letters*, 594). In 1898 he wrote to Robert Ross: "To have altered my life would have been to have admitted that Uranian love is ignoble. I hold it to be noble—more noble than other forms" (*Letters*, 705). In recent years critics of a homophobic frame of mind have suggested that Wilde is an unlikely candidate for canonization by gay critics precisely because he sued for libel when he was publicly described as a sodomite. Such critics ignore the fact that most gay men are rightly offended by the term *sodomite*, and these writers also ignore the fact that the libel suit was not motivated by Wilde's shame but by Douglas's hatred of his father. We need only read *De Profundis* to realize that Wilde was quite pleased with his sexuality.

Where desire between men ceases to become noble and is instead shallow and stupid is not always clear in Wilde's writings. The main thrust of *De Profundis*, however, is not the condemnation of his homoerotic amours, but their glorification as both splendid sins and noble loves, and this glorification is effected through an ingenious appropriation of Christian discourse. His love for Douglas becomes the mode of his salvation: "The gods are strange. It is not of our vices only they make instruments to scourge us. They bring us to ruin through what in us is good, gentle, humane, loving. But for my pity and affection for you and yours, I would not now be weeping in this terrible place" (440). Wilde begins with a confession of his sins and culminates with a confession of his martyrdom. Through a subtle revision of that archetypal Roman Catholic genre, the confession, he alters all the terms by which he was condemned. Once accused of posing as a sodomite, he poses here as Christ. Without straying from the Bible, he reinterprets the figure of Christ as a romantic artist like himself, a fascinating personality with an affinity for sinners, a man whose entire life was "the most wonderful of poems" (477) or the "palpitating centre of romance" (482). Christ is the "true precursor of the romantic movement in life" (484), he is "just like a work of art," he has an "intense and flamelike imagination." Wilde simply describes himself in his finer moments. A faint aroma of homoeroticism attends his description of the Savior as a "young bridegroom with his companions" (478) but with no bride, apparently a reference to the mystical matrimony of Christian discipleship. Even his discussion of Christ's conception of love reads like a sermon on the Love that dare not speak its name: "All that Christ says to us by way of a little warning is that *every* moment should be beautiful, that the soul should *always* be ready for the coming of the Bridegroom, always waiting for the voice of the Lover" (486).

Wilde maintained his peculiar odor of sanctity and sinfulness even after prison. He may have borrowed the paradox from Baudelaire, who in *La Fanfarlo* raises the question "What is that charm so magical with which vice casts its halo around certain creatures" (499). Wilde renamed himself Sebastian Melmoth, a name at once pious and demonic. Presumably, it refers to Saint Sebastian, whose beautiful and arrow-ridden body is still a commonplace of homoerotic art, but also to Maturin's anti-Catholic gothic novel *Melmoth the Wanderer,* whose Byronic hero sells his soul to the Devil. Once again the saint and the sinner are locked in a dialectical embrace. In a hagiographic mood, Wilde wrote to Robert Ross: "Love can canonise people. The saints are those who have been most loved" (*Letters,* 577). Of "The Ballad of Reading Gaol," he wrote: "Without it my beatification as a saint would have been impossible, but I shall now live as the Infamous St Oscar of Oxford, Poet and Martyr" (720). On a similar note, Wilde regarded *De Profundis* as a kind of encyclical letter and himself, no doubt, as its infallible papal author: "If the copying is done at Horton Street the lady typewriter might be fed through a lattice in the door like the Cardinals when they elect a Pope, till she comes out on the balcony and can say to the world '*Habet Mundus Epistolam;*' for indeed it is an Encyclical Letter, and as the Bulls of the Holy Father are named from their opening words, it may be spoken of as the *Epistola: In Carcere et Vinculis*" (*Letters,* 513).

Wilde developed a great fondness for the pope, whom he regarded, like Christ, as a great artist and, apparently, a beautiful work of art as well: "He was wonderful as he was carried past me on his throne, not of flesh and blood, but a white soul wrapped in white, and an artist as well as a saint" (*Letters,* 821). This image could serve as the decadent counterpoint to Zola's indictment of the pope as an anachronism at sea amidst the paganism of Vatican sumptuousness. Indeed, at this time Leo XIII must have looked uncannily like Des Esseintes in his ecclesiastical vestments, the very symbol of a spiritual empire in its decadence. Certainly, a number of his biographers have remarked on the delicateness of the pope, his advanced age, the slenderness of his fingers, and the richness of his robes beside his pallid skin. Toward the end of his life, Wilde declared himself a violent papist. With shades of Huysmans, he could claim with his usual wit that there was only one thing standing between himself and Rome: "It is a curious, and therefore a natural thing, but I cannot stand Christians because they are never Catholics, and I cannot stand Catholics because they are never Christians. Otherwise I am at one with the Indivisible Church" (*Letters,* 831).

With his deathbed conversion and the publication of the Christian section of his *Epistola* as *De Profundis,* many of Wilde's readers assumed that he repented of the sexual crime for which he was imprisoned. Although some were predictably outraged, most reviewers were far more respectful with this text than with any of his earlier publications. In fact, Hugh Walker, a theologian, wrote a surprisingly astute and sensitive essay on *De Profundis* in the Anglican *Hibbert Journal,* claiming that the letter detailed the rebirth of a soul: "Out of the depths to which he had sunk, or from the heights towards which he was rising, Wilde proclaimed this startling gospel, that sin and suffering are beautiful holy things and modes of perfection."[34] The assertion is a fair description of the religious dimension of Wilde's aestheticism, though one would think by the sound of it that Walker was reviewing the confessions of Saint Augustine. Wilde was certainly aware of various efforts to read his life as a model Christian narrative of sexual transgression followed by remorse and bourgeois piety. He wrote to Frank Harris: "I believe they would like me to edit prayers for those at sea, or to recant the gospel of the joy of life in a penny tract" (*Letters,* 780).

Contrary to such popular expectations, *De Profundis,* as a confession, presents Wilde's sexuality as the site of his sanctity no less than his shame. Certainly, in gay criticism, Wilde is not only canonical but canonized. He has, with good reason, attained a virtually hagiographic reputation, though he may strike us as overdressed for the role—"a St. Sebastian with too many arrows," to borrow a phrase from Ronald Firbank.[35] Wilde seems to have recognized his own sanctity long before anyone else did. In 1898 he wrote to the "uranian" poet George Ives on the subject of what we would now refer to as gay liberation or gay rights, and the letter expresses his hope for the repeal of the law through which he was sentenced to prison: "Yes: I have no doubt we shall win, but the road is long, and red with monstrous martyrdoms. Nothing but the repeal of the Criminal Law Amendment Act would do any good" (*Letters,* 721). Sexual freedom, thus cast in Christian terms, is no less powerful than it is appropriate in the context of Wilde's imprisonment, his own martyrdom, and his romantic vision of Christ.[36]

# TWO

# *Huysmans Mystérique*

## Unconscious Unction

La mystérique: this is how one might refer to what, within a still theo-logical onto-logical perspective is called mystic language or discourse. Consciousness still imposes such names to signify that other scene, off-stage, that it finds *cryptic*.　　　　　　Luce Irigaray

I have thus far, in these few pages, spoken of *A Rebours* mainly from the point of view of literature and art. I must now speak of it from the point of view of Grace and show how large a role the unconscious, the workings of a soul ignorant of itself, may often play in a book.

J.-K. Huysmans

In 1903, having completed the last of his series of autobiographical Catholic novels, Huysmans returned to his early success, *A Rebours* (1884), and published the above passage as part of a new preface. What catches my eye is his use of the word "unconscious" *(inconscience)* to describe the workings of grace in his own conversion to Catholicism. Although he knew nothing of Freud,[1] Huysmans' description of his conversion bears a striking resemblance to the psychoanalytic conception of the unconscious. Elsewhere in the preface he speaks of the "perfect unknowing"[2] from which emerges the prayer, perhaps even the conversion, of his decadent hero Des Esseintes in the final pages of *A Rebours*. Huysmans also remarks that his life and his writings "have an element of passivity, of the unknown [*inconnu*], some trace of direction from outside myself that cannot be questioned" (xxv). Indeed, like the paranoiac, he sometimes experienced the influence of the divine Other in the form of an active assault: "he harasses you, tracks you down, 'grills' you, to use a forceful phrase of the police" (xxvi). Huysmans grew increasingly sensitive to the mystical aspect of his own writing—the sense in which, like Freud's hysteric, he experienced the unconscious, the unnamable Other, speaking through him in ways he could not always comprehend.

Huysmans' most vivid characters wander along an always already transgressed boundary line between conversion and mysticism on the one hand and hysteria and perversion on the other. In the late nineteenth century, theorists of hysteria, especially Jean-Martin Charcot and his followers, were eagerly rewriting the history of ecstatic phenomena in materialistic and psychosexual terms. The religious and the psychological discourses existed side by side in highly politicized opposition, and Huysmans appropriated elements of both in defining his own decadent aesthetic, with its peculiar oscillation between the hagiography and the case study. Like Irigaray's ecstatic hysteric *la mystérique*, Huysmans celebrated the distinctly fin de siècle conjunction of the mystic and the neurotic in highly perverse and fragmented texts that strain after an obscure and even brutal *jouissance*.

Traditionally, Huysmans' work has been divided into three phases: naturalistic, decadent, and Catholic. In his early naturalistic phase, he wrote a few gritty novels in a style similar to that of his friend and mentor Emile Zola. In 1884 Huysmans published *A Rebours*, a highly ornamented, oneiric, satirical novel about a dandy who, in a neurotic fit of ennui, retreats into a monastic yet sumptuous solitude. Two other novels followed, the nightmarish *En Rade* (1887) and the satanic *Là-Bas* (1891), both of which are notoriously erotic and bizarre. In 1892, much to the surprise of many readers, Huysmans converted to Catholicism, and the novels that followed—*En Route* (1895), *La Cathédrale* (1898) and *L'Oblat* (1903)—trace the spiritual development of Durtal, one of Huysmans' alter egos, from his life as a jaded sinner in *Là-Bas* to his later incarnations as a penitent convert, connoisseur of religious art, and Benedictine oblate. Huysmans also wrote some non-fictional works, most notably his account of the pilgrims at Lourdes and his hagiography of Blessed Lydwina, that amply demonstrate the sincerity of his faith and his intention to place aesthetics at the service of the Church.

As has often been noted, however, these three phases, convenient as they may be for literary historians, are by no means pure. Although the stylistic shift from naturalism to decadence is a radical one, the shift from decadence to Catholicism is not. The histrionics of the great hysterics and perverts of his decadent phase, characters like Salomé in *A Rebours* or Gilles de Rais in *Là-Bas,* are readily apparent in the erotic dreams of Durtal or the grotesque maladies of Lydwina. Moreover, Huysmans' preoccupation with Christian mysticism and the Church begins not with his formal conversion to Catholicism but rather with *A Rebours* and his conversion to decadence. In fact, both *A Rebours* and *Là-Bas* are Christian conversion narratives, replete with the sort of scholarly disquisitions on mysticism, the liturgy, and Church architecture that are characteristic of his post-conversion work. Although the later novels are less frenetic, less explicitly sexual, than the work of his so-called decadent phase, they nevertheless share many of the same intricacies and idiosyncrasies of style. They share the same passion for ecstatic reverie, aesthetic ornamentation, physical pain, and spiritual torture. Indeed, with their vivid catalogs of suffering and disease, his books on Lourdes and Lydwina can be even more nauseating than the sadistic and demonic *Là-Bas,* in which children are murdered and eviscerated.

With *En Route* Huysmans redeemed himself in the eyes of many Catholics, though there has always been a lingering doubt about the sincerity of his conversion. He was by no means a model bourgeois in his piety, fascinated as he was by the more sadistic and ecstatic extremes of religious experience. In a letter of 1904, he writes that one of his intentions in writing the preface to *A Rebours* was to confront what he saw as the "imbecility and bigotry" of the Catholic response to his pre-conversion novels.[3] What he is saying, in so many words, is that his decadent style was essentially a spiritual, even Catholic, rebellion in literature. He insists that the seeds of his 1892 conversion were present in *A Rebours,* however unconsciously, and he complains that the press and the Catholics were "harping again on that same old string—the destruction of my earlier books. I told them to go to hell in one or two interviews, and to my astonishment this doesn't appear to have pleased them." He also defends his lingering fondness for such doyens of decadence as Gustave Moreau and Odilon Redon, arguing their value from a perspective at once aesthetic and Catholic. He reasserts the truth of the pungent remark he made about Barbey d'Aurevilly in *A Rebours*—that he was the only stallion among the "geldings of religious art." In the same year he wrote the preface, Huysmans also published an edition of Paul Verlaine's religious poetry with an introduction that extols the poet and his work. While he himself thought Verlaine "a great poet, the only Catholic poet," he was aware that many other Catholics dismissed him as a drunkard and a sodomite. Huysmans exasperated his Catholic critics precisely because he insisted upon the paradox of decadent Catholicism, what he called the "medieval" coexistence of the perverse and the divine, brutality and grace, hysteria and mysticism, in Verlaine no less than in himself.

Huysmans was able to exploit a certain degree of religious naïveté and nostalgia in his various discussions of mysticism. He was writing at a time when Christianity could still hold sway over the imagination as a kind of archaic aristocracy, a poetic possibility in its decline, ever losing ground to bourgeois materialism and modern psychology. The Church had always maintained an anxious relationship to mysticism, eager to exploit the implications of its religious language while at the same time embarrassed by its erotic effusions. In the late nineteenth century, with the increasing ideological power of psychology as a scientific field, the Church's investment in mysticism became even more problematic. Suddenly, beginning with Charcot, some of its most distinguished ecstatics, in particular Saint Teresa of Avila, Saint Catherine of Siena, Blessed Christina of Stommeln, and Saint John of the Cross, were cast in an unprecedented and very political shadow of prurient suspicion and psychological inquiry. Charcot's controversial effort to refigure Christian mysticism and demonic possession as forms of hysteria was a radical strategy at the time, though it has now become so commonplace that it is virtually impossible to read mystical works like "The Obscure Night of the Soul" without grinning uncontrollably.

In the twentieth century the argument has become far more sophisticated, and a number of French psychoanalytic theorists have sought to refine the libidinal reading of mysticism through a conversion of their own—a conversion to Freud, who has attained through their writings a distinctly Catholic *odeur de sainteté*. Saint Teresa, in particular, has enjoyed a considerable cult following among Freudians. Accounts of her ecstasy as hysteria, or (as Marie Bonaparte would have it) simply orgasm, have given way to the more subtle work of Georges Bataille, Jacques Lacan, and Julia Kristeva, among others, in which mysticism is conceived as an effect of language, a symbolic confrontation with death, or a profound experience of disruption and limits within a libidinal economy. Bataille, probably drawing on his knowledge of Huysmans, focuses on the eroticization of death and the Catholic concept of "morose delectation," while Lacan speaks of a peculiarly "feminine *jouissance*," and Kristeva of "sublime Eros."[4]

The work of these later psychoanalytic theorists is by no means irrelevant to a study of Huysmans. In his emphasis on language, on the very textuality of faith and desire, he is closer to modern psycho-analysis than to Charcot, though Freudian atheism would have offended him. Unlike Charcot, who assumed that the chatter of his hysterics was nonsense, Huysmans pays close attention to the symbolic content of hysterical discourse, especially dreams. Despite his ignorance of psychoanalysis, he intuitively developed a profoundly textual understanding of hysteria and the perversions that resonates uncannily with Freud's work. He argues that it is precisely the "unconscious," in the religious and proto-Freudian sense he gives the word, that is absent from the writing of Zola and the naturalists. It is the linguistic effect of this divine "unconscious," realized through the peculiarities of ecstatic and obsessive language, that Huysmans strives to articulate as early as *A Rebours*.

Whether he is describing himself, Moreau's hysterical Salomé, the satanical pervert Gilles de Rais, or the mystical Lydwina, Huysmans was fascinated by the "unconscious" as it speaks in reveries through the ecstatic body. In his frequent use of the word *hysteria* and similar psychological terms of his time —*hystero-epilepsy, monomania, neurosis*, and so on—he was much influenced by Charcot and his disciples. In both his fiction and his letters, however, he discusses Charcot as the progenitor of a naive and mechanistic psychology that did little to explain the mysteries of the soul. In *Trois Primitifs* (1905), a collection of religious-art criticism, Huysmans also mentions the work of Paul Richer, who wrote a book with Charcot comparing medieval accounts of mystical union and demonic possession with modern accounts of hysteria in the Salpêtrière, the asylum with which Charcot was associated. In preparation for writing *A Rebours,* Huysmans read Eugéne Bouchut's *Du Névrosisme Aigu et Chronique et des Maladies Nerveuses* and Alexandre Axenfeld's *Traité des Névroses,* both of which are exhaustive textbooks on the subject of hysteria and other nervous illnesses.

Axenfeld describes in great detail the four phases of the *grande hystérie* as Charcot defined them: the *période épileptoïde,* the *période de clownisme,* the *période des attitudes passionelles,* and the *période terminale.* Axenfeld refers to the epileptoid phase as a "demonic attack," emphasizing the muscular contractions and emotional outbursts that Huysmans would ascribe to the acrobatic conversion of the satanist Gilles de Rais. Axenfeld also refers to the phase of *attitudes passionelles* as an "attack of ecstasy," and he adds that, while not all ecstasies are pathological, a great many ecstatics are hysterics. In this ecstatic phase, the patient, "self-absorbed, immobile, silent, remains for hours, even entire days in a sort of mute contemplation," not unlike the weirdly catatonic prayers of the monks that Durtal trips over in *En Route.* In Axenfeld's description of the feminized male hysteric, "beard not very thick, voice feeble, sickly and soft, skin fine, color pale, genital organs underdeveloped, eyes moist and shining, etc.," we might easily recognize the effete and neurotic aristocrat Des Esseintes.[5]

Huysmans was not, of course, the only French writer of his time to take an interest in the psychological discourse of hysteria. As Jan Goldstein has pointed out, Baudelaire, Sand, Flaubert, and Gourmont, among others, were appropriating the perverse and androgynous elements of hysteria in order to weave their own fashionable mythologies of neurotic genius.[6] The hysteric had already become a creative and sensitive *artiste.* Nevertheless, like Huysmans, these writers also maintained a wise distrust of medical wisdom. Baudelaire was diagnosed a hysteric, though in fact he was suffering from tertiary syphilis. He remarked with evident amusement on the elasticity of the term and its power to hide our ignorance of all things. "The illness persists," he wrote; "and the doctor pronounced the great word—hysteria. In good French, that means I'm raving mad."[7]

Rémy de Gourmont was perhaps the most explicitly erotic of these writers, and the closest in sensibility to Huysmans. In books like his study of medieval mysticism, *Le Latin Mystique,* and his series of erotic prose poems, *La Fantôme,* he explored the sensuality and erotics of Catholicism. The latter work in particular is a virtual catalog of Catholic fetishism, as two libertines explore the pleasures of incense, organ music, Christian symbolism, and flagellation in a church. His remarks on the psychology of grace are intended as a commentary on a physiological study by Paul Chaboneix, but they are virtually indistinguishable from the insights of Huysmans' preface to *A Rebours.* In an essay he published in 1900 on what he calls subconscious creation, Gourmont claims, "In conversion the will can act only after a long effort on the part of the subconscious and when all the elements of the new conviction have been secretly assembled and combined," and he concludes, "Grace is subconscious."[8]

Huysmans' relationship to psychology was far more ambivalent and religious. The medical influence on his work was perhaps an inevitable effect of his early discipleship with Zola, who is known to have attended the theatrical public lectures in which Charcot presented his therapeutic technique, not to mention his favorite hysterics. Huysmans closely associated Charcot with Zola, referring to both as materialists who denied the spiritual dimension of literature and human consciousness. With *A Rebours,* Huysmans criticized the naturalism of Zola as an aesthetic dead-end, and he grew increasingly skeptical of those psychologists—Charcot, in particular—who could offer only positivist, biological explanations for hysterical phenomena, even when the symptoms appeared to have no somatic basis. In *Là-Bas* he speaks dismissively of Charcot's practice of pressing women's ovaries to control hysterical fits, and in *En Rade* he describes various other "charlatans" who treat hysteria with metal plates or "Green Electricity." Jacques Marles, the hero of *En Rade,* is utterly baffled by his own nightmares, and he finds the theological and the psychological explanations for them equally troubling:

> Is one obliged at last to allow for supernatural explanations, to believe in the designs of a Providence that incites incoherent turbulations in dreams, and to accept in the same breath the inevitable visits of incubi and succubi, all the archaic hypotheses of demonologists, or is it still more convenient to constrain oneself to material explanations, to regard as entirely external forces, as stomach trou-

bles or as involuntary movements of the body, these damnable diva-
gations of the soul? (60–61)

In his later work, Huysmans is less hesitant in favoring the religious
explanation. In *Là-Bas* one of the characters asks, with evident exas-
peration, "is a woman possessed because she is hysterical or hysterical
because she is possessed? The Church alone can answer, science cannot" (233). In the same novel, he even suggests that hysteria and
mysticism are symptomatic of a materialistic age that offers no vent
to the spiritual aspirations of the people. "It is just at the moment
when positivism is at its height," he writes, "that mysticism rises again
and the madness of occultism begins" (151). After his conversion,
Huysmans' attack on materialism and Republican anticlericalism became all the more fierce. Indeed, his book *Les Foules de Lourdes*
(1906) may be seen as a belated counterpoint to Zola's 1894 book
*Lourdes,* a decidedly more materialistic account of the daily miracles
to be witnessed among the pilgrims at the famous shrine. Psychologists
and naturalist writers responded to Huysmans' novels with harsh
criticisms of their own—so much so that in 1891, after the publication
of *Là-Bas,* Huysmans wrote to his friend Arij Prins: "Charcot and the
materialist school have come down hard on me, treating me as a mystic
and a madman . . . And Zola, not at all pleased, is getting his little
naturalists to protest, crying out that the book is superb but insane!"[9]
Despite a Catholic revival in French literature—what Richard
Griffiths has referred to as a "reactionary revolution"—the progressive
anticlerical impulse remained a powerful literary force throughout
Europe. "And is not the Church itself the Catholic madhouse as an
ultimate ideal?—The earth as a whole converted into a madhouse?"
Nietzsche asks in *The Antichrist.* "The kind of religious man which
the Church aims at producing is a typical decadent."[10] Although
Nietzsche was convinced of his originality in this observation, the fin
de siècle produced a great many theorists who found the distinction
between faith and madness, or between the Christian and the decadent, a tenuous one at best. In the field of literary criticism, Max
Nordau was perhaps the most famous of these theorists, and he singled
out Huysmans as a target for his wrath. Nordau's immensely popular
book *Entartung* (1892), quickly translated into both English and

French, was a mammoth diatribe against the hysteria and occultism of contemporary art and literature. While Nordau's antiquated degeneracy theories and his own hysterical tendency to repetition and tirades have made him something of a period curiosity, he nevertheless articulates with great moral outrage the connections he found between hysteria, Catholicism, and decadent style. In so doing he also unintentionally demonstrates the limits, indeed the dullness, of the clinical view of decadent writing. He is as vague in his categorization as he is broad in his condemnation: "All these new tendencies, realism or naturalism, 'decadentism,' neo-mysticism, and the sub-varieties, are manifestations of degeneration and hysteria, and identical with the mental stigmata which the observations of clinicists have unquestionably established as belonging to these."[11]

Having little patience for religion, Nordau accepts the psychological view of his time that Saint Teresa and other mystics are the victims of "over-excited brain cells" (68) and "supersensuousness" (61). In his work mysticism is less a religious experience than an erotic and literary phenomenon. It is the ecstasy of imbeciles; the rebellion of weak minds against reason; the bewildering juxtaposition of what is mutually exclusive; a penchant for the cloudy and the chaotic; the Baudelairean perception of occult correspondences between different sounds, colors, and words. "Neo-Catholicism," as he calls it, is especially to blame for the mystical style. He locates the first outbreak of this degenerative malady in, of all places, the England of the Oxford movement, then traces it through the Pre-Raphaelites to the symbolists. Baudelaire and Verlaine are key targets, and "Wagnerism" is abused at great length as a neo-Catholic cult of diseased sensibilities. Huysmans, who is dubbed "the classical type of the hysterical mind" (302), is one of many writers Nordau attacks when he indicates that, "to the reader who has followed the arguments on the psychology of mysticism, it is intelligible that, with these romanticists, the ebullitions of piety are accompanied by a sensuousness which often amounts to lasciviousness" (73). From Nordau's clinical perspective, Catholic mysticism, decadence, hysteria, and sexual perversion were all of a piece, and Huysmans was one of their most prolific voices.

This eagerness to redefine mysticism as hysteria is itself a symptom of late-nineteenth-century anticlericalism, the popular movement to resist the political power of the Church in the name of democracy and science. As Jan Goldstein has demonstrated, the hysteria diagnosis was politically volatile, especially in the France of the Third Republic. The debate over hysteria and mysticism contained implicitly "all the rudiments of an anticlerical campaign" and touched a raw nerve in a nation divided between progressive Republicans and reactionary Catholics.[12] After 1870 the Republicans sought to undermine the power of the Church in French politics, particularly in its stronghold on public education. Around the turn of the century, much to Huysmans' disgust, they staged a statutory assault on monastic orders. Charcot was an important figure in Republican anticlericalism, even though he recognized the therapeutic value of Catholicism and had a number of powerful friends among the clergy. He was the most influential figure of the time in a widespread movement to establish psychology as a rigorous science with the power to redefine sexual and ecstatic experience in purely materialist and pathological terms. If religious experience could be shown to have biological or even hysterical origins, the metaphysical claims of the Church, not to mention its considerable political power, might be seriously challenged. Despite the *Ralliément* and the pope's rather unconvincing efforts at compromise, this political rift became increasingly entrenched. Zola's central role in the Dreyfus scandal might help to explain why Huysmans sided with the conservative Catholic opposition, railing against democracy, Jews, Protestants, Freemasons—railing even against the Church itself for being weak and liberal. In his attacks on Zola and Charcot, he clearly regarded himself as the artistic vanguard of Church politics.

Following closely on the work of Charcot, the midcentury deluge of psychological treatises on hysteria was followed in the 1880s by another deluge of psychological treatises on the more emotional aspects of religious experience, especially conversion, demonic possession, and mysticism. In these studies, usually medical in tone, conversion was closely associated with pubescence and discussed with respect to the trauma, nervous illness, or sexual panic that seemed inevitably to precede it. Mysticism and demonic possession were even more popular as targets for psychologists. D.-M. Bourneville, one of the most ardent popularizers of Charcot's work, edited nine volumes of the *Bibliothèque Diabolique,* a scholarly series that sought to reinterpret early modern accounts of possession and mysticism through the hysteria diagnosis. His arguments were explicitly anticlerical in tone.

For example, in his 1886 essay on a sixteenth-century nun, he writes that the clergy, in regarding a hysterical delirium as proof of "the doctrine of the Real Presence," sought to "exploit public ignorance and superstition" in accordance with "all the self-interested traditions of Catholicism."[13] As Bourneville knew, these traditions were alive and well even in his own time. He wrote in similarly clinical terms about Louise Lateau, a devout Belgian woman who, in the 1870s, began to exhibit the stigmata and who was later described by Huysmans in *En Route*.

A few years earlier in 1883, the year *A Rebours* was written, R. P. G. Hahn published his controversial essay "Les Phénomènes Hystériques et les Révélations de Sainte Thérèse," in the *Revue des Questions Scientifiques*. Although he was a Jesuit, Hahn's essay was placed on the Index. In his reading of *The Interior Castle,* he finds he is able "to trace a very nice line of demarcation between the hallucinations of hysterics and the visions of Saint Teresa," and he adds that, "from the physical point of view, she was afflicted with an epileptiform malady in which we have recognized all the organic symptoms of the *grande hystérie*."[14] In 1880 Charles Richet, another devotee of Charcot, published a two-part article, "Les Démoniaques d'Aujourd'hui" and "Les Démoniaques d'Autrefois," in the influential intellectual journal *Revue des Deux Mondes*. In this article Richet refigured the great doctor as a sort of exorcist who could solve the centuries-old riddle of demonic possession. Like Bourneville, Richet traced the convulsive spasms of the modern hysteric gesture-by-gesture onto early modern accounts of demonic possession.

In 1887, a few years before Huysmans' depiction of satanism in *Là-Bas,* Charcot himself published a book with Paul Richer that reasserted the earlier arguments of his various disciples. This book, *Les Démoniaques dans l'Art,* seems calculated to aggravate the temper of someone like Huysmans, especially in its method of placing sketches of modern hysterics alongside reproductions of medieval paintings representing demonic possession. The authors make a tenuous assertion in a concluding chapter that Christian mystics such as Saint Catherine of Siena and Blessed Christina of Stommeln resemble hysterics, especially during the phase of *attitudes passionelles.* A number of the illustrations, especially those that depict various saints as they heal the possessed, bear a remarkable resemblance to the pictures of

Charcot's Tuesday lectures in which a female hysteric appears to swoon at his command (Figures 3 and 4). In this work of "retrospective medicine," the reader is invited to recognize in Charcot a materialistic savior come to free hysterics from their demonic stigmata through purely physical manipulations. By the turn of the century, Charcot and his disciples had excited a flood of studies on the psychology of mysticism and conversion, not only in French (Janet, Lemesle) but also in German (Nordau, Freud) and English (Leuba, Starbuck, James, Coe).

Huysmans clearly knew Charles Richet's work, since he refers to it explicitly in *Là-Bas*. As a counterpoint, he simply made his usual claim that the psychologist is good at categorizing nervous illnesses but fails to recognize their supernatural origins and their religious cure. He recruits Durtal's friend Des Hermies to present his argument. Des Hermies admits that Richet has correctly identified the symptoms of the *grande hystérie,* complete with the *arc de cercle* and muscular convulsions, among the nuns of Loudun and Poitiers who were possessed by demons. "Fine, but what does this demonstrate?" he asks. "That these demonomaniacs were hystero-epileptics? Certainly. The observations of Dr Richet, so learned in such matters, are conclusive; but in what way do they invalidate Possession?" (233).

De Hermies has the same religious counterpoint for Charcot: "Yes, without a doubt, Charcot determines quite well the phases of the attack, notes the irrational and passionate attitudes, the clonic movements; he discovers hysterogenic zones, can, by adroitly manipulating the ovaries, arrest or accelerate the crises, but when it comes to preventing them, when it comes to understanding their sources and motivations, when it comes to curing them, that is another thing altogether!" (234). This rather facile argument is difficult to contradict, perhaps impossible, since it simply posits a divine motivation behind every physical mechanism. Nevertheless, whatever his apprehensions about Charcot, it is evident even in this passage that Huysmans took great pride in his clinical knowledge of hysteria. Psychological jargon was part of his decadent passion for neologisms and other startling or obscure words that delight the reader with their strangeness. He also deployed Charcot's terminology as a "reverse discourse," turning psychological jargon against itself. He makes an essentially religious argument with all the pretensions of modern science.

Huysmans' aesthetic investment in hysteria and Christian mysticism is not only scientifically rigorous but also disturbingly beautiful. He originated an aesthetic of mystical and hysterical fragmentation—physical, sexual, psychological, spiritual, cultural, and, above all, textual fragmentation. He sought to demonstrate the movements of the "unconscious," the enigmatic symptoms of the divine, in a broken language at once ecstatic, maniacal, and perverse. In the famous opening chapter of *Là-Bas,* he articulates a brilliant apologia for his tortured and decadent style as a "spiritual naturalism" or "mystical realism," taking the ecstasy and horror of Matthias Grünewald's painting of the Crucifixion as his model (Figure 5). Through his juxtaposition of mysticism and naturalism, Huysmans presses the style of Zola into the service of decadent Catholicism. It is precisely Grünewald's unsparing "naturalism," his passionately detailed brutality, that mesmerizes Huysmans. Paradoxically, through the unbearable horror of the body in pain, through enigmatic gestures that exceed the reflexive convulsions of the flesh, Grünewald offers a glimpse of the

Fig. 3. Engraving of Charcot during a lecture on hysteria at the Salpêtrière (courtesy of the Wellcome Centre for Medical Science, London).

Fig. 4. Drawing of Saint Philip casting out a demon, from Charcot and Richer's book on hysteria and demonic possession, *Les Démoniaques dans l'Art* (1887).

spiritual. Huysmans finds sadistic inspiration in detailing the suffering of Christ on the cross. He defines the spiritual through images of splitting and fragmentation. He speaks of wounds dripping with blood and pus, arms dislocated and ripped from their sockets, straining muscles, labored tendons, fingers contorted into a gesture of supplication, reproach, and benediction. Grünewald's Christ appeals "with the cry of an infant" to the mother he has lost (16). His convulsions acquire an aura of sanctity: "Around this ulcerated head there filtered a glowing light; and a superhuman expression illuminated the effluescence of the skin, the epilepsy of his features" (18–19).

As with the hysteric, sensation and meaning are perversely and painfully redistributed along the body according to the dictates of an unknowable, unconscious language. The effect is erotic, though not necessarily genital or even pleasurable. One critic put it most succinctly when she said, "What Huysmans portrays is not desire, but rather the decomposition of desire."[15] Christ, already literally the irruption of the

Fig. 5. Matthias Grünewald, detail from *The Crucifixion* (1512–1516) (Staatliche Kunsthalle, Karlsruhe).

Real on earth, appears as the Word incorporated in the flesh. He is also, in this instance, the flesh incorporated in the word, in the work of art. He is a text, a painting, a biblical figure. Huysmans believed that art—even the body as art, or nature as art—is the primary mode of mystical reverie. What Huysmans discovered in Grünewald's brutal Crucifixion is a spiritualization of the hysterical symptom. The symptom, in other words, as a work of religious art. For the hysteric also experiences through the symptom an irruption of the Real on the body, a fragmentation of the familiar fantasy of the body to make way for another, more occult fantasy.

The symptom, as work of art, is itself the Real as word incorporated in flesh. It is like the jewel-encrusted tortoise in *A Rebours*. The tortoise is a paradox of organic tissue and lapidary design. It exists only as a function of style, only as a textual counterpoint to the beautiful carpet on which it walks. It lives in the text, but only by virtue of the jewels that eventually kill it into art and dispell into the past the spark of life that once might have distinguished the ornamental shell from organic tissue. The symptom as Real, like the body of Christ, is a thing jeweled over with a decadent superabundance of brutal words and violent meanings that kill it into text; for the jewels on the expired tortoise and the stigmatic wounds on the dead body of Christ are what mark and constitute the textual effluence of the Real as such, whose spark of life they have already displaced into the past, into another place.

For Huysmans, the irruption of the Real is often a religious spectacle of torture and murder. He endows the dead tortoise with a distinctly religious significance when he likens it to "a jeweled ciborium" (78), an ornamental vessel that contains the host. This icon of decadent ornament bears within it, figuratively speaking, the miracle of transubstantiation, the Real presence as it is experienced on earth. So too, the hysterical symptom is an irruption of the Real, a dislocating wound, an obscure enjoyment that gestures elsewhere, toward an unconscious scene, *au-delà* or perhaps *là-bas*, to use Huysmans' terms. The symptom is the private and enigmatic language of the hysteric spelled out elaborately in incapacitating hieroglyphics through the body. Nordau and Charcot no doubt recognized the mystical aspect of the clinical symptom when they referred to the "stigmata," the distinguishing signs on the body of the hysteric like those on the body of Christ and the saints. Lacan is playing a similar game with words when he speaks of the symptom as *sinthome,* eliciting from the French *symptome* the ghost of Saint Thomas, of the Thomists, restoring to the clinical term a mystical Christian symbolism.

Hysterical fragmentation is, above all, a textual experience for Huysmans. It is his signature, the very essence of his later style, whether we call it "spiritual naturalism," decadent, symbolist, satanic, or Catholic. His explanation of "spiritual naturalism" is itself based on a text, or a text of a text—not just some imagined conception of Golgotha as a real place, but his elaboration on Grünewald's highly allegorical elaboration on a biblical account of the Crucifixion. The same is true of Salomé in *A Rebours:* she is Huysmans' elaboration on Moreau's elaboration on a story in the Bible in which Salomé is not named as such and hardly appears. "But neither St. Matthew, nor St. Mark, nor St. Luke, nor any other evangelist had enlarged on the delirious charms, on the active depravities of the dancer" (83), he observes, as if to say that even the biblical text from which all other Salomés are drawn is an artistic failure, less a body than a mere textual suggestion to be embroidered by minds of neurotic sensitivity. In this naturalism *à rebours,* unmediated nature—the body of Christ or the body of woman—is displaced by a gorgeous textuality, perhaps even an infinite regress of textuality. The body as a natural phenomenon is displaced by the more exquisite delirium of art.

The naturalism of this "spiritual naturalism" is revealed to be its opposite—a textual strategy, estranged from nature but, in Huysmans' hands, certainly not estranged from the Real, which returns through the hysterical peculiarities of his style. Huysmans experiences the return of the Real in the body of his text, not to mention on the text of his body, so numerous were his own neurotic maladies. His decadent style, recognizable at twenty paces, even in English translations, is distinguished by tortuous syntax, archaisms, neologisms, jargon, proper names of obscure people and places, bizarre names for beautiful things that can kill any plant or animal into a work of poetry. His style punishes, seduces, and baffles. It suggests far more than it understands. Rae Beth Gordon's account of his style is especially astute: emphasizing the paralysis, hallucination, and *horror vacui* associated with neurosis, she describes Huysmans' view of hysteria as a "mystical, creative force that would revitalize the novel." Furthermore, she adds, "The contortions of the syntax, the profusion of detail, the superimposition of images through metaphor, all of these elements bring about a paralysis of the narrative line, overwhelmed by the top-heaviness of this movement and superabundance."[16] Huysmans' meandering plotlessness, broken up by conversations, mired down by endless disgorgements of obscure information from his library, leaves us with a fin de siècle sensation of paralysis, of winding down or of getting wound up in the tangle of a text, the tangle of text upon text, as they come apart at the seams. After the fashion of Paul Bourget's definition of decadent style in which the book is sacrificed to the page, the page to the line, and the line to the word, individual words leap out of Huysmans' prose and command attention. They perform histrionics. They act out. And like the symptom, they puzzle the reader with their obscurity and their paradoxes.

Style becomes a symptomatic experience of the "unconscious," figured by Huysmans as divine. His conception of a hysterical grace, an unconscious unction, certainly derived much of its realism from the work of Charcot and his followers, not to mention his own naturalistic discipleship under Zola. But his development of a distinctly decadent aesthetic along mystical lines preserved something of the mystery of religious experience, an ineffability that psychoanalysis has come to celebrate rather than to vulgarize in its own cult of desire. His departure from the materialist presumptions of naturalism and psychology was never more elegantly described than in the preface to *A Rebours,* where the chthonic rumblings of an almost Freudian *inconscience* are sublated into the enigma of grace:

> As for Psychology, the thing is otherwise. If we envision it, as I envision it, from the point of view of a conversion, it is, in its preliminaries, impossible to unravel; certain corners may be tangible, but the rest, no; the subterranean workings of the soul elude us. There was without a doubt, at the time I wrote *A Rebours,* a turning of the soil, a rooting in the earth to lay the foundations, but I can render no account of it. God was digging a place for his filaments and was at work only in the shadows of the soul, in the night. Nothing was perceptible; it was only years later that a spark began to run the length of these filaments. (xxvi)

Huysmans never quite freed himself from his debt to Charcot. The traces of a mechanistic psychology are there even in this passage—the invisible wires and electric spark of a human machine—but there is now a deus ex machina. Judge Schreber, Freud's classic paranoid schizophrenic, uses much the same imagery when he feels the filaments of the godhead under his skin, buzzing with static, approaching him in an arc from the horizon like the rays of a spiritual father whose intentions are unknown. The self is penetrated by the Other, who remains unnamed, perhaps even insidious, though possibly divine. This mysticism, like a form of madness, always gestures beyond the body, beyond explanation, to a religious and erotic *au-delà* at once enacted and encoded in its own text. The movements of grace are never wholly visible, never wholly above ground, but its extraordinary sensation may be felt in the obscure wiring of Huysmans' texts and the aesthetic, almost electrical shock of decadent style.

## Conversion Hysteria

> The difficulty is to be in the desired state of soul—though I have seen, in all this, such curious things, and for that matter I have such a hysterical soul, that I believe I might find a retreat to La Chartreuse exasperating from that perspective—and to cast aside all this carnal filth that tempts me not immoderately.  J.-K. Huysmans

All the books in the decadent and Catholic phases of Huysmans' career—a period extending from the publication of *A Rebours* in 1884 to his death in 1907—celebrate the hysterical and mystical body in some way. They are also, many of them, narratives of religious conversion. Des Esseintes, Gilles de Rais, and Durtal are all converts, as is Lydwina, in the sense that she comes to recognize the significance of her faith in the miraculous course of her suffering. When we think of Huysmans' religious conversion, we generally focus on a brief period in his life, his retreat to a Trappist monastery in 1892, as it is fictionalized in *En Route*. Inevitably, what springs to mind is Barbey d'Aurevilly's famous line about Baudelaire and *Les Fleurs du Mal*, which he applied to Huysmans after the publication of *A Rebours*: "After such a book, it only remains for the author to choose between the muzzle of a pistol and the foot of the cross." Huysmans even quotes this line approvingly in his preface (xxvii). He did, of course, choose the foot of the cross, and so for that matter did Barbey, whose prose was no less bizarre and erotic after his conversion. But there are a number of problems with Barbey's formulation.

First of all, Huysmans did not convert after *A Rebours*, but eight years later, after an even more diabolical book, *Là-Bas*. Barbey also implies that Catholicism brought an end to Huysmans' decadent phase, whereas it is clear from the preface that Huysmans himself regarded Catholicism as a peculiar manifestation of his decadent phase. Furthermore, despite the sincerity of his conversion, Huysmans found that prostration at the foot of the cross was not a position he could maintain with any comfort as an artist. Although he became a

Benedictine oblate, his Catholic novels depict a man, Durtal, who is forever stuttering with unbelief, troubled by feelings of spiritual dryness, irritated by the stupidity of the clergy, or bored by the dreariness of monastic life.

What Huysmans sought in art and in Catholicism were the visionary flights of imagination and inspiration that he found in early modern mystics and satanists. He sought respite from mediocrity and atheism. Like the oscillations between shame and piety that characterize the work of Barbey, Verlaine, and Wilde, faith is constantly in flux in Huysmans' work, marked by dramatic shifts between spiritual abjection and spiritual ecstasy, the extremes of which are realized in passionate fits. The three great converts of his fiction—Des Esseintes, Gilles de Rais, and Durtal—all have in common a histrionic longing to embrace the faith, a longing that they articulate through choking, fainting, convulsions, and other symptomatic maladies generally attributed to hysteria.

Near the conclusion of *A Rebours,* a physician finally prescribes hydropathic treatment for Des Esseintes. Ironically, the same medical advice was given to Huysmans himself by some of his readers: "Other would-be critics," he writes in the preface, "were kind enough to advise me that I would profit from confinement in a hydropathic institution, where I might suffer the punishment of cold showers" (xxviii). The advice was probably more reasonable than they knew, given the long litany of his own afflictions, neurotic and otherwise. In addition to his serious somatic illnesses, such as dysentery and cancer, he suffered from countless other ailments, many of them neurotic, that dogged him throughout his life: impotence, headaches, neuralgia, neurasthenia, melancholia, and interminable dyspepsia. As his formal conversion neared, he began to speak of his nervous maladies in ever more religious terms. He became obsessed with religious purity, calling out in his letters for a carbolic for the soul, phenol, cupric solution, prodigious bleach, exceptional solvents. Moreover, he associated this need for purity with hysteria and the demonic excesses of *Là-Bas.* He wrote to Jean Lorrain: "I shall purge myself, and with a clean body I shall go to confession—after which I shall, I think, be in a state of candor that will permit me to vent my hysteria in a reversal, an 'A Rebours' of *Là-Bas.*"[17]

Huysmans often characterized this "hysteria" as a demonic attack.

As might be expected, these attacks resembled paranoid persecution fantasies. His perennial fear of women, Jews, Protestants, and Freemasons was complemented by his terror of lascivious female "succubi" who were wont to visit him in his sleep. After the publication of *Là-Bas,* he had recurrent fears that satanists were plotting against him. He experienced strange "effluvia" that enveloped him. He wrote quite seriously about malevolent microbe-like demons called "larvae" and complained that the sanctimonious old woman who lived above him was trailing them around in her petticoats all day. Like Louise Marles in *En Rade,* Huysmans experienced strange electrical sensations in his face, and apparently the same sensations afflicted his cat. He asked his friend Leclaire to bring him white tapers from Lourdes to fight off demonic attacks. He told his spiritual mentor, Abbé Mugnier, that he was being driven to suicide by the devil. Zola was convinced that his former disciple had literally gone off his head.

Huysmans also tended to surround himself with religious people who might also be described as neurotics. There were not only satanists but also pious visionaries in his retinue, and they intrigued him by the fine line they walked between reason and madness. Most notable among the satanists was Berthe Courrière, one of the women on whom he based the demonic Hyacinthe Chantelouve in *Là-Bas.* Not only was Courrière a satanist who, according to Rachilde, fed consecrated hosts to stray dogs from her shopping bags, but she was also committed to insane asylums, in 1890 and again in 1906, and published a vitriolic attack on Charcot entitled "Néron, Prince de la Science." On a much sadder note, one of the few women for whom Huysmans had an enduring affection was Anna Meunier, on whom he based the hysterical Louise Marles and whom he visited every Sunday in the asylum where she eventually died of a "general paralysis."

In short, Huysmans knew a great deal about hysteria from his own experience, beyond what he read in clinical texts. Furthermore, the close association between hysteria and religious conversion in his life finds its complement in his various fictional personae, all of whom seem to vacillate on the verge of faith and madness. Des Esseintes, for example, is characterized as a classic male hysteric from the opening pages of *A Rebours,* and he seeks refuge from his nervous illnesses in pious reverie that is itself a malady. Huysmans intended *A Rebours* to be "a very strange novel, vaguely clerical, a bit pederastic, the story of the end of a race devoured by memories of a religious childhood and nervous illness." In a letter to Zola he describes Des Esseintes as a "Christian and pederast" and "a Catholic through atavism."[18] In his portrait of the quintessential decadent, Huysmans applies virtually everything he learned from Bouchut and Axenfeld about the degenerative nature of hysteria. Des Esseintes is "a frail young man of thirty, anemic and nervous, with hollow cheeks, eyes of a cold steely blue, a dull but still straight nose, and long slender hands" (2). Charcot compiled a long list of symptoms characteristic of hysteria, a list that would have aroused the envy of the endlessly afflicted Des Esseintes: blindness, deafness, paralysis, inability to talk or walk or eat, strange pains and swellings, numbness, fever, bleeding, vomiting, fainting, somnambulism, and so on. Des Esseintes's list of complaints is no shorter, and they are mostly "nervous" by his own diagnosis: chlorosis, anemia, fainting, neuralgia, trembling, choking, spasms, nausea, near-fatal reveries, legendary nightmares, an inability to eat, a dry and nervous cough, and a condition of the bowels at once uneasy and constipated.

Huysmans also describes the portrait of one of Des Esseintes's ancestors, a court "minion" with a "world-weary countenance" (2). We learn of his "cosmetic commas of rouge" and his "painted neck." Cosmetics, effeminization, incest, the exhaustion of the race, all the benchmarks of fin de siècle degeneracy theories are here. Even syphilis makes an entrance later on in the figure of a diseased and disfigured woman in a nightmare. Charcot and Nordau spring to mind, and their notion of hysteria as hereditary, a form of degeneracy—not only of the body but of history itself, the history of a race or a family coming apart at the seams. The Duke and Duchess, Des Esseintes's parents, also confirm the hereditary aspect of their son's neurotic afflictions. They live and die in their introduction. "The mother, a tall woman, silent and pale, died of nervous exhaustion." She is a ghostly figure confined to a shuttered bedroom, a chronic invalid who cannot endure light and noise without suffering from nervous attacks. For his part, the father succumbs to "some vague malady" when Des Esseintes is nearly seventeen (3). Des Esseintes's childhood memories of his father are also religious, since his father is displaced by paternal Jesuits at his school.

In the preface, Huysmans claims that when he wrote *A Rebours* he had never set foot in a church, nor did he know any priests. He also writes: "I was never pious in my youth, and the moments I remember from childhood, of first Communion, of religious education, which often assume a place of importance in conversion, had no effect on mine" (xxiv). Nevertheless, such memories play an important role in Des Esseintes's conversion, especially since, unlike Huysmans, he has had a Jesuit education. The Jesuit fathers surrender any hope of holy orders for their pupil, and Des Esseintes finds that he is "scarcely aware of the priests' paternal yoke" (6).

And yet he recalls the fathers in odd moments of hysterical fancy. For example, he remembers a homoerotic scene, in which he seduces a boy, Auguste Langlois, into a life of debauchery and crime; this scene gives way, unconsciously and uncontrollably, to a second phase of memory in which he recalls a pederastic idyll of life among the priests and boys at school. The subtle discipline of the priests, who insinuate themselves into the lives of the boys, is placed in odd juxtaposition with Des Esseintes's own homoerotic seduction of the putatively innocent Auguste. Odd, and we might even say incestuous, given the Jesuits' displacement of the absent father in a family that has suffered a progressive "effemination of the males" (2). Des Esseintes seeks to seduce Auguste and, without his understanding how, lead him into a life of crime; in the same way, he begins to feel in himself the unconscious germination of the Catholic seed planted in him in his childhood by the Jesuits:

> "There was nothing left to say," thought Des Esseintes, trying to reason with himself, to follow the path of this recurrence at Fontenay of the Jesuit element; "Ever since my childhood, and without my knowing it, I have had this leaven fermenting in me; even this penchant that I have always had for religious objects is perhaps proof of it." (118)

Religious sentiments overtake him like a nightmare, their origin and mechanism ever mysterious. But in the juxtaposition of the priests with Des Esseintes's flirtation with Auguste, the curious appeal of Catholicism reads like a homoerotic seduction.

Toward the end of the novel, the Jesuits reappear in an equally symptomatic fashion. In a fit of hitherto unknown symptoms, of nightmares, eye troubles, and coughs, Des Esseintes is afflicted with aural hallucinations. He hears the sound of running water and buzzing wasps, the humming of a lathe that grows more and more shrill until it becomes the silvery note of a bell. Suddenly, he is plunged into the religious atmosphere of his youth, and he launches into his disquisition on religious music, especially the simple plainchant and the organ music of the Jesuit school. This synesthesic memory occurs as a Catholic reverie: "The chants he had learned among the Jesuits came back to him, invoking the college chapel where they had been sung, and echoing their hallucinations onto the sense of sight and smell, which they veiled in clouds of incense and the tenebrous rays that filter through stained-glass windows under lofty ceilings" (306). Not insignificantly, this reverie immediately precedes the notoriously anal-erotic passages about peptone enemas, one of Des Esseintes's more humorous inversions of nature. Like his favorite monastic chants, the peptone enemas offer him yet another avenue for his paradoxical disgust with nature and the body, at once a flight from the senses and a perverse indulgence in them.

Des Esseintes's interest in conversion is a recurrent and increasingly intense preoccupation that he explicitly associates with his nervous illnesses: "These recurrences of belief, these apprehensions of faith tormented him more particularly since his health had begun to deteriorate; they coincided with certain nervous disorders that had recently arisen" (128). Catholicism itself is experienced as a hysterical disorder. First, there is the deterioration of the Church as an institution, its impure and ineffectual language fallen into decadence. Des Esseintes is adrift in ideological and spiritual confusion: "In fact, for some days he found his soul in an indescribable state. For a second, he was a believer, an instinctive convert to religion, but then, after the shortest interval of reflection, all his attraction toward the faith would evaporate" (116).

Even sacred literature has the capacity to turn into its opposite, to torture and lead astray the reader who is anxious to believe. Huysmans frequently returns to the paradox, immensely popular among the decadents, that the Church itself was contributing to the destruction of Catholic faith through the tediousness of its dogma, the materialism of its clergy, and the vulgarity of its art. As Des Esseintes reads the works of various theologians, losing his peace of mind amid their labyrinthine arguments and abstractions, Catholic discourse takes on a fragmented and hysterical countenance: "Fragments of these schisms, scraps of these heresies, which for centuries divided the Church between Occident and Orient, resounded in his mind" (122). His brain seethes with "paradoxes and subtleties, puzzling over a host of hair-splitting distinctions, wrestling with a tangle of rules as complicated as so many codes of law, open to any interpretation, to any play of words, leading up to a system of celestial jurisprudence of the most tenuous, the most burlesque kind" (122–123). Through the bizarre chatter of theologians, through the cracks in his own piety, Des Esseintes experiences the return of the demonic, a manic resurgence of his interest in magic, witchcraft, and the black mass. His body responds psychosomatically through a renewed onslaught of his nervous weakness, his trembling hands and neuralgic agonies. The symptoms abate only with the relinquishment of the texts. His nerves are calmed with medicines and outdoor walks.

To say that Des Esseintes's religious experiences are hysterical is not, however, to say that they are not genuine. Concomitant with the hysterical degeneration of Church rhetoric is an equally hysterical resurgence of Catholic spirituality and a sincere need for faith in an otherwise materialistic world. Precisely because of his doubts, because of his persistent rejection of Church teaching, Des Esseintes experiences his moments of faith in fragmented fashion as disruptive enigmas, as symptomatic expressions of the truth that transfigure his aesthetic and erotic sensibilities with a religious significance. Fragmentation and disruption are essential, since Catholicism, whether in its demonic or mystical capacity, is regarded by Huysmans as an interruption, a spiritual wound, in the materialist fantasy of a purely physical world.

At one point, Des Esseintes looks upon Christianity as "a superb legend, as a magnificent imposture" (119), but through his textual engagement with the Church, through his aesthetic indulgence in its literature and its plainchant, he finds this imposture is one in which he fervently wishes to believe. Throughout decadent literature, whether in Verlaine and Huysmans or in Pater and Wilde, conversion to Catholicism is subject to this peculiar tenuousness, this interminable wavering, this feeling that one is embracing an improbable and anachronistic aristocracy of the spirit, now sadly in decline. Des Esseintes speaks of his tendency to oscillate "between skeptical ideas and sudden fits of conviction that recurred from time to time under the subtle impulse of his childhood memories" (329). This oscillation, these fits, are not so much heretical as they are simply the fate of Catholicism in the cluttered mind of modernity.

In brief glimpses that come upon him like a convulsion, Des Esseintes recognizes the mystical faith he longs for, the touch of magic and sadism, but he sees also a Church that has sold its mystical soul to bourgeois liberalism and commerce. "Business negotiations have invaded the cloister," he observes, adding that "in the guise of antiphonaries, huge account-books were placed on the lecterns" (328). Even the bread of the Eucharist is compromised, since it is manufactured cheaply by secular dealers who use potato flour instead of wheat. The desire for faith is an essential one, even a perverse and instinctual one, but it is lost amid the distractions and dullness of modern life, both religious and secular. There is a romantic agony in Des Esseintes's fits of Catholic faith, a melancholic celebration of the *amour de l'impossible* whose bright gleam begins to fade the moment it is recognized: "As his hunger for religion augmented, as he appealed to all these forces as a ransom for the future, as a subsidy for his new life, he passionately craved this faith that now revealed itself to him, though the distance separating him from it appalled him, doubts crowded into his fevered mind, upsetting his unsteady will, rejecting on grounds of common sense and by mathematical demonstration the mysteries and dogmas of the Church" (330). The very syntax of this sentence is fragmented, constantly interrupting itself and very nearly losing its way. Doubt invades his every outburst of faith even before it is fully articulated.

The final passionate prayer of *A Rebours* is by no means a resolution to Des Esseintes's oscillations. It is, rather, an inconclusive repetition in a circular narrative that rearticulates over and over the same eccentric sensibility in different words, through flowers and perfumes and fragrant books, in chapters that are virtually interchangeable. For an embrace of the faith, the prayer is oddly desperate and hopeless: "Like a tide-race, the waves of human mediocrity mount to the heavens and will engulf this refuge, for I am opening the floodgates in spite of myself. Ah! but my courage fails me and my heart is sick within me!—Lord, take pity on the Christian who doubts, on the unbeliever who wants to believe, on the galley-slave of life who puts out to sea alone, in the night, beneath a firmament no longer lit by the consoling beacon-fires of the ancient hope!" (337).

The conversion of Des Esseintes, if we may call it that, seems less the logical conclusion of a decadent life than a recurrent thread in decadent spirituality. The prayer is certainly less a conclusion to *A Rebours* than a final repetition, we might even say a hysterical repetition, an outburst, of the same improbable longing after faith. The repetition continues, I would argue, through the four Durtal novels, in which Huysmans, even after his own formal conversion, is at pains to reconcile his own mystical vision with the modern sensibilities of the artist.

Durtal himself, especially in *Là-Bas,* where he first appears, seems to experience the same crisis of faith as Des Esseintes. His inability to decide between faith and doubt is frequently characterized as an interminable vacillation. "He found himself once again at the same impasse," pausing at the threshold of mystical faith but unable to enter (20). He is envious of the robust faith of his friend Carhaix, a pious medievalist and bell ringer who lives in the tower of Saint-Sulpice, and he exclaims, "It is tiresome all the same to be always vacillating" (222). Indeed, his spiritual malady is peculiarly fin de siècle: "But it has always been the same; the tail ends of centuries all resemble one another. All of them are periods of vacillation and uncertainty. Just as materialism is running rampant, magic re-emerges" (152).

To say that the conversions of Gilles and Durtal are histrionic is an understatement. Huysmans draws on a full roster of hysterical symptoms to give the impression of penitence as a mystical convulsion of the soul. Although Durtal is not as absurd a figure as Des Esseintes, they share much the same decadent disposition. He has become completely "hystericized" (153) over the mysterious Mme. Chantelouve, who promises to bring him to a modern-day black mass and who is herself "hysterical of body, nymphomaniacal of soul" (166). As for Gilles, he is described as "the Des Esseintes of the fifteenth century" (77), a perverse mystic, an avid collector of gorgeous surplices and sacerdotal ornaments, and a vampiristic lover of young boys. Huysmans' satanists, whether medieval or modern, are also impeccably decadent and stylishly hysterical.

The confession of Gilles de Rais is a protracted spasm. Huysmans builds up to it with a lengthy account of Gilles's crimes—the invoca-

tions of Satan, the studied debauchery, the rape and murder of children, all evoked in copious naturalistic detail. There is a limit to the
ecstatic possibilities of evil, however, and Gilles soon reaches it. He
dreams in vain of unique violations, of more ingenious tortures, but
with no law left to transgress, he has reached a spiritual dead end. He
is suddenly overwhelmed with remorse and wrenched by nights of
expiation. Like an inmate of the Salpêtrière, the asylum whose name
is repeatedly invoked in this novel, Gilles is besieged by phantoms and
"howls like a wounded beast. He is found rushing along the solitary
corridors of the château." He escapes into the forest, where his mind
disintegrates into a hysterical fragmentation: "But in this spirit, mobile
and exalted, ideas superimpose themselves, one atop the other, and
those that disappear leave their shadow on those that follow" (18).
His confusion is projected onto the trees around him, as they resolve
into human bodies and split into pieces: "Here a tree appears to him
as a living being, standing on its head, its root tresses buried in the
ground, its legs tossed in the air and spread wide, subdividing then
into new thighs open themselves in their turn, becoming smaller and
smaller with the lengthening of the limbs" (19). He suffers a few pages
of hallucinations, which culminate in a vision of Christ that recalls
Grünewald's painting in the opening chapter. In an evocation of Charcot's convulsive *arc de cercle,* he writhes and "rebounds in a somersault, then he crawls like a wolf on all fours and, howling, he gnaws
at the foot of the crucifix" (21). In his *période terminale,* Gilles trembles, sobs, and weeps, after which Durtal, "emerging slowly out of the
vision he had imagined," closes his notebook. In short, Gilles passes
through all four phases of the *grande hystérie.*

"Then, in its white splendor, the soul of the Middle Ages burst forth
radiant in this room," Huysmans writes of Gilles's public confession
at his trials, but of course it reads like another histrionic bout of
hysteria. In a labored voice, choked with tears, he recounts his crimes.
"And with the eye of a somnambulist he looked down at his fingers
and shook them as if they were dripping with blood" (139). Women
in the courtroom scream and faint, having gone mad with horror. As
he finishes his confession, he breaks down completely, falling to his
knees and sobbing. He cries out for forgiveness and beats his forehead
on the flagstones. A wild terror and commotion ensue as the crowd,
driven beyond the human limits of horror and pity, tosses and surges.

The judges struggle to contain themselves. Not even the Salpêtrière was ever this exciting.

The celebration of the black mass, which Durtal attends with Mme. Chantelouve as his guide, is another ritual of hysteria. The defrocked priest Canon Docre presides over the scene, invoking a Christ who is a lascivious figure of horror, "Guardian of strident Neuroses, Leaden Tower of Hysteria, bleeding Orifice of Rapes!" (163). Like Charcot, Docre need only give the appropriate signal, the tinkling of prayer bells in his case, and some of the women taking part in the ritual are suddenly reduced to abject howling:

> Some women fell to the carpet and rolled around. One of them, who seemed to be worked by a spring, threw herself prone and waved her legs in the air; another, suddenly struck by a hideous strabism, clucked, then, suffering aphonia, stood with her mouth open, the tongue turned back, the tip cleaving to the palate; another, inflated, livid, her pupils dilated, lolled her head back over her shoulders and then jerked it brusquely erect, tearing at her throat with her nails; yet another, sprawling on her back, undid her skirts, displayed her naked belly, meteorized, enormous, and then twisted her face into a horrible grimace and stuck out her tongue, which she could not control, a white tongue bitten around the edges, harrowed by red teeth in a bloody mouth. (166)

The ritual culminates in a general pandemonium of this sort—what Durtal, with a shudder, refers to as the "aura of the *grande hystérie.*" Again, Huysmans is drawing on clinical material to describe a scene of hysteria that he intends the reader to interpret as demonic possession, not so much psychosomatic as supernatural.

In *Là-Bas* Huysmans suggests the spiritual life of Durtal largely through his association with various satanists, both medieval and modern. In *En Route* Huysmans focuses almost exclusively on Durtal himself, in about three hundred pages of religious vacillation, moral self-reproach, and aesthetic musing. Even more than in *Là-Bas*, Durtal begins to resemble Des Esseintes. The novel begins in the cathedral of Saint-Sulpice, where Durtal's mind is wandering from the dullness of an ineloquent priest to the grandeur, "the cry of absolute desolation and terror" (15), that is the Dies Irae. The music excites in him "the magnificent and barbarous image" (18) of the earth belching flames

and constellations bursting into shards. Immediately, we are re-intro-
duced to his apocalyptic passion for mystical reverie. Huysmans even
returns to the degeneracy theories of fin de siècle psychology that he
exploited in *A Rebours*. Among his reasons for conversion, Durtal
includes "love of art, heredity, weariness of life" (33). He suffers from
neuralgia. He mentions his ancestry and the "atavism of an ancient
and pious family strewn among the monasteries" (34). His passion for
the simple plainchant is at once hysterical and decadent: he finds its
music to be "thin, sharp, nervous, like the work of the Primitives . . .
the resonance of its coloring, the brightness of its metal hammered out
with the barbaric and yet charming art of gothic jewels" (185).

Durtal's confession recalls the spasmodic public confession of Gilles
de Rais and completes his identification with the magnificent sadist
whose conversion preoccupied him in the previous novel. Durtal also
contemplates his affair with Mme. Chantelouve, "the demoniacal
adulteress who had precipitated him into frightful excesses" (63).
Before he meets with the priest, he rehearses his account of his sins,
and "without any need of probing it his life shot forth in jets of filth"
(63). He sweats with anguish and then nausea. He dashes around the
monastery, weeping with shame, "then, like a hunted animal that
thinks itself discovered, he sprang up and, perturbed by his fears,
moved by a wind of disorder, he thought to flee, to pack his bag and
dash for the train" (65). Conscience, not to mention temptation, is
repeatedly depicted in paranoid terms as an insidious presence that is
watching him or reading his mind. On the morning of his confession,
he wakes with the impression that someone has been looking at him
in his sleep. He is afraid he will suffocate and, in speaking of Mme.
Chantelouve, he chokes with disgust.

The serenity of Durtal's faith is riddled at times with strange outbursts of desire. He is suddenly possessed with an overwhelming urge
to defile the Virgin or to contemplate with pleasure the indecencies of
his past. He has nightmares about a scented and shadowy woman
named Florence, another hothouse bloom. His various temptations
usually occur in conjunction with moments of great piety, as if to
underscore the one overarching theme of Huysmans' decadent and
Catholic work, the eternal oscillation between the ecstatic-hysterical
extremes of satanism and piety. In *En Route* the most striking of these
conjunctions occurs when Durtal is wakened by a succubus. He is
sure that the succubus is too vivid to be a mere wet dream. He thinks

he glimpses her as he wakes, and he notes that his orgasm takes place "with a singularly painful acuteness, a spasm of unheard-of relief" (48). Durtal finds the "rape of such larvae" so troubling that he wanders outdoors to enjoy a cigarette.

In a wonderfully gothic passage, complete with a spiral staircase and a red moon illuminating a dark chapel, he stumbles over a body. He discovers a "battlefield" of monks, kneeling or flat on their faces like "combatants mowed down by grape-shot" (51). He is especially impressed by a motionless old man among them, and in a typical slippage from life to art Durtal compares him to "the faces in ecstasy in Primitive masters":

> In this old man the soul did not even take the trouble to reform his physiognomy, to ennoble it; she contented herself in annihilating it with her rays; it was, after a fashion, the nimbus of old saints remaining no more about the head, but extending itself over all the features, pale, almost invisible, bathing his whole being.
>
> He saw nothing and heard nothing; monks dragged themselves on their knees, came to warm themselves, to take shelter near him, and he did not move, he was dumb and deaf, so rigid that you might have believed him dead, had not his lower lip stirred now and then, lifting in the movement his great beard. (52–53)

In his slippage from the spasmodic sexual indulgence with the succubus to the catatonic self-annihilation of the monks, Huysmans offers very little in between. Durtal hopes that conversion will be a flight not only from the dullness of bourgeois life in Paris but also from the dullness of his round of monastic duties. He is not content with being religious, he must be ecstatic. His interminable vacillation is not a sign of his failure as a Catholic, but rather is further evidence of his virtually monastic discontent with the world—his decadent, we might say hysterical, search after an intensity of sensation, whether it be aesthetic, erotic, religious, or all three.

## Christianity by the Back Door

> At the bottom of satanism, he told me, there is sodomy; it is that which gives force to filth.　　　　　Abbé Mugnier on Huysmans

> Satanism itself, so far as not merely an affectation, was an attempt to
> get into Christianity by the back door.                    T. S. Eliot

Although it was originally applied to Baudelaire, Eliot's remark about satanism seems even more appropriate when applied to Huysmans. I presume that Eliot was aware of the historical association between satanism and sodomy, and so I am intrigued by his notion that Christianity has a demonic "back door," curiously ajar, through which one might enter the *sanctum sanctorum* of the Church by an inversion of its mystical tradition. His assertion is fraught with all the sexual meanings of sodomy as anal penetration, male homosexuality, sexual inversion, and of course evil. Ironically, Huysmans used the same homoerotic door metaphor to describe his own paranoid relationship with the devil. In *En Route* Durtal is told that his spicy imagination "will be the badly closed door of your person, and it is through there that the devil will enter and expand himself in you" (94). In *L'Oblat* the image is even more vivid. The devil "simulates an assault on the armed ramparts, consenting even to withdraw, claiming he has been defeated, but at this moment he penetrates by the postern door that has been left undefended because it was believed to be safe from danger and shut tight; and his presence remains unperceived until he is already strutting about inside the place" (156).

In his letters and in pre-conversion novels like *A Rebours* and *Là-Bas,* Huysmans was far more explicit about the connection between sodomy and satanic mysticism. Sodomy is "the force in filth"—that is to say, the evidence of evil, of a supernatural presence, in human sexuality. By *sodomy* he seems to mean any deviation from procreative sex, though sex between men appears to enjoy a privileged status within his definition. As his use of the term would imply, his understanding of those pleasures that he labeled as sodomy is largely Christian. Though they have always been popular with gay men, Huysmans' novels are alarmingly homophobic. Sex between men is regarded in his books with a typically fin de siècle mixture of religious and medical horror. It is a sin, a crime, a perversion, a symptom of sexual inversion and hysteria, and a sign of physical and cultural degeneration.

In 1893 Huymans wrote a letter to a psychologist, Paul Sérieux, whose studies of sexual anomalies he admired, and recounted his own harrowing experience in "the frightful world of sodomy." He exclaims: "Frightful! That is the word, and if demonic action were to exist, that is where it would be found. I believe they are just about all candidates for the madhouse, but stab wounds ensure that they die in hospitals rather than in mental asylums."[19] Nevertheless, he was himself given to homoerotic flirtation, and he maintained friendships with a number of homosexual men, Paul Verlaine, Jean Lorrain, and André Gide among them. Moreover, he was so curious about sex between men, so intrigued by his own homoerotic impulses, such an aficionado of anal eroticism, that it is difficult not to notice the thinly disguised pleasure lurking behind his often homophobic frame of reference. Like Baudelaire, Verlaine, and Rimbaud, who mined all the mystical possibilities of sin and shame, Huysmans found in sodomy a supernatural force, an object for what the Church has called "morose delectation," the morbid and obsessive contemplation of evil. While androgyny is evident among his saints no less than his satanists, sodomy is a sexual inversion and an erotic indulgence that is entirely on the side of evil in Huysmans' work. In *A Rebours* and *Là-Bas*, as well as his critical essay on Félicien Rops in *Certains* (1889), Huysmans defined a mystical and erotic experience of evil through sodomy. If hysteria was the mystical neurosis, sodomy was the mystical perversion.

Throughout the eighties and nineties, French psychologists were virtually unanimous in their assertion that sexual inversion was an innate and hereditary predisposition, a physiological impulse in the brain that was eventually triggered by an environmental stimulus. The groundbreaking article on the subject was Charcot and Magnan's "Inversion du Sens Genital" in 1882. In this article, as in Magnan's 1885 book on sexual perversions, inversion is regarded as a form of hereditary degeneration, and the afflicted men are described in virtually vampiristic terms as "customarily lucid madmen, unbalanced individuals whose appetites and interest control their will and drive irresistibly towards the satisfaction of unhealthy needs."[20]

Along the same lines, Charles Féré presented an even more distinctively decadent portrait, declaring that inversion was a form not only of physical degeneracy but also of cultural degeneracy, and that it would become increasingly common as society became more civilized. André Raffalovich took issue with Féré and, in his 1896 book *Uranisme et Unisexualité*, offered his own theory that inversion or uranism, while hereditary, was simply a harmless sexual deviation and not necessarily degenerate at all. Nevertheless, in a book called *Perversion et Perversité Sexuelle* published the same year, a certain Dr. Laupts, given to writing under the suggestive pseudonym of "G. Saint-Paul," countered such speculations with his own theory that inversion is the result of a lapse in Catholic faith. He cites Oscar Wilde as a pervert who would inevitably benefit from his prison sentence, forgetting all about his depraved thoughts and returning to normal habits and simple pleasures. As Foucault has suggested, sex between men in the late nineteenth century was regarded for the first time as the perversion and pathology of a sexual minority. These various medical texts demonstrate that it could also still be regarded as a sin and a crime. It was, not unlike hysteria, an overdetermined site where the discourses of Christianity and secular psychology overlapped. In the work of Huysmans, the religious conception of sodomy relies for its peculiar fin de siècle flavor on psychological conceptions of inversion, degeneracy, and hysteria.

We should also keep in mind that inversion in men, like hysteria in men, was defined in part by gender ambiguity. In fact, at times, the two discourses are virtually indistinguishable. In her study of "sexual anarchy" in the fin de siècle, Elaine Showalter discusses the case study of a male hysteric, Louis V., a patient in the Rochefort Asylum in France, who apparently upset his doctors when he tried to caress them. In *A Rebours* Huysmans draws heavily on this medical connection between inversion and hysteria in men, though he was wont to slip into the religious language of sodomy and demonic possession. The effeminate Des Esseintes is not only a hysteric but, on occasion, he also aspires to inversion. Apparently, both impulses originate from the same degeneracy of the family line. The dandy ancestor of the opening pages, the "minion" with his "ambiguous look of the eyes" and languid expression (2), is offered as a hereditary pretext for Des Esseintes's pink boudoir and his passion for cosmetics, not to mention his turning away from the "stale caresses of women" to plunge into "exceptional amours" and "deviant pleasures" (11–12).

In Huysmans' work, inversion or sodomy is the privileged sign of fragmentation along the lines of gender and sexuality. Through its incitement to androgyny and to the performance of gender roles presumed to be inappropriate to one's anatomical sex, inversion is also figured as a subversion of nature in favor of text. Des Esseintes's progression through a number of androgynous sexual objects is marked by gender reversals and highly self-conscious sexual role-playing. His relationship with the American acrobat Miss Urania is a case in point, her very name presumably a reference both to "Urania," the muse of poetry, and to "uranism," a euphemism for inversion. She is brought to Des Esseintes's mind through his sense of taste, in particular by violet bonbons that contain a drop of "feminine essence" (155) and that are known as "Pearls of the Pyrenees" ("pearl," as Huysmans noted in letters to Arij Prins, was at the time a slang term for a homosexual).[21]

Through the bonbon, Des Esseintes is able to induce a memory, indeed a reverie, of himself as feminine. Miss Urania is extraordinary for her masculine features, her "muscles of steel, arms of iron," and they are a stimulant to Des Esseintes's imagination. "In a word, after being a woman to begin with, then, after some hesitation, becoming something like an androgyne, she now seemed to become definitely and precisely and completely a man" (157). Meanwhile, Des Esseintes has become more feminine and sexually passive, "craving for her as an anemic young girl will for some great hercules whose arms can crush her in their embrace" (157–158).[22] In the end, however, he cannot sustain the fantasy, and he discovers the banality of a Miss Urania who is, when all is said, "purely feminine" (158).

A few pages later Des Esseintes meets a ventriloquist whose voice, mysterious as an incantation, has both a religious and a hysterical quality as she reproduces from Flaubert's *La Tentation de Saint Antoine* an imaginary conversation between the Chimera and the Sphinx. For a while, she fascinates him with her "deep, guttural tones, now raucous, now shrill, like superhuman voices" (162), voices that seem to gesture toward an unrepresentable, seemingly spiritual beyond. In order to insure the homoerotic element in Des Esseintes's fascination, Huysmans describes the woman's hair as "plastered on her head with a brush, and parted on one side near the temple like a boy's" (160–161).

These instances of sexual inversion and polymorphous perversity do not, however, touch upon the religious horror that Huysmans was wont to attribute to sex between men, nor, for that matter, upon the mystical significance of androgyny. Sexual inversion was simply a fin de siècle pleasure or malady, depending on the ethical perspective, but

Huysmans was fascinated with sodomy and all the Christian fire and brimstone the word implies. As he defined it in his critical essay on Rops in *Certains,* sodomy still shared a common ground with hysteria within the Roman Catholic concept of morose delectation. Rops was a decadent artist who created demonic and virtually pornographic illustrations for books like Barbey d'Aurevilly's *Les Diaboliques* and Péladan's *Le Vice Suprême.* His heretical drawings of bestial women and phallic Christs, pictures with titles like "Calvary" and "Icon," gave full rein to Huysmans' cerebral fascination with evil, not to mention his misogyny.

Since he was quite sure that Rops did not actually engage in the carnal and occult excesses depicted in the illustrations, Huysmans speculated instead on the mere contemplation of evil, itself a sin—the obsessive and morbid drive to look upon what is horrible. "I am speaking exclusively of the Spirit of Lust," he writes, "of isolated erotic ideas, without material correspondences, and without the need of any animal pursuit that might appease them" (71). He waxes poetic, speaking of the same sort of mystical and hysterical fascination for evil that he found in Gilles de Rais, "an impulse toward a supernatural debauchery, a plea for those convulsions that elude the flesh, rebounding into a spastic beyond" (71–72). The sin of sexual perversity becomes not so much an orgasmic delight as a prolonged malady of acute desire, impossible to gratify, aggravating itself entirely within the realm of the imagination and the soul. Desire is rendered corrupt, but also spiritual. Above all, it becomes a work of aestheticism—"filth for filth's sake," as he calls it (72)—for art is the only possible site for its expression. It is a sexual excitation that is eminently textual, a purely discursive or imaginary dissipation without end that stimulates the body to exhaustion but not gratification.

Huysmans is, as usual, dissatisfied with the psychological explanation for this phenomenon as a perversion and a form of hysteria: "Erethism of the brain, says science; and if this state persists and becomes aggravated, provoking certain disorders in the organism, she pronounces the word 'mental hysteria' and prescribes emollients, lupulin and camphor, potassium bromide and cold showers" (72–73). He delights in his own clinical language, but immediately redirects our gaze toward a religious interpretation. "The Church, on the other hand, finds herself in her own element; she recognizes the sinuous stirring of ancient sin. This mental hysteria she calls a morose Delectation, and she defines it: 'The enjoyment of an evil deed, present to the imagination, without desire to commit it'" (73).

Morose delectation is at the heart of Huysmans' depiction of sodomy. Strangely, it is a sodomy without sex. But Huysmans has a secret that he wants everyone to know: sex is almost always a nauseating bore. His characters very rarely have an orgasm. When they do, it is usually a dream or a disappointment. The body is too dumb, too inelegant, too disgusting. The difference between sex as sex and sex as art is the difference between a woman and Salomé or between a man and Des Esseintes. If you want a woman and a man, you can read Zola, or for that matter any of Huysmans' many forgettable naturalistic accounts of farmers, tradespeople, prostitutes, and grumpy monks. Those of us with a morbid inclination to romance would rather read about Salomé.

In place of sex, Huysmans presents the art of chastity or the dance of the virgin temptress. Chastity in the Rops essay is somewhat more insidious, however. Huysmans observes that "there are no really obscene persons except the chaste ones. Everybody knows, of course, that continence engenders frightfully libertine thoughts, and that the man who is not a Christian and who is therefore involuntarily pure overheats in such solitude, goes mad and begins to rave; until then, in his mind, in his waking dreams, he comes to the point of orgiastic delirium" (70). Huysmans does not specify what happens to the Christians in this passage. For that, we have to read *En Route* and *Sainte Lydwine*. They become mystics, a "mental hysteria" of a different sort.

Sodomy, as morose delectation, is sex for art's sake. We can already glimpse it in *A Rebours* in the highly aestheticized episodes with Miss Urania and the ventriloquist. The sixth and ninth chapters are noted for their homoeroticism, and they are the only ones that Huysmans claimed to regret after his conversion. Sodomy is presented not as a sexual act but as a memory text that descends like a nightmare and leaves the dreamer exhausted. Auguste Langlois, the virginal boy that Des Esseintes picks up in the street, is one of the more extraordinary objects of delectation. His interest in the boy is at once homoerotic and vampiristic. He takes perverse pleasure in corrupting him and inspiring in him a self-destructive addiction to evil. But in dreaming of Auguste, Des Esseintes remarks how he lived on himself and fed on his own substance even in the boy's absence. The homoeroticism re-mains unconscious at first, implied simply by the boy's wonderfully available pose with a cigarette and Des Esseintes's eagerness for his company. When he brings the boy to a brothel, the madam exclaims, "I get it; you sly dog, you like them young, do you?" (108)—thus cornering Des Esseintes into unpersuasive denial. He does make clear, however, that it is not sex that he wants so much as the delight of seeing Auguste imperil his soul.

Later, Des Esseintes is possessed by another homoerotic memory that follows closely upon his account of the ventriloquist. He recalls another boy that he picked up in the street, a schoolboy whose femi-nine attractions are underscored by "long black hair," "liquid eyes," and "fleshy lips divided by a line in the middle like a cherry" (166). He apparently has sex with this one. He enjoys a prolonged relation-ship with the boy, claiming that he had never known such delightful exploitation, never run such risks, never known such "distressing sat-isfaction" (166). But at this point, his description emphasizes his mere recollection of the boy and makes an unexpected leap into the pleas-ures of Catholic theology. Sodomy gives way to the superior pleasures of theological texts about sodomy, texts that are necessary to complete the satisfaction he finds in his homoerotic reminiscences:

> Among the memories that besieged him in his solitude, his recollec-tion of this reciprocal attachment dominated the others. There fer-mented in him all the leaven of insanity that can oppress a brain overexcited by neurosis; and, as a complement to these memories, to this morose delectation, as theology names this recurrence of past iniquities, he added to his physical visions the spiritual lusts inflamed by his former reading in those casuists, in Busenbaum and Diana, in Liguori and Sanchez, who treat of sins against the 6th and 9th com-mandments of the Decalogue. (166–167)

Ironically, Des Esseintes has not actually committed the sins of the sixth and ninth commandments, and the sins of the sixth and ninth chapter are quite different. What is important here, rather, is the contemplation of sin, a purely textual pleasure. The potent brew of sodomy and Sanchez, this weird juxtaposition of the erotic and the religious, excites in Des Esseintes an "extrahuman ideal," a demonic

mysticism whereby "licentious and mystical obsessions merged together to haunt his brain" and plunge him into "original ecstasies, into
paroxysms celestial or accursed, but equally exhausting in the waste
of phosphorus they involved" (167). Inspiration and depletion come
in the same breath, and Des Esseintes is left completely shattered and
half dead.

It is not until *Là-Bas*, however, that Huysmans gives full rein to his
sodomitical muse. Sodomy as demonic homosexuality is rife in this
novel. He did not need to add it to the biography of Gilles de Rais,
since it was already a central issue in the documentation of his trials.
It is also a biographical fact in the life of Abbé Louis Van Haecke, on
whom Huysmans based Canon Docre, the satanic priest who celebrates the black mass. In his preface to Jules Bois's *Le Satanisme et la
Magie* (1895), Huysmans claims that Van Haecke initiated his followers into sodomitical practices, having seduced them with the help of
hypnotized women and lavish meals. Huysmans also maintained an
acquaintance with the ex–Abbé Boullan, on whom he based the character of Dr. Johannès and whom he referred to as "a demonic priest
and sodomite who says the black mass."[23] Indeed, sexual inversion
and textual inversion (hanging the crucifix upside down, for example)
traditionally go hand in hand in the black mass.

As in *A Rebours*, sodomy in *Là-Bas* is less a sexual indulgence than
a highly aestheticized and textual experience of morose delectation. In
fact, most of the references to sodomy occur in connection with Gilles
de Rais, who is himself the text of a text of a text. He is Huysmans'
discussion of Durtal's discussion of early modern transcripts of the
trials of Gilles de Rais; that is to say, he is a classic object of the
decadent passion for research into the morbid and obscure byways of
Church history. Sodomy is a textual obsession. Morose delectation
becomes a topic of conversation in *Là-Bas*, though it is referred to
with terms like "cerebral hermaphrodism" or "self-fecundation" (36)
or "cerebral erethism" (51). Durtal's ideal of bliss, already familiar to
us from the essay on Rops, involves the obliteration of the earthly
object of desire in favor of a mystical, spiritual one. All that remains
is a melancholic pleasure: "These real and intangible loves, these loves
made up of distant melancholies and regrets, are the only ones that
count" (52). Art is brought into the discussion with Durtal's lecture
on "Pygmalionism," a form of "cerebral onanism and incest" (34) in
which an artist makes love to his own artistic creation: "the father

violates the daughter of his soul, the one thing that is purely and really his, the one thing that he can impregnate without the aid of another" (35). In a line reminiscent of Oscar Wilde, Durtal declares that he has invented a new sin. As Pygmalion, however, Durtal apparently seeks congress with the sons of his art rather than the daughters.

When she learns of this new sin that Durtal has invented, Mme. Chantelouve eagerly asks, "Can I commit it?" (34). Although a woman, she is essential to the novel's male homoerotic dynamic. It is through her that Huysmans is most successful at establishing sodomy and demonic mysticism as textual experiences. Her first name refers to a mythical homoerotic icon, the beautiful youth Hyacinthus, beloved of Apollo. Durtal observes, "Mme. Chantelouve has a boy's name that suits her well: Hyacinthe" (164). After the androgynous Miss Urania and the equally ambiguous ventriloquist, we begin to recognize a recurrent theme in Huysmans' depiction of the decadent mistress. Woman is the site not only of feminine evil, but of sodomitical evil, the horrors of lust between men. It is through the sodomitical Mme. Chantelouve that Durtal enters into the world of satanism. After the black mass and her final attempt at coitus with Durtal, he is disgusted to find fragments of the host in her bed. Presumably, she has hidden the host in her vagina in the hope that Durtal would defile it.[24] Although he claims not to believe in transubstantiation, the assumption here is that, in having sex with Mme. Chantelouve, Durtal is also defiling the body of Christ, though it is a hysterical and sexually inverted Christ, fragmented like the host, penetrated by a man, and inhabiting the body of a hysterical woman. The host itself, in this context, is at once a miracle and a symptom, especially since, for the faithful, transubstantiation transcends the symbol, marking an irruption of the Real, the Word incarnate in the flesh. It really is the body of Christ, not a symbol. As Canon Docre intones during the black mass, "Hoc est enim corpus meum."

Through this defilement Mme. Chantelouve is poetically linked with the sodomitical orgy of the black mass, in which Canon Docre also defiles the host, the body of Christ, presumably with his own semen, given his jerky and "tumefied" state at the altar. A similar scene is described earlier by Durtal's friend Des Hermies:

"These priests, in their baseness, often go so far as to celebrate the mass with great hosts that they then cut through the middle and afterward glue to a parchment, arranged in the same manner, and use abominably to satisfy their passions."

"Divine sodomy, in other words?" (111)

Through the manipulation of the host, the sublimated figure of Christ, his body already marked with effeminizing wounds, is perversely presented as a vulnerable rectum, and the celebration of the mass as a sodomitical ritual. Christ himself, in Canon Docre's black mass, is figured as a satyr and seducer during the celebration. His face is painted into a mean laugh, and he has a "virile member projecting from a bush of horsehair" (157). This figure is attended by sodomite choirboys who are lascivious and hideous. Huysmans refers to one of them sardonically as a *petit Jésus,* and he describes another as hollow chested, "racked by coughs, withered, made up with white greasepaint and vivid carmine" (158). Inevitably, we recall Durtal's fascination with the brutalized and fragmented Christ of Grünewald's painting. The sodomitical defilement of the host makes the paradox of the first chapter all the more glaring and it invites us to reflect back on Durtal's spiritual yet sadistic reverie before the Crucifixion and question the unconscious homoerotic motivation for his fascination with the suffering of Christ.

It is important, however, that the black mass is a ritual and, above all, a ritual in which Durtal does not take part, except as spectator, as a devotee of morose delectation. Mme. Chantelouve appears to seduce him only insofar as she can lead him to the black mass, the whereabouts of which he is ignorant. She has a text to offer him, a theatrical spectacle of sodomy and hysteria. She casts a spell only as a producer of perverse texts. Like Miss Urania, she demonstrates Huysmans' contention that the sexual relation, if it exists at all, is a disappointment. Following a protracted and spicy seduction, coitus with Mme. Chantelouve proves a dismal experience for Durtal. All he can think of is unwanted pregnancy, the corpse-like coldness of her body, and the absurdity of corsets. He is filled with revulsion as he recognizes the collapse of his dream of her.

In fact, his fascination with her is most intense before they have even met. His first love is her texts, her letters, not just what she says in them but the sensuous existence of her words themselves. He is entranced by their scent of heliotrope and by the very peculiarity of the ink, myrtle green, very thin, very pale. He abandons himself to a passion for a woman he has not met. Indeed, he speaks of a "sensual resurrection" in reading her letters, a suggestive phrase given her connection with Christ in this novel, not to mention her age, thirty-three, the same age at which Christ was crucified. Even Mme. Chantelouve seems to have caught on to the unconscious homoerotic dimension of her relationship with Durtal, when she discovers he is more interested in Canon Docre than in herself. As she points out, "it is not very flattering to a woman, I suppose, to be able to entertain a man only by telling him about another man" (133).

Huysmans himself, especially while he was writing *Là-Bas,* was fascinated with sodomy. In fact, at this particular point in his life, he was questioning whether he might not have a taste for it himself. In letters to Paul Sérieux and André Raffalovich, Huysmans describes in lurid detail a tour he made through the homosexual underworld of Paris. Jean Lorrain, a decadent writer who was better acquainted with this milieu, acted as his guide for the tour. In these letters Huysmans speaks with his characteristic mixture of distaste and utter fascination. In earlier letters to his friend Arij Prins, Huysmans is much more playful about this episode, which he regarded as part of his research for *Là-Bas.* He describes with a sense of triumph his penetration into the underworld of men he called *tapettes, perles,* or *pédérastes.* When he writes of his research into satanism that "all this gets mixed up a little with sodomy, as you might imagine," he means it.[25] He was much disappointed, however, when he could find neither queens nor butcher-boys nor circus strongmen to his liking, no matter how much they flirted with him. "Decidedly I am not a sodomite," he concludes, but then adds teasingly, "a pederast maybe, with a young boy clean-shaven, but with these hulking mustachioed fellows, 30 years old, nothing happens."[26]

Prins himself fancied an ice-skater he had met, and his accounts of the young man occupied Huysmans' imagination for about a year. "I dream of your ice-skater sometimes," he writes, or "Your ice-skater is decidedly given over to the joys of Sodom" or, more wistfully, "Ah! if only your ice-skater!"[27] At one point he even exhorts his friend to even greater sexual boldness: "Come my friend, a little courage, deflower the mouth of Sodom!" Huysmans also indulged this fascination with the "mouth of Sodom" in exploits with women, in particular Berthe

Courrière, who inspired his depiction of Mme. Chantelouve. He writes: "Her delicious and terrifying anus haunted me. I devoured it without respite," and further notes how difficult it is to come by a suitable female buttocks in Paris, a "little lilac and rose hole" that he could kiss.[28] He points out, however, that he would prefer the ice-skater to Berthe. As the editor of the Arij Prins letters opines, the unembarrassed playfulness of the banter between the two friends suggests that they found in sodomy merely a ripe subject for verbal virtuosity. Whatever the likelihood of this explanation, it is certainly true to Huysmans' preference for a purely textual homoerotic pleasure.

Of Huysmans' many sodomitical icons, Gilles de Rais is surely the most alarming. Durtal finds in Gilles what Huysmans finds in Durtal and Gilles both: sodomy, hysteria, fragmentation, the mysterious workings of the unconscious and the spiritual, and the uncanny power of the textual. Durtal emphasizes the contradiction, the strange disjunction, at the heart of his study of Gilles, not to mention his study of Mme. Chantelouve: "Gilles de Rais divides himself, like her, into three different beings" (96). Mme. Chantelouve is at once a good drawing-room companion, a harlot, and a satanist. Similarly, Gilles is a brave warrior, a great criminal, and a penitent mystic. How does one reconcile the Gilles inspired by Joan of Arc and the Gilles who was a notorious sadist?

Durtal restates the problem as a question of spiritual conversion: why did he convert to satanism seemingly overnight? Something is missing from the scene, something remains mysterious. In Durtal's account of Gilles, sodomy becomes the mystical element in satanism, not to mention one of the abominable sins that lends force to his final confession. Sodomy, for the most part unconscious in Durtal, becomes a spectacle of horror in the life of Gilles de Rais. Gilles travels through the countryside, picking up children, mostly boys in this account, whom he rapes and tortures. He has the children eviscerated as he masturbates over their bodies. He holds a beauty contest of severed heads. He is called a vampire. The horrible rending of the body that is a sign of faith in the Grünewald painting of Christ becomes a sign of the workings of Satan in Durtal's book.

Gilles's crimes end in hysterical hallucinations. Under the burden of his own sins, consciousness cracks. In tears, he swears to God he will do penance, but then he debauches another child, gouging out its eyes. He escapes into the forest, where he sees the trees making concrete the perverse fragmentation of his mind. "It seems that nature perverts itself before him, that his very presence depraves it; for the first time, he understands the motionless salaciousness of trees, discovering priapi among the leaves" (19). The trunk of the tree is an enormous inverted phallus, plunging upward into the leaves and downward into the belly of the ground, but it is also an obscene and bestial anus: "beside the bifurcations of the branches there are yawning holes, puckered orifices in the bark, simulating obscene emunctoria or the gaping sex of beasts." Sexual parts bloom from the lines of the trees— the parts of men, women, and animals, all thrown together in confusion. "They accord with the somber bulging of the foliage, in which now there are only images of giant or dwarf hips, feminine triangles, great V's, mouths of Sodom, glowing cicatrices, humid vents!—And this landscape of abomination changes. Gilles now sees on the trunks aggravated polyps, horrible wens" (20). Images of sexual perversity refigure themselves as images of pathology. Gilles's conversion comes about in a hysterical somersault, the blood pounding in his veins, but all he hears in the end are the cries of the dead children calling out for their mothers, like the infantile cry that Huysmans ascribes to Grünewald's Christ.

The holy Passion of Christ meets the satanic passion of Gilles de Rais in a poetic juxtaposition of one violence with another. The perverse resemblance seems not to trouble Huysmans. As early as *A Rebours,* he praises Barbey d'Aurevilly for his celebration of sadism and mysticism, the two extremes of spiritual aspiration. Years later, Georges Bataille would dwell upon the same paradox in his own commentary on the trial of Gilles de Rais: "It may be that Christianity would not want a world from which violence was excluded. It makes *allowances* for violence; what it seeks is the strength of soul without which violence could not be endured."[29] In the course of *Là-Bas,* Durtal comes to recognize the dialectical tension between sadism and mysticism as a paradox rather than a simple opposition. He despairs of finding any mundane biographical explanation for the dramatic shift from Christ to Satan and back again in Gilles: "I have already told you that there are no documents to bind together the two points of this life so strangely divided." The division becomes a mystical and unconscious one: "Now from exalted Mysticism to base Satanism there is but one step. In the Beyond all things touch" (82).

Having finished *Là-Bas,* Huysmans retreated to a Trappist monastery to undergo his own process of conversion to Catholicism. He said that, having written a work of black magic, he would now write a work of white magic. Demonism and mysticism, sodomy and chastity, are placed in dialectical opposition to each other, two different expressions of the same longing for the intensity of a spiritual life. Whether or not *En Route* qualifies as a work of white magic is open to question, but Huysmans succeeded nonetheless at entering Christianity by the back door.

## Refined Thebaids

> There comes a time when *one needs to make oneself suffer,* to hate one's flesh, to throw mud in its face, so hideous does it seem. If it were not for my love of form, I might perhaps have been a great mystic.
>
> Gustave Flaubert

When the decadents read Flaubert, they gravitated predictably toward the romantic splendor of works like *La Tentation de Saint Antoine* and *Salammbô.* Huysmans was surely the most indulgent in his appreciation of the mysticism and orientalism in these particular works, even though Flaubert's atheism relegated them to a catalog of profane literature in *A Rebours.* Des Esseintes lingers over the incomparable pages of the two books, admiring "the Asiatic glories of ancient times, their mystical ejaculations and prostrations, the dementias of their idleness, the brutalities of their boredom, that oppressive boredom that emerges from opulence and prayer even before their pleasures have been fully enjoyed" (182). Huysmans slips with great subtlety from aberrations to mystic ardors, from pleasures to prayers, within a context of degeneration, paganism, and ennui. The slippage from malady to mysticism, typical of Huysmans throughout his career, corresponds well with Flaubert's beleaguered Saint Antony, tortured and delighted as he is by prurient and religious visions. Like Huysmans, Flaubert read both theological and medical works, Saint Teresa's autobiography as well as Esquirol's *Des Maladies Mentales,* while writing the *Tentation*. In Flaubert's Antony, Huysmans found another neurotic with spiritual aspirations.

The most extraordinary decadent appropriation of the *Tentation* is the scene in *A Rebours* in which Des Esseintes, motivated as much by aesthetic and spiritual considerations as by erotic ones, invites the female ventriloquist to perform the roles of the Sphinx and the Chimera. He is spellbound by Flaubert's prose, which incites in him an *amour de l'impossible* that the ventriloquist can gratify neither with her body nor her voice: "Ah! it was to him that this voice spoke, as mysterious as an incantation; it was for him that it recalled the feverish desire for the unknown, the unsatisfied longing for an ideal, the craving to escape from the horrible realities of life, to cross the frontiers of thought, to grope after a certainty without ever finding one, in the misty regions of art!—All the miseries of his own efforts came back to him and weighed upon his heart" (163). Beginning with *A Rebours*, Huysmans endeavored to realize this incantatory, mystical, religious capacity of art. He sought for the artist, whether inside or outside the Church, whether a satanist or a Benedictine oblate, the status of eremite and visionary, a Saint Antony imprisoned in the Theban cave of his imagination, tortured and enlivened by dreams from another world, images of lust and death, pagan gods and the basilisk, Hilarion and the devil, and ultimately the face of Christ resplendent in the disk of the sun. Flaubert's Antony was, for Huysmans, a paradigm for the mystic as artist.

Unlike some of his contemporaries, Huysmans did not seek to make of art a substitute for religion; rather, he hoped to heal the rift between religion and art, a disjunction that he blamed on the Renaissance. In *A Rebours* he asserts that religious writers of his own day like Bloy and Hello lack talent, while secular writers lack faith. In the later Durtal novels, Huysmans tries to reconcile the artist and the monk in himself, but his efforts are continually frustrated by his own doubts, discomfort, and erotic fantasies. In his final novel, *L'Oblat,* he is still trying to define the eremitic role of the Catholic artist that he first touches upon in *A Rebours*. Durtal is convinced that art is essential to the Church. He proclaims that it was art "that spoke the Gospel and embraced the masses; that thrust them, happy in their joyous prayer, to the foot of the cross" (150), and it was art again that made them ecstatically adore the newly risen Christ on Easter Sunday. He speaks of how bloodless the Church has become since it has forsaken art.

Durtal is attracted to monasticism, but it is clear to him, as it was to Huysmans, that monastic life does not lend itself to the freedom of the imagination he requires to write well. He focuses, therefore, on the liminal figure of the oblate, a sort of monk manqué who is connected with a monastery but is free to pursue certain secular interests, such as literature. As visionary-in-residence in the monastery, Durtal hopes to enjoy both religious inspiration and artistic freedom. He seeks to return art and his own aesthetic impulses to their former transcendent role: "Religious art, so tainted, so dead as it is, can be revived, and if Benedictine oblates have a reason to exist, it is precisely to create it anew and elevate it" (151).

In all of his novels from *A Rebours* to *L'Oblat*, Huysmans re-enacts the role of the artist as eremitic visionary that Flaubert rendered paradigmatic in the *Tentation*. Each novel presents a neurotic hero cloistered in a secluded sanctuary, where he indulges in dreams, fantasies, obscure scholarship, and intellectual speculation, usually with a penchant for all things Catholic. Des Esseintes retreats to Fontenay, where he can decorate his rooms according to his monastic tastes and read from his highly spiced collection of religious literature. In *En Rade* Jacques Marles retreats with his hysterical wife to the Château de Lourps, where he also indulges in ecclesiastical decoration and mystical dreams. In *Là-Bas* Durtal converses about satanism with his friends Carhaix and Des Hermies in the bell tower of Saint-Sulpice. In *En Route* he finds sanctuary in a Trappist monastery, in *La Cathédrale* it is Notre-Dame de Chartres, in *L'Oblat* it is the Abbey of Solesmes—all of which become dream spaces for Durtal's neurotic Catholic sensibility.

Victor Brombert has defined Huysmans' various dream spaces as "romantic prisons" and regards them as largely narcissistic or solipsistic. But Huysmans' self-imprisonment, however neurotic, was also voluntary, and the oneiric retreats of his characters are a genuinely religious echo of the *Tentation*. Huysmans longed for a Theban cave with all the comforts of home and all the freedoms of the modern artist. Like Des Esseintes in *A Rebours,* he longed for "a refined Thebaid, a comfortable desert hermitage" (10): "Like an eremite, he was ripe for solitude, harassed by life and expecting nothing more of it; like a monk indeed, he was overwhelmed by an immense lassitude, by a longing for peace, by a desire to have no further contact with the

profane, who in his eyes comprised all utilitarians and imbeciles"
(102).

Like Antony, Durtal retreats from the world to wrestle with his own
hallucinatory demons. In *En Route,* for example, he is assailed with
"priapisms" that people the space before his eyes: "He tried to fix his
gaze on the statue of Saint Joseph, before which he kept himself, and
he wanted to see nothing except that, but his eyes seemed to revolve,
to see only within, and were filled with indecencies. It was a medley
of apparitions with undecided outlines, with confused colors, that
gained precision only in those parts coveted by the secular infamy of
man" (196–197). Durtal is unfortunately more of a victim to his
temptations than was Antony. He is not rewarded with the same
epiphany, the same solar countenance of Christ, that reassures the
reader of Flaubert that faith has persevered. Nor can Des Esseintes
sustain for long the ascetic pretensions of his boudoir, even though he
has dreams to rival anything to be found in Theban caves. His reveries
seem always to collapse into the mundane dreariness of everyday life.
Baudelaire describes much the same failed aspiration in his prose poem
"La Chambre Double": "A bedroom resembling a reverie, a bedroom
truly *spiritual,* where the stagnant atmosphere is faintly tinged with
rose and blue." But always he must eventually recognize his own
gloomy windows, his own dusty furniture: "Horror! I remember! I
remember! Yes! this hovel, this abode of eternal ennui, is indeed my
own."[30] This grim state of wakefulness, this all too clear perception of
the world's dullness, is the fate of all Huysmans' fictional alter egos.
*L'Oblat* ends as *A Rebours* ends, with the desperate prayer of a soul
in doubt and a dispiriting return to the mundane troubles of Paris.

Huysmans was a cynical and jaded Antony. His dreamers suffer
from an incurable malady, part mysticism and part hysteria, and their
various retreats, their refined Thebaids, reflect the fragmentation of
consciousness in their very architecture, dream after dream, novel after
novel. Huysmans' interiors have visions for walls. What is more, this
mystical-hysterical architecture, which is almost always ecclesiastical
in some way, stands as a decadent metaphor for the crumbling and
fragmentation of Roman Catholicism itself. The later novels depict the
Church as an institution adrift, divided against itself, its miracles half-
forgotten by an ignorant clergy, its monasteries emptied by an anticlerical government. Huysmans regarded Catholicism as the last hope

of the mystical imagination, but it is an imagination grown archaic, a bit senile, a bit perverse, tortured by doubt and desire. The hysterical architecture of modern Catholicism is depicted not only in the retreats of his decadent heroes—Fontenay, the Château de Lourps, and Saint-Sulpice—but also in the brilliant dream visions of his pre-conversion work: the cathedral in which Salomé dances in *A Rebours,* the palace of Esther in *En Rade,* the forest at Tiffauges where Gilles de Rais finally learns to repent in *Là-Bas.* But even after his conversion, when he turned his attention to ever more pious subjects, such as Blessed Lydwina and Notre-Dame de Chartres, Huysmans retained his essentially decadent conception of the Church as an uncertain Thebaid that bears within its very architecture the signs of degeneration and the spiritual maladies of its modern visionaries.

Of all Des Esseintes's visions in *A Rebours,* the passage on Moreau's Salomé (Figure 6) is the most extraordinary instance of hysterical architecture as a sign of spiritual decadence. She is, of course, the "goddess of immortal Hysteria" (84), jeweled over like the tortoise with an ornamental carapace that kills her into art. Her body is shaken by a mysterious catalepsy, rendered in the language of hysterical fits—whirling, swarming, twitching, quivering. At the sight of the head of Saint John the Baptist, she "tries to thrust away the terrifying vision that grips her, immobile, balanced on the tips of her toes; her eyes are dilated, and her hand claws convulsively at her throat" (87). The spasms of hysteria are complemented by a further disjunction: the eviscerations and embalmment of her body in an Egyptian sepulchral ritual. Des Esseintes imagines how "chemists and priests lay out the dead woman's body on a slab of jasper, then with curved needles extract her brains through her nostrils, her entrails through an incision made in her left side" (85), and so on. Through a pagan ritual, sumptuous and solemn, the hysterical body of Salomé is reduced to a dismembered and reconstructed objet d'art.

Huysmans also goes to great pains to establish the Tetrarch's palace in which she dances as a fragmentary extension of her hysterical body. The palace already has a Christian significance as a biblical setting, but Huysmans further compares it to a "basilica of an architecture at once Moslem and Byzantine." He further compares Herod's throne to "the high altar of a cathedral" with "almost Romanesque columns" (80). He lends to the palace a religious, even Christian, aura that is

Fig. 6.  Gustave Moreau, *Salomé Dancing before Herod* (1876) (courtesy of The Armand Hammer Collection, UCLA at the Armand Hammer Museum of Art and Cultural Center, Los Angeles, California).

historically inappropriate, but he also complicates matters further by a confusion of styles and a confusion of cultures. The same edifice is described as Romanesque, Moslem, and Byzantine. Herod himself is compared to a Hindu. Huysmans suggests that Moreau has intentionally jumbled together disparate cultural references in order to place Salomé outside history, but there is also the suggestion that she is an overdetermined figure, replete with contradictory meanings, many of them religious:

> Moreover, the painter seemed to have wished to assert his intention of remaining outside the bounds of the centuries, of giving no precise indication of origin, country, epoque, setting his Salomé inside this extraordinary palace with its confused and grandiose style, clothing her in sumptuous and chimerical robes, crowning her with a curious diadem like Salammbô's in the shape of a Phoenician tower, and finally putting in her hand the scepter of Isis, the sacred flower of Egypt and India, the great lotus-blossom. (84–85)

Phoenician, Egyptian, Indian? Like the hysterical symptom, which is in its own way "outside the bounds of the centuries," Salomé is an "ancient fantasy" lost to history and "accessible only to brains fragmented, sickened, as though rendered visionary by neurosis" (83). She is the wandering—we might say the dancing—*hyster* of medical lore, the evocation of an eternal feminine that defies the specificities of race or country or period. Like the hysteric, her body and the architecture within which she dances are a heterogeneous confusion of historical markings that place her and fail to place her at the same time. Contradictory meanings exist side by side, vying for attention. She belongs to the "theogonies of the extreme Orient" (85) no less than to the Bible, and Des Esseintes further discovers hints of Mantegna, Leonardo, and Delacroix in Moreau's painting.

Through this confusion of origins, which only further stimulates the scholarly Des Esseintes, Moreau generates "architectonic fusions, his luxurious and unexpected amalgamations of dress materials, and his hieratic and sinister allegories, burning with the mad perspicuity of a neurosis altogether modern" (90). The Christian possibilities of Salomé can only be glimpsed as fragments, like the sparkle of the gems on her body as they are lit by "sunlight filtered through stained-glass

windows" (89). The Christian meanings are only one thread of signification among many that can be elaborated by the hysterical sensibility of Des Esseintes, a thread that may ultimately snap under the
strain of contradiction.

This hysterical architecture is also a grammatical or literary experience for Des Esseintes. He is attracted to Latin literature in its decadence, the historical moment at which paganism falls to pieces and
Christianity articulates itself through the decomposing fragments. He
is especially fond of writers like Tertullian, Saint Cyprian, and Com-
modianus of Gaza, who embody this pagan instability in their prose:
"It was a slow and incomplete decay; there were awkward attempts
to return to the emphases of Cicero; as yet it had not acquired that
special gamy flavor that in the IVth century, and even more in the
following centuries, the odor of Christianity was to give to the pagan
tongue as it decomposed like venison, dropping to pieces at the same
time as the civilization of the ancient world, falling apart while the
Empires succumbed to the barbarian onslaught and putrified in centuries of pus" (51). Des Esseintes speaks of Christianity in ghoulish
terms, picking at the "decaying carcass" of the Latin language, preserving a few choice expressions, "marinating in the brine of their new
idiom" (56). A year after *A Rebours* was published, Walter Pater
would return to the same period in Church history in *Marius the
Epicurean,* and he too would delight in the euphuism of early Christianity, the peculiarities of the language with its odd outbursts of pagan
beauty.

The irony, of course, is that writers like Huysmans and Pater were
celebrating the decadence of Catholicism in their own time, delighting
in its archaic grandeur, its obscure moments of ecstasy, the ripeness of
its decomposition, as it was displaced and dismantled by secular hu-
manists. The decadents were preserving fragments of Catholicism like
museum pieces and pickling them in the brine of their own fragmentary, heterogeneous idiom. The decadent passion for the early Church
fathers is not only a delight in the decay of paganism but also, paradoxically, a delight in the decay of Christianity as well. The decadents
were enthusiasts of the lustrous and gem-like twilight of paganism and
Christianity both.

The Church as romantic ruin, as fragmentary Thebaid, is rendered
most explicit in *En Rade.* The neurotic hero, Jacques Marles, is a kind

of mystic, assaulted by his own nightmares. The most Christian among them is the elaborate vision of Esther, and it rivals Des Esseintes's daydream of Salomé in its evocation of a perverse or hysterical Christian architecture. The dream chapter begins as Jacques, suffering from a vague spiritual exhaustion, retires to bed. He sees the design in the wallpaper dissolve into a magnificent, gem-encrusted palace that, like the Tetrarch's palace in *A Rebours,* is more like a shrine with gilded ceilings. Finally, a king and a virgin appear, and it is only in a later chapter that Jacques recognizes them as Ahasuerus and Esther. The King is another Herod, jaded by sensual indulgence and unattainable aspirations, his gaze lingering with evident delectation on the virgin. Esther is another Salomé, a hysteric more pagan than Jew. With her arms "clenched behind her back, the muscles tensed in the nape of her neck, which was tilted backwards, she was perfectly still except for the passing shivers that shook her and made the eyes of sapphire in her dress tremble and sparkle amidst their silky pupils with every heave of her breast" (34).

In the Bible the presentation of Esther is recounted with admirable economy, and her twelve months of cosmetic preparation are a mere parenthetical remark. In Huysmans' work, however, the Bible is always a peculiar stimulant to the imagination. Jacques muses on "the silent King in pursuit of fornication, Esther macerated twelve months long in aromatic spices, bathed in oils, rolled in powders, led naked by Hegai the Eunuch before the redemptive bed of an entire people" (58). Her body is literally transformed into ornament, not only by the jeweled tightness of her dress and the unnatural pallor of her painted lips, but even by her perfumes, which have the power "to decompose the pigments of the skin, altering forever the tissue of the dermis" (33). The presentation of Esther is, in the nightmare, a religious ritual of rape and blood sacrifice: "The transports of an irreparable union, abusing the skin that had been ennobled with balms, crushing her unblemished flesh, desecrating, violating the tight ciborium of her thighs" (35), and so on. The tight ciborium of her thighs? Only rarely does the Bible aspire to such poetic license.

As with Salomé, the hysterical shudders and eroticized rending of Esther's body are reflected also in the architecture of the palace. It is a dream palace that emerges from the design of the wallpaper in Jacques's bedroom and resolves into a screen of water, then terraces and esplanades which split open and evaporate into hallways paved with porphyry. During a fireworks display at Esther's presentation, the great hall is shrouded in mist and "the palace became larger, took flight, and lost itself in the sky, scattering its stones pell-mell like seeds in the black fields above, where there scintillated a fabulous harvest of stars" (36). All that is solid melts in air. The very walls take shape according to the neurotic sensibility of the dreamer and the grotesque ritual he imagines. Even the ornamentation of the palace, like the hysterical symptom, like the perfumes of Esther, rigidify organic tissue into art. The riotous vines that cover the palace are heavy with gems that have obscure and wondrous names. They even become gems, "nourished by the mineral embers of leaves in different shades of green—in the luminous green shade of emerald, prasinous green peridot, glaucous aquamarine, yellowish zircon, cerulean beryl" (30).

Esther is literally a symptom for Jacques, a latent suggestion from the Bible, "incubating" in his unconscious and suddenly bursting forth as an "unfathomable enigma" or a "mysterious flower." And the symptom is inexplicable in the terms of modern psychology: "Is one not forced to posit, on the contrary, some essential association of ideas so tenuous that the thread snapped upon analysis, a hidden thread laboring in the obscurity of the soul, one that produced a spark of light that would suddenly illuminate forgotten caverns, reuniting chambers unvisited since childhood?" (60). Huysmans is at his most Freudian in this novel, and yet his maladies are ultimately super-natural.

The imagery of "forgotten caverns" and "chambers unvisited," not to mention the visionary palace of the nightmare, is further elaborated in the hysterical architecture of the two real edifices that Jacques explores, namely, the Château de Lourps, where his dreams take place, and a nearby church, where all the Lourps are buried. The château is itself a gothic pile straight out of a Radcliffe novel, "mournful and decrepit, sordid and somber" (53). This decay is associated with the Church as well, not only through the dream of Esther, but also through Jacques's plan, reminiscent of Des Esseintes, to redecorate a room with ecclesiastical ornaments and the bust of a praying penitent. He does not act upon this plan. When he visits the church, however, his fascination with a Catholicism in decay is unmistakable. Having stolen the key and entered by way of the cemetery through a postern door,

Jacques finds himself in a gothic chapel "half-demolished by time and further mutilated by masons" (231). The interior is fragmented and decaying: "The points of the lancets were broken, patched up with lumps of cement and ends of brick, the stained-glass windows had been replaced by panes of glass divided into a fake lozenge with lead foil or else left empty such that the blistering vaulting, strained and curbed by the weight of the roof, shed scabs from its skin of plaster" (230). Tawny owls have left the remains of mice and shrews behind the tabernacle, such that an odor of decaying flesh clings to the altar. Amid the wreckage Jacques finds the chalice, a ciborium, and a tin box containing a few wafers. What is extraordinary is that the church is still in use, a gothic ruin and yet still a house of prayer. Even the religious language of this church is itself in decay, and Jacques imagines a hurried priest who lets the place rot. Even the gothic script on the graves, fascinating though it is to Jacques, is rendered indecipherable with age on many of the stones.

This sense of Catholicism in ruins, gasping prayers in the throes of a terminal illness, is by no means a peculiarity of Huysmans' pre-conversion novels. The so-called Catholic novels have a decadent architecture of their own. Like his hysterics, Huysmans' saints and mystics are also icons of perversity. In *En Route* he says of Saint Teresa: "She caresses the soul; she is a Bacchante of divine love, a Maenad of purity" (141). Blessed Angela of Foligno impresses him precisely because of her rise from the depths of adultery and shame. *La Cathédrale* ends with a prayer to the Virgin, "Holy Temptress of men" (297). Durtal has a "wild desire" for faith. "It is plain that as I have drawn near the Church, my filthy desires have become more frequent and more tenacious," he remarks in *En Route* (67). Clearly, the art and soul of the Church, what Durtal calls the burning zone of pure and exalted mysticism, is ringed with an aura of perverse eroticism.

Huysmans' later work is peppered with mystics, almost always female, and his accounts of their lives betray all the visionary weirdness of modern clinical case-studies. For example, there is Blessed Christina of Stommeln in *La Cathédrale*. The devil turns her food to vermin when she tries to eat it, and he finally fastens himself to her bosom in the form of a giant toad in order to persecute her. There is also Mary Margaret of the Angels, who suffers paralysis, loss of speech, and loss of sight; she even binds herself in chains with points on the links, and one winter she lets her legs freeze. "Her body was one wound," Huysmans exclaims, "but her soul was radiant" (188). His mystics, especially Blessed Lydwina, are all artists of exquisite suffering. The very name Lydwina is taken from a Flemish word that means "to suffer." In her case Huysmans spares no details. As a girl she injures a rib in a skating accident, but it never heals. Instead she is assailed by God with pain and every imaginable disease from leprosy to epilepsy to the plague—even Huysmans' pet maladies, neuralgia and toothache, make an appearance. An abscess breaks inside her, and she vomits pus and blood. She is covered with ulcers, strips of flesh fall from her body, black-headed worms swarm under her skin, and there is a recurrent concern that she will fall to pieces if her body is moved. Recognizing the workings of grace in the decomposition of her body, she waxes beatific and prays for increased suffering, which is granted her in the form of the stigmata, a holy trinity of ulcers. In her ecstasy she attains the power of duplicating herself and traveling the world in spirit. Her rotting flesh paradoxically gives off a sweet perfume, the odor of sanctity.

For Huysmans, the investment of the Lydwina hagiography in decadent stylistics goes well beyond the pleasure of nauseating his audience. Most important, Lydwina's body is another instance of the spiritualization of sadism and hysteria in Huysmans.[31] Lydwina is the Salomé and the Esther of Huysmans' later works. She is a martyr to Christianity but also a virgin grotesque. Her diseased body, even more effectively than that of the hysteric, again marks the irruption of the Real, the mark of God's will written in her flesh. Her disfigurations are themselves figurations: like the hysterical symptom, they mark a displacement from the unconscious to the conscious, from the supernatural to the natural. Huysmans had been fascinated for years by the Catholic doctrine of "mystical substitution," which he exploited for his own aesthetic purposes. Lydwina was able to free the people around her from suffering by taking onto herself the burden of their sins. This mystical substitution, in Huysmans' account, becomes a spiritualization of hysterical substitution, but on a national scale.

The opening chapter of the hagiography is usually dismissed, even to a degree by its author, as a senseless and artless jumble of historical facts about medieval Europe. It may be seen, however, as a procession, a stylistic quirk frequent enough in Huysmans, that finds its precedent in his many decadent lists, his catalogs of obscure junk from his library. These fragments have the effect of embedding in his very style the fragmentations of European civilization itself in the fifteenth century. We learn that France was "convulsed" and "split into two camps," riddled with the signs of plague and debauchery. England is in revolt. Flanders is wasted by internal struggles and strewn with bones. The sexual monstrosities of Gilles de Rais are mentioned, thus rendering explicit the connection of Lydwina to *Là-Bas*. Even worse, the Church itself suddenly becomes "two-headed," with one pope in Rome and another at Avignon. In short, it was "the most absolute disorder; and Christianity had never been reduced to such chaos" (22).

These violent divisions, both of style and of history, are embodied by Lydwina herself in an effort at expiation through mystical substitution and suffering. Like the body of Lydwina, Huysmans' hagiography is itself a wounded grotesque, a spectacle of suffering that seeks to take on the sins of the modern world. Fragmentation of the body, the spirit, and the state gives rise through an obscure process of displacement to a symptom, to the saint who embodies the symbolic disorder of the world's sins. She needs only to be interpreted through the art of hagiography for an entire people to recognize the source of their redemption. Like Salomé and Esther, Lydwina is tortured into text. Out of the horror of her wounds rise reveries that read like allegorical fragments, narratives recounted by Huysmans as though they were written in stained glass or an illuminated Gospel. In one of her visions, Christ shows Lydwina the tiara that he intends to give her in heaven, pointing out the gems that represent each of her sufferings. The medieval symbology of gems becomes virtually indistinguishable from decadent ornamentation. Lydwina is the symptom, the *sinthome*, bearing on the elaborate text of her body the sign of an entire culture falling to ruin from the inside out, just as the hysteric, through the medium of literature and the case study, had become virtually emblematic of the apocalyptic, fin de siècle anxiety about cultural degeneration.

If Lydwina is a Catholic Salomé, so Chartres Cathedral is a Catholic version of the Tetrarch's palace. It is Huysmans' most elaborate work of decadent architecture. The text of *La Cathédrale* pores over the surfaces of Chartres like a Baedeker gone mad. The edifice itself represents an androgynous conflation of Christ and the Madonna, encrusted and jeweled over with religious texts, some pious, some grotesque, in a gloriously overdetermined and often enigmatic profusion. Indeed, Huysmans' obsession with medieval Catholic symbolism in *La Cathédrale*—his little essays on the science of symbolism and the meanings of certain colors, gems, and flowers—recall the passages on gems and flowers in *A Rebours*. Rose pink, for example, is the color for the love of eternal wisdom, while yellow is the color for idleness. Amethyst is the mirror of humility, while chalcedony is an emblem of charity. Bramble and aconite represent envy, though aconite is more precisely assigned to calumny and scandal. What are we to make of all this information, presented as it is in page after page of exhaustive detail? Is it art for art's sake or dogma for dogma's sake? As Durtal is aware, religious symbolism was always arbitrary and contradictory, and in this context it is simply arcane. We learn that "an innocent color may be read in a perverse sense, and vice versa" (250). We learn also that the "hermeneutics of gems are vague; it is based on mere fanciful resemblances, on correspondences between ideas reunited only with great pain" (262).

This Catholic symbolism seems to draw us inevitably back to a decadent conception of "correspondences," the sort of enigmatic juxtapositions that Max Nordau condemned as hysterical. Durtal draws a suggestive connection between Saint Augustine's theory of symbolism and the symbolist poetics of Mallarmé: meaning is set forth in allegory for a more impressive and pleasing effect. The comparison, he realizes, is whimsical at best. Modern symbolism "is really not symbolism at all," he concludes (46). The difference is in the monolithic correspondence of symbol to spiritual referent, which the obscurities of decadent and symbolist style are wont to undermine. Mallarmé's symbolism, like Huysmans' scholarly account of medieval symbology, is evidence of the symbol in decay.

I am reminded of Julia Kristeva's characterization of the passage from the Middle Ages to the Renaissance as a fall from symbol into sign, with its concomitant rediscovery of pagan beauty. Huysmans never forgave the Renaissance for that fall, and yet his own medieval sensibility suffers from a fin de siècle of its own, a decomposition that Huysmans and Durtal are powerless to prevent. A priest finally points out the absurdity of the cathedral's symbolism: the evidence of an excess of signification, paradox, double meaning, enigma. "It is the very dementia of symbolism!" Durtal cries out, and the priest responds, "It is, in any case, a meticulous excess of it" (174). A rigid political and religious regime is no longer in place to determine the context in which the symbol may be clearly understood, and there is some doubt that it ever was. The Church can no longer maintain control over the production of meaning. Durtal immerses himself in a medieval dream, a hermeneutic indulgence, within the confines of the cathedral. Its architecture, however, is an unruly and confusing text, and when at odd times he breaks its spell on him, he recognizes its failure to signify in the modern world: "On one's emerging from the cloister the liturgical meaning of colors was weakened; it lost its original rigidity and became pliant" (250). In the development of a lofty Catholic aesthetic out of the ruins of a satanic one, Huysmans managed to preserve a number of important elements of decadent style—among them, the fetishistic pleasure of the symbolic fragment, preserved like a curio, a museum piece, by a modern sensibility that recognizes in its sensuous form only a thrilling and enigmatic remnant of the spiritual order that gave it meaning.

This failure of the Catholic signifier is most dramatic in *L'Oblat,* even though Huysmans wrote the novel late in his life, at a time when he was most secure in his faith. In the opening pages, Huysmans describes a daydream that Durtal has during a service in the church of Val-des-Saints. The church is not in ruins, as in *En Rade,* but it is strangely divided between medieval and modern in a manner that grates on Durtal. "Yes, the belfry and the porch date from the fifteenth century," he observes, "but all the rest of the church is modern. The interior has been restored more or less haphazardly; disfigured by hideous stations of the cross and lighted, except at the end, by plain windows" (36).

Through the vulgarity of the present day, Durtal captures only fragmentary glimpses of a more inspired time, the century of Gilles de Rais and Lydwina. The daydream he has in the church is inspired by the divine office, but it invokes all the passionate faith and demonic horror that Huysmans found to be lacking in modern Catholicism. Like the reveries on Salomé and Esther, Durtal's daydream of "Chosroes, the robber of the Holy Cross," depicts a tyrant who invents an artificial universe in which he hopes to be worshiped as God the Father. Durtal's mind wanders from Chosroes to the choir, which is just then singing the Vexilla Regis and the Magnificat. The vulgarity of the church has briefly been transfigured by this dream of a very different architecture, a dream inspired by the liturgy and the sacred music.

Durtal's role as oblate and Catholic artist, however genuine his faith, is an inadequate expression of his spiritual ideal. Monasticism proves to be an improbable Thebaid. He re-enacts old faults, chewing over the same cud of sin in the confessional. He begins to find his attempts at holiness absurd. "Alas!" he exclaims, "such vows are drunken vows, and such pious castles in the air can never stand" (156). He wants to be Saint Antony, but he seems more like Chosroes; his ideal is no more convincing than the false firmament of beaten gold he dreams of during mass. *L'Oblat,* like all of Huysmans' later novels, is troubled by a persistent acedia, a peculiarly Christian ennui that subverts Durtal's religious aspirations. The Church itself is incapable of inspiring mystical faith. *L'Oblat* was written shortly after enactment of the Communities Bill, an effort to legislate monasticism out of existence in France. Durtal hopes to celebrate his submission to a Benedictine order, even as the monks themselves are packing their bags to emigrate to Belgium. The very institution of monasticism appears to expire even as he embraces it.

The final chapters of the book are a melancholy confusion as the monastery is dismantled. "It seemed as if each packing case that they were nailing down was a coffin in which lay one he loved" (208). Durtal's vows are a religious dream that comes of nothing. What is meant to be a rallying cry for Catholics reads more like a jaded cry of defeat. "Val-des-Saints is dead," he laments (273). Both religion and science have left modernity spiritually hollow. Durtal heaves a sigh as he remarks that all is falling apart: "it is a failure in every camp, failure of materialistic science, failure of education in the great seminaries and Orders, soon there will be a general bankruptcy that nothing can delay" (243). The final prayer of *L'Oblat* is hauntingly reminiscent of the final prayer of *A Rebours.* Durtal intones: "It seemed as if You were guiding me to a haven of safety. I arrive—after many hardships!—I sit down at last, but then the chair breaks!" (274). Like Des Esseintes, he returns to Paris in despair.

Huysmans' novels, whether we define them as decadent or Catholic, are ultimately about the failure of faith in a modern context. The language of Catholicism continues to glow with a gem-like splendor, but its symbolism no longer has the force of meaning. Faith is apprehended as a brief and fragmentary reverie, a mystic dream of Theban intensity that nevertheless leads nowhere. Despite the sincerity of Huysmans' religious aspiration, we are drawn by the perversity and wistfulness of his novels back to a persistent feeling of despair, degeneration, and depletion. Des Hermies voices the sensation most poetically in *Là-Bas,* when he claims with evident ennui, "I believe, alas, that a dotard Heaven maunders over an exhausted Earth" (200).

# THREE

# *Pater Dolorosa*

## Pater Noster

> Pater was a sort of domesticated Verlaine, a Protestant Verlaine, I
> might say a vicarage Verlaine.        George Moore

George Moore's portrait of Walter Pater, though whimsical at best, has the virtue of gathering into one place some of the paradoxes that have made Pater especially difficult to define, both as a man and as a writer. Still, there remain the perennial questions of Pater criticism: Was he a florid decadent or a timid aesthete, a daring epicurean or a scholarly monk? Was he Catholic or Protestant, Christian or pagan, Hebrew or Hellene? Was he homosexual or . . . not? In his eulogy poem "Walter Pater," Lionel Johnson is surprisingly confident in his claim to know the real Pater, although we might wonder at Johnson's hagiographic portrait of his mentor as a saintly Christian and scholar:

> Patient beneath his Oxford trees and towers
>     He still is gently ours:
> Hierarch of the spirit, pure and strong,
>     Worthy Uranian song.[1]

In what sense is he "ours," *Pater noster,* this patient recluse, who meanders serenely but evasively through every biographical account, eschewing conversation, burning letters, suitably reserved behind his ever burgeoning mustache, always waving to us from a distance with

169

his hand neatly gloved? The "pure" Christian saint of Johnson's account masks the Pater who sometimes scoffed at Christian dogma like
a veritable Voltaire, while the hint of homosexual inspiration implied
in the word "Uranian" marks a man who may well have been chaste
his entire life. Virtually no one could claim to know Pater intimately;
indeed, one of his early companions, J. R. McQueen, likened him to
an actor with a dual personality.

In defining Pater it is important to preserve the sensuous mobility
of his mind, his eternal tenuousness, his perennial ambivalence, and
what he would have called the Heraclitean flux of his impressions and
his ideas. Only with numerous qualifications do I claim Pater as a
decadent, a homosexual, and an Anglo-Catholic. In my reading of *The
Renaissance* (1873), *Marius the Epicurean* (1885), and a few of his
shorter "imaginary portraits," I will focus on two recurrent and related themes in his writing—namely, homoerotic friendship and virgin
motherhood. The dialectic between Christian and Greek, Hebrew and
Hellene, one forever modified by the other, is the most frequently
examined aspect of Pater's work; but there is another, closely related
dialectic—that between birth and death, artistic creativity and cultural
disintegration. The frequency of Pater's allusions to infants and pregnancy is strange, given the utter maleness of his texts, but even stranger
perhaps is the romantic, even decadent, shadow of death that passes
over virtually every representation of love he ever described. In Pater's
world of Heraclitean flux, every artistic creation, every beautifully
conceived moment, is brought into being from the ruins and fragments
of its predecessors and, indeed, meets the same fate, perhaps even as
it is realized. His "Conclusion" to *The Renaissance* is a call to the
enjoyment of beautiful impressions as they pass, impressions "unstable, flickering, inconsistent, which burn and are extinguished with our
consciousness of them."[2]

In Pater the beautiful impression is evanescent, "a tremulous wisp
constantly reforming itself on the stream." The thrill of its apparition
is scarcely distinguishable from the sorrow for its passing. Subjectivity
itself is in flux, in "that strange, perpetual weaving and unweaving of
ourselves" (236). At the heart of this dialectic between birth and death,
creation and dissolution, Pater places the passionate desire and pitiful
mourning of one man for another. His ideal of this homoerotic love is
based not only on mythic male figures of comradeship and mourning,

such as Apollo and Hyacinthus, but also on maternal archetypes: the Christian Mary or the Greek Demeter, a mother but also a *mater dolorosa,* a mother who mourns.

Before I elaborate on this reading of his texts, I should first say something about Pater himself and how he has traditionally been perceived. In making what must seem an enormous leap from the excesses and ecstasies of the French *décadents* to the quieter effulgence of Pater, I should begin with the question of whether his aestheticism is indeed decadent, as many have suggested. Pater's name was on the most decadent lips of the 1890s, buoyed by the worshipful praise of Oscar Wilde, George Moore, and Lionel Johnson, among others. After the modernist damnation of nineties decadence, however, Pater's reputation was everywhere in peril. Notable among antagonistic modernist readings of Pater were those of Paul Elmer More, who dismissed Pater as unwholesome, sterile, and voluptuous (More's sexual distaste is evident), and T. S. Eliot, who claimed that Pater was "incapable of sustained reasoning," was "not wholly irresponsible for some untidy lives," and had nothing to do with "the direct current of religious development," whatever that is.[3] He was, in other words, a hedonist without mind or soul. Somewhat later, especially in the work of Ruth Child, an all too serious effort at critical redemption recast Pater as less an impressionistic aesthete than a stylist noted for his reserve, shyness, emotional sensitivity, maturity, and critical discrimination. Endless comparisons were made to Keats and Arnold, even Newman, while the modernist disparagement of fin de siècle decadence remained firmly in place. Critics sought to dissociate Pater from some of his more controversial friends and acquaintances—Simeon Solomon, Oscar Browning, Oscar Wilde, Lionel Johnson, A. C. Swinburne, and André Raffalovich, among others. His influence on Wilde and his circle was construed as a lamentable misreading, and therefore irrelevant for the most part to any serious discussion of Pater himself.

This redemptive reading of Pater has been commonplace until fairly recently; nevertheless, many of the arguments that seek to sanitize his reputation are less than persuasive. Pater did criticize Dorian Gray as a failed epicurean—but his main objection was not to Dorian's sins but to the narrowness of his experience. He withdrew the famous "Conclusion" from the second edition of *The Renaissance* (later restoring it, with minor changes) because he had been told it was likely to corrupt the young men into whose hands it fell; and yet the most homoerotic passages were in the chapters on Michelangelo, Leonardo, and Winckelmann, all of which remained intact. The tenor of Pater's days was presumably as serene as the tone of his prose; nevertheless, his contemporaries were more astute than some of his later critics when they sensed something subversive and decadent about his work.

Pater's repeated call for "art for art's sake" would seem to make his aesthetic allegiances clear enough. George Eliot thought *The Renaissance* "quite poisonous in its false principles of criticism and false conceptions of life," while John Wordsworth declared with evident horror that the book was an incitement to unbelief.[4] Others used some of the same pathological terms that were applied to Verlaine and Huysmans. The decadents themselves recognized a kindred spirit in Pater. Wilde called his essays "the holy writ of beauty," while George Moore extolled *Marius* for its "combinations of words for silver or gold chime, and unconventional cadence, and for all those lurking half-meanings, and that evanescent suggestion, like the odour of dead roses, that words retain to the last of other times and elder usage."[5] Surely, not all his contemporaries can be accused of misreading. On the subject of Huysmans, Pater was heard to exclaim, "Beastly man!"[6]—and yet he shared with Huysmans a decadent taste for the elegant but elusive style, for obscurity and tortuous syntax, for androgynous men and vampiric women, for Catholic ritual and the sublime violence of the gothic.

Apart from his reverie on *La Gioconda,* his most famous icon of perversity, his description of Marguerite of Valois in the recently published "Anteros" chapter of *Gaston de Latour* (1895) could have been lifted from *A Rebours*: "If Queen Margaret's chamber was like some place of strange worship, herself at once its idol and priestess, its chief relic was as ghastly as church relics usually are, a dead man's face, with the stamp of his violent end, mummied and brown, set there exposed among the best prized objects of the lady's personal property, mounted in a kind of shrine or pyx of good goldsmith's work, and set with gems picked from milady's own jewel-case."[7] Continuing his discourse on sadomasochism—what he calls "cruel love" (286) or "love for love's sake"—Pater turns his attention to a deliciously cruel love between two men, Jasmin and Raoul, before ending in the vaguely religious martyrdom of Raoul, his self-sacrifice, torture, and execution, rendered with a delight in suffering typical of Huysmans. In the work of recent critics, such as Linda Dowling and John R. Reed, Pater is seen as a quintessential English decadent by virtue of his style, but in many ways he is decadent in his subject matter as well.

Until recently, another redemptive tendency in Pater criticism has been the elision of homosexuality as an issue in serious discussions of his work.[8] What little biographical information there is regarding Pater's emotional attachments suggests that he formed sentimental, sometimes passionate, probably chaste, relationships with a number of men. Furthermore, what is apparent in his life is readily obvious in his prose—most notably in his portraits of Michelangelo, Winckelmann, and Montaigne, although homoerotic friendship was a recurrent theme in Pater, from Amis and Amile to Emerald Uthwart and James Stokes. Pater's homosexuality was an open secret for many who knew him, and some of the more confident whisperings have made it into print. As Pater's biographer Michael Levey has pointed out, Ingram Bywater, who later succeeded Benjamin Jowett as Regius Professor of Greek at Oxford, spoke privately of "a certain sympathy with a certain aspect of Greek life" in Pater that was not confined to his interest in Winckelmann.[9] Sidney Colvin, at one time a friend of Pater's, warned at least one young man against knowing him; and Mark Pattison, the rector of Lincoln College, noted in an acerbic tone the feminine-looking youths who accompanied Pater and Oscar Browning at tea. Pater maintained friendships with a number of homosexual literati, and he was very supportive of Browning, who had left Eton in a homosexual scandal. He was also loyal to his friend Simeon Solomon, the pre-Raphaelite painter, even after Solomon was arrested for indecency in a public lavatory in London.

The earliest of Pater's more ardent attachments occurred in his school days, when he was especially fond of Joseph Haydock, an aristocratic boy whom he once referred to adoringly as a "handsome and ferocious young bull," though the admiration was not mutual. As an adult Pater demonstrated no sexual interest in women. On the contrary, he was a solitary figure, apparently attracted only to men. Richard Jackson, an eccentric man who claimed to be Pater's closest friend and the model for Marius, is an important figure in Thomas

Wright's account of Pater's life, as is another young admirer, Walter Blackburn Harte. Jackson's sentimental lines to Pater are certainly affectionate, if somewhat lame:

> Your darling soul I say is enflamed with love for me;
> Your very eyes do move I cry with sympathy:
> Your darling feet and hands are blessings ruled by love,
> As forth was sent from out the Ark a turtle dove![10]

The best documented of Pater's erotic relationships with men was his affection for a nineteen-year-old Balliol undergraduate, William Money Hardinge, whose indiscretion about his homosexuality led Jowett to request his withdrawal from the college. One of Hardinge's friends, Alfred Milner, describes in a letter not only Hardinge's "filthy" and "unnatural" poetry, but also his account of his relationship with Pater:

> When a man confesses to lying in another man's arms kissing him & *having been found doing it,* as there is the strongest evidence to prove, or when letters pass between them in wh. they address one another as "darling" & sign themselves "yours lovingly," & such a letter *I* have seen, when verses are written from one man to another too vile to blot this paper, what hope can you have, that a criminal act, if not committed already, may not be committed any day?[11]

Pater and Hardinge appear together, along with Jowett, as Mr. Rose and Robert Leslie in W. H. Mallock's popular satirical novel *The New Republic* (1878). Hardinge's presence in the novel makes sense only in connection with Jowett and Pater, since he is certainly out of his league among the other characters in the book, who are satirical portraits of Carlyle, Ruskin, and Huxley, among others. Mallock offers a number of tantalizing hints regarding Mr. Rose's religious opinions and sexual tastes. Most notable among them is a poem, read aloud by Mr. Rose and written by "a boy of eighteen" whose education he has directed. The poem is a "true and tender expression of the really Catholic spirit of modern aestheticism, which holds nothing common or unclean," and it equates the speaker's passion for Narcissus and Venus with the passion of Aquinas for Christ.[12] Furthermore, it was probably Mallock who informed Jowett of Pater's relationship with Hardinge, causing Pater to lose a university proctorship that had been virtually promised to him. Keeping in mind this dismal display of Victorian homophobia, it is much easier to sympathize with Pater's chilly reserve, not to mention the close association of homoeroticism with death in his work.

I speak at length about Pater's homosexuality, first of all to clarify its existence, but also to suggest its relevance to any discussion of his religious experiences. As early as 1949, Graham Hough, in an essay on Pater, remarks upon the intersection of homosexuality and Christianity in late-romantic aesthetics, although he does not elaborate much on the phenomenon. He speaks of a "morbid" temperament and "some half-developed sexual deviation" in Pater, by which he means not only homosexuality but also masochism, "some obscure alliance in the natural world between love and pain, something beyond the pleasure principle . . . constructed so ingeniously to play pain-fugues on the delicate nerve-work of living creatures."[13] While his characterization of Pater's sexuality veers predictably toward accusations of immaturity and pathology, Hough seems to be searching for a language or a historical framework in which to consider the connections between Pater's sexuality, his aesthetic, and his fascination with Christianity.

In a remarkably candid comment, he spells out the connection:

Remembering too the continual evidence of homosexual feeling in Pater's life and writing, one almost inevitably begins to form a composite picture of a kind of temperament in which more or less suppressed erotic fantasy, combined perhaps with the frustration or diversion of normal sexuality; a preoccupation with the periphery of religious experience; a tremulous sensitiveness to aesthetic impressions; a conscious pursuit of beauty, and the conscious cultivation of a precious elaborate style, all play a major part; and the more usual kinds of adjustment and efficiency become unimportant.

Hough set the critical table, but no one came to dinner. The continuum of sexuality, literary style, and religion that he describes is otherwise unremarked in Pater criticism and remains mysterious to Hough himself, who backs away from the issue with the claim that the phenomenon is probably "congenital" (170–171). His comment is an excellent example of how literary and religious criticism turns into a pseudo-psychological case study as soon as the specter of homosexuality is raised. In its association with "deviant sexuality," religion itself becomes a pathological symptom.

Despite Hough's contention that Pater "cultivates an aesthetic admiration for the Church, not only for its ceremonies, but for its doctrines, for the writings of the fathers and modern theologians" (197), his case study format leads him to suppose that aesthetes and decadents are only interested in the "periphery of religious experience." The presumption that socially marginalized sexualities can only go hand in hand with peripheral religious experiences is part of a larger critical tradition of dismissing the religiousness of aesthetes and gay people as an affectation, even when there is considerable evidence of their faith and theological interests. Erotic and aesthetic pleasure are seen to taint and therefore invalidate any religious experience, no matter how orthodox, spiritual, or ethically motivated.

The word *orthodox* itself poses a problem here, not the least because it is a historically relative and unstable term. In Pater criticism it is also in large part negatively defined, construed less by what it is than by what it is not. It is defined by what it succeeds in repressing—namely, sex and sensual beauty. In this way Pater's genuine interest in Church history, monasticism, and ritual is a mere perversion of Catholicism and therefore irrelevant if it coincides with his expressions of aesthetic and homoerotic pleasure. His interest in Catholic ritual, for example, is unjustly dismissed as "lust of the eye," to use a biblical phrase he once remarked upon in Saint Augustine. The Foucauldian irony that the Church tacitly produces and exploits the very sexual and aesthetic pleasures that it officially represses and disavows is certainly relevant here. When it comes to sensual effusions and flights of masochism, the Church could leave even Pater with a blush. When we restrain our urge to pathologize and, furthermore, when we look beyond the unlikely sexual presumptions that often accompany the term *orthodoxy,* we find a very different Pater. We can begin to question his early, and notoriously untrustworthy, biographers. Thomas Wright, for example, acknowledges Pater's appreciation of ritual but makes the improbable claim that Pater never troubled about "what it was all for."[14] A. C. Benson, himself a homosexual ritualist, balked at Pater's Catholic leanings, citing his alleged failure to recognize the importance of Christianity's "detachment," its "corporateness of humanity and the supreme tie of perfect love," its "sense of comradeship," and its "brotherhood of God."[15] A mere glance at *Marius* should have told Benson that all these aspects of Christianity were much on Pater's mind and were indeed at the very foundation of his interest in the Church.

Pater eagerly sought to reclaim a Christianity he could live with, to reconstruct what is called Christian orthodoxy, according to his own ideas about modernity, sensual beauty, and the love of men for men. His tendency to Hellenize the Hebrew, especially later in life, was not so much an effort to displace Christian faith in favor of art and paganism as it was an effort to rethink Christianity as he knew it through an insistence upon the aridity of dogma and the paradoxical spirituality of the sensuous. The very distinction between matter and spirit was not in Pater's view an essentially Christian one, but rather a Manichaean or Scholastic peculiarity. In his essay on Dante Gabriel Rossetti, Pater elaborates on his own Christian aestheticism, which he finds at work already among the Pre-Raphaelites:

> Spirit and matter, indeed, have been for the most part opposed, with a false contrast or antagonism by schoolmen, whose artificial creation those abstractions really are. In our actual concrete experience, the two trains of phenomena which the words *matter* and *spirit* do but roughly distinguish, play inextricably into each other. Practically, the church of the Middle Age by its aesthetic worship, its sacramentalism, its real faith in the resurrection of the flesh, had set itself against that Manichean opposition of spirit and matter, and its results in men's way of taking life.[16]

Pater might have found much the same distinction presented as a witty paradox in Baudelaire, who writes of the dandy hero in *La Fanfarlo*, "He loved the human body as a material harmony, as a beautiful work of architecture, full of movement: and that absolute materialism was not far removed from the purest idealism."[17]

For Pater, however, this paradox was not a joke but a historical fact. Unlike Baudelaire and Wilde, he did not see the spirituality of the material as an incitement to epigrammatic wit. He saw himself as only mildly revisionary of certain regrettable religious trends, however radical or heretical he was taken to be by his contemporaries. Among the more astute critics of Pater's religious ideas is U. C. Knoepflmacher, who speaks of Pater's search for a "religion of sanity" and locates him firmly within a Victorian tradition of religious humanism that also includes George Eliot and Samuel Butler.[18] Another reading I find especially forceful is Hilary Fraser's critique of the scholarly tradition (Eliot, Hough, DeLaura) that posits a "normative" Christianity profoundly antagonistic to art and the body and that obliges us to choose between Pater the aesthete and Pater the Christian ethicist. For Fraser, Pater's "religion of art," like his Christianity, is at once sensuous, spiritual, and ethical: "For the aesthetic and spiritual appeal of Christianity for both Pater and Wilde fused in one undeniably authentic source—the shared sense of the beauty of Christ incarnate."[19]

Whether it is the body of Christ or Apollo, however, Pater's aesthetic aspirations are also spiritual ones. Religion is for Pater not so much a "department of art" (Wright) or a categorical confusion that privileges art (Eliot) as it is the very model for aesthetic experience at its most perfect—a diaphanous faith that lends a new and essentially spiritual intensity to our experience of sensuous forms. Pater's so-called religion of art is also inherently ethical in that it is a search for spiritual perfection and beauty in life, especially in his preoccupation with monastic discipline, Greek *ascêsis,* and male comradeship.

Pater's religious ideas were themselves often in flux, although they find their most rigorous elaboration in *Marius the Epicurean,* with its tenuous embrace of a great many ancient philosophies, Christianity among them. Edmund Gosse described most succinctly Pater's ambivalence toward the Greek and Christian religions when he said, "He was not all for Apollo, or all for Christ, but each deity swayed him, and neither had that perfect homage that brings peace behind it."[20] This remark calls to mind Lord Alfred Douglas's homoerotic poem "Rejected," in which the speaker exclaims that he will have none of Christ, but Apollo will have none of him. The constant shuttling between Christian and Greek was no less a matter of sexual ethics than a matter of religion or aesthetics. Many homosexual aesthetes cast themselves adrift between these two respectable, if improbable, modes of sublimation. For Pater this drift began early in his childhood. Although he was the first Pater son not to be brought up a Roman Catholic, he was so pious as a child that his school friends referred to him as "Parson Pater" and punned on his name. J. R. McQueen vaguely recalled that Pater performed sermons, complete with surplice and procession, with his mother and grandmother as an audience. His schoolmaster feared that the boy's extreme High Churchmanship would lead him to Rome. Among his juvenilia are poems to Saint Elizabeth of Hungary and a saintly Gertrude of Himmelstadt.

His faith dissipated quickly and mysteriously at Oxford, giving way to an adolescent skepticism that delighted in shocking others. He still seriously considered taking holy orders, but his flippant remark, "What fun it would be to be ordained and not to believe a single word of what you are saying," incited the ever pious McQueen to block his ordination. His paradoxical shifts from piety to profanity as a young man are summed up by Wright: "In one breath he would make utterances that befitted a Voltaire, and in the next express the hope that he would be buried in the robes of a Capuchin."[21] I am reminded of Symonds's description of the Oxford undergraduates who were "farcical ritualists" well after the decay of Tractarianism—the incense, the sky-blue surplices, ivory crucifixes, presumably with their suggestion of ecclesiastical camp. Beyond this irreverent humor, however, is the role of Roman Catholic and especially Anglo-Catholic traditions in providing a religious haven, even a sense of community and mutual recognition, for English homosexuals.

At a time when ritualism was a major political battle, when altar candles at Saint Alban's literally incited riots, a High Church faith was paradoxically both an earnest orthodoxy and a scandalous affront to Victorian Evangelicalism. *Unwholesome, gushing, effeminate, sentimental, very poor specimens of men* were some of the epithets that disapproving Protestants applied to the young men who, like Pater, sought out ritualistic churches. As David Hilliard writes in his groundbreaking study of Anglo-Catholicism and homosexuality: "Some were drawn by the Anglo-Catholic idea of the church as a divinely constituted religious society and by its emphasis on tradition, dogma, and visible beauty in worship. Others, of radical temperament, found in Anglo-Catholicism a religion 'freed from the respectability and the puritanism of the churches in which they had grown up.'"[22]

A skeptical aesthete and yet drawn to Christianity, homosexual and yet in a respectable professional position at Oxford, Pater must certainly have recognized the various paradoxes of Victorian Anglo-

Catholicism. After the publication of *The Renaissance,* he slouched back toward Anglo-Catholicism, drawn by the beauty of the services in such notoriously ritualistic churches as Saint Austin's Priory, Saint Alban's at Holborn, and Saint Barnabas at Oxford. In *Marius the Epicurean* he wrote at great length about the fascination of his two heroes, Marius and Cornelius, for Christianity. Near the end of his life, he wrote extensively on the Greeks but was also planning a three-part study of religion with titles like "Hebrew and Hellene," "The Genius of Christ," and "The Poetry of Anglicanism." Despite his early opinions, he maintained a sober respect for the Church throughout much of his adult life.

Given the extravagance and panic of Victorian "No Popery" rhetoric, Pater's interest in ritual, not to mention the alleged effeminacy of that interest, must have seemed a political and spiritual outrage. Mallock's Mr. Rose in *The New Republic,* with his languid evocation of the beauties of Catholic ritual, is a notable attempt to depict Pater's Catholic aestheticism as an affront to Victorian piety and manliness: "The dim religious twilight, fragrant with the smoke of incense; the tangled roofs that the music seems to cling to; the tapers, the high altar, and the strange intonation of the priests, all produce a curious old-world effect, and seem to unite one with things that have been long dead."[23] This description may seem to modern readers a perfectly tame, if affected, rendering of an Anglo-Catholic service, but it manages to list every aspect of Christian ritual that horrified Victorian Evangelicals. Mallock's book was published only a few years after adoption of the Public Worship Regulation Act (1875), which, in a climate of widespread anti-Catholic panic, led to the prosecution of several ritualistic priests in the Church of England during the seventies and eighties. In fact, ritualism proved a serious political bugbear well into the Edwardian period. Pater's ritualism was indeed what many Victorians, including Victoria herself, had deeply feared at least since the Oxford movement thirty years earlier.

Evangelicalism aside, Pater's aestheticism, with its singular views on Catholic dogma, gave even some of the ritualists of his acquaintance cause for alarm. Father Nugée, for example, who delighted Pater by modeling the services at Saint Austin's on those of the early Church, saw fit to take Pater aside and explain to him that beautiful ritual is merely an outward symbol of what is in the hearts of the faithful. Of course, Father Nugée was accused of the same insincerity by his many critics, and this can only make us wonder at the motive for his little lecture. His concern, however, was part of a wider confusion about Pater, a presumption that there was nothing in his heart, that his aesthetic reveries and his effeminate effusions militated against his seriousness and his religious appreciation of the service.

Whatever doubts they might have entertained, however, Pater's contemporaries could not agree on whether he, or even Marius, was Christian, and they tended to see him as ever on the verge of a conversion. If Marius had lived a little longer, so the argument goes, the book would have been Pater's *Apologia Pro Vita Sua*. Or, as Gosse said of Pater, "it is my private conviction that, had he lived a few years longer, he would have taken orders and a small college living in the country."[24] Pater himself elaborates on this uncertainty in *The Renaissance,* in the first chapter of his first book, in which he seems to find in the medieval Abelard a reflection, perhaps even a premonition, of his own position with respect to the Church:

> When Abelard died, like Tannhäuser, he was on his way to Rome. What might have happened had he reached his journey's end is uncertain; and it is in this uncertain twilight that his relation to the general beliefs of his age has always remained. In this, as in other things, he prefigures the character of the Renaissance, that movement in which, in various ways, the human mind wins for itself a new kingdom of feeling and sensation and thought, not opposed to but only beyond and independent of the spiritual system then actually realised. (7)

The reference to Tannhäuser here is especially suggestive, given the decadent cult of Wagner and the fascination with the great sinner whose staff miraculously bloomed in the pope's sight. Like Tannhäuser, Pater was ever on his way to Rome. But on this twilight journey, Pater and Abelard rediscover the Venusberg of "feeling" and "sensation."

In Pater's view, the opposition between Christian faith and the more humanistic or pagan faith in the senses is a historical peculiarity of the Middle Ages and the Enlightenment. He turns to the Renaissance to rediscover their elusive harmonies. Pater's humanistic vision is not opposed to the old faith, which he refers to critically as "system for its own sake"; it is beyond that faith, "beyond the prescribed limits of that system, though in essential germ, it may be, contained within it" (7). He insists on the paradox of being, at once, wholly within and wholly beyond Christian doctrine and practice as he knew it. The Renaissance is for Pater a perfect religious reconciliation of the spirit and the senses that is not necessarily in conflict with Christianity: "Here there are no fixed parties, no exclusions: all breathes of that unity of culture in which 'whatsoever things are comely' are reconciled, for the elevation and adorning of our spirits" (27).

Pater's revival of the Renaissance is not so much a classical gesture as a decadent one, especially in the way that it juxtaposes two traditionally antithetic essences, such as the spirit and the senses, and insists upon a unity that is in no way readily apparent. Similarly, his perpetually deferred religious conversion, his seeming ever on the verge, precariously positioned between two worlds and partaking of each, is an important aspect of the decadent experience of religious faith—or for that matter the decadent experience of art, history, and subjectivity. Pater's faith, like his vision of human consciousness, is evanescent, fragmented, inconclusive, always in a state of subjective transformation. The chapter in which Abelard appears, called "Two Early French Stories" in all but the first edition, is itself a collection of literary fragments, and even the word *fragment* is frequently repeated. Pater's spiritual ideal is only glimpsed at odd moments, in buried texts, in passages of a peculiarly sensual delight. In this way Pater locates in the Renaissance something of that fragmentary vision, the realization of the soul through the body, that Barbey d'Aurevilly and Huysmans sought in gothic literature and the violent ecstasies of the Middle Ages. Furthermore, as in Huysmans' slow progress through the four autobiographical Durtal novels, ever taking up new spiritual positions, ever wavering between ardent faith and spiritual dryness, progressing from epiphany to epiphany or deferring in a glow of hope any such supreme moment of insight, Pater maintained this tenuous spiritual flame to the end of his life.

Unlike Huysmans, however, Pater embraces the uncertainty and flux of faith rather than painfully and cynically resigning himself to it. The illusion of a simple, fundamental, immutable faith quite easily falls to pieces in decadent writing. Pater entertained Christian faith as a "possibility" throughout much of his life. Dogma is subjugated to practice, and the impressionistic fragments of doctrine, ritual, religious art, mystical certainty, and sensual reverie are all "weaving and unweaving" themselves, self-destructing and reconstructing in a relentless subjective process of *becoming*. Late in his life, Pater conceived of the experience most beautifully in his 1890 lecture on Prosper Mérimée: "Fundamental belief gone, in almost all of us, at least some relics of it remain—queries, echoes, afterthoughts; and they help to make an atmosphere, a mental atmosphere, hazy perhaps, yet with many secrets of soothing light and shade, associating more definite objects to each other by a perspective pleasant to the inward eye against a hopefully receding background of remoter and ever remoter possibilities."[25] This sentence loses sight of its beginning, drifting into a wonderfully suggestive, teasingly vague, "hopefully" inconclusive realm of possibilities that seem themselves to be drifting beyond our field of vision. I have read this passage a hundred times, and I still have no idea precisely where it is headed. But there are *possibilities*, however remote—that much is clear. In the hazy mental atmosphere of fragments, mystically related—these queries, echoes, afterthoughts— the subject-in-process is free to remake itself in relation to God, or to be remade. Art, faith, and desire cease to sustain their orthodoxies, their immutable and mutually exclusive status as pure and distinct categories.

Pater found that this tenuousness actually brought him closer to the feelings of love and hope that Christianity is generally thought to foster. Especially interesting in this regard is his review of Mrs. Humphry Ward's immensely popular religious novel *Robert Elsmere,* in which he notes that many people have doubts about the sacred story, but many people also have doubts about their doubts: "For their part, they make allowance in their scheme of life for a great possibility, and with some of them that bare concession of possibility . . . becomes the most important fact in the world. The recognition of it straightaway opens wide the door to hope and love."[26] Again, this uncertain but unavoidable belief in a divine "possibility" allows for all that is noble and felicitous in the Christian religion, but faith is still side by side with skepticism in an irrepressible motion of the mind that Pater regards as peculiar to modernity.

Pater once made a passing remark that I think is his most succinct expression of his Christian philosophy, that paradoxical orthodoxy without a doctrine. In observing some scaffolding on a church, he noted, "I have a great fondness for a church in progress."[27]

## Renaissance and Resurrection

*"La maladie est l'état naturel des Chrétiens,"* says Pascal himself.

Walter Pater

In speaking of Pater's religious and aesthetic preoccupation with mobility, becoming, and subjective transformation, I am suggesting that Pater's Catholicism, his view of art, his very style, are lively and creative. At the same time, however, he is a decadent writer, not only because of his tortuous and exquisite style, his fascination with the objet d'art and the fragment, but also because of his preoccupation with death and decay. It is one of the paradoxes of decadent literature that life and death, creativity and decay, are often aspects of the same artistic gesture. The theme of death and decay is also linked with homoeroticism, though Pater spares us the connection between sodomy and satanism so often pursued by the French *décadents*. Virtually every representation of love between men in Pater is haunted by the grave—and the stronger the suggestion of homoerotic desire, the more eagerly Pater seems to want to see one of the two men dead.

Nearly every Victorian story of a romance between men ends in death, and Pater is a touchstone for the tradition. The list of men with dead comrades in Pater's work is a long one: Amis and Amile, Winckelmann and Goethe, Marius and Flavian, Marius and Cornelius, Emerald and James, Apollyon and Hyacinthus, Montaigne and Etienne, and Jasmin and Raoul, to name a few. Love between men and women, however rare in Pater, and love between parents and children fare no better. Consider Marius's dead mother and father or, in the same book, Aurelius and his son, or the widows Cecilia and Faustina. To read Pater with pleasure is to be a little in love with death. Like Huysmans, he is concerned less with desire than with the decay of desire. The object of love is ever passing beyond a mortal boundary into the intriguing otherness of the deceased. For this solitary lover, desire is mournful, melancholic, even spiritual. Indeed, the sexual relation has been virtually replaced by mourning. La Gioconda is only one of the many lovers in Pater for whom fantastic reveries and exquisite passions survive only as the traces of loss that fret the hands and tinge the weary eyelids.

While Pater frequently used the word *morbid* to attack particular works of literature that offended him, many of his readers have applied the same word to him. Even today the term retains a homoerotic nuance, and it was frequently used to describe homosexuals in psychological studies from Krafft-Ebing onward. John Addington Symonds—who also had a tendency to the morbid in his descriptions of his own homosexuality, whatever his distaste for the decadents—found himself at once seduced and repelled by Pater's funereal eroticism. In commenting on *The Renaissance* in a letter, he wrote: "There is a kind of Death clinging to the man wh. makes his music (but heavens! how sweet that is!) a little faint & sickly. His view of life gives me the creeps, as old women say. I am sure it is a ghastly sham; & that live by it or not as he may do, his utterance of the theory to the world has in it a wormy hollow-voiced seductiveness of a fiend."[28] In this jarringly ambivalent portrait, Pater resembles Des Esseintes's nightmare of the Pox in *A Rebours*. Another reviewer of *The Renaissance* declared that the book was misnamed, that it depicts "a morbid abhorrence of life and health, and fondness for death and artifice."[29]

Pater did much to justify these remarks, as in this passage from his imaginary portrait "Duke Carl of Rosenmold" (1887): "Youth even, in its sentimental mood, was ready to indulge in the luxury of decay, and amuse itself with fancies of the tomb; as in periods of decadence or suspended progress, when the world seems to nap for a time, artifices for the arrest or disguise of old age are adopted as a fashion, and become the fopperies of the young."[30] Duke Carl walks the earth even after his own funeral, but he is only one instance of Pater's recurrent interest in the undead. Persephone and Michelangelo are likened to the "revenant." The word "vampire" is applied to Apollo and La Gioconda in the same book, while elsewhere Gilles de Rais is the "werewolf" of France and Dionysus Zagreus is the "sarcophagus," the eater of flesh. Marius has a yen for buried ancestors, and Denys exhumes his mother's corpse. In his prose Pater is neither afraid of death nor repelled by it. His various forays among the dead are usually drawn with melancholy delectation, as in his delicate and muscular

Trypho, who emerges from the tomb a "still active soul," or the mournful Greek, who experiences "deep joy" at the sight of his own youth "still red with life in the grave."[31] Necrophilia finds its sweetness and light in Pater. Not with any great surprise do we discover that his favorite haunts in Paris were the Louvre and the Morgue.

Death is, however, as much a starting point as it is an ending for Pater. Like many a romantic poet before him, fascinated by the dead and the revenant, he sees the grave as a site of inspiration and creativity. Birth and death are for Pater concomitant phenomena, two aspects of the same beautiful gesture in art. Out of the ruins and fragments of dead civilizations, out of the perceived decay even of his own age, Pater engenders a modern cultural ideal, a decadent sensibility in which birth is always more precisely a perpetual rebirth, a renaissance or a resurrection. His womb presumes a tomb. He knows no annihilation without flux, no fragmentation without reconfiguration, no grave without its revenant waking as if from a sleep and wandering abroad with the stain of burial still visible on its countenance. Moreover, Pater's images of birth and regeneration have a highly unconventional, even decadent, sexual significance. Throughout his work, from *The Renaissance* on, Pater constructs a sexual ethics of his own, a new chivalry at once autoerotic and homoerotic.

Sexual reproduction, not to mention its modus operandi the nuclear family, suffers a curious extinction in his work—curious, I say, because it seems to expire without a gasp. In *Marius the Epicurean* Pater speaks sentimentally about family life, but what has he done with all those big happy bourgeois families so abundant in the Victorian novel? Pater himself grieved at the loss of his father when he was a child, and even more the loss of his mother and brother. His work is a veritable parade of dead fathers, dead mothers, even dead infants. He seems more interested in the decay of the family than in the family itself. Furthermore, sexual experience begins to lose its gendered and familial parameters. Motherhood is no longer limited to women. Marriages occur between men. Women attain an erotic self-sufficiency, an iconic aura of completeness apart from men.[32]

The homoerotic and autoerotic tendency of this sexual play has often been defined critically as morbid or sterile. For example, in his recent book on aestheticism and deconstruction, Jonathan Loesberg draws a problematic opposition between sexual inversion and creativity:

> To the extent that Pater's philosophy suggested indulgence in sensation, even if it was the fairly intellectualized sensation of aestheticism, it represented a turning inward away from the world, thus an "unnatural" inversion—inversion rather than perversion was the psychological flaw they thought inherent in homosexuality—a turning away from outwardly productive and reproductive sexuality toward inverted enjoyment of and repetition of private sensations.[33]

Furthermore, he adds, "both homosexuality and sign proliferation, being essentially sterile and enclosed, can reproduce only through an unnatural tainting process." Loesberg's definition of "inversion" is alarmingly inaccurate, since as a psychological term it referred to an inversion of gender. Nevertheless, his analysis has a trace of historical truth, however homophobic. Ironically, it is precisely gender inversion, a sort of androgyny, that was regarded by many Victorian and modernist aesthetes as a stimulant to artistic creativity. In homophobic minds, then as now, the homosexual, unjustly judged to be sterile, unnatural, and tainted, is thought to reproduce himself through an erotic act of conversion or proselytization—what Pater and Wilde were wont to refer to vaguely as "influence." Similarly, decadent writing transforms what is already there, taking the ruins and fragments of things living and dead as material for a creative effort that confounds sexual reproduction in something more like a cultural reproduction.

But Pater's prose is by no means a mindless and self-enclosed mechanism of repetition. He literally reclaims the metaphor of sexual reproduction to define the singularly homosexual inspiration he finds in literature and art; and in so doing, he subverts the conventional notion of homosexuality, autoeroticism, and aestheticism as somehow sterile. He presents us with the paradox of virgin childbirth, of male motherhood and conception between men, essentially deconstructing the trite and untenable equation of artistic and imaginative creativity with procreative heterosexuality. Autoeroticism and homosexuality, which had already been relegated to a vampiric domain in the Victorian imagination, rise from the grave in Pater's work and become the new starting point, the beginningless beginning, for a new conception of culture.

The opening chapter of *The Renaissance* presents in embryo these revised sexual tropes, which Pater continued to elaborate in every book that followed. The story of Amis and Amile, flanked by Abelard and Heloise on one side and Aucassin and Nicolette on the other, is a Christian romance of love between men. Even their names suggest their love and their twin-like similarity. Pater immediately introduces the homoerotic and narcissistic *doppelgänger* theme, "the romantic circumstance of an entire personal resemblance between the two heroes, through which they pass for each other again and again." Underscoring their fraternal "inward similitude" are the two cups they possess, "exactly like each other—children's cups, of wood, but adorned with gold and precious stones" (9). Beyond the womb symbolism of their association with birth and childhood, the cups are the ornate souvenirs of Amis and Amile's baptism by the pope—apparently a double baptism suggestive here of a wedding ceremony, complete with grateful parents.

An allusion to Saint Francis of Assisi's notions of chivalry and romantic love opens the chapter, and indeed it is the chivalry of their love that Pater emphasizes when he speaks of Amis taking the place of Amile in a tournament for life or death. Pater returns to this theme of homoerotic chivalry with the Christian knight Cornelius, for whom Marius undertakes a similar self-sacrifice. Another foreshadowing of *Marius* occurs when Amis falls ill with leprosy and is tended by Amile, just as Flavian is tended by Marius. Both Amis and Amile have wives, and Amile also has children, but the responsibilities of a husband and a father are secondary to the love between the two friends. At one point Pater notes that the two men are sleeping together, that they "lay in one chamber without other companions," and he further adds that, when Amis was ill, "his wife would not approach him, and wrought to strangle him" (10). In a few subtle strokes, Pater sketches a domestic arrangement familiar to many a married homosexual of his day, Paul Verlaine and Oscar Wilde among them.

The angel Raphael appears to the men as they lie in bed together. If Amile wishes to see Amis healed of his leprosy, the angel tells them, he must kill his own children and wash Amis in their blood. "But I conjure thee," says Amile to his friend, "by the faith which there is between me and thee, and by our comradeship, and by the baptism we received together at Rome, that thou tell me whether it was man or angel said that to thee" (13). In thus recalling their double baptism, this scene with the angel becomes a second and more profound christening, the pope replaced by an angel, water by blood, the baptismal act itself taken over by Amile as a testament to his love for Amis. Amile is obliged to make a choice between what is construed as two conflicting allegiances: a man's love for a man as opposed to his love for his wife and children. The emotional conflict inherent in the arrangement of the men's households is not permitted to stand as such. After much agonizing and weeping, Amile does the deed, exclaiming, "Alas, my children! I am no longer your father, but your cruel murderer," as he cuts off their heads. If we miss the sense of the double baptism as wedding the first time around, it is unmistakable the second time around. With Amile's prayer to Christ, Amis is cleansed of his leprosy with blood that Amile carries to their bed from the bed of his children.

After the christening Amile seems to play bridegroom to his friend: "And Amile clothed his companion in his best robes; and as they went to the church to give thanks, the bells, by the will of God, rang of their own accord" (14). To this miraculous thanksgiving, Pater brings all the blessings and ritual accoutrements of a Victorian middle-class wedding. Amile's wife appears, and he does not explain to her the secret of Amis's health, effectively excluding her from the symbolic significance of the scene. Even more extraordinary than God's blessing on the murder and the male bond of love is the reappearance of the children: "And in going in alone to the children to weep over them, he found them at play in the bed; only, in the place of the sword-cuts about their throats was as it were a thread of crimson" (15). The homoerotic rebaptism and remarriage are followed by the rebirth and resurrection of the children, presumably a gift to Amile not only for his faith but also for his love of his comrade. Love between men, with the aid of Christian faith and a Christian miracle, re-engenders children. The children are presented again to the wife, who is then told the secret of the angel's commandment. Family happiness is restored, but Amis's affective position within that family has been strengthened by a symbolic, even symbiotic, bond that has rechristened him through Christian faith as an additional spouse and parent.

In Amis and Amile, Pater finds an early modern romance in which the erotic and spiritual seem to be in perfect harmony. Chivalric homoeroticism is seen to be wholly in keeping with Christian idealism. As he passes on to the story of Aucassin and Nicolette, Pater emphasizes the contention between the erotic and the spiritual. Aucassin represents the "ideal intensity of passion," but ends up suffering from "that great malady of his love," virtually sleepwalking into the ranks of his enemies (23–24). Pater compares this Renaissance passion to the emergence of Venus from the caves of the Venusberg in the story of Tannhäuser: "In their search after the pleasures of the sense and the imagination, in their care for beauty, in their worship of the body, people were impelled beyond the bounds of the Christian ideal; and their love became sometimes a strange idolatry, a strange rival religion" (24). Pater speaks of a "rebellious and antinomian element" even within the "Age of Faith" (25). He is clearly fascinated by this "rival religion," but it is to the homoerotic love story of Amis and Amile that he returns in order to define his own ideal, one in which "the harmony of human interests is still entire" (27). We learn of the martyrdom of Amis and Amile—"in the *House Beautiful* the saints too have their place" (26)—and Pater lingers on the irony that, despite its "liberty of the heart," the story is in fact a hagiography written by a monk, *La Vie des Saints Martyrs Amis et Amile*. Indeed, the "earthly comradeship" is a "monkish miracle" (27).

The chapter ends with the account of another miracle attesting to the love of Amis and Amile. Although wives and children are nowhere in sight, the two men are united in life as in death. When Amile's coffin is brought to Saint Peter's Church, it somehow migrates to the side of Amis's coffin in Saint Oseige. Because of this supernatural sign of their "wondrous amity," they are honored not only by the bishop but also by the king and queen. Love between men is construed as itself a reawakening, a resurrection, something that occurs on the other side of the grave. It is strangely dependent on the threat of death, at times even a passage through death—by tournament, by illness, by child murder—a romantic death that demands a testament of faith and love. The lover is then revived, and in a sense he is reborn and rechristened in the name of his love.

In a later chapter, the portrait of Michelangelo, Pater develops the themes of homosexuality, faith, death, and maternity as they are initiated in the essay on Amis and Amile. Michelangelo's sexual behavior goes against the grain of the chivalric ideal established in the earlier essay. Pater's homoeroticism, however intense and seductive, is chaste at heart, and he circumnavigates any acknowledgment of orgasm; but his mild distress at Michelangelo's sexuality is probably feigned: "He who spoke so decisively of the supremacy of the imaginative world of the unveiled human form had not been always, we may think, a mere Platonic lover. Vague and wayward his loves may have been; but they partook of the strength of his nature, and sometimes, it may be, would by no means become music, so that the comely order of his days was quite put out" (81). Pater redeems the "less tranquil affections" through an assertion of genius "in harmony with itself." Furthermore, he attributes to Michelangelo an artistic creativity that is maternal and paternal at once. He focuses on the artist's treatments of spontaneous generation, whether in Christian myths or pagan ones. He is especially taken with the myth of man's creation in Genesis, noting apparently without irony that it has always had a certain "pregnancy of expression" (91). He comments on the artist's "languid" and "satyr-like" Adam, finger to finger with his Creator on the ceiling of the Sistine Chapel. And the Almighty himself appears to be pregnant "with the forms of things to be, woman and her progeny, in the fold of his garment." On a more Hellenic note, he mentions the painting of Leda, "the delight of the world breaking from the egg of a bird" (76)—a suggestive image for an artist who speaks of "the nest where he was born" (81).

Michelangelo even leaves on his work the traces of their birth struggle and his own labor. There is an intentional incompleteness about his sculpture, "something of the unwrought stone about them," such that the spectator must "complete the half emergent form" (76). The statue of David, according to Pater, has something like a navel positioned oddly on his head, a fleshly souvenir of the quarry and the artist's hand: "on the crown of the *David*'s head there still remains a morsel of uncut stone, as if by one touch to maintain its connection with the place from which it was hewn" (77). To emphasize the homoeroticism of his engagement with Michelangelo, Pater positions himself as a receptive spectator, while juxtaposing birth metaphors with suggestions of the artist's virility, his "strength," his "convulsive energy," his "penetrative" imagination. "And it is in this penetrative suggestion of life that the secret of that sweetness of his is to be found," he explains. In what follows, it is difficult to tell who is pregnant with the "warmth and fulness of the world," the painting or Pater: Michelangelo "penetrates us with a feeling of that power which we associate with all the warmth and fulness of the world, the sense of which brings into one's thoughts a swarm of birds and flowers and insects. The brooding spirit of life itself is there; and the summer may burst out in a moment" (77).

Michelangelo's wombs, however, always presume a tomb. "Some of those whom the gods love die young" (88), Pater writes. He mentions the deaths of Julius, Lorenzo, Christ, La bella Simonetta, the youthful and princely Marquess of Pescara and Cardinal Jacopo di Portogallo. He claims that the association of creativity with the grave is a distinguishing characteristic of the Italian Renaissance itself: "It has been said that all the great Florentines were preoccupied with death. *Outre-tombe! Outre-tombe!*—is the burden of their thoughts, from Dante to Savonarola" (92). In his art Michelangelo seems to be recovering life, redeeming it, rather than creating it. "With him the beginning of life has all the characteristics of resurrection; it is like the recovery of suspended health or animation, with its gratitude, its effusion, and eloquence" (75). Pater's juxtaposition of birth and death is even more paradoxical on the following page: "This creation of life—life coming always as relief or recovery, and always in strong contrast with the rough-hewn mass in which it is kindled—is in various ways the motive of all his work . . . ; and this, although at least one-half of his work was designed for the adornment of tombs—the tomb of Julius, the tombs of the Medici" (76). Pater eroticizes Michelangelo's relationship to the dead, not only by commenting on their youthful beauty, but by literally betrothing him to a feminine figure of death who functions as a kind of muse: "For, like Dante and all the nobler souls of Italy, he is much occupied with thoughts of the grave, and his true mistress is death" (88). Michelangelo himself is designated at one point as the "executioner" for the strength of his bitterness, and we learn also that he once tried to starve himself. Not only does he beget beauty by death, he is himself a ghostly figure at the height of his own creativity. In the Catholic revival he deems himself a spectral stranger in his own land. Pater often depicts Catholicism, especially in its "frozen orthodoxy," as a dead weight, inimical to the fluent and harmonious human spirit of the Renaissance. In this new milieu Michelangelo becomes the revenant, the undead, "a ghost out of another age, in a world too coarse to touch his faint sensibilities very closely" (90).

Despite his ignorance of Roman Catholic doctrine, Michelangelo has an intuitive and sensuous understanding of the Church's beauty. Like Pater, he is a stranger in the faith, but a comfortable and inspired stranger, "consoled and tranquillised, as a traveller might be, resting for one evening in a strange city, by its stately aspect and the sentiment of its many fortunes, just because with those fortunes he has nothing to do." Michelangelo's Christianity is alive and creative, but it is also a thing of mourning, alive among the dead. Paradoxically, in his role as revenant, he experiences generativity only as a dead and mournful man: "Dreaming, in a worn-out society, theatrical in its life, theatrical in its art, theatrical even in its devotion, on the morning of the world's history, on the primitive form of man, on the images under which that primitive world had conceived spiritual forces" (90). In other words, through the worshipful offices of the dead, through the prosopopoeia of a life as symbolic simulacrum or death mask, Michelangelo and Pater glimpse a more primitive and even pagan origin for religious experience, one that does not deny the body, the beautiful "form of man." But this glimpse itself partakes of the speech of that ritualistic death mask, having grown sleepy in that evening in a strange city, its eyelids heavy in that worn-out society; it does not witness the morning of the world's history, but dreams of it.

When Pater turns to Michelangelo's Madonna, therefore, it is not the Madonna of Bruges, the bliss of nurturance on her countenance, but the Madonna of the *Pietà*. Her presence is prefigured in this chapter by Vittoria Colonna, "an ardent neo-catholic, vowed to perpetual widowhood" (83), who also prefigures the mourning rituals of Marius's mother. She too, like the revenant, like the vampire La Gioconda, "is a woman already weary, in advanced age, of grave intellectual qualities" (87). She transforms sorrow and disappointment into a dispassionate calm, a meditative sweetness. In this way she is like the mistress death herself, "death at first as the worst of all sorrows and disgraces, with a clod of the field for its brain; afterwards, death in its high distinction, its detachment from vulgar needs, the angry stains of life and action escaping fast" (88).

Michelangelo's relationship with Vittoria is Pater's self-conscious refiguration of homosexuality as a dolorous and maternal desire. In John Addington Symonds's book on Michelangelo, the author's interest in desire between men in general and between Michelangelo and Tommaso Cavalieri in particular is abundantly clear, despite the defensive and sublimating tone. If we demand the same from Pater, we are disappointed. Despite the copious biographical and literary material on Michelangelo's love for men, Pater prefers to focus on Vittoria. He is not, however, heterosexualizing Michelangelo. Rather, he elides sex between men or between men and women and valorizes instead a more phantasmatic and maternalized desire, an erotic engagement with death and art that is virtually indistinguishable from male homoeroticism in Pater's work. Through Vittoria, Michelangelo's unruly passions are made cool and serene, sublimated perhaps, transfigured into a more refined sensuousness, an indifferent perception of form. He perceives "the new body," to use Pater's vague expression, a body that is itself spiritualized and dreamlike, diaphanous—"a passing light, a mere intangible, external effect, over those too rigid, or too formless faces; a dream that lingers a moment, retreating in the dawn, incomplete, aimless, helpless; . . . a breath, a flame in the doorway, a feather in the wind" (96).

This new body, this more delicate and polymorphous passion, plays over the harder surfaces of the world like an appreciative glance. But it is a resurrected body, a revenant gaze, not body or spirit alone, but the body spiritualized in all its sensuousness. Something must die for it to be born. Its passion is a form of mourning or pity. "*Pietà,* pity, the pity of the Virgin Mother over the dead body of Christ, expanded into the pity of all mothers over all dead sons, the entombment with its cruel 'hard stones';—this is the subject of his predilection" (94). The discovery of beauty is for Pater the recognition of an absence, a loss, a sensation of utter solitude and abandonment, through the contemplation of what is present but has no life of its own. In this sense Pater's Madonna resembles Huysmans' description of Grünewald's *Crucifixion.* In a crisis of sorrow, hopelessness, physical anguish, the body itself is transfigured into a sublime object. The pity of Michelangelo's Madonna appears "always as a hopeless, rayless, almost heathen sorrow—no divine sorrow, but mere pity and awe at the stiff limbs and colourless lips" (94). Pater first depicts Michelangelo's passion as something unruly, insufficiently platonic, but nevertheless in-spired, strong, a generative homoerotic desire. Through the figure of the *Pietà*, however, he presses this homoeroticism even farther into the sublime and impossible, until it becomes a perpetual and unspeakable demand, the melancholic pity of a virgin mother for her dead son, for all dead sons.

The essay on Leonardo da Vinci continues this juxtaposition of death and the maternal in Pater's portrait of another homosexual artist. "A feeling for maternity is indeed always characteristic of Leonardo" (114), Pater writes, and yet that feeling also seems to draw the artist into the secrets of the grave. The portrait of Leonardo is the most decadent in the book, given his "life of brilliant sins and exquisite amusements" (109). It teems with fragments of the grotesque and the sublime. Like Michelangelo, Leonardo embraces "extremes of beauty and terror" and is "smitten with a love of the impossible" (104). His occult gaze renders nature a grotesque, fragmented and breaking open, revealing its inward secrets in a weird prosopopoeia. Leonardo's silver harp is "shaped in some curious likeness to a horse's skull" (108). Women, children, and maternity become somewhat gothic figures, uncanny and beautiful, in their association with death. "Legions of grotesques sweep under his hand; for has not nature too her gro-tesques—the rent rock, the distorting lights of evening on lonely roads, the unveiled structure of man in the embryo, or the skeleton?" (105). Embryo and skeleton? Leonardo sees a little skull like a seashell in the head of the Christ child, as it peeps sideways in half-reassured terror at a griffin with bat-like wings. He is deeply disturbed when the Duchess Beatrice dies in childbirth, and he paints Beatrice d'Este "with some presentiment of early death, painting her precise and grave, full of the refinement of the dead, in sad earth-coloured raiment, set with pale stones" (112). The Medusa is portrayed as the dream of a child, as "the head of a corpse, exercising its powers, through all the circum-stances of death. What may be called the fascination of corruption penetrates in every touch its exquisitely finished beauty" (106).

Finally, there is La Gioconda, who is not only a vampire but also a mother, even the mother of the Virgin Mother. She is a mother to both Christianity and Hellenism, since she, "as Leda, was the mother of Helen of Troy, and, as Saint Anne, the mother of Mary" (125). In La Gioconda Pater captures most poetically the maternal countenance of

death. She is an embodiment of Huysmans' dictum in *Là-Bas* that in
the Beyond all things touch. She offers a glimpse, faint as the sound
of lyres and flutes, of innumerable fallen days, in which she has died
many times and been a mother many times. She is another *Pietà*,
though less mournful than simply weary. Her son is missing from the
scene because her son is Leonardo or Pater or whatever man meets her
vampiric maternal gaze. Her smile, treacherous as that of John the
Baptist, may be an invitation to a resurrection, but more likely it is an
invitation to identification, to that "feeling for maternity" of which
Pater speaks. Like the mother, the son will be dead many times in what
amounts to a perpetual life, sweeping together ten thousand experiences, gathering all the ends of the world on his head. Christ is undead
in La Gioconda's arms, an aesthete, another god in exile, continually
re-enacting his resurrection in the manner of Pater's epicurean.

Pater's portrait of Leonardo leads almost inevitably to Freud's essays
on Leonardo and the Medusa. In part through a reading of Pater,
Freud offers a psychoanalytic explanation for the connections among
death, homosexuality, and motherhood in Leonardo. Richard Dellamora has written of Leonardo's Medusa, Saint John the Baptist, and
La Gioconda as transvestite portraits, even self-portraits, in Pater's
critique, discovering in Leonardo the "wish to be a woman," an
erotically transformative identification with femininity. Dellamora further notes that Pater's fascination with death "suggests the possibility
of a new life that lies on the other side of the death to the self that the
entry into sexual desire and activity portends."[34] He dismisses as homophobic Freud's comments on the "unhappiness" of Leonardo's sexual life; nevertheless, whatever Freud's clinical intentions, the association of maternity with death is abundantly clear in Pater and Leonardo
both. In Freud's essay on Leonardo, male homosexuality is indeed the
death of the masculine self through identification with the fantasy of
a phallic mother. Leonardo fixates narcissistically on his own prehis-
tory, symbolically realized through his fascination with death. He
becomes a diver in deep seas, regressing to an idyllic and oceanic
dream of gender indifference, the dream like that of Freud's Little
Hans, in which the mother has a phallus and the son has a womb.

Pater finds a similar movement in Michelangelo when he writes that
the poet is "still alive, and in possession of our inmost thoughts—
dumb inquiry over the relapse after death into the formlessness which

preceded life, the change, the revolt from that change, then the correcting, hallowing, consoling rush of pity" (96). The virgin mother, especially as *Pietà,* looms large in this religious, "hallowing" experience. For Pater, it is a dreaming child that engenders the horrible snakes and androgynous fascination of the Medusa, not to mention the sinister smiles of La Gioconda and Saint John the Baptist. Freud quotes Pater's contention that the mysterious dream of a smile finds its origins in Leonardo's own childhood: "From childhood we see this image defining itself on the fabric of his dreams" (124).[35] Pater continues, remarking on the homosexual significance of the smile: "and but for express historical testimony, we might fancy that this was but his ideal lady, embodied and beheld at last." Freud speaks of John the Baptist's "secret of love" and the "mystical air" of Leonardo's "beautiful youths of feminine delicacy and with effeminate forms; they do not cast their eyes down, but gaze in mysterious triumph, as if they knew of a great achievement of happiness" (67).

Where Freud finds unhappiness and sublimation, Pater finds a seduction. Pater delights in a masochistic pleasure, eager to fall victim to the treacherous smile of the androgynous Christian saint whom he says "no one would go out into the wilderness to seek" (118). Leonardo's desire for other men excites Pater's interest in desire as a transgressive fusion of two men, of self and other, a fusion that Freud defined as narcissistic. "Andrea Salaino, beloved of Leonardo for his curled and waving hair" is said to have "identified himself so entirely with Leonardo, that the picture of *Saint Anne,* in the Louvre, has been attributed to him" (116). Pater conceives homoerotic desire here as a subjective and creative fusion mediated by the Christian maternal figure of Saint Anne. Salaino is only one of the princely young men in Pater's account who were initiated into Leonardo's "secret, for the sake of which they were ready to efface their own individuality." Even in his relationship to his own art, Leonardo seeks a "self-love" that is also a "self-forgetfulness" (117).

In the Winckelmann essay Leonardo's homoerotic gaze of occult maternal knowledge becomes the gaze of the aesthetic historian and critic who, like Pater, awakens from the grave of his own time the fragments and ruins of a Hellenic ideal of male beauty. Like Heine's god in exile, like Pater himself, Winckelmann is a stranger in his own time, a passionate Hellenist hoping to find a profession within the uncertain confines of the Church, undergoing a conversion with Voltaire in hand. For Winckelmann, Roman Catholicism appears to be the last hope of paganism. With its "antique and as it were pagan grandeur," Catholicism seems to have "reconciled itself to the Renaissance" better than "the crabbed Protestantism, which had been the *ennui* of his youth" (187). "Mystic passion" and "monastic reverie" are evoked as the attraction of medievalism, and yet their negative impulse "deflowered the flesh." Pater finds in the Enlightenment Winckelmann a Renaissance harmony and completeness of body and soul, a merger of the religious and the aesthetic, "a more liberal mode of life" that transcends both classical and medieval limitations (184).

As Pater makes clear, the physical ideal that Winckelmann hoped to introduce into his own age is Hellenic and homoerotic. "That his affinity with Hellenism was not merely intellectual, that the subtler threads of temperament were inwoven in it, is proved by his romantic, fervent friendships with young men. He has known, he says, many young men more beautiful than Guido's archangel" (191). Beyond this relatively explicit passage, however, there is a homoerotic and auto-erotic suggestiveness, a metaphorical phallicism, wandering and diaphanous, that eroticizes Pater's gaze at Winckelmann, not to mention Pater's gaze at Goethe's gaze at Winckelmann. Variations on the word "penetrate" abound once again as the adjective of choice for Winckelmann's aesthetic. We learn that his force and enthusiasm are by no means "flaccid" (181), nor are they vague and diffuse, but "rays, in themselves pale and impotent, unite and begin to burn," prefiguring the hard, phallic, gem-like flame of the "Conclusion."

Following Hegel, Pater remarks several times on a certain "new organ" that Winckelmann discovered: "He is to be regarded as one of those who, in the sphere of art, have known how to initiate a new organ for the human spirit" (177), and Pater wonders "what kind of man it was who thus laid open a new organ" (178). We might wonder also whether the organ belongs to himself or someone else, or whether indeed it is a phallus or an orifice. Regarding Winckelmann's relationship to nature, Pater writes: "And that world in which others had moved with so much embarrassment, seems to call out in Winckelmann new senses fitted to deal with it. He is in touch with it; it penetrates him, and becomes part of his temperament" (194). This innocent immodesty in touching the phallus is one of the peculiar virtues of Winckelmann. He is "shameless and childlike." He knows nothing of the sensual intoxication of Christian transgression, typified by a certain famous biblical line that also intrigued and amused Wilde with its curious suggestion of homosexual fellatio: "I did but taste a little honey with the end of the rod that was in mine hand, and lo! I must die." From this intoxication Winckelmann is free. Pater writes that Winckelmann "fingers those pagan marbles with unsinged hands, with no sense of shame or loss" (222). Greek poetry bears a similar pleasure, phallic and homoerotic, yet shameless and spiritualized: "Hitherto he had handled the words only of Greek poetry, stirred indeed and roused by them, yet divining beyond the words some unexpressed pulsation of sensuous life" (183).

Variations on the word "pregnant" also abound in this essay. Pater is playing, of course, on Plato's *Symposium,* in which images of child-birth are appropriated for a discussion of cultural generation, a homoerotic parthogenesis that takes place between men. Diotima characterizes the soulful inspiration that one man feels in the presence of a beautiful youth as a kind of pregnancy:

> When he attaches himself to someone beautiful, I believe, and associates with him, he gives birth and brings forth what he was pregnant with before, both while in that person's presence and while remembering him when he is absent. Together with him he nurtures the offspring produced, so that such men have much more to share with each other and a stronger friendship than that which comes from rearing children, since they share in the rearing of children who are more beautiful and more immortal.[36]

This pregnancy between men who are lovers goes to the very heart of Pater's aestheticism, as is most evident in the Winckelmann essay. For example, there is Pater's account of the beautiful multitude of male figures blending and folding together on the Panathenaic frieze: "This colourless, unclassified purity of life, with its blending and interpenetration of intellectual, spiritual, and physical elements, still folded together, pregnant with the possibilities of a whole world closed within it." And what is the result of the "interpenetration" and "pregnancy" among all these men? A child, of course. "Everywhere there is the effect of an awaking, of a child's sleep just disturbed" (*Renaissance,* 218).

The pregnancy metaphors are especially suggestive with regard to Goethe, who is singularly receptive to Winckelmann's new organ. We learn that "Goethe's fragments of art criticism contain a few pages of strange pregnancy on the character of Winckelmann" (177). For Pater, to read Winckelmann with inspiration is to make of him a bridegroom for our own passage into an aesthetic of male homoerotic desire. Goethe waits for the arrival of Winckelmann, "expecting his coming, with that wistful eagerness which marked his youth" (195):

> Goethe, then in all the pregnancy of his wonderful youth, still un-ruffled by the "press and storm" of his earlier manhood, was await-ing Winckelmann with a curiosity of the worthiest kind. As it was, Winckelmann became to him something like what Virgil was to Dante. And Winckelmann, with his fiery friendships, had reached that age and that period of culture at which emotions hitherto fitful, sometimes concentrate themselves in a ritual, unchangeable relation-ship. German literary history seems to have lost the chance of one of those famous friendships, the very tradition of which becomes a stimulus to culture, and exercises an imperishable influence. (197)

This passage is a masterpiece of homoerotic suggestiveness, ripe with words like "friendships" and "influence" that Oscar Wilde would later render more voluptuous.

This hymn to Platonic male friendship is like a palimpsest through which we can glimpse the celebration of a wedding between a homo-sexual art critic and his devoted reader. Winckelmann is finally able to tame his "fiery friendships," a coy allusion to his sexual passions for other men. He finally settles down with a good man and, under his stimulus and influence, Goethe brings his cultural pregnancy to term. But alas, this marriage, this "ritual, unchangeable relationship," never quite happens. Pater loves this part of the story. Death is Goethe's bridegroom since, on the way to Leipzig, Winckelmann is murdered, probably by a male prostitute—what Pater calls a "fellow-traveller"—suggestively named Arcangeli. The murderer recalls the treacherous Saint John the Baptist, "Guido's beautiful archangel," and the archangel Raphael's visit to Amis and Amile as they lay in bed together. In Pater's work, the male beloved is more often than not a fair-haired Apollo or a Christian angel, and his message of birth or rebirth is always also a message of death.

## Virgin Marius

*Pietas* was a passion with him.          Lionel Johnson on Pater


This is a typical and very strongly expressed grotesque. It is ambivalent. It is pregnant death, a death that gives birth.

Mikhail Bakhtin


In *Marius the Epicurean,* Pater elaborates on the discussion of maternity, male comradeship, and aesthetics that he initiated in *The Renaissance,* but he demonstrates a more profound engagement with the possibilities of religious faith. *Marius* contains some of Pater's most assertive remarks on Christian humanism and the historical development of ritual. Like Huysmans, Pater is fascinated by a decadent degeneration and regeneration of language and faith in the period of the early Church. Unlike his French contemporary, however, Pater is attracted to this particular moment in Church history as much for its humanism as for its literary and liturgical peculiarities. "As if in anticipation of the sixteenth century," he writes, "the church was becoming 'humanistic,' in an earlier and unimpeachable *Renaissance.*"[37] Pater emphasizes the expansiveness and inclusiveness of the Church and its reconciliation of the spirit and the flesh:

> With her full, fresh faith in the *Evangele,* in a veritable regeneration of the earth and the body, in the dignity of man's entire personal being for a season at least, at that critical period in the development of Christianity, she was for reason, for common sense, for fairness to human nature, and generally for what may be called the naturalness of Christianity . . . It was by the bishops of Rome, diligently transforming themselves, in the true catholic sense, into universal pastors, that the path of what we must call humanism was thus defined. (210)

Pater further notes that the Church delighted in its own aesthetic charm, "'the beauty of holiness', nay! the elegance of sanctity . . . , her evocative power over all that is eloquent and expressive in the better mind of man, her outward comeliness, her dignifying convictions about human nature" (210). Religious and aesthetic experience are deeply intertwined here, if not wholly indistinguishable. Moreover, Pater reasserts his notion of Christianity as a practice in flux, a practice that reforms itself with history rather than a doctrine that remains steadfast and static. In the Winckelmann essay Pater discusses the natural origins of ritual as a sentimental attachment to "certain usages of patriarchal life, the kindling of fire, the washing of the body, the slaughter of the flock, the gathering of harvest, holidays and dances" (*Renaissance,* 202). The solemnity of ritual, its sadness, reflects the human confrontation with death, "whenever its thoughts wander far from what is here, and now" (201). Ritual slowly takes on a "religious motive, losing its domestic character, and therefore becoming more and more inexplicable with each generation" (202).

In *Marius* Pater returns to his contention that Christian ritual retains the traces of its natural and pagan origins. Moreover, doctrine follows upon religious practice, continually transformed by it: "Our creeds are but the brief abstract of our prayer and song." In a particularly suggestive passage, Pater describes the sweetness and moderation—indeed, the spirit of appropriation—with which the early Church dealt with pagan influences: "The faithful were bent less on the destruction of the old pagan temples than on their conversion to a new and higher use; and, with much beautiful furniture ready to hand, they became Christian sanctuaries" (*Marius,* 211). Conversion becomes something more like acquisition in a decadent storing up of ruins and fragments, a "generous eclecticism" that assembles bits and pieces from various sources, "Gnostic, Jewish, pagan, to adorn and beautify the greatest act of worship the world has seen." With shades of Darwin, Pater describes the development of ritual through a natural evolutionary process: "Ritual, in fact, like all other elements of religion, must grow and cannot be made—grow by the same law of development which prevails everywhere else, in the moral as in the physical world" (212).

Pater elaborates on this evolutionary view of religion, and especially of ritual, in a bildungsroman and conversion narrative that follows the same law of development. Marius is a Paterian aesthete, an epicurean, who undergoes a series of conversions, from the pagan religion of Numa, through Epicureanism and Stoicism, toward the Roman Church. The religion of Numa is the very archetype for that "domestic" and "patriarchal" ritualism from which Pater believed the Christian religion originated. He offers a glimpse of High Church ritualism, the services he admired at Saint Alban's and Saint Barnabas, in the pagan rites of White-nights, Marius's childhood home. But amid the cloud of incense, the monotonous intonation of the liturgy, the antique vestments, we find the priests' "bearing ears of green corn upon their heads" (5), recalling this distant mirror of modern Catholicism to its origins in nature and pagan ritual.

Even more suggestive, I think, is the powerful presence of Marius's mother in the opening chapters of the novel. His father is dead and the solemn rituals of the religion of Numa, for whose significance the dead father acts as symbolic guarantor, weigh heavily on the son. His mother, however, is a figure of identification for the boy. She is defined by her role as *mater dolorosa,* perpetually in mourning for the dead father, tending to his memory as she tends to her young son, providing the archetype for Marius's conception of love as maternal and melancholic. She is a symbolic and originary presence in the novel, and she leaves her trace on every phase of Marius's life—his every conversion, his various religious and aesthetic philosophies—informing not only his view of women but also his love for men. Like the religion of Numa, the *mater dolorosa* as embodied by his mother is a figure to which Marius continually returns. Freud's reading of homosexuality through Pater and Leonardo—homosexual desire as the recurrence of the maternal trace in an enigmatic smile—is certainly relevant here. Pater has accomplished something rarely glimpsed in literature: while Christianity has traditionally presumed an identification with the paternal Word, Pater has chosen instead an affective Marianism, a faith inflected by homoerotic desire and maternal identification. The Christ of *Marius* is indeed the suffering figure of the New Testament, but envisioned only through the eyes of his mother, the Blessed Virgin.

Marius's own mother is his archetype for the Virgin Mother whom he later discovers among his Christian friends. She is the makings also for a new Gioconda; she is the recollection of the pagan and natural world in his every spiritual ambition; she will live and die many times through her son; her outlines are traceable not only in the spouseless

mothers Faustina, Cecilia, and the martyr Blandina, but also in
Marius's fondness for his many heroes, the priest of Aesculapius,
Flavian, Marcus Aurelius, and Cornelius. The outline of Marius's
religious humanism, however vague, is well known. But the matrix of
erotic fantasy through which this Christian web is threaded has been
virtually ignored.[38] In discussing the intersections of the religious with
the erotic and aesthetic in the story of Marius, I will limit myself to a
few remarks about his relationships with men and a reading of three
particularly dense and interconnected moments in the text: his childhood at White-nights, his visit to the tombs in Cecilia's house, and his
return to the tombs of his ancestors shortly before his death and
martyrdom.

In the opening paragraph of the novel, Pater reintroduces the juxtaposition of birth and death that he initiated in *The Renaissance*.
Although it emphasizes fertility and the harvest, the patriarchal religion of Numa is evidently in decay, a dying fragment of an earlier age
that survives in remote places despite the "triumph of Christianity."
Pater also speaks of the miraculous asexual birth of the child Romulus
from a spark and the "birthday sacrifice" in his honor. While the
religion of Numa appeals to Marius's "native instinct of devotion"
and his passion for beautiful ritual, it nevertheless leaves him feeling
ambivalent and alienated. Not only is he moved with pity at the
spectacle of the sacrifice and the terror of its victims, but there is also
a funereal hollowness in the "year-long burden of forms" (*Marius*, 4).
Even the liturgy itself had "long since become unintelligible" (5), read
from a scroll kept in a painted chest with the family records that is
reminiscent of the family urns to which Marius pays service.

Marius is ambivalent even toward his dead father, from whom he
has inherited his religion and his name. Far from identifying with the
senior Marius, the son regards his father and the deity itself with a
"devout circumspection" (11) and a fear of punishment that develops
into a paranoid fear of persecution, of an unnamed evil that dogs his
footsteps. Marius, like Pater, has only a vague recollection of his
father. He remembers a "tall, grave figure above him in early childhood," a man he found "a little severe and cold" (7). Marius desires
to be free of the punishing and authoritative father: "The feeling with
which he thought of his dead father was almost exclusively that of
awe; though crossed at times by a not unpleasant sense of liberty, as

he could but confess to himself, pondering, in the actual absence of so weighty and continual a restraint, upon the arbitrary power which Roman religion and Roman law gave to the parent over the son" (11). Marius has virtually traded places with his father, who is not only powerless to enforce his religious will but is also relegated to a childlike position, dependent on his own son for his sustenance in the grave, for the violets and honeycomb and the cake dipped in wine that accompany the daily service to the dead. Without this sustenance, the dead wander helplessly through the house, "crying sorrowfully in the stillness of the night" (7).

To complete the oedipal disruption of paternal authority, Marius takes his father's place beside his mother. He is free to identify with her: "Helping her with her white and purple wools, and caring for her musical instruments, he won, as if from the handling of such things, an urbane and feminine refinement, qualifying duly his country-grown habits" (13). In the soft lines of the white hands and face, set among the many folds of the veil and stole of the Roman widow, Marius finds the "typical expression of maternity" (13). In this line Pater establishes his recurrent symbol of whiteness and of the veil. Whiteness is something perfect, ideal, and imaginary, closely associated with maternity and the grave throughout his work; and the veil is for Pater what it has often symbolized in Western metaphysics: the boundary between life and death, the symbol and its referent, the aesthetic object and its spiritual significance, and, most of all here, the son and the sacred gaze of the mother. The white face of Marius's mother behind her mourning veil will be the type of all hidden and beautiful things in the novel. As in *The Renaissance,* mourning is an essential aspect of motherhood. Marius shares his mother's position of mourning for the father, who lives only through their grief. He enjoys a "subjective immortality," a kind of rebirth in death, "that secondary sort of life which we can give to the dead in our intensely realized memory of them" (13).

Marius's father is again refigured as the son, resurrected, reborn through a mother's love and mourning. But Marius inhabits the same position as his father in the sense that he too is the object of his mother's love, even her mourning, in a typically Paterian blending of death and maternal care: "And Marius the younger even thus early came to think of women's tears, of women's hands to lay one to rest, in death as in the sleep of childhood, as a sort of natural want" (13).

Love, as embodied by Marius's mother, is melancholic, "languid and shadowy," a "sustained freshness of regret," a "costly self-sacrifice" (11). But it is also spiritual and regenerative in a way that Marius thinks is impossible for men and yet available to him through identification with his mother: "It was a feeling which had in it something of religious veneration for life as such—for that mysterious essence which man is powerless to create in even the feeblest degree." This maternal, life-giving capacity for pity and for sympathy with the suffering and the dead begins in Marius as a love for animals, and "at the desire of his mother" he disengages his hunting traps (14). His mother likens his soul to a white bird entrusted to the safety of his bosom—a Christian and maternal metaphor recalling the conception of Christ in Mary by a dove in medieval painting.[39]

The Virgin Mother is an important figure for Pater precisely because of her tenderness, mercy, and pity, which modify the severity of patriarchal law. Marius may be seen in part as the humanistic progress of the patriarchal deity from the paternal to the Paterian, a slow conversion to his maternal ideal. Elsewhere, in his essay on Notre-Dame d'Amiens, Pater even associated patriarchal severity with Christ and designated Mary as the humanistic intercessor: "Nay, those grand and beautiful *people's* churches of the thirteenth century, churches pre-eminently of 'Our Lady,' concurred also with certain novel humanistic movements of religion itself at that period, above all with the expansion of what is reassuring and popular in the worship of Mary, as a tender and accessible, though almost irresistible, intercessor with her severe and awful Son."[40] Maternal tenderness becomes the spiritual prototype of all love for Marius, and his mother's presence, which so pervades White-nights, becomes a womb-like shrine to which he often returns, physically and symbolically: "And as his mother became to him the very type of maternity in things, its unfailing pity and protectiveness, and maternity itself the central type of all love;—so that beautiful dwelling-place lent the reality of concrete outline to a peculiar ideal of home, which throughout the rest of his life he seemed, amid many distractions of spirit, to be ever seeking to regain" (*Marius,* 14).

White-nights, the "beautiful dwelling-place" that seems like an extension of the maternal body, is itself a fine example of decadent architecture, permeated with Pater's peculiar understanding of the feminine. The house is "but the exquisite fragment of a once large and sumptuous villa," now in decay (12). In his description of the villa, Pater mentions Venus twice and the villa's famous head of the Medusa, that familiar icon of the horror of the feminine gaze. White-nights has been taken over by the oddly Marian spirituality of Marius's mother. "Something pensive, spellbound, and but half real, something cloistral or monastic, as we should say, united to this exquisite order, made the whole place seem to Marius, as it were, *sacellum,* the peculiar sanctuary, of his mother" (13).

White-nights is at once a religious space and a dream space, a convergence of the maternal and the imaginary, not unlike the paradoxical nonspace of maternal identification in psychoanalysis—what Julia Kristeva, troping on Plato, refers to as the maternal *chora.* This dream quality of the villa is even reflected in the etymology of its name, which suggests "nights not quite of blank forgetfulness, but passed in continuous dreaming, only half veiled by sleep." Pater repeats the "half-real," the image of the veil, and the sleep of children in his description of Marius's relationship with his mother. Maternal identification is a dream of sorts, an afterthought rendered visible in the house of the patriarchal real, itself in decay. For Marius, the dream is of his own generative capacity for life, even through his own self-sacrifice. And it is also the dream of a new vocation, his preparation for a priesthood beyond the religion of Numa. Pater describes the "white mass," which is "celebrated by young candidates for the priesthood with an unconsecrated host, by way of rehearsal" (9). White-nights is Marius's "church in progress," the ghostly and maternal beginning of his progression of philosophical conversions, his perpetual spiritual rehearsals.

Marius's ideal of love is not only maternal and melancholic but also virginal and homoerotic. However erotic Marius's attachments to young men are, Pater insists upon a Platonic self-restraint and moderation. After his night with the priest of Aesculapius, Marius recoils from any thought of excess in sleep, diet, or taste, "still more from any excess of a coarser kind" (21). His love for Flavian is romanticized into the "pure and disinterested friendship of schoolmates" (29), though we have to maintain a certain naïveté and historical blindness for that analogy to succeed. Marius's pleasures, especially in other men, have a strong masochistic and autoerotic element, displacing sex

in favor of self-sacrifice, *ascêsis,* mourning, and maternal identification. He spiritualizes his pleasures, and Pater speaks of "the sort of
mystic enjoyment he had in the abstinence, the strenuous self-control
and *ascêsis*" (15) of his priestly habits. Behind Pater's Christian ideals,
behind his Christian knights like Cornelius, there is the Platonic ideal
of Greek pederasty, disguised like Heine's gods in exile in the new
religion. Marius seems to panic at the thought of actual sexual contact
between men, or even between men and women. This anxiety is first
glimpsed in Marius's mysterious phobia regarding snakes, a fear that
has its antecedent in Pater's own childhood.

Significantly, Marius first learns of his phobia when he sees snakes
breeding, after which he can neither eat nor sleep. From a psychoanalytic perspective, the first explanation that springs to mind is "castra-
tion anxiety," and there is ample evidence in the text to support it.
Marius's horror of snakes, especially breeding ones, is associated with
a patriarchal religious presence, "the heavenly masters" who excite in
him a vague and paranoid fear of "unexplored evil, ever dogging his
footsteps" (14). Moreover, the phobia militates against the love for
animals inspired by his mother. The snakes recall the head of the
Medusa in White-nights and the legend of a feminine gaze turned to
a thing of horror in the patriarchal imagination. Eve and the serpent
also writhe nearby, though only implicitly.

The snakes seem to represent for Marius a ghostly paternal grimace,
a religious injunction against a certain pleasure in looking, a certain
lust of the eye. The very language with which the snakes are described
suggests a distinctly sexual punishment, as though Marius were in
danger of looking upon the phallus itself, naked and unveiled, as he
looked with an identificatory gaze at the whiteness of his mother's face
and hands behind her veil: "It was something like a fear of the supernatural, or perhaps rather a moral feeling, for the face of a great
serpent, with no grace of fur or feathers, so different from quadruped
or bird, has a sort of humanity of aspect in its spotted and clouded
nakedness. There was a humanity, dusty and sordid and as if far-gone
in corruption, in the sluggish coil, as it awoke suddenly into one
metallic spring of pure enmity against him" (15). The snakes are
especially difficult to interpret. On the one hand, they would seem to
connect Marius's distaste for the sexual act, whether between men or
between men and women, with a patriarchal prohibition. On the other

hand, this phobia soon disappears or, rather, is reconfigured as itself a veil, a mirage, to be pulled aside in the search for perfect love and perfect beauty in other men. Behind this veil of sexual panic stands the priest of Aesculapius and Flavian. I am reminded of Hélène Cixous's essay on the laugh of the Medusa. Through the eyes of the father we see only the face of a gorgon with snakes for hair, but behind that symbolic veil of horror the woman is laughing.

Marius's first contact with what he presumes to be a mysterious priest of Aesculapius, who is neither named nor seen again, occurs immediately after a feverish dream that is excited by the snake symbol of Aesculapius himself. Marius fears the healing god, however unjustifiably, as he fears the patriarchal deity of White-nights. Waking from this feverish dreaming, he sees a beautiful youth by his bedside instead of the snake he anticipated. Pater's description of the youth recalls Marius's relationship with both his mother and his father: "Ever afterwards, when the thought arose in his mind of some unhoped-for but entire relief from distress, like blue sky in a storm at sea, would come back the memory of that gracious countenance which, amid all the kindness of its gaze, had yet a certain air of predominance over him, so that he seemed now for the first time to have found the master of his spirit. It would have been sweet to be the servant of him who now sat beside him speaking." (19) The kind and gracious bedside manner of the priest recalls the protective hands of Marius's mother laying him to rest in the sleep of childhood. The room where he sleeps is white-walled with a white and serpentine road leading up to it, and it shares the dream-like, cloistral quality of the *sacellum* of Marius's mother. But in his predominance and mastery over his willing servant, the priest resembles Marius's father. In his attraction to certain men—the priest, Flavian, Aurelius, and Cornelius—Marius seems to be searching for an androgynous ideal, like the man with the flowing hair in the classical frontispiece to *The Renaissance*. Pater has maternalized and homoeroticized the father, replacing the grave and severe countenance with a sweetly Hellenic one: a youth who lectures from Plato's *Phaedrus,* who speaks of the amusements of young men, of certain influences diffused by fair things and fair persons visibly present.

Marius is not altogether sure he has not dreamed the encounter, since the next morning he cannot find his night visitor anywhere. What he finds instead are the *"Houses of Birth and Death,* erected for the reception respectively of women about to become mothers, and of persons about to die; neither of those incidents being allowed to defile, as was thought, the actual precincts of the shrine" (21). There is a certain patriarchal aggression toward mothers among the "brotherhood of Asclepidae" (22), and their cult is one of sanity, the eternal youth and health of the male body. The priest of the dream, with his discourse on vision and beauty, appeals to the "morbid religious idealism" of Marius mentioned in the first sentence of the chapter. Death and birth, like the mothers and the dying, like the priest of Marius's dream, remain invisible in the shrine. Despite Marius's renewed health, the chapter ends with the death of his mother, whom he has slighted in a "sudden, incomprehensible petulance" (25).[41]

The snakes as a veil of horror over perfect love also figure in Marius's fondness for Flavian. Marius has the same master-servant relationship with Flavian, who dominates him with the privilege of a natural aristocracy even though he is a "lad of servile birth" (29). Flavian is a paragon of pagan spirituality and male beauty who seems to embody the various forms of matriarchal worship around him. He is at once the serpent and the glimpse of the ideal beyond its veil. Marius dwells on the paradox: "How often, afterwards, did evil things present themselves in malign association with the memory of that beautiful head . . . To Marius, at a later time, he counted for as it were an epitome of the whole pagan world, the depth of its corruption, and its perfection of form" (31). He embodies the maternal concurrence of corruption and rebirth. His fascination with euphuism, which is essentially the philosophy of decadent style, is at once a celebration of the decay of Latin literature and a "sacred service to the mother-tongue" (56). He is delighted by the macabre, "that species of almost insane preoccupation with the materialities of our mouldering flesh, that luxury of gazing at corruption" (36), and yet his great poem is a "nuptial hymn, which, taking its start from the thought of nature as the universal mother, celebrates the preliminary pairing and mating together of all fresh things in the hot and genial springtime" (64). He stands between a dying Latin tongue and "the rhyming middle age, just about to dawn," envisioning the "decrepit old Roman architecture about him rebuilding on an intrinsically better pattern" (64–65).

All the matriarchal goddesses of this chapter are a little cruel, and their countenances are tinged with a knowledge of death. Most important is Venus, a figure recalled from White-nights, but also the subject of Flavian's nocturne, *Pervigilium Veneris,* and the cruel mother of Apuleius's story, who sends Psyche on a journey into Hades. There is also the "archaic beauty, though a little cruel perhaps," of the Siren Ligeia. In Apuleius's story, we find Ceres, the goddess of fertility, who mourns for her daughter Proserpine, the mistress of death in Hades. Isis is described as "that new rival or 'double,' of ancient Venus," and her brotherhood of devotees bear with them the all-consuming sacred flame of the "mother-hearth" in another of Pater's numerous pagan revisions of Catholic ritualism. In his almost Bacchic enthusiasm for Isis, Flavian is stricken with the fever that eventually kills him, and his "pagan end" is the most moving part of the book. Marius tends to Flavian vigilantly as life slips away; he weeps over him and climbs into bed with him to lend him the warmth of his body, recalling from White-nights the women's tears and women's hands that "lay one to rest, in death as in the sleep of childhood." In Flavian's death Marius realizes in himself the love of the *mater dolorosa* he recognized in his own mother, and in an odd play on pregnancy and his mother's mourning ritual, he carries away "the urn of the deceased in the folds of his toga, to its last resting-place in the cemetery beside the highway" (68).

The tale of Cupid and Psyche, quoted at length from Apuleius, is another important development of the motherhood and serpent themes with respect to homoerotic friendship. The tale functions as an allegorical comment on Marius's own thinking, especially with regard to Flavian. Marius draws from the tale an understanding not only of perfect love and flawless beauty but also of "the fatality which seems to haunt any signal beauty, whether moral or physical, as if it were in itself something illicit and isolating: the suspicion and hatred it so often excites in the vulgar" (53)—a comment that reads like a sidelong glance at Victorian homophobia. Flavian and Marius read the book together in a romantic setting—"How like a picture!" (33)—in an old granary, buried among heaps of corn (echoing the corn of Ceres in the tale) that are transformed by the sunlight into heaps of gold (echoing Psyche's golden castle).

In the story, Psyche offends Venus, "the benign mother of the world" (37), by being so beautiful that she outshines the goddess herself. She is therefore forced into a marriage, a "deadly bridal" with an "evil serpent-thing" (38). She never sees her bridegroom because he comes to her only as an invisible but "unclothed" voice in the night, making love to her and then departing hastily at dawn (39). She loves the serpent in spite of herself, delighted that she carries its child, but her sisters convince her to strike off its head as it sleeps. In attempting the deed, however, she finds that the serpent is in fact Cupid, Love himself, the son of Venus. He fears she wishes to wound him, and he punishes her by flying away. Venus intervenes, insisting that Psyche demonstrate her worthiness to be the mistress of Love by performing various impossible tasks, including stealing an urn of water from the serpents by the river Styx. She must also bring a casket to Ceres's daughter Proserpine in Hades, and she is nearly killed when she opens it and finds only the sleep of death. She is finally exonerated by the "father of the gods" (52), though he is vexed by Cupid, and Venus dances sweetly at the wedding of Psyche and her son.

In Pater's story Marius becomes the Psyche figure, presuming to take the place of the mother of Beauty and Love. The story of her tasks becomes a devotion to Venus in both her maternity and cruelty, a devotion that sends her pregnant among the shadows of the dead. Pater uses a heterosexual myth of Beauty smitten by a male figure of Love to modify the love between Marius and Flavian. Marius is again envisioned as maternal, just as Psyche is sometimes deemed masculine, such as when she puts by her sex to kill the serpent or when she plots to dress like a man and seduce Venus. Most suggestive, I think, is the great "serpent-thing" that functions as a veil for Love himself, recalling Marius's phobia of snakes. As with the priest of Marius's dream, the fear of the serpent is a veil, an unjustified fear that gives way to a beautiful man, the very embodiment of perfection; and this time he is a youth of classic Paterian androgyny: "She sees the locks of that golden head, pleasant with the unction of the gods, shed down in the graceful entangle behind and before, about the ruddy cheeks and white throat" (44). Through Marius's love for Flavian, Pater develops a new ethic of desire, beauty, language, and spirituality that, however "virile," retains the traces of identification with a maternal ideal.

The visit to Cecilia's house is especially dense with references to death and motherhood, and Cornelius, who guides Marius through the house, represents the final Christian phase of Pater's homoerotic ethic. As with the priest and Flavian, Cornelius's appearance on the scene is preceded by Marius's usual paranoia, an echo of his childhood religion and fear of snakes. He likens his mysterious distress to the fear of a child at the coming of night, and he feels the "touch upon his heel" of a falling stone—an image suggestive of the serpent of Genesis, fated to bite man on the heel. "That was sufficient just then to rouse out of its hiding-place his old vague fear of evil—of one's 'enemies'" (95). Like the voice of the priest, the voice of Cornelius comes to Marius as an antidote to his fear as he lies in bed at night. In dreams he hears the "youthful voice, with a reassuring clearness of note," calling his name (96). Unlike the priest, Cornelius is still there the next morning, and he is the first thing Marius sees upon looking out the window. More than Flavian, Cornelius is a spiritualization of the male body, his physical beauty qualified by a military *ascêsis* and idealism that the pagan sensualist lacked. Although Marius's love for Cornelius seems even more virginal than his love for Flavian, Pater leaves little doubt as to the homoeroticism of the attraction. The long passage in which Marius watches Cornelius dress in full knightly regalia is especially suggestive and ends with the line: "And as he gleamed there, amid that odd interchange of light and shade, with the staff of a silken standard firm in his hand, Marius felt as if he were face to face for the first time with some new knighthood or chivalry, just then coming into the world" (97). This new chivalry as homoerotic ethic is not only an echo of the "chivalrous conscience" (55) awakened in Flavian but is also a suggestion of the sexual ethic of certain late-Victorian homosexual apologists, especially Charles Kains-Jackson, whose essay on male sexual comradeship "The New Chivalry" reads like a parody of Pater's novel.[42]

Pater sees the relationship between Marius and Cornelius as an aestheticization of marriage and maternal love—a White-nights dream given palpable masculine form. Their love is the same but different. Marius speaks of his "intimate companionship" with Cornelius, who reminds him of his mother's story of the soul as a white bird. At one point Marius finds himself among a multitude of mothers, all straining "to touch the lightning-struck image of the wolf-nurse of Romulus—so tender to little ones!—just discernible in its dark shrine" (*Marius*, 106–107). Marius is not gazing at the icon, however, but at Cornelius, as his friend turns away, singing. Pater repeats the image at the somewhat funereal wedding ceremony that opens the chapter entitled "Manly Amusements." The marriage of Lucilla and Lucius Verus is ironically balanced with the ritual sacrifices at the end of the chapter—animal slaughter in which the young are ripped from their mothers' bosoms. Marius turns from the wedding celebration to find himself face to face with Cornelius: "It was a relief to depart with him—so fresh and quiet he looked, though in all his splendid equestrian array in honour of the ceremony—from the garish heat of the marriage scene" (133). Cornelius is the homoerotic Christian refiguration of maternity, the marriage bed, and traditional manly amusements.

The ideal of maternal love that Cornelius turns toward is a Christian one, especially as it is embodied in Saint Cecilia, who seems to model herself after the Virgin. In a visit to Cecilia's house, Marius finally discovers the Christian secret behind Cornelius's beauty and strength and peers behind his enigmatic "veil of reserve." (194) Like Whitenights, the house is an "expansion of the body" of Cecilia, who is also a mother in mourning for her husband, himself a saint (194). The house is also another example of decadent architecture, and Pater's description recalls La Gioconda, not to mention the cathedral of Huysmans' Salomé:

> It was the old way of the true *Renaissance* . . .—conceiving the new organism by no sudden and abrupt creation, but rather by the action of a new principle upon elements all of which had in truth already lived and died many times. The fragments of older architecture, the mosaics, the spiral columns, the precious corner-stones of immemorial building, had put on, by such juxtaposition, a new and singular expressiveness, an air of grave thought, of an intellectual purpose, itself aesthetically very seductive. (196)

Conception and creation become virginal and maternal acts of artistic reconfiguration of dead things. Pater describes the house as a "bride adorned for her husband," and yet Cecilia's husband is dead. Pater also marvels at the paradoxical thought of "chaste women and their children" (197) and "the virginal beauty of the mother and her children" (202), without so much as a hint of irony. Close by this maternal house are the family tombs, a "hollow cavern or crypt" accessible from the rest of the house by a "narrow opening cut in the steep side" (197), suggestive once again of Pater's association of womb and tomb.

Cornelius gives Marius a guided tour of this "necropolis," and their passage into the narrow cavern is construed poetically as a return to the mother and White-nights. They come to an "altar-tomb" adorned for some "anniversary observance" that lends a strange nuptial quality to their macabre procession together. Pater does not spare us any of the necrophiliac sensuality of this tour, such as when Marius finds himself "cheek to cheek" with the dead in a narrow corridor (198). There are many children, both in the house and in the tomb. The singing of the children of Cecilia's household reminds Marius of Cornelius's enigmatic singing and connects its mystery with the Christian inscriptions of hope on the children's graves. The singing children and the dead children are linked in Marius's imagination, and later he sees Cecilia actually burying one of the children. He is filled with pity and—the word pervades the final chapters of the book—with hope.

Marius experiences neither disgust nor horror in the tombs, but rather a sense of rebirth through Christian hope: "About one sepulchre in particular, distinguished in this way, and devoutly arrayed for what by a bold paradox was thus treated as *natalitia*—a birthday" (199). His raising of Cornelius's "veil of reserve" and his discovery of the meaning of Christian hope are construed in images of male marriage and maternity amid the inspiring fragments of dead things. *"Yet hast Thou brought up my life from corruption"* (200) reads a biblical inscription on a grave (Jon. 2:6), offering a glimpse of Cornelius's parental role in the ideal toward which Marius is converting. The Christian hope of resurrection, or even a pagan and rather vampiristic waking of the dead, impresses Marius as a spiritual possibility. With the lifting of Cornelius's veil, Pater makes another reference to the Medusa, at once recalling and diffusing at last Marius's old anxiety about snakes, death, and the feminine gaze: "Might this new vision, like the malignant beauty of pagan Medusa, be exclusive of any admiring gaze upon anything but itself? At least he suspected that, after the beholding of it, he could never again be altogether as he had been before" (202).

Marius begins to conceive of a deity through his ideal of homoerotic friendship, in particular through Cornelius, moving from that "mere fantasy of a self not himself, beside him in his coming and going, to those divinations of a living and companionable spirit in all things" (179). This new companion is certainly a sublimation of his friendships with Flavian and Cornelius: "besides Flavian, besides Cornelius even, . . . some other companion, an unfailing companion, ever at his side throughout" (178). He likens this companion to the Father of Men in the New Testament, but finds his origins in the love of his male comrade, just as "one builds up, from act and word and expression of the friend actually visible at once's side, an ideal of the spirit within him" (179). This new companion is, like the other ones, a reconception of the father as brotherly, creative, even maternal. His new ideal recalls the generosity and hope of his mother, rather than the severity of his father.

Marius's identification with Christ is also an identification with the *mater dolorosa*. Christ himself, like Marius's mother, is "mournful"— "a figure which seemed to have absorbed, like some rich tincture in his garment, all that was deep-felt and impassioned in the experiences of the past" (217). He is also, like Marius's mother, a figure of ritual self-sacrifice, surrounded by Marius and other male worshipers who surrender their youth, their greatest gifts, even themselves, for the feeling of hope he affords. Marius also finds a model of self-sacrifice in Cecilia and, more dramatically, in Blandina, the mother and saint who undergoes all manner of torments for her faith. Pater's descriptions of Blandina recall Huysmans' fascination with torture and saintly suffering, as she is hung from a stake and offered as food to wild beasts. Witnesses see through her the Christ of the Crucifixion. Through the power to inspire conversion, the Virgin Mother, like the virginal mothers Blandina and Cecilia, gives life in a manner like resurrection: "such as were fallen away retraced their steps—were again conceived, were filled again with lively heat, and hastened to make the profession of their faith" (250).

Marius's maternal identification is further suggested by his return to White-nights shortly before his own martyrdom. He returns to the tombs, where he sees an infant moldering in a fractured coffin. He notices that, side by side with his mother, there is a boy of his own age, a serving boy who "had taken filial place beside her there, in his stead" (257). In this revision of the opening chapters, Marius is now the one who mourns, both for his mother and for his place beside her as the beloved child, even as the child for whom she mourns. This renewed desire for his mother's love after the visit to the tombs is physical to the point of necrophilia: "Dead yet sentient and caressing hands seemed to reach out of the ground and to be clinging about him" (258).

Marius's final self-sacrifice, risking his own life to save Cornelius, is a further effort at renewing maternal identification. It is a longing for death that is at once a longing to take his place with his mother and also to take her place as *mater dolorosa,* she who suffers to give life to her beloved. It is a masochistic longing for death that is a longing for rebirth. Marius's love for Cornelius takes on a parental tone: "'More than brother!'—he felt—'like a son also!'" (258). Marius achieves a new life through this son. "Identifying himself with Cornelius in so dear a friendship, through him Marius seemed to touch, to ally himself to, actually to become a possessor of the coming world; even as happy parents reach out, and take possession of it, in and through the survival of their children" (259).

Marius even begins to suspect that Cornelius, if saved, will marry Cecilia, such that Marius would be in effect bringing about the marriage between the virginal mother and the Christ figure, recalling his own relationship with his mother. This giving of oneself to save one's friend is a recurrent homoerotic gesture in Pater, from Amis and Amile to Jasmin and Raoul. Here it also becomes Marius's final realization of his mother's old dream, to give the beloved new life through her suffering. In doing so, Marius also becomes something of a child to be mourned, his mind wandering sleeplessly in fever, "like a child, thinking over the toys it loves, one after another" (266). He is left to die among Christians whose gentle fingers "applied to hands and feet, to all those old passage-ways of the sense" (267), recall the women's tears and women's hands of his mother at White-nights. Marius's conversion to Christianity is only an implicit and tenuous one, the entertainment of Christian hope as a possibility. His martyrdom, moreover, is virtually accidental, the interpretation given to his life by the Christians who bury him. Nevertheless, through Marius, Pater succeeds at evoking in Christian forms the traces of maternal and homoerotic desire that, like Heine's pagan gods in exile, find another vocation under the new dispensation.

## Monkish Miracles

Every age of European thought has had its Cyrenaics or Epicureans, under many disguises: even under the hood of the monk.

Walter Pater

To the eye of true taste, an Aquinas in his cell before a crucifix, or a Narcissus gazing at himself in a still fountain, are—in their own ways, you know—equally beautiful.

Mr. Rose

Despite his preference for the Renaissance over the Middle Ages, Pater began to take a greater interest in gothic art later in his life. His imaginary portraits are populated by a number of monks, even though medieval asceticism, unlike Greek *ascêsis,* is often associated in his early work with lifeless dogma and the denial of the body. Monasticism attracted Pater for several reasons. First, its association with mysticism lends an emotional and imaginative idealism to the severity of its rubric. Also, its paradoxical blending of chastity and sensuousness resonates with Pater's own virginal aestheticism. In *Marius the Epicurean* Pater draws only the finest of lines between the saint and the epicurean, bringing Marius to the verge of Christian martyrdom. He writes that "the saint, and the Cyrenaic lover of beauty, it may be thought, would at least understand each other better than either would understand the mere man of the world. Carry their respective positions a point further, shift the terms a little, and they might actually touch" (152). If, as Huysmans' wrote, even the satanist and the mystic touch in the Beyond, so might the aesthete and the monk, each aspiring to that gem-like intensity of experience that transcends the banality of modern life.

In his portrait of Giordano Bruno in *Gaston de Latour,* an unfinished romance, Pater explores the possibility of aestheticism even under the cowl of a monk. Monasticism also provides Pater with a chaste homoerotic ideal. He was intrigued by the notion of a male community whose shared idealism and love for one another is organized around the suffering and androgynous figure of Christ or the melancholic and maternal figure of the Virgin, and he might have found the outline of such a homosexual community in the Anglo-Catholic services he attended. In two of his stories, "Denys l'Auxerrois" (1886) and "Apollo in Picardy" (1893), Pater explores the possibilities of desire between men in a monastic setting, drawing as well upon images of death and maternity such as inform his earlier work. Furthermore, in both these stories, we can also glimpse Pater's gothic side. He was attracted to the violence and eroticism of gothic style, although he often criticized it as rude or grotesque.

In *Gaston de Latour* Pater follows an autobiographical pattern not unlike that of *Marius*, tracing the development of a priestly child from a naive Christianity, to skepticism, to an epicureanism that includes Christianity within its scope. He again challenges the distinction between the spiritual and the sensuous, and Catholic ritual is one of the sites of their reconciliation. Pater's description of Chartres Cathedral prefigures Huysmans' *La Cathédrale* in its passion for ritualism, vestments, and holy relics. Like Huysmans' novel, *Gaston de Latour* is an erotic and philosophical museum, a decadent collection of old French fragments, intellectual and emotional curiosities presented as imaginary portraits of Ronsard, Montaigne, Giordano Bruno, and Marguerite of Valois, among others. Pater offers for consideration not only the cruel "love for love's sake," sadomasochistic desire as a rival religion exemplified by Jasmin, Raoul, and the Queen of Navarre, but also the aging Ronsard, "the priest who should have sacrificed a goat to pagan Bacchus"[43] and the "undulant" Montaigne, in mourning for his friend Etienne de la Boétie (another Flavian, it seems) and leaning effortlessly toward the Roman Church.

The artists and historical figures of *Gaston,* like many of those in *Marius,* bring the soul to the surface. They make it visible for the pleasure and contemplation of the one unifying consciousness, that of Gaston himself, a passive and receptive figure who, like Marius, is capable of embracing a number of different ideas at once in tenuous juxtaposition. Christianity is articulated within a decadent aesthetic of cultural and subjective fragmentation, and it figures as a recurrent possibility in an inconclusive series of religious and philosophical conversions. The novel even begins in a singularly decadent setting, a house that recalls Des Esseintes's retreat at Fontenay even more than White-nights does, though Pater is quick to point out the absence of any "social decadence" (4) in Gaston's family. Like the romance in which it appears, Gaston's house, the Château of Deux-manoirs, has been left unfinished. Its gothic peculiarities are numerous, and Pater notes the doubleness of the house, its "irregularity of groundplan," and its tendency to "architectural caprice" (2). The house also has a homoerotic origin, for one of its halves is called the Château d'Amour and, united with its other, marks the union of two brothers who could not bear to be apart.

From a description of Deux-manoirs, spiced with a familiar odor of decadence and medieval Catholicism, Pater leads us through a progression of imaginary portraits that reflect transformations, or perhaps accumulations, in Gaston's thought. In one of these portraits, that of the monk Giordano Bruno, Pater is especially adept at navigating the blurry line between mysticism and eroticism, not to mention Catholic faith and aesthetic pleasure. The chapter is condescendingly called "The Lower Pantheism," but it reverberates with Pater's own conceptions of Christianity. He moves back and forth from what appear to be distinct and mutually exclusive conceptual registers—between the spiritual and the sensuous and between the religious and the aesthetic—in an effort at complicating any such essential boundary.

Bruno is the Paterian aesthete with a monk's tonsure. He is inspired with a "dangerous mysticism" (140), a pantheistic diffusion of God throughout the sensible world and an artistic reconception of himself as a participant in the divine creative function. As a teacher, he means to move men's minds and "bring them to birth" (157). He appears in Pater's book just at the moment when Gaston despairs of the sterility of Catholicism, the preoccupation with the empty tomb and the death of Christ, unmediated by "the gaieties of Easter morning, the congratulations to the Divine Mother" (134). Bruno, through a certain "maternity of soul" (161), reintroduces Gaston to the sensuousness and creative spirit of Roman Catholicism—a religious joy, an exalted inebriation, and an unmistakably erotic enthusiasm. Bruno is inspired by pagan literature and is therefore yet another of Pater's gods in exile. From Plato and the Christian Platonists, he derives the "analogy between the flights of intellectual enthusiasm and those of physical love, with an animation which shows clearly enough the reality of his experience of the latter" (146). His religious verse is amorous, speaking of union and of man as the spouse of God, treading that highly contested ground between spiritual love and chivalric eroticism. He has a passion for ritualism—all the "influences of the convent, the sweet, heady incense, the pleading sounds, the sophisticated light and air, the grotesque humours of old gothic carvers, the thick stratum of pagan sentiment beneath all this,—*Santa Maria sopra Minervam!*— are indelible in him" (147–148). Complementing the sensuality of his religion is the sensuality of his language, which seems the very epitome of decadent style: "His rank, un-weeded eloquence, abounding in play of words, rabbinic allegories, verses defiant of prosody, in the kind of erudition he professed to despise, with here and there a shameless image . . . was akin to the heady wine, the sweet, coarse odours, of that fiery, volcanic soil, fertile in such irregularities as manifest power" (156).

Pater insists upon Bruno's monasticism despite his liberation from the stricter confines of his order. "Bruno, the escaped monk, is still a monk; and his philosophy, impious as it might seem to some, a religion; very new indeed, yet a *religion*" (153). In his portrait of Bruno, Pater comes closest to his French contemporaries Verlaine and Huysmans and their nostalgia for a medieval religious enthusiasm and a more boldly physical experience of faith. Pater is finally critical of Bruno not for any lapse in orthodoxy, but rather for a failure to make finer distinctions, to recognize difference, nuance, and proportion. It is not a moral fault, but an aesthetic one, a failure to distinguish "what was right and wrong in the matter of art" (161).

"Denys l'Auxerrois" is another portrait of a monk that addresses the conflict between the sacred body and the profane body, though it is far less optimistic. Renaissance harmony gives way to the violence of the gothic grotesque. Pater's notion of the Renaissance as a triumphant resurrection of a more sensuous spirituality within Roman Catholic discourse is an aspect of both "Denys l'Auxerrois" and "Apollo in Picardy," but within the generic context of the gothic, this rebirth is suffered to abort. The portrait of Denys begins in a typically decadent fashion, with a scholarly narrator searching among antique relics. The story of Denys is pieced together from fragments of medieval tapestry and stained glass that are dutifully hunted down by a visitor to the the cathedral town of Auxerre. This textual grave-digging complements another grave-digging within the medieval narrative itself, the unearthing of a Greek coffin in which is found an old bottle of Roman wine. The wine generates a virtual Renaissance among the townspeople, who are thereby inspired to complete their unfinished cathedral. The wine is also closely associated with the appearance of the beautiful youth Denys and is one of the ways by which Pater associates the birth of Denys with both the resurrection of Christ and a profane and vampiristic awakening of Dionysus from the grave.

The Paterian *mater dolorosa* is another important figure in this story. The wine bottle, which is also compared to the Holy Grail, glows green like an emerald fetus among the ashes in the exhumed coffin. Denys, the embodiment of this regeneration, is born twice more in the story. His first appearance in the cathedral is construed poetically as a rebirth among men—significantly, on Easter Day. The scene is a ball game, a "peculiar usage" of dubious origin, celebrated with solemnity by the canons and various children. When Denys appears out of nowhere to join the game, the clergymen are suddenly filled with enthusiasm, "a delightful glee which became contagious."[44] "Amazing levity" and "boisterous amusement" ensue (58), and even the eighty-year-old Dean of the Chapter lifts his purple skirt to play. The homoeroticism of Denys's presence is further underscored by the uncanny charm he exercises on the monk Hermes, whose name recalls the guide of departed souls to Hades. The third and last account of Denys's resurrection is his actual birth. He is born a bastard, and in childbirth his mother is struck dead by lightning. He emerges literally from the dead and profane body of his mother. He is a Christ figure, charismatic, regenerative, humble, his birth a kind of resurrection, and yet Pater inverts the New Testament story, making Denys a pagan and Bacchic Christ, born into a hostile Christian world that he will transform.

If Christ revitalized the soul for humankind, Denys rejuvenates the body for the pious townspeople. Auxerre experiences another golden age and, with the inspiration of some miraculous wine seasons, the beautiful cathedral is completed. This familiar gesture of Renaissance harmony is confounded, however, by the failure of the spirit and the flesh, the sacred and the pagan, to coexist peaceably. The gothic violence of this story is far more disturbing than anything in Pater's earlier studies of the Renaissance. Pater reveals an essential horror in both sensuality and spirituality, insofar as they are wholly divorced from each other. Denys is both a Christ figure and a pagan threat to the people of Auxerre. He is the wine god, the beautiful Hellenic youth born outside the Church; but he is also the town's redeemer, even their Holy Grail, and his sacrificial murder in monk's dress is reminiscent of Christ's Passion: "Denys certainly, with all his flaxen fairness about him, was manifestly a sufferer" (67). The pious respond to him as though he were a demon, but their Christian outrage seems strangely brutal and pagan. Like vampires, they are excited to murderous frenzy at the sight of blood on Denys's lip. In their superstition, they bury a child alive in the cathedral. Religion denies the body, and the body rebels against religion.

Perhaps the most decadent figure of this discord is the unnamed saint whose improper burial is thought to have brought misfortune on Auxerre. His body has shriveled away, as though from severe penance even after death, and its mere presence acts upon Denys like an exorcism. This image of the body wholly spiritualized is nevertheless a perverse and gorgeous figure of horror and Catholic decadence. The ghastly features of the corpse are still recognizable, and the odor of its moldering remains is distinguishable through the clouds of incense in the cathedral. The saint is reinterred in a new shrine, ornamented by goldsmiths and lapidaries. This second burial of the saint, which suggests a symbolic effort to reconcile the body to the spirit, complements another reinterment in the story, that of Denys's mother. Denys digs up his mother, who, because of her sexual crime, has not been given a Christian burial, and he reinters her within the cloister where he lives. Pater again presents an echo of the *Pietà*, here inverted—the son in mourning for the mother. Pity and tenderness seem to be missing from Christianity, and their recovery is likened to the recovery of a lost and profane body, a maternal body, by a devoted son in a transgressive act at once necrophiliac and incestuous. The medieval narrative ends on a keynote of fragmentation and discord as the people of Auxerre tear to pieces the body of Denys, the Dionysus with a tonsure, but then bury his heart in the cathedral. Pater makes no redemptive gestures in the modern narrative that frames the story of Denys, but rather leaves it to his narrator to note the medieval atmosphere of certain days on which the tortured figure of Denys can be seen among modern men.

"Apollo in Picardy" is no less violent, though it ends on a note of Christian hope. It is another allegory of the harmony and discord of body and spirit in which Hellenic figures act as gods in exile within a Christian context. It is also one of Pater's most homoerotic stories and is, indeed, an allegory of Greek pederastia in exile within a repressive Christian context. Desire between men becomes in this story a visionary and musical experience—not only physical, but spiritual and textual—as it breaks through repression in images of male beauty. This disruptive desire is also captured in Pater's recurrent symbol of the golden ring, at once mystical and natural, which appears most spectacularly as the dream of a circlet of flame surrounding the earth, but also as an aurora, a golden moon, a halo, a discus, even the tonsure of a beautiful monk. This resonant symbol of the golden ring, whether mystical or marital or sphincteral, suggests a lost pleasure, a sensation of wholeness, that seems to herald the return of the sensuous and erotic body into the repressive monastic world of the main character, Prior Saint-Jean.

As with "Denys l'Auxerrois," Pater begins this story with textual fragments, a bit of Teutonic scholarship on the Hyperborean Apollo and "a certain manuscript taken from an old monastic library in France at the Revolution."[45] Volume Twelve of Prior Saint-Jean's scholarly work is notably strange. We learn of its "confusion," "baffling inequalities," and "irregularly formed pages" (122–123). It breaks off with an unfinished word. Its peculiarities seem to be symptomatic of an episode in the life of some madman. The prior's volume bears all the marks of a decadent text. The sensuousness and music of the written word rebel against its own denotation, even its own crabbed script: "Soft wintry auroras seemed to play behind whole pages of crabbed textual writing, line and figure bending, breathing, flaming, into lovely 'arrangements' that were like music made visible; till writing and writer changed suddenly, 'to one thing constant never,' after the known manner of madmen in such work" (123). These soft wintry auroras are the textual correlative of Prior Saint-Jean's well-deserved vacation from the monastery and his concomitant discovery of male beauty and childlike pleasure in the form of his young companion, the monk Hyacinthus, "the pet of the community" (125), and another monk he meets, Apollyon.

"Apollo in Picardy" is a conversion narrative in that Prior Saint-Jean moves from the repressive rubric of his life as a monk toward a Paterian harmony of body and spirit within a monastic community of men. His very name suggests the Saint John of the Gospels, that most Greek celebrant of Christian love. The narrative follows Pater's typical movement from gothic discord to Renaissance harmony, but the conversion ends in violence and failure. The monastic order in which the prior has grown up is a strictly spiritual and textual domain, an abode of prayer and scholarship, guarded from the secular world by fortified medieval walls. As the prior looks down from his high tower at the stifling streets below, it is clear that his denial of the body has extended to a denial of the body's maternal origin, since he realizes only vaguely that one of those streets is the street where he was born.

The very idea of a trip to the Grange, a temporary move to the country "for the benefit of his body's health," fills his mind with strange misgivings and thoughts of pagan wickedness. The dream that the prior has the night before his departure is especially suggestive of paranoid pleasure, the concomitant feelings of fear and sexual excitement in the loosening of repression:

> He saw the very place in which he lay (he knew it! his little inner cell, the brown doors, the white breadth of wall, the black crucifix upon it) alight, alight softly; and looking, as he fancied, from the window, saw also a low circlet of soundless flame, waving, licking daintily up the black sky, but harmless, beautiful, closing in upon that round dark space in the midst, which was the earth. He seemed to feel upon his shoulder just then the touch of his friend beside him. "It is hell-fire!" he said. (125)

This dream passage unites the sacred and the profane in a single mystical vision. The burning circlet is at once a crown, "harmless, beautiful" as it closes on the head of Christ, itself reconfigured here as the earth; but it is also a ring of fire that turns the earth into the dark abyss of hell. Richard Dellamora is wise to note the suggestion of homoeroticism in the touch of the friend, not to mention the hint of "analingus and anal copulation" in the brown doors, the licking flame, and the round dark space of the earth.[46]

I would add that the ring around the dark earth, construed symbolically as an orifice, is another example of Pater's numerous womb-as-tomb images closely associated with the feminized male body. The dream is generated by his fear of returning to the world of his birth outside the monastic walls, but we might also consider other references to birth in which life and death, or sin and redemption, are juxtaposed—often with homoerotic undertones. In a feudal tower, for example, the monks keep a pigeon-house in which the birds are "encouraged to grow plump, and to breed, in perfect self-content," even though in the same paragraph Pater refers to the birds as a "feathered brotherhood" ("Apollo," 136). Later, Apollyon brutally slaughters the birds on Christmas, leaving them to soak in "pale milky blood" (137)—a scene that Pater ironically juxtaposes with the Feast of the Nativity. The appearance of Apollyon himself is likened to the asexual birth of Adam and the taint of original sin, "the old Adam fresh from his Maker's hand" (127). Apollyon has extraordinary curative power and is at one point depicted with a newborn lamb in his arms; but he is also thought to "scatter seeds of disease" from his "serpent-skin bag" (133). His very name is a misreading by the prior, who mistakes Apollo for the Apollyon of Revelations, the king of the bottomless pit.

The prior's dream is followed by a description of Hyacinthus and a passage into another orifice, the landscape of the so-called *vallis monachorum,* or monksvale. In a reconfiguration of the dream vision, Pater describes the vale as an "oval cup" over which shines a "golden moon" and pearly clouds with light and heat "in their hollows" (126). The vale is an idyllic place of springtime and awakened sexual desire, but also open graves and white gravestones. Once they enter it the monks become childlike in their pleasure. "By night chiefly, in its long, continuous twilights, Hyacinth became really a boy at last, with immense gaiety," Pater writes, qualifying this return to childhood innocence with the ominous presence of twilight shadows (134).

The homoeroticism of the monksvale world is obvious from Pater's numerous allusions to the myth of Apollo and Hyacinthus, and it is reinforced by the prior's fondness for Hyacinthus and his fascination with Apollyon, whose every appearance before the prior reads like a paean to androgynous male beauty: "Could one fancy a single curve bettered in the rich, warm, white limbs; in the haughty features of the face, with the golden hair, tied in a mystic knot, fallen down across the inspired brow?" (127). In giving way to this sensual pleasure in the company and the bodies of their companions, Hyacinthus and Prior Saint-Jean seem to be giving birth to themselves anew from their own heads. "Making what was really a boy's experience, he had a wholly boyish delight in his holiday, and certainly did not reflect how much we beget for ourselves in what we see and feel, nor how far a certain diffused music in the very breath of the place was the creation of his own ear or brain" (128). This rebirth is qualified, however, by murder. The image of the open grave is another reconfiguration of the dream vision. It is a dark orifice intended for a child and, in it, a golden discus is discovered. When Apollyon throws the discus, "it seems to burn as it goes," recalling the circlet of fire (142). In a Christian revision of the Greek myth, Apollyon's discus is taken by a demonic wind and crashes into the skull of the boy-monk, Hyacinthus, who is then buried in the open grave.

The prior himself is no better at translating classical inspiration into his own Christian text. Pater offers a glimpse at the writing of the prior's decadent Volume Twelve. He captures the prior's inspiration, his mystical vision, in another ring metaphor, that of a halo that will not be captured: "If he set hand to the page, the firm halo, here a moment since, was gone, had flitted capriciously to the wall; passed next through the window, to the wall of the garden; was dancing back in another moment upon the innermost walls of one's own miserable brain, to swell there—that astounding white light!—rising steadily in the cup, the mental receptacle, till it overflowed, and he lay faint and drowning in it" (141). I am reminded of Des Esseintes's feverish reading of medieval visionaries. The halo, with its astounding white light, recalls the prior's earlier vision of the circlet of fire, while the innermost walls, the swelling of the halo, and the overflowing cup echo the other eroticized images of male orifices. Homoerotic desire has exceeded the monk's capacity for textual control. The text is seen as the symptom of the prior's madness, and he is "detained in a sufficiently cheerful apartment, in a region of the atmosphere likely to restore lost wits" (145).

The ending of "Apollo in Picardy" is archetypal of Pater's view of Christianity after *Marius*. With the violence of Apollyon, it is clear that Pater is criticizing the Hellenic golden age that he evokes, as well as the dreary Christianity of the monastery. In Apollyon Pater finds not only the beauty of the male form, but also all the violence of the Greeks—the anger of Apollo at Marsyas and the brutality of Dionysus Zagreus. The horror of the body and spirit in disjunction culminates in the madness and alienation of Prior—now simply Brother—Saint-Jean. But Pater concludes also with a leap of faith or, more precisely, hope. Brother Saint-Jean's apartment gives him a view of the *vallis monachorum,* the origin of his pleasure and his madness. He is no longer the monk in the tower, looking down with dismay on the profane world of his birth. He now looks with longing and weeps. It is a longing for a rebirth that never quite happens: "He is like the damned spirit, think some of the brethren, saying 'I will return to the house whence I came out'" (146). It is also a desire for male beauty reconfigured as mourning, as he sees the blue hyacinths and recalls his dead companion. In other words, it is the mourning of a damned spirit for a pleasure that was widely demonized in the time that Pater lived and wrote.

*Hope* is the word that reverberates through Pater's late writings, especially *Marius*. The blue of the hyacinths becomes the blue in the gown of the Virgin Mother: "blue, as he observed, was the colour of Holy Mary's gown on the illuminated page, the colour of hope, of merciful omnipresent deity." In this final appearance of the Virgin on the illuminated page, the themes of Christianity, homoeroticism, textuality, rebirth, and resurrection come together in a startling vision of hope. The man who desires other men is again the *mater dolorosa.* Pater glimpses in a maternal icon one of those "remoter and ever remoter possibilities" that remain for him as an afterthought, an echo, as he peruses the ruins of Christian faith. Ever on the verge of a conversion that never happens, ever in mourning for a male beauty out of reach, Pater may seem to us now a bit of a renegade monk himself, though perhaps less mad than melancholic and terminally hopeful. Like Brother Saint-Jean, he seems to have died, as he lived, in expectation of a vision: "Brother Saint-Jean died, standing upright with an effort to gaze forth once more, amid the preparations for his departure" (146).

# FOUR

# *The Temptation of Saint Oscar*

## Christ for Christ's Sake

My existence is a scandal.        Oscar Wilde

Like his aesthetic mentor Walter Pater, Oscar Wilde believed that Christianity was an extraordinary invention. Wilde brought his singular synthesis of Roman Catholicism, aestheticism, and eroticism to every book that he ever published. I say singular, though he took many of his cues from Pater and Huysmans. Like his two great precursors, Wilde seemed ever to waver on the verge of conversion. He was well read in theology and yet suspicious of dogma, enamored of Christ yet despairing of Christians, seduced by the beauties of Catholic ritual and art but appalled by the philistinism of the pious. Wilde even repeated Pater's favorite observation from Heine: "The old fable that the Greek gods took service with the new religion under assumed names has more truth in it than the many care to discover."[1] Wilde also shared with Pater a fascination with ritual, and even his moments of doubt have all the symbolic theater of the Catholic mass. One passage in particular from *De Profundis* (1897), his prison letter to Lord Alfred Douglas, recalls Pater's description of the "white mass" at the beginning of *Marius the Epicurean*: "When I think about religion at all, I feel as if I would like to found an order for those who cannot believe: the Confraternity of the Fatherless one might call it, where on an altar, on which no taper burned, a priest, in whose heart peace had no

229

dwelling, might celebrate with unblessed bread and chalice empty of wine."[2]

Although Wilde often wavered in typical decadent fashion between piety and heresy, this passage is most often quoted as proof of his atheism. As such, it is inadequate; indeed, it is one of his more paradoxical and Christian statements. It should be read in the context of *De Profundis*, his extended and brilliant meditation on Christ, his own martyrdom, and the value of mysticism in literature. Wilde celebrates an enigmatic God who has, in a tragic and beautiful gesture, hidden his face from man. And this very modern man has lost his faith. Nevertheless, in a gesture no less tragic and beautiful, he never tires of going to church to look for it. In this passage Wilde demonstrates a wistful doubt that is commonplace in decadent literature, a melancholic aspiration toward a faith that is always already in decay, imperiled, and improbable. Furthermore, it also demonstrates Wilde's theatrical mastery of Catholic rhetoric and Catholic gestures. Even more than Pater, he appreciated the performative dimension of religion, and he found in Catholicism what a great many have found there: a site of self-transformation.

Wilde also saw in Catholicism the last hope of paganism in modern times and, after the fashion of Pater, he expounded on the spirituality of sensuous forms. "Those who see any difference between soul and body have neither," he writes, summing up a Paterian theme in a pithy epigram (1205). On a similar note, Lord Henry Wotton advises Dorian Gray, "Nothing can cure the soul but the senses, just as nothing can cure the senses but the soul" (31). Among Wilde's early poems, written when he was torn between his allegiances to the Vatican and to Ancient Greece, we find that even his forays into antiquity read like improbable efforts at escaping Christian morality, while some of his Catholic poems betray a golden thread of homoerotic Greek idealism. The juxtaposition is a dissonant and sometimes contradictory one in his early work, and this is one reason why most critics have dismissed his first volume, *Poems* (1881), as badly flawed. Only in prison did Wilde discover the sorrow that he was never able to recognize in either Pater or the Greeks. In *De Profundis* he complemented Pater's melancholic Marius with another Hellenized Christian icon, the figure of Christ himself as the Son of Man, perfected through his suffering, a speaker of Greek who could have conversed with Socrates.

Most important perhaps, Wilde shared with Pater a conviction that Christianity is a mode of becoming, a work of art subject to historical revision and artistic recontextualization. In *The Renaissance* and *Marius the Epicurean*, Pater offered a historical and evolutionary account of Christianity and religious ritual, one that emphasized the spiritual and creative practices of individuals. Wilde also had this artistic tendency to remake the Church in his own image, and to mark religious discourse with his own signature. When he writes that "Art has a soul, but man has not," he does not deny the existence of the soul but rather, in a well turned paradox, reveals its textual essence.[3] Religion is the imaginative work of great artists: "History ends with a few bare facts; Religion with a few undeniable Doctrines—beyond that all is invention."[4]

Unlike the discreet and taciturn Pater, Wilde had a genius for drama, in his life as well as on the stage. He had a genius for dandyism, scandal, public confession, and even martyrdom. His very conversation was like a scripted and highly polished event. Like Christ, he spoke in proverbs and parables of a sort, although in true decadent fashion he called them paradoxes and prose poems. To propagate his aesthetic beliefs, he mastered the open letter to the editor. To advertise his sexuality, he mastered the open secret. In many ways, Roman Catholicism provided Wilde with an ideal stage. For his dandyism and his aestheticism, there was beautiful ritual and passionate faith. For his taste for scandal, there was a discourse of sin. And for his aesthetic and sexual martyrdom, there was the language of penitence and hagiography.

I am not, however, going to claim that Wilde's Catholicism was a meaningless pose, or that he was somehow immune to faith, doubt, shame, or remorse, all of which he described in religious terms with considerable eloquence. Those critics who have characterized Wilde as a consummate poseur have been especially eager to trivialize his religious beliefs. From Robert Ross and André Gide to the standard biography by Richard Ellmann, I see an unfortunate tendency to regard Wilde as essentially a "pagan" and aesthetic clown, whose writings on religion are all shallow and insincere. Here "pagan" presumably means unchristian rather than Greek, since Wilde would surely have made Athenian sages blush no less than his prudish contemporaries. But if Wilde was simply a "pagan," why did he consider conversion so often? Why did he attend Catholic services so often? Why did he return again and again to Christian themes in his work? How could he have written about Christ as sensitively as he did in his prison letter to Douglas?

Another strategy, which has become increasingly popular of late, has been to discuss Wilde as though he were Cardinal Newman, to apologize for his lapses in orthodoxy and to remark on the biblical allusions in his work. Recently, an article on Wilde's Christianity was published in a periodical called *The Journal of Ultimate Truth and Meaning*—an irony that was lost on the author of the essay but would surely have delighted Wilde. Both of these critical approaches are hostile in varying degrees to Wilde's homosexuality and to his less conventional religious opinions. Both are obliged to debate the genuineness of his Christian beliefs according to some presumed standard of orthodoxy that is itself highly questionable.

There is ample evidence for Wilde's religious sincerity and Christian faith, just as, to his credit, there is ample evidence for his doubt. A line from his early poem "Theoretikos" is sometimes cited as evidence of his Paterian aloofness from Christianity:

> It mars my calm: wherefore in dreams of Art
> And loftiest culture I would stand apart,
>
> Neither for God, nor for his enemies. (716)[5]

The line sounds more like wishful thinking, however, when we consider Wilde's deathbed conversion alongside his more blasphemous humor, his fascination with Christ alongside his mockery of clergymen, his horror at sin alongside his indulgence in it. Like many decadents, he was sometimes for God and sometimes for his enemies. I think it wiser to conclude that Christianity played an important, though by no means dominant, role in his life and his work. Like Pater, Wilde always entertained the prospect of faith, with varying degrees of enthusiasm, as a poetic possibility. He once characterized Roman Catholicism as the most romantic college in the great university of the world's religions. He embraced Eastern mysticism alongside Greek gods and Freemasonry, shoring up religious fragments and not always troubling to reconcile their contradictions. If anything, he saw it is a point of honor to preserve their contradictions. G. K. Chesterton, a far more conventional convert, once said of Wilde, "He was so fond of being many-sided that among his sides he even admitted the right side. He loved so much to multiply his souls that he had among them one soul at least that was saved. He desired all beautiful things—even God."[6]

Those who deny the seriousness of Wilde's interest in Christianity must nevertheless at some point come to terms with his remarkable theological erudition, not to mention his subtle and challenging interpretations of the Gospels in *De Profundis*. When the Christian argument of the letter was first published in 1905, one reviewer remarked: "All his reflections upon Christ remind one of an educated pagan, who admired whilst not believing, but yet are true and just, so just, one wonders why one never thought them for oneself."[7] The familiar questions—whether Wilde's deathbed conversion was genuine, whether Wilde was "orthodox," whether he was a good Christian or not a Christian at all—are not my primary interest here. The answer is usually yes and no, and we invariably learn more about the religious opinions of the critic than about Wilde.[8] I am more concerned here with Wilde's profound attraction to Catholicism as a work of art.

Wilde often spoke of Christ and the Church in the same way he spoke of beautiful objects and beautiful boys—in the language of fascination and seduction. It comes as no surprise that Flaubert's *Tentation* was one of his favorite books. He claimed that whenever he was in a strange town, he ordered a copy of the *Tentation* and a packet of cigarettes, and was happy. In prison he requested a copy of the *Tentation*, as well as *Salammbô* and *Trois Contes*, and upon his release he made plans to translate it. "I never read Flaubert's *Tentation de St Antoine*," he said once, "without signing my name at the end of it."[9] Like the hero of Flaubert's proto-decadent drama, Wilde's fictional personae are ever on the verge of sin, ever troubled by temptation. Like other decadents, Wilde found in Roman Catholicism a florid and profound discourse of sin that gave shape and moral significance to transgression. For Wilde, however, the Catholic Church was itself a troubling and exquisite vision, like the visions of pleasure and torment that appear before the eyes of Flaubert's eremite. Wilde was tempted by the romantic figure of Christ. He was tempted by the beauty of the Church, its art and poetry and ritual, and he was tempted by the power

, poetry to transform his consciousness, to reinterpret his passions, . )estow a religious meaning on his actions, and to scandalize his family. Above all, he was tempted by Catholicism as the most beautiful lie ever told. Coming from the author of an essay called "The Decay of Lying" (1889), this is no small praise.

Faith for Wilde is a passion that concerns itself with the beauty of a religion, not the truth of its doctrines. "For what is Truth?" he writes. "In matters of religion, it is simply the opinion that has survived." He made a number of similar assertions. Farther along in the same essay, he takes ironic note of Newman's alliterative claim, "Forms are the food of faith," and adds, "The Creeds are believed not because they are rational, but because they are repeated." Elsewhere he writes: "Religions die when they are proved to be true. Science is the record of dead religions."[10] Such epigrams are scandalous. They are scandalous in the cynical sense of the word—laying bare the lie that one is nevertheless content at times to live by. They are also evidence of what Wilde called the "antinomian" quality that he claims the aesthetic critic shares with the mystic: the valorization of faith over the apparent truth of moral law.[11] Any fool can believe what is true; the real challenge to faith is to believe what is improbable, if not patently untrue.

The capacity to believe what is untrue for the sake of its beauty is a central theme of "The Portrait of Mr. W. H." (1889), Wilde's speculative essay on the enigmatic dedication of Shakespeare's sonnets. In this essay, which is really a short story about literary critics, Wilde suggests a homoerotic, highly seductive, though improbable, theory about Shakespeare's inspiration, and then describes how a critic who believes in the theory has generated a forgery to support the claim. Wilde repeatedly casts the capacity to believe the theory in religious terms. We must have faith in the theory, we must be converted to it or be skeptical. In other words, a religion, like an improbable literary theory, requires a few good lies to convince us of its beautiful truths. Faith in the improbable becomes a form of martyrdom: "Martyrdom was to me merely a tragic form of scepticism, an attempt to realise by fire what one had failed to do by faith. No man dies for what he knows to be true. Men die for what they want to be true, for what some terror in their hearts tells them is not true" (1201). The observation is a cynical one. At various times in his life, however, Wilde's critical cynicism coexisted peacefully with a willingness to risk faith, to entertain Catholicism as a glimmering possibility and a thing of genius, to enter into the sphere of its influence and fashion himself anew—in short, to live the lie more or less on its own terms.

For Wilde, Catholicism was as inevitable as sin, and no less disturbing in its fascination. For this reason, the Bible, no less than Pater's *Renaissance* or Huysmans' *A Rebours,* was a poisonous and seductive book for Wilde, the one volume to which he would return again and again in his own writing. "When I think of all the harm that book has done," he quipped, "I despair of ever writing anything to equal it."[12] André Gide, who was himself given to playing Saint Antony to Wilde's various temptations, was especially astute about his friend when he remarked: "The Gospel disturbed and tormented the pagan Wilde. He did not forgive it its miracles."[13]

As he suggested even in some of his earliest remarks on Christianity, Wilde found something remarkably artificial, even decadent, in religion. In 1875, while he was still a student at Oxford, he seriously contemplated conversion to Catholicism, and even traveled to Rome with that intention. He wrote a letter to his friend William Ward that prefigures much of his later writing on the artistry of Christianity: "Faith is, I think, a bright lantern for the feet, though of course an exotic plant in man's mind, and requiring continual cultivation" (*Letters,* 20). To the biblical lamp-metaphor, lifted from Psalms, Wilde appends another image of faith as some sort of hothouse flower. Faith is unnatural, foreign to the human mind, a beautiful thing of "cultivation." Wilde eventually developed this notion into the more sophisticated response of the creative or artistic critic. He echoed Pater's evolutionary approach to religion by claiming, "And what is true in regard to races is equally true when applied to individuals, I mean individuals who can claim individuality—each one makes his own God, and I have made mine."[14]

Wilde's most important strategy for making his own God was to rewrite or reinterpret the Bible. Indeed, Max Beerbohm once remarked of *Salomé* (1893), "If Oscar would re-write *all* the Bible, there would be no sceptics."[15] Wilde was always careful to emphasize the literary dimension of the Bible. "Do you know," he once said, "the Bible is a wonderful book. How beautifully artistic the little stories are!"[16] According to Coulson Kernahan, Wilde insisted upon his own earnestness when outlining his ambition to free Christianity from the stylistic disasters of modern cant. Although we might wonder at the accuracy of Kernahan's memory of Wilde's conversation, the ideas and tone are certainly familiar:

> Shall I tell you what is my greatest ambition—more even than an ambition—the dream of my life? Not to be remembered hereafter as an artist, poet, thinker, or playwright, but as the man who reclothed the sublimest conception which the world has ever known—the Salvation of Humanity, the Sacrifice of Himself upon the Cross by Christ—with new and burning words, with new and illuminating symbols, with new and divine vision, free from the accretions of cant which the centuries have gathered around it.[17]

Although *Salomé* is probably the most famous example of Wilde's revisionary approach to the Bible, this quotation sounds more like his reinterpretation of the Gospels in *De Profundis*. Wilde also planned to write a play entitled "Ahab and Isabel," as well as another work that he called the "Epic of the Cross"—"the Iliad of Christianity, which shall live for all time."[18]

His prose poems, often written in the language of the King James Bible, begin like the parables of Christ, although they end with a paradox that, however edifying, is purely Wilde. Some of the prose poems actually take as their subject matter the scandal of Christianity as art. For example, Kernahan also recalled a prose poem that Wilde never published, in which the body of Christ is found today in the very rock-sepulchre in which Joseph of Arimathea had laid it. A crisis of faith occurs when the doctrine of the Resurrection is revealed to be a poetic lie. In one of his published prose poems, "The House of Judgment" (1894), Wilde describes the appearance of "the Man," a great sinner, in the House of Judgment. The Man insists that God cannot send him to Hell because "in Hell I have always lived." When God asks why the Man should not be sent to Heaven, he replies, "Because never, and in no place, have I been able to imagine it," thus confining religion to the limits of each man's imagination (866). This assertion is similar to a comment Wilde once made to Robert Sherard: "Imaginative people will invariably be religious people for the simple reason that religion has sprung from the imagination."[19]

Wilde even allowed that the Church, no less than himself, was capable of propagating this imaginative quality of religion. Although he was often dismissive of actual clergymen, he did not despair of the Church altogether. Priests were often the butt of his mockery, as with Canon Chasuble in *The Importance of Being Earnest* (1895) or the stern and dogmatic priest in "The Fisherman and His Soul" (1891). He reacted with great bitterness to the prison chaplains, whose hollow and tyrannical piety he satirized as the kiss of Caiaphas in "The Ballad of Reading Gaol" (1898). Popes fare a little better, adored one minute, but the next minute dismissed as tyrants of the soul. Nevertheless, on the clergy as an abstract concept, Wilde could speak appreciatively, though perhaps a bit condescendingly. "As for the Church," he writes in "The Decay of Lying," "I cannot conceive anything better for the culture of a country than the presence in it of a body of men whose duty it is to believe in the supernatural, to perform daily miracles, and to keep alive that mythopoeic faculty which is so essential for the imagination" (989).

It was Christ himself, more than his official representatives, who embodied for Wilde the romantic ideal of the artist. In "The Soul of Man under Socialism" (1895) and, especially, *De Profundis*, Wilde offers an interpretation of the Gospels in which Christ is valorized as an aesthete, a mouthpiece for Wilde's own theories about art, individualism, imagination, love, sorrow, and faith. In *De Profundis* Wilde recalls having said to Gide in a café that there was "nothing that either Plato or Christ had said that could not be transferred immediately into the sphere of Art, and there find its complete fulfilment" (*Letters*, 476). Having delineated an intimate and immediate connection between the true life of Christ and the true life of the artist, Wilde declares that "Christ's place is indeed with the poets" (476–477). But Christ is not only an artist but a work of art, for the image of the Man of Sorrows has "fascinated and dominated Art as no Greek god ever succeeded in doing" (481). Wilde refers to the life of Christ as an "idyll" and to his Passion as a "tragedy," the playing of which is the supreme office of the Church (478). These observations appear on the same pages with allusions to Pater's *Marius* and Arnold's *Literature and Dogma*, and certainly the aesthetic impulse to harmonize the Christian and the Hellenic takes its cues from these two Oxonian predecessors. When Wilde asserts that the very basis of Christ's character "was the same as that of the artist, an intense and flamelike imagination" (476) or boasts that his creed relies on Gods who "dwell in temples made with hands" (468), the shadow of Pater looms large. In addition to his theory that Christ spoke Greek, Wilde claims that "the ultimate survival of the Greek Chorus, lost elsewhere to art, is to be found in the servitor answering the priest at Mass" (478).

Such remarks are Wilde's style of "creative" criticism at its best, high critical fiats of dubious accuracy that nevertheless have a poetry all their own. As in Arnold and Pater, Wilde's Hellenism here is an effort to rescue Christ in the name of a late-Victorian humanism that buried its scholarly roots in Renaissance art. In addition, there is a homoerotic motive to this Hellenization and aestheticization of Christ. A few pages earlier, Wilde remembers how he compared Lord Alfred Douglas to Hylas or Hyacinth, Jonquil or Narcissus, just as, in a letter he wrote upon his imprisonment in 1895, he called Douglas—we gasp in amazement—"the golden-haired boy with Christ's own heart in you" (*Letters*, 397). As is well known, Wilde extolled the virtues of homosexuality through comparison to classical models, and *De Profundis*, with its references to Greek marbles and Plato's *Symposium*, is no exception. By a similar act of interpretation, he transfigured the Victorian Savior into a classical pederast and aesthete. As Richard Ellmann phrases it, "Christ had become a kind of boy lover."[20]

Wilde's rejection of Christ's divinity is another effort at Hellenizing him. "The divinity of Christ," he once said, "in its generally accepted sense, I, of course, do not believe, but I see no difficulty whatever in believing that he was far above the people around him as though he had been an angel sitting on the clouds."[21] For Wilde, Christ was eminently the Son of Man and not the Son of God. Christ's divinity is apparent not in his pedigree but in his perfection, just as his truth is neither historical accuracy nor moral righteousness but the poetic truth of art—that is to say, the truth of lies. Wilde had contemplated this artistic truth as early as his undergraduate days, as this quotation from Hegel in his Oxford notebooks demonstrates: "The sensuous and the spiritual which struggle as opposites in the common understanding are revealed as reconciled in the truth expressed by art."[22] The traditional notion of truth as a thing to be revealed is undermined here by a view of truth as art, a fabrication, a dialectical accomplishment.

In *De Profundis* this artistic truth is endowed with a Christian significance: "Truth in Art is the unity of a thing with itself: the outward rendered expressive of the inward: the soul made incarnate: the body instinct with spirit" (473). The aesthetic is essentially Greek, with its emphasis on the perfection of form, but the language is biblical, with the phrase "the soul made incarnate" reminiscent of Christ as the Word made flesh. Christ again provides the model for truth in art when Wilde declares: "For every work of art is the conversion of an idea into an image. Every single human being should be the fulfilment of a prophecy. For every human being should be the realisation of some ideal, either in the mind of God or in the mind of man. Christ found the type, and fixed it, and the dream of a Virgilian poet, either at Jerusalem or at Babylon became in the long progress of the centuries incarnate in him for whom the world was waiting" (481–482). The shifting between Christian and pagan modes of thought is deft and ingenious. Christ is juxtaposed with Virgil, Jerusalem with Babylon, the mind of God with the mind of man, biblical prophecy with Greek idealism. Christ is the realization of an ideal, rumored among prophets for centuries, and Wilde is willing to allow that God, like some men, is a great artist capable of formulating such an ideal. That a divine perfection should inhere in Christ in no way contradicts Wilde's assertion that divinity is realized through perfection of form. Wilde presumes, in fact, that while the ideal of Christ may be found in the mind of God, Christ is the author of his own perfection.

When Wilde speaks of Christ as the "supreme Artist,"[23] he means to equate the ideal with its performance, its sensuous existence, rather than conceiving Christ as the mere physical shadow of a transcendent ideal that exists elsewhere. "And," he notes in *De Profundis*, "it is the imaginative quality of Christ's own nature that makes him this palpitating center of romance. The strange figures of poetic drama and ballad are made by the imagination of others, but out of his own imagination entirely did Jesus of Nazareth create himself." Christ, like the work of art, is the fulfillment, and also the revision, of a prophecy in the mind of Isaiah or John the Baptist, not its accidental resemblance. "The cry of Isaiah had really no more to do with his coming than the song of the nightingale has to do with the rising of the moon—no more, though perhaps no less" (482). In a sense, the realization precedes the prophecy. The perfection of the performance determines the ideal.

Wilde's insistence upon Christ as a personality and an individualist is immensely important. Like the Wildean dandy, Christ offered his personality as a work of art, a rejection of social conformity, and a challenge to moral cant. Wilde found in Christ a kindred soul, one who propagated a cult of himself through religion, much as Wilde had propagated a cult of himself through art. In "The Soul of Man under Socialism," he writes that the message of Christ to man was simply "Be thyself." Again, the perfection of the performance determines the ideal. "What Jesus meant was this. He said to man, 'You have a wonderful personality. Develop it. Be yourself'" (1085). There appears to be a tautological problem here. How could you be other than yourself? Presumably, Wilde distinguished between the self as the shadow or reflection of an ideal essence that lies elsewhere and a more romantic conception of the self as autonomous text, a performative accomplishment that goes beyond the banal limits of mere existence. *De Profundis* also defines spirituality romantically as an emanation from the self: "Only that is spiritual which makes its own form. If I may not find its secret within myself, I shall never find it" (468).

The difference between the person and the personality, therefore, is the difference between realism and romance. Christ demonstrated "that close union of personality with perfection which forms the real distinction between classical and romantic Art and makes Christ the true precursor of the Romantic movement in life" (476). It is also, for Wilde, the difference between bad art and good art. His investment in dandyism should be readily clear in this context. Barbey d'Aurevilly, whom Wilde had read, once declared that individuality, the power to be oneself, was the gift of the dandy. Christ, like the dandy, is an essentially romantic artist because he is the originator of himself both as ideal and form. A great conversationalist and "the most supreme of individualists," he inspires others to be beautiful by virtue of the "charm of his personality" (478–479). He is also himself a great work of art, the ultimate object of aestheticism, a poetic icon whole and complete in himself, a Christ for Christ's sake. His life may have been foretold, but he alone is its realization. He does not seek to change the world, but the world is transformed in his presence. Even the very textuality that constitutes the modern experience of Christ renders him strangely artificial and makes of him an aesthetic object. When Wilde writes that Christ "has all the colour elements of life" or that Christ's words are the translation of a translation, life itself retires in favor of the play of textual possibilities.

For Wilde, the truth of Christ lay in his beauty as a poetic lie. The very intensity of the need to believe in Christ was sufficient evidence that he must be an illusion. As Lord Henry remarks in *Dorian Gray:* "The things one feels absolutely certain about are never true. That is the fatality of Faith, and the lesson of Romance" (161). We need not wonder, then, at Wilde's impatience with other people who spoke of moral imperatives, religious orthodoxy, or the historical accuracy of the Bible. When Robert Ross tried once to convince Wilde of the truth of Christianity, it was no doubt in an ironic tone that Wilde responded simply, "No, Robbie, it isn't true."[24]

## Ritualism and Dandyism

To live is to change, and to be perfect is to have changed often.

Cardinal Newman

He was so High Church. His views were so extremely high! Quite unintentionally, perhaps, he attracted towards us the uncertain climate of Rome.                                      Ronald Firbank

I have mentioned the figure of the dandy in passing, but the subject demands greater elucidation, if only because accusations of dandyism or camp are a commonplace means of denigrating Wilde and denigrating in particular his religious and aesthetic opinions. Wilde was the most controversial dandy of his age, especially in his highly self-dramatizing "aesthetic" phase in the 1880s when he affected a more flamboyant style of dress. Many of his critics have remarked upon the velvet knee breeches he wore around the time of his lecture tour in America, the languid poses in lovely clothes, the Parma violets, the sunflowers, and the lilies. His epigrammatic and conversational style was itself an essential mark of dandyism, and some of his wittiest phrases take the dandy as their subject matter: "Dandyism is the assertion of the absolute modernity of Beauty," he writes, or "A really well-made buttonhole is the only link between Art and Nature"

(1204–1205). He had also mastered the gender ambiguity of the dandy. He favored an indirect and artful articulation of his homosexuality, with a marvelous capacity for the camp gesture of stagy effeminacy. In lines like "At Mrs. Crosby's I will appear in a new departure in evening dress, black velvet with lace," Wilde claimed for himself the dramatic and traditionally feminine language of haute couture. Life is ritual, as Lionel Johnson is said to have proclaimed, and both he and Wilde recognized a taste among Catholics for gorgeous ritual.

I do not wish to minimize the Tyrian thread of dandyism that sometimes distinguishes Wildean Catholicism, but neither do I wish to overemphasize it with the dismissive tone that typifies much critical writing on the subject, both then and now. Rather, I prefer to analyze the ironic gestures of the dandy with regard to the religious and historical milieu in which Wilde in particular performed. As a dandy with a fascination for the Catholic Church, he placed himself center stage in one of the thorniest and most protracted debates in Victorian politics: the battle over ritualism, Tractarianism, and the revival of Roman Catholicism in England.

When Wilde is satirized it is almost invariably for his dandyism and usually by people incapable of appreciating either the wisdom or the parodic humor already inherent in the pose. It is also true that when his religious beliefs are satirized, his ritualism is usually a principal target. Ritualism was inherently farcical, if not wholly shocking, to many earnest Victorians, even though it was defended by a great many nineteenth-century theologians of an Anglo-Catholic or High Church persuasion who cared little about Wilde. The English decadents did not bear the full brunt of British anti-Catholic wrath—that was reserved for the ritualistic priests and bishops themselves—but they did aggravate the issue by playing relentlessly upon its central tensions, the problematic distinctions between ritual and idolatry, spiritual ecstasy and sensual enjoyment, the Word of God and the words of morally dubious men.

The most frequently quoted satire directed at religious dandyism is Gilbert and Sullivan's operetta *Patience*. Since *Patience* was first performed in 1881, the year Wilde published his first book, Gilbert did not have the advantage of reading the most provocative works of the Wildean oeuvre. Most of his religious satire, therefore, consists of jabs at the Pre-Raphaelite medievalism for which Wilde had demonstrated a penchant. Fairly early in *Patience,* Bunthorne explodes the validity of his aesthetic pose through a confession of his own religious fatuity:

> I am *not* fond of uttering platitudes
> > In stained-glass attitudes.
> In short, my mediaevalism's affectation,
> > Born of a morbid love of admiration!

Or, on a more distinctly Wildean note:

> Though the Philistines may jostle, you will
> > rank as an apostle in the high aesthetic band,
> If you walk down Piccadilly with a poppy or a lily
> > in your mediaeval hand.[25]

A less clever parody of Catholic dandyism appears in G. S. Street's comic novel *The Autobiography of a Boy* (1894), in which an annoying and pretentious aesthete, telling the history of his life and opinions, remarks: "From a purely aesthetic point of view, there is much that is acceptable in the Church's ritual and surroundings. Why trouble about the import of her teachings? I never listen to them, or merely smile when some fragment of quaint dogmatism breaks in on my repose." Furthermore, he adds, "I would gladly listen if they talked to me of pale, pure saints and quaint ascetic martyrs, or told me of beautiful, useless miracles which they had read of in their curious lore."[26]

Perhaps the most damning work in this genre was Robert Hichens's novel *The Green Carnation* (1894, published anonymously), which was unusually daring in its depiction of the relationship between Wilde and Douglas, to whom Hichens gives the names Esmé Amarinth and Lord Reggie Hastings. While Esmé expounds in Wilde's epigrammatic style on the lyrical beauties of the Gregorians and the Book of Job, Lord Reggie "mesmerizes" a choirboy with his entrancing buttonhole, a carnation of "astonishing green fascinations." Esmé is decidedly High Church in his passion for ritual, but his religious sincerity is compromised by his unmanly lack of "straight, untrammeled vision." Sometimes the queerness of his vision is quite evident:

> "The high church party are showing us the right way," Mr. Amarinth remarked impressively, with a side-anthem glance at Lord Reggie

which spoke volumes. "They understand the value of aestheticism in religion. They recognize the fact that a beautiful vestment uplifts the soul far more than a dozen bad chants by Stainer, or Barnby, or any other unmusical Christian."[27]

Indeed, that side-anthem glance does speak volumes, mostly about Victorian homophobia. But what is strange about this passage is the paradoxical truth of what Esmé says. No doubt beautiful vestments *are* more uplifting than bad chants. If it were not for Hichens's satirical tone, which descends upon Esmé on all sides, it would be difficult to argue with the Wildean witticisms.

Less parodic treatments of Wilde usually attribute his dandyism to his admiration for French decadents such as Baudelaire, Barbey d'Aurevilly, and Huysmans (who were themselves revising English models from Beau Brummell to Thackeray and Disraeli). Although these writers developed a Catholic strain within the dandy tradition, Wilde's dandyism seems also to partake of another source: the Oxford movement. Indeed, in *The Green Carnation* Hichens is far less concerned with the mysticism and diabolism of French literature than with the British ritualists, the High Church and Anglo-Catholic inheritors of Tractarianism. He mentions Stanton and Bishop King, names that actually meant something in Anglican circles in 1894. While a student at Oxford in the 1870s, Wilde was first introduced to the dandyism inspired in large part by the Oxford movement, not to mention its more recent ritualistic scion. As Walter Bagehot once remarked, "The English have ever believed that the Papist is a kind of *creature;* some think that the Oxford student is its young."[28] Although by the 1870s the Tractarian enthusiasm was a fading memory, Oxford was still reverberating loudly with its echoes. In fact, Wilde's first attempt at conversion took place while he was still at Oxford and was inspired in part by Manning's conversion that same year. Wilde and a friend, David Hunter-Blair, got caught up in the excitement of the debates over the declaration of papal infallibility by Pius IX. This particular doctrine outraged many in the Church of England, and Hunter-Blair was particularly impressed by Manning's public defense of it against Gladstone.

The French decadents and the Oxford movement had more in common than is generally supposed, especially for Evangelicals, though I do not wish to strain the comparison. Both may be seen as romantic approaches to the connection between faith and art, and both Baudelaire and Newman are read today more for their style than for their religious opinions. Decadence was an often diabolical aesthetic perfected by a few artists, while Tractarianism was an earnest religious movement founded by a group of theologians, but they both scandalized their generation and inspired no small degree of religious panic in their critics. Although the Tractarians themselves were anxious not to be perceived as ritualists and enthusiasts, the enormous deluge of anti-popery and anti-ritualist literature of the time cast them into a role usually reserved for decadents: they were vehemently attacked as degenerate idolaters and sensualists. Both movements were called to task for what seemed a dubious interest in mysticism, ritual, vestments, and all the other peculiarities of Catholicism that many Victorians found distasteful. Both may be seen as a reaction against an increasingly materialistic and faithless age. Like the Oxford movement, the French decadents had their share of converts to Roman Catholicism. Moreover, both movements, like the dandy, posed a challenge to Victorian gender roles, not only because of the constant refrain of homosexuality that resounds through their respective histories, but also because of the androgyny and celibacy of some of their chief personalities.

These two movements, so foreign to each other in many ways, nevertheless converged upon the aesthetes of the English fin de siècle, saturated as they were with French and Oxonian cultural influences. This convergence brought about a strange and unprecedented commingling of sincere faith and theological scholarship with a fascination for sin and artistic beauty. Thus we find Lionel Johnson retreating to his room with its bust of Newman and its well-thumbed theological texts, even as he lived a life of alcoholism and homosexual guilt rivaled only by Verlaine. Ernest Dowson, like Johnson an alcoholic and a convert to Rome, could claim that Catholicism was the only beautiful ism left in the world, even as he numbered his days of wine and roses. John Gray was probably the finest master of this contradiction, having led two lives, first as a decadent poet and vaguely homosexual companion of Wilde, and ultimately as a Roman Catholic priest and vaguely homosexual companion of André Raffalovich. But Oscar Wilde will always be the most famous figure upon whom these two seemingly disparate traditions converged. In his life no less than in his prose and poetry, he defined for his age the dandy as Roman Catholic ritualist.

The diabolical aspect of the dandy's Catholicism is obvious enough. The tendency to satanism and sexual perversity is so often remarked upon in decadent literature (not to mention libertine literature and the gothic novel) that we are not surprised when we recognize the more insidious and purely sensuous fascination with ritualism in Wilde. This is the diabolical dandyism that Barbey d'Aurevilly made popular, despite—or perhaps because of—his conversion and his more pious theological interests. Even in old age Barbey wore flamboyant clothing of a nostalgic cut. Although his biographers label him heterosexual, he maintained a circle of male disciples who excited rumors of his homosexuality. To these rumors Barbey responded in a typically Wildean fashion, remarking that "my tastes can bear it and my principles permit it, but the ugliness of my contemporaries disgusts me."[29]

Not only did Barbey write the groundbreaking theoretical text on dandyism, *Du Dandysme et de George Brummell* (1844), but he also brought to the tradition a religious quality—a mere spiritual fragrance, some would argue—that it never had before. As Ellen Moers points out, "The quest for 'something superior to the visible world' was Barbey's own," and she adds that he was the first to exhibit the anomaly of the dandy-priest.[30] Barbey's Catholicism in many ways prefigured that of Huysmans and Verlaine, if only for his fascination with mysticism and the interdependence of sin and grace. His was also a strikingly paradoxical faith. His interest in ritual is evident in his joining the Société Catholique, a lay organization devoted to the aim of refurbishing the liturgy. He was also an editor of the *Revue du Monde Catholique*. Verlaine referred to him as a *formidable* Catholic, a learned man given to public theological debate. Like Huysmans, he was willing to embrace the more violent and grotesque extremes of religious experience, and did not shy away from depictions of sin and sexual obsession. He believed that Catholicism was capable of embracing the entirety of life, without lapsing into prudery or pedantry.

Barbey's most famous work is a collection of short stories, *Les Diaboliques*, in which the dandy as rake or sensualist abounds. Missing from this collection is the mystical horror of the earlier gothic novels, in which Barbey delights in the figure of the priest as ritualist and demonic seducer. In *L'Ensorcelée* (1852), *Un Prêtre Marié* (1864), and *Une Histoire sans Nom* (written about the same time but not published until 1882), Barbey offers a heady mixture of sexual obsession, mysticism, neurosis, satanism, and Catholicism that predictably excited the fervent admiration of Huysmans. The dandy in each of these novels is a priest who, through some enigmatic and perhaps demonic influence that prefigures the sway of Lord Henry over Dorian, spiritually and sexually awakens a woman who then lapses into a form of hysteria virtually indistinguishable from demonic possession. Barbey marks the type in his description of a Capuchin in *Une Histoire sans Nom:*

> The incredulous epicureanism of the century had enervated creeds and customs. Orders renowned for their holiness no longer possessed that austerity which rendered them imposing even to the impious. In the town where Mme. de Ferjol danced her first contredances with the adorable baron, she remembered meeting a Capuchin whose beauty was so intriguing that it was impossible not to notice it, Capuchin though he was, and who, while he had come, as Father Riculf had, to officiate during Lent, exhibited in the garb of poverty and renunciation the affectations of a dandy.[31]

The passage is remarkable, not only for its explicit association of the demonic priest with the dandy, but also for its decadent style and setting: the tortuous syntax, the historical sketch suggesting sensuality and moral degeneration, the paradox of piety and seduction, and the paradox of monastic poverty and flamboyant style.

Wilde was equally adept at evoking this priestly and satanic aspect of the dandy. He once said that "the history of Theology is the history of madness," thus recalling the connection between mysticism, diabolism, and hysteria that was mined by his French contemporaries.[32] Wilde enjoyed telling spicy tales of the early Church, and one such tale, on the death of Pope John XXII, which his friend Hamilton Grant has recalled, is very much in the fashion of Barbey. While browsing through the library of a country house, Wilde claims to have come across a "musty, calf-bound volume of ancient European history" that contains the story of how the pope granted absolution to a man with murderous intentions.[33] Later, during a secret tryst with a mistress, the pope is murdered by that same man. The ironic ending echoes Wilde's assertion in "The Ballad of Reading Gaol" that each man kills the thing he loves—though in this case a dandy-priest is killed by the thing he blesses. Wilde also wrote a scenario for a play along the same lines, "The Cardinal of Avignon," a tragedy of illicit love and betrayal that focuses on the vices of an ambitious cardinal and his bid for the papacy.

More explicitly demonic is the dandy Satan who makes a brief appearance in Wilde's tale "The Fisherman and His Soul":

> It was a man dressed in a suit of black velvet, cut in the Spanish fashion. His face was strangely pale, but his lips were like a proud red flower. He seemed weary, and was leaning back toying in a listless manner with the pommel of his dagger. On the grass beside him lay a plumed hat, and a pair of riding-gloves gauntleted with gilt lace, and sewn with seed-pearls wrought into a curious device. A short cloak lined with sables hung from his shoulder, and his delicate white hands were gemmed with rings. Heavy eyelids drooped over his eyes. (254)

The fine clothes, listless manner, delicate hands, pale face, and drooping eyelids are all part of an iconography of the homosexual decadent that Wilde helped to propagate.

The most memorable dandy ritualist in Wilde is, of course, Dorian Gray. In fact, when Ellmann loses patience with Wilde's attempts at conversion, he quotes from the ritualistic passages in *The Picture of Dorian Gray,* as though Dorian were the last word on Wilde's religious sincerity. Indeed, Wilde invited comparisons between himself and Dorian when he claimed in a letter that the novel "contains much of me in it. Basil Hallward is what I think I am: Lord Henry what the world thinks me: Dorian what I would like to be—in other ages, perhaps" (*Letters,* 342). But as Walter Pater pointed out, Dorian is a failed epicurean. He is a creature of pleasure only, blind to the spiritual beauties of sorrow and the soul. Particularly in his later work, Wilde expressed an emphatic unwillingness to part with his soul, and he might well have agreed with Pater's assessment of Dorian. Nevertheless, Wilde often reveled in the Christian belief that sensuality leads to damnation. He also recognized that remorse and repentance are essential to the beauty of the sinner; otherwise, "he would be unable to realise what he had done" (*Letters,* 487).

Like Barbey, Wilde could distinguish between art and his own conduct, and he was aware that the best Catholic art is unafraid of evoking sins and heresies. He also shared with Barbey a realization that, the usual clerical vices aside, Catholic ritual was itself seductive. The ritualism of *Dorian Gray* plays continually on this vague line between piety and idolatry, as Wilde's descriptions become increasingly insidious. Consider the two most ritualistic passages, in which Wilde imitates the decadent reveries of *A Rebours.* In the first, a note of religious inspiration is evident amid Dorian's aesthetic speculations:

> It was rumoured of him once that he was about to join the Roman Catholic communion; and certainly the Roman ritual had always a great attraction for him. The daily sacrifice, more awful really than all the sacrifices of the antique world, stirred him as much by its superb rejection of the evidence of the senses as by the primitive simplicity of its elements and the eternal pathos of the human tragedy that it sought to symbolise. He loved to kneel down on the cold marble pavement, and watch the priest, in his stiff flowered vestment, slowly and with white hands moving aside the veil of the tabernacle, or raising aloft the jewelled lantern-shape monstrance with that pallid wafer that at times, one would fain think, is indeed the '*panis caelestis*', the bread of angels, or, robed in the garments of the Passion of Christ, breaking the Host into the chalice, and smiting his breast for his sins. The fuming censers, that the grave boys, in their lace and scarlet, tossed into the air like great gilt flowers, had their subtle fascination for him. (105–106)

The exquisiteness of this passage can immediately excite the puritan in any reader, and one suspects right away that the ritual is simply another piece of fashionable clothing for Dorian. In a more prurient frame of mind, we might also notice the subtle enactment of fellatio suggested by Wilde's language—the kneeling, the "stiff" vestment, the unveiling, the *panis caelestis* raised aloft. And yet some of the lines, especially the references to tragedy and symbolism, could have been written by Newman, so suggestive are they of the transcendent meaning of the Mass. Beyond the sensual beauty of color and scent, their is a symbolic beauty that appeals to the ambivalent capacity of the potential convert to apprehend the significance of the invisible and to embrace it.

The second ritualistic passage takes place in Dorian's house rather than in a house of God. Here there is no mention of the authority or rituals of the Church, since Catholicism itself has been virtually displaced by the gorgeousness of its own vestments. No longer do they serve to spiritualize his eroticism and aestheticism:

> He had a special passion, also, for ecclesiastical vestments, as indeed he had for everything connected with the service of the Church. In the long cedar chests that lined the west gallery of his house he had stored away many rare and beautiful specimens of what is really the raiment of the Bride of Christ, who must wear purple and jewels and fine linen that she may hide the pallid macerated body that is worn by the suffering that she seeks for, and wounded by self-inflicted pain . . . Another cope was of green velvet, embroidered with heart-shaped groups of acanthus-leaves, from which spread long-stemmed white blossoms, the details of which were pieced out with silver thread and coloured crystals. The morse bore a seraph's head in gold-thread raised work. The orphreys were woven in a diaper of red and gold silk, and were starred with medallions of many saints and martyrs, among whom was St. Sebastian. He had chasubles, also, of amber-coloured silk, and blue silk and gold brocade, and yellow silk damask and cloth of gold, figured with representations of the Passion and Crucifixion of Christ, and embroidered with lions and peacocks and other emblems. (110)

And so on! The repeated "he had" of this passage emphasizes the possessive, hoarding quality of Dorian's interest in the vestments. As in Huysmans, the long sentences collapse and grind to a halt under the sheer weight of exotic names. While this piling of detail upon exquisite detail may produce a sublime effect, it is one of excess and ennui rather than spiritual grandeur. Also, the repeated references to pain—the Church as self-lacerating Bride, the martyrdom of Sebastian, the Crucifixion—suggest a violent masochistic pleasure that is for the most part disengaged from its Christian significance. Wilde is signaling to us that Dorian has missed the point. He has not even followed Lord Henry's Paterian advice to cure the senses with the soul and the soul with the senses. The chapter ends with a piling up of sins and vices in which there is no explicit mention of Christianity apart from the "pagan church for Christian worship" built by Ginevra d'Este in honor of a "shameful passion" (115). The progression from ritual as the poetry of the soul to ritual as the poetry of the senses is complete.

Wilde was certainly not the originator of the idea of Church ritual as the poetry of sensuality and evil. Indeed, the ritualistic passages from *Dorian Gray* may be seen as Wilde's parody of the immensely popular Evangelical attack on Catholic ritual, confession, and the so-called Papal Aggression—the re-establishment of a Roman Catholic hierarchy in England with Cardinal Wiseman at the helm. The figure of the Catholic priest as dandy and decadent flourished in Victorian anti-Catholic pamphlets and sermons, especially around the time of the Papal Aggression in 1850 and the Vatican Decrees of 1869–70. Throughout the 1870s, while Wilde was at Oxford, thousands of books and pamphlets were published condemning popery, with accusations of treason, sexual immorality, effeminacy, and cultural degeneration. Even a High Churchman like Gladstone could pen a number of anti-Catholic tracts, among them his *Essay on Ritualism* (1874), in which he condemns Catholic efforts to convert Englishmen by seductively parading "every rusty tool she was fondly thought to have disused." He also wrote *The Vatican Decrees in Their Bearing on Civil Allegiance* (1875)—145,000 copies were printed the first year—which claimed that popery sought to undermine the British constitution. Victoria herself, whose sympathies were Broad Church and decidedly anti-ritualist, responded to the Papal Aggression with the exclamation, "Am I Queen of England or am I not?"

Conspiracy theories abounded, as did horror stories about the Inquisition, sex in monasteries, and the torture and imprisonment of women in convents. As the historian E. R. Norman has summarized it: "Although superstitious belief and idolatrous worship were frightful enough, Protestants also supposed the 'Man of Sin' [the pope] to be inextricably involved with vile practices. Monks and nuns, confessors and popes were all popularly imagined to indulge themselves with contemptible vices. The Protestant tradition certainly suspected that the rule of celibacy was largely a fiction and the seclusion of monastic cells invited (almost) unthinkable practices."[34] Degeneracy theories, which became increasingly popular in medical texts and social criticism as the end of the century neared, lent an aura of scientific credibility to the condemnation of British Catholicism, especially in the physiognomic assertion that Jesuits were inherently secretive and deceptive and in the representation of Irish-Catholic immigrants as apelike and subhuman. *Fraser's,* in response to the Papal Aggression, noted the "marks of degeneracy, which history records as having been . . . the fall of all great and powerful empires," and another newspaper described the papacy as an "effete, dull, and soulless anachronism."[35]

Gladstone himself argued that "popery" and ritualism, "in a succession of generations if not even in the lifetime of individuals, tend to emasculate the vigour of the mind."[36] As one historian has noted, "Implicit in this was the assumption that those who had not accepted salvation were, at the very least, morally and spiritually unregenerate, at worst, degenerate," and he concludes that this pseudo-scientific method represented Catholicism "as a degenerative and corruptive creed which bred gross physical deformities as well as moral and emotional perversity."[37] From the puritanical language of the "No Popery" movement, it is but a small step to its ironic transvaluation as a decadent discourse in *The Picture of Dorian Gray.*

Anglican anxiety over Catholic ritual began with the reintroduction of certain ritual practices by the Tractarians and culminated with the Church Association, founded in 1867 specifically for the purpose of suppressing ritualism (or "Puseyism"); the Ritual Commission, which published a series of reports between 1867 and 1870 that investigated and condemned ritualism in Anglican churches; and the passage of the Public Worship Regulation Act of 1875, the law through which the Church Association prosecuted ritualistic priests for the remainder of the century. Contrary to popular beliefs about them at the time, Newman and Pusey were not great champions of ritual. In fact, Newman expressed his dismay at his Anglo-Catholic followers who he thought were too much concerned with *"showy works,"* and he once observed: "I think we are in great danger of becoming . . . *theatrical* in our Religion. All true attention to rites must be founded of course on deep inward convictions, and this makes me dread the fine arts when disjoined from what is practical and personal."[38] Nevertheless, those who were crying "No Popery!" asserted, with good reason, that the Tractarians were responsible for introducing into the Church of England an enthusiasm for every bit of idolatry they claimed to distrust.

Despite the increasing momentum of the Anglo-Catholic movement during Wilde's lifetime, the publication of laudatory Tractarian biographies in the 1890s, and the steady flow of converts to Rome (about ten thousand a year in the 1890s, by one count), this suspicion of Catholic ritual still persisted toward the end of the century. In fact, even around the time of Wilde's death in 1900, scholarly diatribes against the Tractarians were still being published, the best known of which was *The Secret History of the Oxford Movement* (1899), one of about a half dozen books about "the Romeward movement" written at the turn of the century by Walter Walsh. *Secret History* in particular details in a scandalized tone the insidiousness with which Pusey, Manning, Faber, and others propagated Roman Catholic practices within the Anglican Church. Among the numerous sacred props and gestures singled out for execration, not to mention prosecution, were the wearing of Roman Catholic vestments by a priest or bishop, his assumption of an eastward position during the Holy Communion, auricular confession, sacerdotalism, Marianism, incense, bells, lighted altar candles, and the mixed chalice.

The relative theatricality of ritualistic services was profoundly shocking to many, and the connection with dandyism was frequently made. In his 1867 diatribe *Ritualism, the Highway to Rome,* J. Cumming writes: "Prodigious efforts are being made by the Ritualists to enlist converts, or rather I should say perverts. Young men and young women are captivated and charmed by beautiful music, by a gorgeous ceremonial, by rich and variegated dresses, which also, whether at the ball or at the opera, or in a Ritualistic Church, are no doubt very attractive."[39] Charles Kingsley, the great theorist of "muscular Christianity," was more explicit in his gender anxiety about Anglo-Catholics: "[There] is an element of foppery—even in dress and manner; a fastidious, maundering, die-away effeminacy, which is mistaken for purity and refinement; and I confess myself unable to cope with it, so alluring is it to the minds of an effeminate and luxurious aristocracy; neither educated in all that should teach them to distinguish between bad and good taste, healthy and unhealthy philosophy or devotion."[40] The magazine *Punch* virtually declared war on ritualism (see Figures 7 and 8). In a brief unsigned article entitled "Parsons in Petticoats" (1865), it was noted that clergymen of "extreme High Church proclivities are very fond of dressing like ladies. They are much addicted to wearing vestments diversified with smart and gay colours, and variously trimmed and embroidered."[41] As David Hilliard has made clear, many Victorians thought the Anglo-Catholic ritualists "unenglish and unmanly," and attacks on their "effeminacy" were a smear that was typical of the homophobia and gender panic of the age.[42]

The sexual ambiguities of the Oxford movement have been well known since Geoffrey Faber, in *Oxford Apostles* (1933), interpreted the chivalric cult of virginity and male friendship among the Tractarians as essentially homosexual in motivation. Faber's reading of Newman's sexlessness and Hurrell Froude's guilt as evidence of homosexuality may seem strained, but it is nevertheless clear that both men presented a challenge to Victorian gender norms. Faber recounts William Wilberforce's famous dream of Newman as a woman who conversed with him from behind a veil. Newman was often described in feminine terms, and he presented a figure of the celibate priest as somehow, like the androgynous and erotically self-sufficient dandy, "outside sex."

Frederic William Faber, another Tractarian, is the very pattern of

**HEIGHT OF FASHION.**

*Ardent Ritualist.* "OH, ATHANASIUS, IT'S CHARMINGLY BECOMING!"

Fig. 7. "Height of Fashion" (1866), cartoon from *Punch*.

the dandy ritualist. His passionate and Italianate tastes in religious aesthetics made even Newman and Pusey anxious, and he was a guiding spirit behind the establishment of that fulsome icon of ecclesiastical aestheticism, the Brompton Oratory. As is evident from his poetry and his romantic friendships with various men, Father Faber was homosexual, though probably in a chaste and highly sublimated way. His poetry caused alarm among his acquaintances for its effusions of sentiment toward men. Lines like these to his friend George Smythe were especially suggestive:

> Ah, dearest!—wouldst thou know how much
> My aching heart in thee doth live?
> One look of thy blue eye—one touch
> Of thy dear hand last night could give
> Fresh hopes to shine amid my fears,
> And thoughts that shed themselves in tears.

SELLING OFF!!

Fig. 8. "Selling Off!!" (1851), cartoon from *Punch*.

Faber felt the need to defend himself against his own brother's accusations that his poetry was unhealthy. "Strong expressions towards male friends," he wrote, "are matters of taste. I feel what they express to *men:* I never did to a born woman. Brodie thinks a revival of chivalry in male friendships a characteristic of the rising generation, and a hopeful one."[43] I have already pointed out the decadent significance of this "chivalry," but it is also evident in other homosexual poet-priests inspired by Tractarianism, such as Digby Dolben and Gerard Manley Hopkins.

The most significant ritualism scandal in England was the ecclesiastical trial in 1890 of Edward King, who was chair of Pastoral Theology at Oxford when Wilde was a student there and who later became bishop of Lincoln. He is the same bishop of Lincoln that Hichens mentions in *The Green Carnation* as the very embodiment of High Church principles, and he was, along with Father Mackonochie of Saint Alban's, Holburn, one of the most famous clergyman to be prosecuted for ritualistic practices. King's most recent biographers have concluded from various suggestive remarks he made on schoolboy friendships and the conversion of plowboys that he was homosexual but strictly chaste. He is also noted for the spirit of romantic love he engendered among his male disciples. His Oxford appointment was troubled by rumors of his ritualism as principal of Cuddesdon seminary; some claimed that "Cuddesdon curates were 'unmanly' and that their training bred effeminacy." It was thought that his arrival at Oxford would scandalize the undergraduates, but as King himself observed, "All the dear things did was to hang up a surplice on the lamp-post outside my house." His appointment as bishop of Lincoln was also cause for consternation, although one of his admirers, Henry Scott Holland, a High Church theologian well known for his own romantic devotion to young men, was enthusiastic about the prospect. He wrote to King, "Blessings, blessings, blessings, on your dear, dear head, dearest of friends," and added, "It shall be a Bishopric of Love." Bishop King was eventually tried for such ritualistic practices as the eastward position, lighted altar candles, and mixed chalice. Indeed, King was and continued to be after his trial undaunted by attacks on his "odd gestures, posturings, candles and so on," and he was the first bishop since the Reformation to wear a miter in the cathedral. The trial was a cause célèbre, spurred on by King's saintly bearing, and the fact that he went virtually unpunished proved a major victory in the ritualist cause. The similarity between King's defense of ritualism and Wilde's defense of aestheticism is uncanny, not the least for the subtle homoeroticism they share: "We live in an age of decoration," King wrote. "Look at the working-boys in the streets, how elaborate are their Sunday button-holes! It is in all matters, not merely ecclesiastical ones, that the spirit of adornment has caught hold of us, and unless there is positive wrong in any of these things, we have no call to repress them."[44]

As Edward King demonstrated, neither effeminacy nor aestheticism was essentially incommensurate with piety in the career of a priest, despite protestations to the contrary among the Low Church party. Nevertheless, simply by acting on what they saw to be a doctrinal imperative, men like King walked an unstable line between saintliness and ignominy in the public eye. It was precisely this line that Wilde often walked throughout his career, much to the bafflement and dismay of many of his friends and readers. To obtain a better grasp of his paradoxical relationship to Catholicism, we might take a closer look at his various attempts at conversion. In the accounts of his flirtations with Rome, I find not only a degree of religious sincerity, but also an acute awareness of transgression, a realization that his allegiance to Rome was shocking to a great many people. Lady Wilde had in fact had both her sons baptized during one of her own eccentric moments of enthusiasm for Rome, but her husband, no doubt with an eye toward English standards of respectability, was firm in his conviction that Oscar should be raised a Protestant. More than forty years later, Wilde was received into the Church and given the Last Sacraments by a Roman Catholic priest—ceremonies to which he apparently gave his consent despite his being virtually comatose on his deathbed. In between these two events were a number of periods in his life when he slouched rather heavily toward Rome but never formally converted. Most notable among these periods were his trip to Rome in 1875 while he was still an undergraduate, his confession at the Brompton Oratory in 1878, upon his release from prison in 1897, and in Paris and Rome shortly before his death. At these times Wilde demonstrated the paradox that is central to his conception of faith: he could speak with evident sincerity of his eagerness to convert and yet at the same time gesture ironically toward the scandal of Catholicism as art.

When Wilde first set off for Rome to be converted in 1875, he wrote to his friend Reginald Harding, affectionately known as "Kitten," to say, "This is an era in my life, a crisis." This stagy adieu, which sounds as though he were leaving for battle rather than a pleasurable trip, is typical of the public drama with which Wilde announced his every step in the direction of the Roman Catholic Church. On the road to Rome, he was waylaid with an almost allegorical flair by his classics tutor, Mahaffy, a veritable Lord Henry Wotton, who swayed him with anti-popery arguments and whisked him off to Greece to make a proper pagan of him. Wilde eventually did make it to Rome, and he did pay obeisance to Pius IX. But his poems and letters from the period resound with his torn allegiance between Greece and Rome, with his instincts straining more toward the bright sunlight of the former rather than the exquisite guilt and sorrows of the latter.

That said, I do not think it wise to underestimate the sincerity of his Catholic enthusiasm, since it resurfaced again and again later in his life. Because of his tendency to engage absolutely everyone he knew in the interminable spiritual push and pull of his prospective conversions, Wilde's religious opinions have been documented in surprising detail. A priest who knew Wilde at this time claimed that "beneath his superficial veneer of vanity and foolish talk there is, I am convinced, something deeper and more sincere, including a genuine attraction towards Catholic belief and practice." David Hunter-Blair was struck by "how deep, I am sure genuine, was his own sympathy with Catholicism, and how much moved he was by my having taken the step which I did." Others, evidently anti-papist, expressed their dismay. Lord Donald Sutherland Gower, a Magdalene friend who was also homosexual, referred to Wilde as a "pleasant cheery fellow, but with his long-haired head full of nonsense regarding the Church of Rome."[45] Wilde's parents were appalled by a suggestive reference to Saint Aloysius in a letter from a friend, and apparently his father threatened to disown him. As Wilde repeatedly remarked, "I suffer a good deal from my Romish leaning, in pocket and mind" (*Letters*, 43).

Such suffering did not, however, restrain Wilde's behavior, and there is something of the dandy's eagerness to shock in the way Wilde decorated his room not only with pictures on Hellenic themes but also pictures of Pius IX, Manning, and Newman, not to mention a plaster bust of the Madonna and a photograph of Burne-Jones's painting *Christ and Magdalene.* His Catholic poems were the first writings he published, and he sent a copy of "Rome Unvisited" to Newman (who was evidently delighted by it) and a copy of "Urbs Sacra Aeterna" to the pope. He told Hunter-Blair of the Catholic services he attended and the priests in Dublin he befriended, and they both went to hear Manning preach. He debated with Dean Mills, a High Churchman, on the virtues of the Tractarians. He conversed with and wrote to his friends ad nauseam on Catholic matters. He even weepingly entreated his friend Dunlop to pray for him.

In London in 1878 he went through much the same crisis, with no less drama. At the Brompton Oratory, he made a confession to Father Sebastien Bowden, who was, according to Ellmann, known for his conversions among the well-to-do. Bowden was supportive of Wilde's intention to convert, but on the day he was to be formally received into the Church, Wilde did not appear and sent in his place a box of lilies. When he was released from prison in 1897, he again expressed an intention to convert and—after the fashion of Huysmans, whose *En Route* he had recently read—to enter a Trappist monastery as a retreatant. When his application was rejected, he sobbed bitterly in Ada Leverson's drawing room. In the period between his imprisonment and his death, Wilde attended mass frequently, even daily. During his stay in Rome, he sought and received the blessing of the pope no fewer than seven times. The effort would certainly imply a great degree of sincerity, but seven times? Throughout his life, Wilde demonstrated a fascination with ritual and vestments. At Oxford he dabbled in the rituals of Freemasonry. He offered his opinions on the proper attire for missionaries in Africa. In France after his prison term, he regularly attended services at a nearby church and befriended a priest there: "He showed me all his vestments: tomorrow he really will be charming in his red" (*Letters,* 598). Even in his most pious moments, Wilde kept the Church in ironic perspective.

In Wilde's early Catholic poems, there is an emphasis on those sacraments and rituals that were most distressing to the English. His tendency to find the pagan in the Catholic and the Catholic in the pagan recalls the commonplace Evangelical belief that the Roman Catholic Church had gone seriously astray and busied itself with idolatrous rituals that were no better than "wretched sweepings from the deserted shrines of Paganism."[46] His Catholic poetry has a tendency to slip into paganism and homoeroticism on the one hand, and some of the most controversial aspects of Catholicism—kneeling, Marianism, transubstantiation, papal authority—on the other. Wilde speaks admiringly of the pope and his role as the so-called prisoner of the Vatican. In the "Sonnet on Approaching Italy," his papist sentiments are impeccable:

> But when I knew that far away at Rome
> In evil bonds a second Peter lay,
> I wept to see the land so very fair. (725)

Similarly, in "Urbs Sacra Aeterna" he refers to the pope as the "prisoned shepherd of the Church of God" (730), and in "Easter Day" he describes the pope as being like "some great God, the Holy Lord of Rome" (731). With the Vatican's assertion in 1854 that Mary was born without taint of original sin, the adoration of the Virgin also became a point of contention between English Protestants and Catholics, as Evangelicals quoted with disdain from Liguori's *Glories of Mary*. This tension may explain the frequency with which Wilde writes in praise of the Blessed Virgin, such as in "San Miniato":

> And throned upon the crescent moon
> The Virginal white Queen of Grace,—
> Mary! could I but see thy face
> Death could not come at all too soon.
>
> O crowned by God with thorns and pain!
> Mother of Christ! O mystic wife! (725)

I presume that Wilde intended to impress Newman and the pope with his sincerity when he sent them these poems. At the same time, he seems to delight in the paradox by which such pious lines can outrage pious people all over England.

In Wilde's fiction, his fairy tale and conversion narrative "The Young King" is probably his most sophisticated elaboration on the connection between aestheticism and ritualism. In this story he sums up in a parable the paradox of ritual as the sumptuous symbol of the unseen. The young king spends his life in a fabulous and decadent palace. Like Dionysus and Pater's Denys, he springs of an ill-fated and illicit affair, in this case between a princess and an artist who is decorating the cathedral, a "young man of marvellous and foreign beauty, whose hands were tied behind him with a knotted cord, and whose breast was stabbed with many red wounds" (224). Decoration, exoticism, the oddly pagan allusion to Christ and Saint Sebastian—all set the tone for a decadent tale preoccupied with symbols and polished surfaces.

In the course of the tale the king moves from an admiration of various homoerotic and pagan icons—the "slim, fair-haired Court pages," Adonis, Hadrian, Narcissus—to an admiration for a no less glorious crucifix. The progression echoes that of *Marius the Epicurean,* in which homoerotic identifications develop into a religious conviction with oddly pagan nuances and a fascination for the sorrows of Christ. Wilde begins with a decadent pageant of exotic gems and carpets in order to establish a portrait of the king as both a sophisticated aesthete and a materialist who is blind to the suffering of his people:

> All rare and costly materials had certainly a great fascination for him, and in his eagerness to procure them he had sent away many merchants, some to traffic for amber with the rough fisher-folk of the north seas, some to Egypt to look for that curious green turquoise which is found only in the tombs of kings, and is said to possess magical properties, some to Persia for silken carpets and painted pottery, and others to India to buy gauze and strained ivory moonstones and bracelets of jade, sandal-wood and blue enamel and shawls of fine wool. (225)

All this comes in one rambling and glittering sentence, with shades of Pater's Mona Lisa, Flaubert's Salammbô, and Huysmans' Des Esseintes.

With the help of a magical mirror, however, the king is presented with the suffering of his people in a series of dream visions. The mirror is significant for its homoerotic reference to Narcissus, and it is also significant that, like Flaubert's Saint Antony, the king's insights come from visions. Wilde seems to suggest, in true decadent fashion, that homosexuality and a dreamlike textuality are the source of the king's wisdom. When he arrives at a recognition of sorrow and suffering, the young king admires an image of Christ in a passage no less decadent than the one quoted above. The only difference is the Catholic ritualism:

> He stood before the image of Christ, and on his right hand and on his left were the marvellous vessels of gold, the chalice with the yellow wine, and the vial with the holy oil. He knelt before the image of Christ, and the great candles burned brightly by the jewelled shrine, and the smoke of the incense curled in thin blue wreaths through the dome." (233)

With its kneeling, incense, candles, and holy oil, this passage contains everything but an Evangelical standing beside it saying, "What's wrong with this picture?" The young king has discovered that he must give up his regal raiment, part with his riches, and humbly embrace an identification with the poor.

In the final passages, however, the contrite king is reclothed by God:

> And lo! through the painted windows came the sunlight streaming upon him, and the sunbeams wove round him a tissued robe that was fairer than the robe that had been fashioned for his pleasure. The dead staff blossomed, and bare lilies that were whiter than pearls. The dry thorn blossomed, and bare roses that were redder than rubies. Whiter than fine pearls were the lilies, and their stems were of bright silver. Redder than male rubies were the roses, and their leaves were of beaten gold.

The style of this passage is, like that of *Salomé,* somewhere between the King James Bible and Maeterlinck in its mesmerizing symbolist repetitions and exoticism. The most striking paradox, however, is that the young king's spiritual raiment is more gorgeous than his material one. It is not his aestheticism, nor even his effeminacy or homosexuality, that has been sacrificed, only the blindness of his hedonism (though we might wonder how the poor figure into all this). For Wilde, when we put by beautiful words in order to apprehend God, we simply find—more beautiful words. And beautiful raiment and beautiful ritual. The story ends with a decadent sense of the inevitability of textuality, of texts behind texts like a succession of masks without a face. The story is relentlessly pious, and yet we are asked to look upon the face of God as essentially a beautiful and gem-encrusted mask. Even without the pervasive sense of evil that taints the ritualism of *Dorian Gray,* Wilde could express the essentially decadent belief that Christianity, and Catholicism in particular, is a beautiful work of art.

## Seduction and the Scarlet Woman

> He had read in the dark annals of the Inquisition, that a victim who had recanted, and was led to believe that he was to be reconciled to the bosom of Mother Church, approached to embrace the image of the Virgin, when suddenly the arms of the figure opened, and receiving him into her embrace, a hundred knives pierced him to the heart.
>
> Rev. W. Chalmers

Although Rev. Chalmers recounted this tale about a half-century before Wilde wrote "The Sphinx" (1894) and *Salomé,* it is ripe with the sort of violent fear of women that distinguished every phase of fin de siècle decadence and Victorian anti-Catholicism. Evident in the literature of the No Popery movement is a rampant panic about female sexuality that often finds expression in bizarre and paranoid images of seduction and betrayal by the Mother Church. The desire for spiritual righteousness goes hand in hand with a concern for national, racial, and sexual purity in this tradition. A supposedly religious threat is articulated as an invasion, a challenge to the queen and the constitution, a racial disease or degeneracy, a threat to the bourgeois family, a threat to the modesty and virginity of women, or a threat to the sacredness of married life. The fact that there have been queens, constitutions, families, and virgins even in ardently Catholic countries generally escapes the writer's notice. The No Popery movement is an excellent example of the way in which religious and sexual discourses seem inevitably to overlap—the way that religion often presumes a certain discipline or deployment of sexuality.

Instead of a rational comparison of doctrinal claims, anti-Catholic literature offers impassioned rhetoric about the Church as the whore of Babylon, not to mention bizarre and sometimes fabricated stories about monastic satanism, convent brothels, seduction in the confessional, and the sadism of the Inquisition. This preoccupation with the erotic lends to this tradition a peculiar pruriency that puts me in mind of Richard Hofstadter's remark, "Anti-Catholicism has always been the pornography of the Puritan."[47] The Church is seen as vampiric, with all the sexual baggage that term implies. It is represented as seductive, perverse, decadent, often feminine, and certainly fatal. The Victorian deployment of the term "perversion" as virtually synonymous with "conversion" is by no means innocent. Having established the Church as the Scarlet Woman, conversion collapses easily into seduction, and "popery" into sin.

Even traditional theorists of conversion to Catholicism were not immune to conceiving the spiritual tug of the Church in erotic terms. G. K. Chesterton, a contemporary of Wilde and the very archetype of the smug and earnest convert, wrote of the Church as a terrifying and magnetic force that, for its initiates, "begins to take on the tragic and menacing grandeur of a great love affair. The man has exactly the same sense of having committed or compromised himself; of having been in a sense entrapped, even if he is glad to be entrapped."[48] In this context Wilde's recurrent tendency to conversion no longer appears to be at odds with his preoccupation with seduction. Indeed, much of his writing on sexual seduction—for example, *Dorian Gray,* "The Sphinx," *Salomé,* and "La Sainte Courtisane" (a fragment, written in 1893)—is also about the seductiveness and fascination of Roman Catholicism.

The most colorful biblical passages that No Popery literature draws on refer to the doom of Babylon. The description of the whore of Babylon is itself one of the great moments of decadent style in the Bible. I take this translation from a revised edition of the King James Version published in Cambridge in 1885:

> Come hither, I will shew thee the judgement of the great harlot that sitteth upon many waters; with whom the kings of the earth committed fornication, and they that dwell in the earth were made drunken with the wine of her fornication. And he carried me away in the Spirit into a wilderness: and I saw a woman sitting upon a

scarlet-coloured beast, full of names of blasphemy, having seven heads and ten horns. And the woman was arrayed in purple and scarlet, and decked with gold and precious stone and pearls, having in her hand a golden cup full of abominations, even the unclean things of her fornication, and upon her forehead a name written, MYSTERY, BABYLON THE GREAT, THE MOTHER OF THE HARLOTS AND OF THE ABOMINATIONS OF THE EARTH. And I saw the woman drunken with the blood of the saints, and with the blood of the martyrs of Jesus; and when I saw her, I wondered with a great wonder. (Rev. 17:1–6)

This is the moment where Des Esseintes generally fades into a swoon. But these lines had a powerful appeal for puritans as well. They were taken out of context and redeployed by No Popery writers as a condemnation of the Vatican. References to the Church were juxtaposed with pagan imagery in order to bring to light of day what these writers saw as a scandalous idolatry, a bloodsucking barbarity, and a veiled eroticism. "Does not Papal Rome, as well as did Pagan Rome, *abound in images?*" one William Bennett writes in a sermon against the Papal Aggression. "And wherever her influence extends; wherever temples are erected for her worship, *there* are images, and there are prostrate worshippers. Rome is, in very truth, 'the mother'—the fruitful parent—'of harlots and abominations of the earth.' 'With the wine of her golden cup, this Circe has seduced the kings and intoxicated the inhabitants of the earth.'" Needless to say, the pagan Circe does not appear in the Bible, despite the quotation marks here.

Bennett continues along the same lines: "Ignorance is her safeguard: darkness her delight: for then she works unseen, and revels in appropriate deeds. Her name, indeed, is '*Mystery Babylon* the Great, the mother of harlots and abominations of the earth!'" He proceeds in a decidedly vampiric vein: "I hasten on to another and a flagrant and most notorious sin; the *cruelty, and intolerance, and persecuting spirit* of the Babylonish woman: her scarlet robes are stained with blood. 'She is *drunken* with the *blood of saints* and with the *blood of the martyrs of Jesus.*' 'In her was found the *blood* of the prophets, and of saints and of all that were slain upon the earth.'"[49] This imagery is not unlike that of *Salomé*, with the beheading of Saint John the Baptist and of course the fatal dancer herself, her desire figured in terms of hunger and thirst, blood and wine, and a final necrophilic kiss, spiced with the taste of blood.

Probably the most famous No Popery writer of the time was Patrick Murphy, a former Catholic who traveled the country giving lectures and inciting riots. He was finally beaten unconscious in Cumberland by a mob of irate Irish Catholics and died a year later in 1872. His rhetoric was suitably bombastic and inflammatory, and his impact was enormous. Tens of thousands of No Popery tracts, such as the notorious pamphlet *The Confessional Unmasked*, were sold in anticipation of his lectures. In his book *Popery in Ireland*, which went into several editions, he cries out: "Oh, Popery! Popery! thou curse of my country! where once religion, fostered by heavenly influences, flourished with unsullied beauty; how hast thou degraded it in the eyes of every nation in the world! How hast thou dyed the pages of its history with deepest, blackest stains of crime! Alas! . . . Go to, thou mistress of sorcerers; cease from thy superstitious mummeries and abominations." He recounts how he was singled out for the priesthood: "O, miserable infatuation! Not less fascinated was I than the unconscious bird, that is fixed by the eye of the reptile, till it falls a victim to its cunning enemy." With similar melodrama he describes a woman abducted into a convent: "Caught in the gorgeously woven net of Rome, for a time the victim drooped and languished," though later, we discover, "That church which trades in scarlet and crimson draperies, musical exhibitions, and silly mimicries, fascinated her."[50]

Wilde sometimes uses a similar language of illicit fascination, temptation, and flirtation when describing the Church, although he adopts a tone of self-conscious irony rather than outrage. Obviously, he had little patience with soapbox Christians, nor would they have had much patience with him. In *The Picture of Dorian Gray*, he satirized the type. Lord Henry passes Marble Arch just as some "prophet" is bellowing "what does it profit a man if he gain the whole world and lose his own soul?" With impeccable ironic detachment, Lord Henry remarks: "London is very rich in curious effects of that kind. A wet Sunday, an uncouth Christian in a mackintosh, a ring of sickly white faces under a broken roof of dripping umbrellas, and a wonderful phrase flung into the air by shrill, hysterical lips—it was really very good in its way, quite a suggestion" (161). Nevertheless, those hysterical lips would find their apotheosis in Wilde's Jokanaan, the incensed and somewhat absurd prophet of *Salomé*. But even while a student at Oxford, seriously considering conversion to Rome, Wilde was intrigued by the "hysterical" phrases of the No Popery movement, which were no doubt a frequent cause for annoyance among the numerous converts of his acquaintance. His friend Hunter-Blair, as I have said, was inspired to convert by Manning's defense of ritualism; and Wilde was, even as a student, surrounded by other converts, among them Williamson, Dunlop, and MacCall. The language of the No Popery tracts, tainted by an ironic tone, seeped into his own letters, such as when he wrote, "I now breakfast with Father Parkinson, go to St. Aloysius, talk sentimental religion to Dunlop and altogether am caught in the fowler's snare, in the wiles of the Scarlet Woman—I may go over in the vac"; and a couple weeks later he wrote of a friend, "He is awfully caught in the wiles of the Scarlet Woman and wrote to Newman about several things" (*Letters*, 30–31, 33).

The very word *fascination* resounds through Wilde's letters and fiction, often in a Roman Catholic context. His Oxford letters to William Ward are especially redolent with the term:

> Still I get so wretched and low and troubled that in some desperate mood I will seek the shelter of a Church which simply enthrals me by its fascination. (31)

Or, somewhat later:

> I won't write to you theology, but I only say that for *you* to feel the fascination of Rome would to me be the greatest of pleasure: I think it would *settle* me. (32)

And on a more Paterian note:

> *Do* be touched by it, *feel* the awful fascination of the Church, its extreme beauty and sentiment, and let every part of your nature have play and room. (31)

We begin to wonder here whether Wilde is the seducer or the seduced, so inviting and effusive are his religious appeals to his friends. Ward himself explained that Wilde's deathbed conversion was not the pathetic and desperate effort of a dying man, but a return to a "first love," one that had "haunted him from early days with a persistent spell."[51]

This fascination almost always carried with it a homoerotic nuance, and Wilde delighted in blurring the distinction between inspiration and seduction among men. Usually, the Scarlet Woman was in fact represented by a man. Having been to the Pro-Cathedral to hear Cardinal Manning, Wilde wrote to Ward: "He is more fascinating than ever. I met MacCall and Williamson there who greeted me with much *empressement*. I feel an impostor and traitor on such occasions and must do something decided" (*Letters*, 16). Of Bishop Wilberforce, he once said, "I fear he tempted me."[52] On another occasion, he gave his opinion of the Bible, declaring, "Christ, Paul, and most of the other characters in the book have for me a singular fascination," and again of Saint Paul, he said, "I fear he tempted me."[53] I am reminded of Dorian's relationship with Lord Henry when I read Wilde's comment upon receiving a letter from Newman, "I am awfully keen for an interview, not of course to argue, but merely to be in the presence of that divine man"—to which he added, "I could hardly resist Newman I am afraid" (*Letters*, 33). What is all this fascination? Why this parade of clergymen dancing before Wilde's eyes like the visionary temptations of Saint Antony?

In *Dorian Gray* Wilde expounded upon his conception of seduction as "influence," and this influence is at once textual, sexual, and religious. Lord Henry, like Wilde in his Oxford days, sees the appeal of the Church as a form of seduction: "Religion consumes some. Its mysteries have all the charm of a flirtation, a woman once told me; and I quite understand it" (85). The identity of this woman, this nameless Diotima, is not revealed, but Lord Henry needs no education on the subject of flirtation. The notion of "influence" is, from the beginning of the novel, homoerotic. In the opening scene, which takes place in Basil Hallward's garden, Lord Henry is introduced to Basil's beautiful young model, Dorian. Basil's fascination with Dorian amounts to a highly sublimated flirtation, but it is also strangely mystical. It is articulated in a language of temptation that is hardly more voluptuous than the prose that Wilde used to describe Newman, the Church, and, later, the figure of Christ. "When our eyes met, I felt that I was growing pale. A curious sensation of terror came over me. I knew that I had

come face to face with someone whose mere personality was so fascinating that, if I allowed it to do so, it would absorb my whole nature,
my whole soul, my very art itself. I did not want any external influence
in my life" (22).

The word *influence* occurs again when Dorian asks Basil's visitor,
"Have you really a very bad influence, Lord Henry? As bad as Basil
says?" And Lord Henry replies, "There is no such thing as a good
influence, Mr. Gray. All influence is immoral—immoral from the scientific point of view" (28). What he means here by "influence" is something more like "imitation," which Wilde claimed to dislike. One who
is thus influenced "becomes an echo of some one else's music, an actor
of a part that has not been written for him. The aim of life is self-de-
velopment" (29). Thus Lord Henry passes on to another sort of
influence: seduction as education, which for Dorian is a leading downward, but also a leading out—out of self-ignorance, and very nearly
out of the closet.

In Lord Henry's presence—through some mystical sympathy between the older man's words and the younger man's consciousness—
Dorian senses something strange stirring within himself, a sensation
that Wilde likens to the pleasures of music, poetic form, anamnesis,
and at a less explicit level, the pleasures of an as yet unnameable sexual
desire:

> Music had stirred him like that. Music had troubled him many times.
> But music was not articulate. It was not a new world, but rather
> another chaos, that it created in us. Words! Mere words! How terri-
> ble they were! How clear, and vivid, and cruel! One could not escape
> from them. And yet what a subtle magic there was in them! They
> seemed to be able to give a plastic form to formless things, and to
> have a music of their own as sweet as that of viol or of lute. Mere
> words! Was there anything as real as Words?
>
> Yes; there had been things in his boyhood that he had not under-
> stood. He understood them now. Life suddenly became fiery-coloured
> to him. It seemed to him that he had been walking in fire. Why had
> he not known it? (30)

This passage is ingenious for the connections it makes between desire
and artistic form with regard to a vague mystical knowledge. Wilde

ascribed much the same appeal to Pater's *Renaissance* when, in *De Profundis,* he called it "that book which has had such a strange influence over my life" (471). Influence is not merely the transference of information or facts, but the "transference of personality" (1196). Influence is seduction, but also inspiration, a call to become oneself, an invitation to creative criticism rather than imitation. The concept surfaces elsewhere in *De Profundis,* this time in a more religious context, when Wilde points out that Christ did not seek to change people, he did not require imitation; rather, Christ was an individualist. Through the beauty of his mere presence, his capacity to say beautiful things, others around him were inspired to realize themselves as well, to be beautiful in their own way.

This Christian influence is also celebrated in *Teleny,* an anonymous pornographic novel that, however dubiously, is sometimes attributed in part to Wilde. A homosexual painter named Briancourt compares Christ to a male model who is sitting for him. "You would be able to fathom the influence He must have had over the crowd," the painter exclaims. "My Syrian need not speak to you, he lifts his eyes upon you and you grasp the meaning of his thoughts. Christ, likewise, never wasted His breath spouting cant to the multitude."[54] Christianity is mesmerizing and dangerous. What Lord Henry is to Dorian, Christ is to Wilde. But it is, once again, a temptation to the antinomian experience of mysticism, a temptation to break rules in the name of the Father, to live by faith rather than by the law. It is also a romantic temptation to allow oneself to be crucified, obliterated, damned, transformed, by the dormant capacities that are awakened within oneself by the presence of beautiful people and beautiful things. Like the Christian, we are born anew at the baptism of mere words and, as Dorian discovers, it is not a "new world, but rather another chaos, that is created in us." It is a temptation to individualism, which, as Wilde defines it, is a "disturbing and disintegrating force" not unlike the workings of grace in a martyr.

The seduction of "mere words" is a temptation of both spirit and flesh. We see this duality not only in Dorian's eroticized apprehension of "formless things" and "subtle magic" in the voice and presence of Lord Henry, but also in Herod's fatal attraction to both Jokanaan and Salomé. Wilde drew on the ambivalence of Herod as suggested in Saint Mark—his incestuous delight in Salomé but also his spiritual admiration for Saint John the Baptist: "For Herod feared John, knowing that he was a just man and an holy, and observed him; and when he heard him, he did many things, and heard him gladly" (Mark 6:20). In *Salomé* Wilde's Herod recognizes Jokanaan's holiness: "He is a holy man. The finger of God has touched him. God has put into his mouth terrible words" (571). Herod, of course, knows the importance of "mere words," since Salomé has put some terrible ones into his own mouth. "I am the slave of my word, and my word is the word of a king," he declares (569), but he is a slave to many words, a confusion of words like the profound and essentially decadent confusion that Huysmans and Pater and Gourmont found in the language of the Latin mystics or the early Church fathers.

*Salomé* supposedly re-creates a moment of cultural conversion, a moment of historical decadence, the death rattle of paganism alongside the birth cries of Christianity. Herod, in his confusion and paranoia, is cast back upon the word, which is now at play, no longer performing its symbolic role as transcendent authority. Wilde has lifted from the Bible a moment in Christian history in which religious instability has obliged a king, under the influence of two lascivious women, a hysterical Christian, and disputatious Jews and Nazarenes, to look to mere words with a new desperation, only to find they mirror his own crisis of meaning. Herod discovers the seduction of mere words, not only in Salomé's dance and her poetic discourse of the body, but also in the hysterical Christian discourse of Jokanaan.

In *Salomé* Wilde has accomplished an extraordinary feat: he has used a biblical text and biblical language to dramatize the decadent and symbolist fascination with the material word. The biblical word exerts a mystical influence; it fascinates and seduces Herod, no less than Salomé herself. Wilde plays upon a paradox of language, and one of the central paradoxes of Christianity: the word is both symbol and sound, both sense and sensuousness, just as Christ is the Word made flesh, the Son of God and the Son of Man. Like Huysmans, Wilde draws on the popular discourse of hysteria as a mode of the signifier run amok. Just as the Salomé of *A Rebours*—which Wilde had read on his honeymoon, ironically enough—is the "goddess of immortal Hysteria," so Wilde's Salomé is "monstrous," to use Herod's word (574). Like the moon that is her virtual familiar, "She is like a madwoman who is seeking everywhere for lovers" (561).

Jokanaan, like the disembodied "hysterical voice" of the Christian that Lord Henry hears at Marble Arch, is reduced to his impassioned voice throughout much of the play. Like the hysteric, and like the one who speaks in tongues, Jokanaan speaks in the voice of the Other, "the voice of him who had cried in the waste places and in the houses of kings" (557). Much of his language is drawn from the Bible, and so he represents the pure and divine Logos, but he carries on like a lunatic or a "drunken man" (566). Herod says, "I cannot understand what it is that he saith, but it may be an omen." Herod has glimmerings of Christian faith—his belief in the prophetic truth of Jokanaan's words—but only in a paranoid fashion, and by the end of the play he is clearly losing his wits. The Jews and Nazarenes, who are yet another reflection of Wilde's distaste for disputatious puritans, are presented as ridiculous rule-bound ideologues whose theological debates are simply babble or the howling of wild beasts. "These men are mad," Herodias finally exclaims. "They have looked too long on the moon" (565). Herodias herself, though a literalist, claims she is driven mad by the words of Jokanaan, and like her daughter, she partakes of a long tradition of what Foucault has called "the hysterization of women's bodies," the qualification and disqualification of the feminine body as being "thoroughly saturated with sexuality."[55] In *Salomé* madness signifies the peculiarly decadent fate of the Word among "mere words."

Beyond the familiar preoccupation with sexual exoticism and cruelty, all the characters in the play are decadent poets: they are solipsistic, their language militates against meaning, they repeat themselves with the eerie symbolist music of a Maeterlinck. Herod lapses into decadent pageantry as he tries to tempt Salomé with all his gems and his peacocks. Jokanaan's speech has an erotic flair, even though it is a panegyric against the sexual transgressions of Herod and Herodias; for example, he dwells with oddly prurient interest on the beauties of the young men of Egypt, their fine linen and purple, their gold shields, their silver helmets, their mighty bodies. Salomé's language constantly veers from its supposed referent, the thing as in itself it really is, into simile after simile, each more absurd than the next.

At the same time, Wilde is playing upon the irony that the decadence of *Salomé* is essentially biblical. In his decadent enumeration of his treasures, Herod mimics the equally decadent biblical account of the New Jerusalem, whose foundations are of jasper, sapphire, chalcedony, emerald, sardonyx, sardius, chrysolite, beryl, topaz, chrysoprase, jacinth, and amethyst. Nor is the vituperation that Jokanaan heaps on Herodias any less decadent than the biblical descriptions of the whore of Babylon. Nor are Salomé's similes more absurd and sensuous than those of the Shulamite bride, who claims that her breasts are like feeding deer and her lover's teeth are like sheep. Wilde mines the seductive and rebellious power of "mere words" even in the Bible. In drawing his style—at least in the English translation—from the archaic and musical King James Version, he reveals the Bible as the ultimate symbolist tragedy.

In rereading the New Testament alongside *Salomé,* I am struck by the constant tension between spirit and body in biblical metaphors, not to mention the fascination with Christ's body. In *Salomé* Wilde is not so much attacking Christianity as he is deconstructing the Bible, making it speak over and over a contradiction that is never resolved, namely, that the spirit only makes itself known through the flesh, the Word through mere words. "And the Word became flesh, and dwelt among us," Saint John tells us (1:14). And the Word has a fascinating and beautiful body. As in *Salomé,* the Gospels engage a wonderfully sensual discourse preoccupied with voice, gaze, and touch. It is a discourse of the symbolic word preoccupied with what is eminently pre-symbolic, with modes of communication and pleasure that precede the child's fall into language.

In the first epistle of Saint John we are told, "For all that is in the world, the lust of the flesh, and the lust of the eyes, and the vainglory of life, is not of the Father, but is of the world" (2:16), and yet the epistle opens with the remarkable lines, "That which was from the beginning, which we have heard, which we have seen with our eyes, which we have looked upon, and our hands have handled, of the Word of life," and so on. This wondrous palpability of the Word is apparent in the Gospels as well. The sheep know the shepherd from the stranger by the quality of his voice. Christ cures those who have lost the physical capacity for sight and hearing. He blesses by the touch of his hand, just as the touch of the baptist elicits the disembodied voice of God. Even beyond the spectacle of his crucifixion, Christ calls attention to his body, especially after his death. "See my hands and my feet, that it is I myself," he says; "handle me, and see; for a spirit hath not flesh and bones, as ye behold me having" (Luke 24:39).

This emphasis on the palpability of his body is not without its homoerotic implications, as suggested by his invitation to the doubting Thomas: "Reach hither thy finger, and behold my hands; and reach hither thy hand, and thrust it into my side: and be not faithless, but believing" (John 20:27). The homoeroticism of discipleship was by no means lost on Wilde, who was evidently delighted by Frank Harris's interpretation of Judas's betrayal as the act of a jealous lover who thought himself abandoned for "that sentimental beast John" (*Letters*, 756). In *Teleny* Briancourt proposes that two of his colleagues pose for a portrait of Christ and John as lovers: "'As I was saying, I shall paint Achmet as the Saviour, and you,' added he to Teleny, 'as John, the disciple He loved; for the Bible clearly says and continually repeats that He loved this favourite disciple.'"[56] All romantic speculations aside, to have faith is literally to partake of Christ's body, as established by his oddly Salomesque invitation, "He that eateth my flesh and drinketh my blood hath eternal life" (John 6:54). Indeed, hunger and thirst are repeatedly evoked in the Gospels as metaphors for the yearning after righteousness.

In this biblical manner, Wilde took voice, gaze, touch, and hunger as central tropes through which, in a spectacle of seduction, the senses are placed in dialectical relation to the soul. As Wilde repeatedly proclaimed, "But the Saint and the artistic Hedonist certainly meet—touch in many parts" (*Letters*, 265). Wilde's contention that ethics and aesthetics, spiritual belief and sensuous beauty, are by no means mutually exclusive is represented allegorically by the saint Jokanaan and the hedonist Salomé. Guy Willoughby has suggested that Salomé is attracted to Jokanaan as a would-be convert. Although the claim is unlikely, it does reflect the experiences of thousands of Victorian ritualists and aesthetes who became faithful converts to the Catholic Church, having first admired its sensual beauty.

Salomé and Jokanaan do exercise a peculiar influence over each other. When exposed to each other's presence, their similarity as well as their ideological opposition is revealed. What transpires is not so much a battle of opposites as a dialectical reversal in which the soul and the senses appear to mirror each other. Wilde set the pattern for this reversal in his unfinished play "La Sainte Courtisane," which, like "The Sphinx," is another parody of Flaubert's *Tentation*. The dramatic fragment takes place in the Thebaid, where the saintly hermit Honorius is tempted by the voluptuous Myrrhina. In a comic reversal, both succeed in tempting and converting each other—Honorius to the delights of sin and Myrrhina to the delights of Christian love:

HONORIUS: Myrrhina, the scales have fallen from my eyes and I see now clearly what I did not see before. Take me to Alexandria and let me taste of the seven sins.

MYRRHINA: Do not mock me, Honorius, nor speak to me with such bitter words. For I have repented of my sin and I am seeking a cavern in this desert where I too may dwell so that my soul may become worthy to see God. (705)

The dialectical reversal of saint and sinner is much more subtle and complicated in *Salomé*. The allegorical positions of various characters in the play give way to a hall of mirrors in which all the characters seem to resemble one another. Similar words are used to describe different characters, especially Salomé and Jokanaan. Even in Aubrey Beardsley's drawings they appear to mirror each other; the black locks and long flowing robe of Jokanaan (John) is like a mirror image of the black locks and long flowing robe of Salomé (Figure 9). Most striking is the structural pattern that both characters share in their relation to the voice. Salomé begins as a body without a voice, admired from afar by the young Syrian, and she is, before her moonlit murder, a voice without a body, literally the "Voice of Salomé," as she celebrates her bloody kisses in the darkness of an unlit stage. Jokanaan is in this sense her inverted mirror image, beginning as the "Voice of Jokanaan," a voice without a body, hidden as he is in the cistern, and ending as a body without a voice, a dismembered head on a silver charger—or as Salomé says, "And thy tongue, that was like a red snake darting poison, it moves no more, it says nothing now, Jokanaan, that scarlet viper that spat its venom upon me" (574).

When Jokanaan and Salomé approach each other on the stage, when indeed they have both voices and bodies, it is not only voice but gaze and touch and taste that define their opposition and their similarity. Their interaction is structured around Salomé's desire to look at

Fig. 9. Aubrey Beardsley, *John and Salomé*, illustration for *Salomé* (1892).

Jokanaan, to speak with him, to touch him, and finally to taste his mouth. He responds passionately in the negative to each of her desires: "I will not have her look at me . . . I will not listen to thee . . . Touch me not," he cries, and to her offer of a kiss, "Never, daughter of Babylon! Daughter of Sodom" (558–559). Apart from the moon, and the evocation of a lunatic gaze, Salomé appears to be the focus of the play's anxiety of the gaze, with its constant refrain, do not look at her, you look too much at her, and so on. But in fact, this pleasure and anxiety of the gaze is dispersed throughout the play, such that Herod has also gazed appreciatively at the young Syrian, though he fears to look on his corpse. The Page has also admired the young Syrian, but must now hide him from the gaze of the moon. In true paranoid fashion, Herod, the perverse subject of the gaze, becomes at last the haunted object of the gaze, a divine surveillance from which he hopes to hide himself.

Jokanaan is also both the subject and the object of a terrible gaze. As Salomé says, "It is his eyes above all that are terrible. They are like black holes burned by torches in a Tyrian tapestry. They are like black caverns where dragons dwell." He is also, like Salomé, a spectacle for the gaze. "He was very terrible to look upon," says one of the soldiers (554). But Salomé is seduced by him. His gaze is as thrilling as it is terrible to her, his voice is like wine to her, she longs to touch and admire his pale and wasted body, which is transvalued in her similes into a moonbeam, a shaft of silver, a tower of ivory, white lilies, then execrated in her anger as the body of a leper, a plaster wall where vipers have crawled, a whitened sepulchre. Salomé reveals the sensual body of Jokanaan, the body that his word both denies and confesses— denies in his passionate rejection of her, but confesses, as I have noted, in his passionate enumeration of her mother's splendid sins. The denotation of his words are pious enough in their denegation of the world, but his voice, his gaze, his body, the taste of his blood, are nevertheless a scandal.

While in Jokanaan we find the sensuous body of the saint, in Salomé we find the unexpected spirituality of the hedonist. Whatever her similarities to the whore of Babylon, Salomé is, like the Madonna, a virgin. The comparison is not a frivolous one, given that the Blessed Virgin was herself suspected by her husband of fornication, as suggested by his momentary desire to "put her away privily" (Matthew

1:19). Salomé also resembles the Blessed Virgin of anti-Catholic discourse and the puritanical diatribes against "Mariolatry" that followed upon the Vatican's recognition of the Immaculate Conception in 1854: despite her virginity, she is the object of considerable idolatry and erotic investment. Salomé makes much of her virginity, as she sees it in the mirror of the moon: "I am sure she is a virgin, she has a virgin's beauty. Yes, she is a virgin. She has never defiled herself" (555). And it is Jokanaan who is the first to scandalize her by the spectacle of his voice, gaze, and body: "I was a virgin, and thou didst take my virginity from me. I was chaste, and thou didst fill my veins with fire" (574). Her final long monologue, spoken to the dismembered head, ends with the line, "Well, I know that thou wouldst have loved me, and the mystery of love is greater than the mystery of death" (574), thus echoing an essentially Christian sentiment, one that she could have quoted almost word for word from the Shulamite bride, who says that love is as strong as death.

Wilde himself said of Salomé that "her lust must be an abyss, her corruptness, an ocean. The very pearls must die of love upon her bosom," but, paradoxically, she must also be chaste, a kind of angel: "The curves of her long, pale body . . . are like those of a lily. Her beauty has nothing of this world about it . . . Thin veils woven by the angels wrap round her slender figure . . . Her eyes shine and sparkle, and are the very stars of hope and faith."[57] Clearly, Wilde had spiritual aspirations for Salomé that his audiences might understandably have overlooked. Wilde plays upon the paradox that the language of spirit always has a beautiful body, that shame and grace stand ever in close proximity, that the saint is often no more than a perfected hedonist.

Wilde strained to see the lovely figure of Christ even in the slim-gilt body of Lord Alfred Douglas. On the eve of his sentencing—his own martyrdom—he wrote a love letter to Douglas, claiming that the boy had Christ's own heart. He lapses into the fragrant biblical language of the Canticles: "I love you, I love you, my heart is a rose which your love has brought to bloom, my life is a desert fanned by your breath, and whose cool springs are your eyes; the imprint of your little feet makes valleys of shade for me, the odour of your hair is like myrrh, and wherever you go you exhale the perfumes of the cassia tree" (*Letters*, 398). Clearly, Wilde also had spiritual aspirations for Douglas that his biographers might understandably have overlooked.

In this letter, he seems to be playing Salomé to Douglas's Jokanaan, and with about the same degree of success. Perhaps the tragic figure of Wilde should be included in performances of *Salomé*, as he is in the film adaptation directed by Ken Russell. In Aubrey Beardsley's illustrations for the play, Wilde haunts the stage in the guise of the moon or a master of ceremonies. The characters of the play already seem to represent a number of his moods and poses, especially with respect to Christianity. I think it fair to say, rephrasing Wilde's famous comment on *Dorian Gray*, that Jokanaan is what he thought he was, Herod what the world thought him, and Salomé what he wished to be—in other ages, perhaps.

## The Confessional Unmasked

> Many have a vague and indefinite notion that some *queer* questions are asked in the confessional, but very few indeed have any idea of the fearful reality as disclosed in the following pages.
>
> *The Confessional Unmasked*

In an exchange between the dandy Lord Illingworth and his sparring partner Mrs. Allonby in *A Woman of No Importance* (1893), Wilde brought together some of his signature themes—confession, flirtation, and masquerade:

> LORD ILLINGWORTH: The Book of Life begins with a man and a woman in a garden.
> MRS. ALLONBY: It ends with Revelations.
> LORD ILLINGWORTH: You fence divinely. But the button has come off your foil.
> MRS. ALLONBY: I still have the mask.
> LORD ILLINGWORTH: It makes your eyes lovelier. (443)

In this exchange, where it is uncertain how much Mrs. Allonby knows or suspects about Lord Illingworth's sexual secrets, Wilde seems to depict a confession, but his revelations seem to involve more masks. Like Mrs. Allonby's eyes, which are rendered lovelier by a mask, by a charming artifice of concealment and display, so the charm of Wilde's dialogue, its titillating breath of scandal, is assured not through the parading of a secret, but through the artful play of suspicions, suggestions, insinuations, that lends a sharpness to the lady's rhetorical foil.

Wilde's playfulness may be seen as a parody of the righteous Victorian Protestant in *The Confessional Unmasked,* who plays his own spicy game of masks and revelations and who would have us know of some queer goings-on in the Roman Catholic confessional. He will spell out his evidence like a good detective in pamphlet after pamphlet, by turns scandalizing and delighting his intended audience with inflammatory prose. The secrecy that surrounds the confessional is an inspiration to him. In language the like of which could be heard in pulpits and lecture halls all over England, he says: "I know no other reptile in all animal nature so filthy, so much to be shunned, and loathed, and dreaded by females, both married and single, as a Roman Catholic priest or bishop who practices the degrading and demoralizing office of auricular confession."[58] A good confession is usually brief and to the point, but a well-wrought suspicion can run through several editions.

Wilde's conception of confession is certainly far more Roman Catholic in its inspiration than my quotation from his comedy might at first suggest. I have already mentioned his confession to Father Bowden at the Brompton Oratory, but there were other times, especially as an expatriate after his release from prison, when Wilde spoke of being in a state of grace. For example, in a letter to Robert Ross in 1897, he writes: "Yesterday I attended Mass at ten o'clock and afterwards bathed. So I went into the water without being a Pagan. The consequence was that I was not tempted by either Sirens, or Mermaidens, or any of the green-haired following of Glaucus" (*Letters,* 583). I presume that Wilde is no longer a pagan here because he confessed and took Holy Communion. Although the remark is witty and ironic, Wilde recognized the potential of beautiful performative acts, such as taking Communion, to determine the imaginative framework through which the world is perceived.

Wilde also at times viewed confession and the Catholic Mass as an outsider. In *The Picture of Dorian Gray,* in the long ritualistic passage where Dorian lingers in a Catholic church to admire the beauty of the mass, Wilde writes: "As he passed out, he used to look with wonder at the black confessionals, and long to sit in the dim shadow of one of them and listen to men and women whispering through the worn grating the true story of their lives" (106). Dorian's gaze at the confessional may be seen as a parody of the English puritan in a Roman or Anglo-Catholic church, peering with wonder and disdain and a more or less prurient fascination at the black closet of the confessional, never having been obliged to participate in that singular contractual arrangement between the priest and the sinner that confession represents. The puritan wonders, though he cannot sufficiently overhear or comprehend. For Dorian, loitering in the half-lights of conversion, the confessional offers a voyeuristic—we cannot quite call it vicarious—pleasure. He is fascinated by the words he cannot quite hear, the "true story" whispered by sinners who appear to have taken off their masks at last.

In the nineteenth century the whisperings of the confessional excited no small degree of interest. Certain French naturalistic writers evoked the sexual dimension of confession, presumably in an effort to disqualify its spiritual significance. For Germinie Lacerteux and Emma Bovary, the confessional holds only the hope of a romantic intrigue with the priest. In decadent literature, however, it is precisely the religious context that gives the spoken sin its splendor, rendering the confessional a stage for exquisite shame. The decadent usually retires to the confessional not to flirt with a priest but to engage with the self-lacerating sensuousness of language itself. Huysmans demonstrates as much in *En Route,* with Durtal's hysterical torrent of shame and self-reproach before his confessor. Nevertheless, in the eyes of many Victorians, the decadent and ritualist fascination with the confessional was sheer prurience. Robert Hichens expresses precisely this suspicion in *The Green Carnation,* when Lord Reggie, his satirical portrait of Lord Alfred Douglas, admits to his confessional habits. Lady Locke questions Lord Reggie on the proper pose of a ritualist: "Should you like to confess all your sins?" she asks him with some surprise. "Immensely," he replies (Hichens, 73).

Wilde approached the confessional not only with the usual ardent shame of the decadent, but also with a sense of irony. He was much in sympathy with that suspicious man who lingers just outside the darkened closet, that curious puritan scarcely aware of the prurience of his own interest. As Wilde knew, the very idea that something appalling was being whispered in the confessional posed a unique challenge to Victorian norms of sexual propriety. The sexual and religious threat of auricular confession had been a matter of public, even parliamentary, outrage at least since its introduction into the Church of England by Pusey in 1838. The outcry reached a feverish pitch in the 1870s with the publication of *The Priest in Absolution,* a training manual for Anglican confessors. The information in this manual was thought to be so controversial that it was published with the utmost secrecy and distributed only to those priests who had the recommendation of well-known ritualists. Even the secrecy with which it was circulated among the clergy was considered scandalous and contributed to Protestant paranoia about a Vatican plot. Inevitably, copies of it fell into the wrong hands, and it was widely decried, not only by anti-ritualist preachers but also by no fewer than ninety-six peers, among them Archbishop Tait, who gave a blistering speech about it in the House of Lords.

Throughout the late nineteenth century, the Protestant Evangelical Mission and Electoral Union reprinted and distributed *The Confessional Unmasked,* which quoted theologians such as Peter Dens and Liguori on the nature of auricular confession and warned that Roman Catholic priests were infiltrating England in order to "convert Eden into a Sodom." They distributed the pamphlet to every member of both houses of Parliament, and later, ironically, it was itself condemned as obscene by the Court of the Queen's Bench.[59] *The Priest in Absolution* instructed Anglican priests in the essentially Roman Catholic practice of confession, but popery was the least of its crimes in the eyes of its opponents. What really captured the public's imagination was the advice given to priests for questioning women about adultery and for questioning children about masturbation and homosexuality. This advice excited the worst Evangelical fears about lascivious priests who would compromise the modesty of attractive English women and prey on innocent English children. Auricular confession was immediately condemned as a threat to the sanctity of the marriage bond, since it was presumed that priests wished not only to seduce wives but also to encourage them to spy on their husbands. Horror stories, which were often themselves confessional in nature, were printed and reprinted, stories about priests who became sexually obsessive through the temptations of the confessional and about penitent women full of shame who fell under the sway of unscrupulous priests.

Anglican priests and bishops condemned the confessional as a "dark den," "the source of unspeakable abominations," "obscene, filthy interrogations," and an institution that exposed "the sacredness of the hearth to a prying and often morbid curiosity."[60] Bishop Jeune claimed, "Confession destroys delicacy, it deadens shame, it quiets remorse."[61] Archbishop Tait found *The Priest in Absolution* regrettable and disgraceful, and he further asserted, "I cannot imagine that any right minded man could wish to have such questions addressed to any member of his family, and if he had reason to suppose that any member of his family had been exposed to such an examination, I am sure that it would be the duty of any father of a family to remonstrate with the clergyman who had put the questions, and warn him never to approach his house again."[62] "Family," I gather, is the operative term in this speech, since the Archbishop repeats it three times in the same sentence. Confession was seen as a challenge to the sacred boundaries of bourgeois family life, in particular the authority of the father over his wife and children and over any secrets they might wish to divulge. Inevitably, it is the patriarch in the family who must remonstrate with the priest. In fact, the former Roman Catholic priest William Hogan, in his No Popery diatribe *Auricular Confession and Popish Nunneries* (reprinted throughout the fin de siècle), includes an engraving of a father who brandishes a revolver as he chases after a priest on horseback. As always, the boundaries of the Victorian family were easily translatable into the boundaries of England itself. A satirical cartoon that appeared in *Punch* depicted the symbolic father of England, John Bull, dragging away a scruffy priest by the ear (Figure 10). In the man's hand is a copy of *The Priest in Absolution,* and in the background is the scandalized matron Britannia.

In his representation of the confessional in *Dorian Gray,* Wilde appears to delight in this middle-class anxiety. He further complicates and compounds the prurient sense of scandalous whisperings by making of his entire novel a kind of dark and suggestive confessional closet. Through frequent scenes of confession, through the very repetition of the word *confess,* Wilde abstracts the Catholic confessional into a confessional mode, disseminating its peculiar language of temptation and transgression, shame and remorse, secrecy and revelation, throughout the narrative. Some of the sins of Dorian Gray are explicit, such as murder and the selling of his soul. Other vices, such as homo-

## "A WOLF IN SHEEP'S CLOTHING."

Mr. Bull (*to* Britannia). "WHENEVER YOU SEE ANY OF THESE SNEAKING SCOUNDRELS ABOUT, MA'AM, JUST SEND FOR ME. *I'LL* DEAL WITH 'EM, NEVER FEAR!!"

Fig. 10. "A Wolf in Sheep's Clothing" (1877), cartoon from *Punch*.

sexuality and opium addiction are hinted at if we are able to read the signs—and a great many Victorian readers were indeed able. Nevertheless, the novel is darkened with the pervasive evidence of the unnameable and the inadmissible, the rumored and the secret.

In *Dorian Gray* transgression is not something one does so much as something one confesses or refuses to confess. Basil Hallward confesses to Lord Henry that Dorian was the one great influence in his life and art: "It was a confession. Now that I have made it, something seems to have gone out of me. Perhaps one should never put one's worship into words" (95). The confession itself, the very magic of the words, grants him absolution, though it also dissolves the pleasure he took in "worship." Dorian attempts a written confession to Sibyl Vane; he also makes a "monstrous confession" (129) to Alan Campbell; he confesses again to Basil when he reveals the portrait to him. In every instance, however, he confesses to someone who will soon die. He knows his secret will never be fully known.

The portrait, as a symbol of conscience, represents the psychological weight of a confession that will not out, that cannot escape the draperies or the secret attic room where Dorian has hidden it. It is like the soul that rankles and sickens with its sin, so often described in confessional literature. The portrait is only a confession of Dorian's sin to Dorian himself, Basil, and the reader; and in this sense it is only the private awareness of sin, not the public confession through which remorse is demonstrated, forgiveness begged, and absolution granted. Wilde is drawing on a commonplace belief to which the practice of auricular confession appeals: the belief that sin is an insistent text that will spell itself out through the body of the sinner, if not through the sinner's words. The portrait is the very image of sin as flesh as text—confession as literally a work of art.

In the last few pages of the novel, Wilde defines a conception of confession that harmonizes well with his morality plot of transgression and punishment. Dorian sees blood on his hands in the horrible portrait, and he wonders: "Confess? Did it mean that he was to confess? To give himself up, and be put to death? He laughed. He felt that the idea was monstrous. Besides, even if he did confess, who would believe him?" (166). Guilt and remorse, however, seem to lead him to a recognition of the universal necessity of confession: "Yet it was his duty to confess, to suffer public shame, and to make public atonement.

There was a God who called upon men to tell their sins to earth as well as to heaven. Nothing that he could do would cleanse him till he had told his own sin." Following this explanation, the scene in which Dorian stabs the portrait becomes the true scene of confession, the horrible cry being the cry of a soul in anguish. The portrait reverts to its previous state, which may be seen as a state of grace, and Dorian's secret is publicly revealed to a policeman when Dorian, now a withered corpse, is recognized by his rings.

Recognizing a man by his rings—the image sticks in my mind, not the least because of its intimation of an effete aestheticism that survives to the last sentence of the book. There are a number of problems with the traditional Christian reading I have suggested. First of all, Wilde's morality plot sits uneasily like a mask on his suggestive and conversational style. Like Mrs. Allonby's mask, this mechanical plot, its machinery grinding all too loudly, simply renders lovelier, as if by a backhanded compliment, Wilde's seductive eyes that look at us from behind it. What exactly is Wilde offering us in this book, revelations or more masks?

Dorian's motivation is another problem. In stabbing the portrait, he is not engaging in an act of contrition or confession. He is trying to reinforce the secrecy of his façade. He is alone, unseen, and he is trying to destroy the portrait, since it is the only evidence of the various sins, especially murder, that he might confess. "Was he really to confess? Never" (166). The revelation has come about against his will. Despite his rejection of the duty to confess, the text reveals itself and the narrative takes its fatal course. Wilde seems to be indicating that even Dorian's reticence and his beautiful face cannot conceal sin. It will out no matter what, by accident or by rumor, if not through confession. But there is also the problem of determining precisely what the final revelation has revealed. The policeman is presented with the loathsome body of a man who was youthful and handsome a moment before, but does the corpse suggest a particular interpretation? Does the decay of the body, like a symptom, always reveal a particular disease, a particular vice, a particular state of the soul, as Ellmann tells us that Wilde's blackened teeth, which he was wont to conceal as he spoke, reveal his syphilis?

It seems to me that the spectacle of Dorian's decay would leave its witnesses utterly baffled. This bafflement would be by no means insignificant in a novel that is playfully reticent about the details of the sexual sins it refers to only vaguely, metaphorically, suggestively, but nevertheless ostentatiously. Sin is not always a specific transgression in this book; sometimes it appears merely as trace of decay in the portrait, a hieroglyphic allusion to pleasure, or an inarticulate gesture of panic or anxiety in the one who knows. Wilde wanted to produce only an "atmosphere of moral corruption." As he wrote in an open letter to the editor of the *Scots Observer,* "To keep this atmosphere vague and indeterminate and wonderful was the aim of the artist who wrote the story" (*Letters,* 266).

Wilde places us in the position of the Protestant lingering with prurient fascination outside the Catholic confessional. We see only a suggestive closet, draped in black and full of whispers. We are quite sure that we are in the presence of sin, or at least the recounting of sin—its careful construction in Christian terms, with due shame and weighty silences. We have our suspicions about the sins that have transpired, but we are not altogether sure. We do not overhear all that we could wish. Much is left to our imaginations. We search faces, gestures, the double meanings of words, as the traces of what we suspect. We wonder, as did some of Wilde's readers, what sort of man "worships" the beauty of another and what sort of man drinks "something with strawberries in it." We wonder at the erotic dimension of the word "influence," at the furry bee that entrances Dorian in Basil's garden, and at the green substance in Dorian's drawer. And some have concluded that there is a certain something unhealthy, mephitic, unmanly, about the book, a certain odor of evil that exceeds definition or, at any rate, ought to.

When pressed to confess the true nature of Dorian Gray's sins—to confess, in other words, about his confession—Wilde played the trump card in his game of secrets and revelations. He confessed publicly, in the pages of the *Scots Observer:* "What Dorian Gray's sins are no one knows. He who finds them has brought them" (*Letters,* 266). He added: "It will be to each man what he is himself. It is the spectator and not life, that art really mirrors." What can we say? It is the old "it takes one to know one" ploy. In this house of mirrors, where the act of reading, like Basil's theory of painting, is purely narcissistic, at whom does one dare point in accusation? Wilde thus revealed the paradox of that curious, *curious* puritan, listening eagerly as all England seemed to be listening, to what may or may not be transpiring in whispered tones in the dark closet of the confessional. He hears only the sins he can imagine, the sins he can recognize, the sins indeed that delight him most. In this way, Wilde's novel not only contains a fairly traditional, even Catholic, representation of the confessional, it is also itself, by virtue of its very form and style, a confessional that excites the guilt and the fascination of the reader through its peculiar deployment of sin, at once ostentatious and inexplicit.

We might claim with hindsight that Wilde's trials drew the curtain from his own picture, thus revealing the truth about *Dorian Gray* as a literary puzzle whose secrecy was motivated by homosexual shame or, more likely, homosexual irony. This claim has certainly been made recently by a number of gay critics, thus perhaps illustrating Wilde's point. We may guess that the truth is out at last. But there remains the curious effect of Wilde's secrecy, the ever present suggestion that the truth is no more than suspicion and that the secret exists only to give us the pleasure of detection.

As Eve Kosofsky Sedgwick has pointed out, the confessional that is *The Picture of Dorian Gray* is an "open secret," a "glass closet," ever on the verge of becoming an "empty secret" and an "empty closet."[63] She sees the tension between the figural and the structural in *Dorian Gray* as an essentially modernist and homophobic strategy of abstract formalism, by which the literary frame is emptied of specific homosexual content. I would argue rather that this tension between the figural and the structural might indicate an essentially postmodernist—or at any rate, decadent—gesture on Wilde's part by which he unmasks the real as a fiction, another mask, essentially textual. In other words, sin is not an act so much as an interpretation. It is an act determined by the practice of interpretation. In this way, the sin is not in the transgression, but in the confession that produces the transgression as such. For Wilde, the confession determines the sin, rather than the sin the confession. Dorian's murder of Basil is certainly a relatively direct representation of a transgressive act, but there are other sins in the novel that seem to be the mere conversational traces of a transgression that is otherwise unrepresented. We get only a confession, a look of shame, a recollection of pleasure. We see the confessional closet, and it might be an empty closet, but that is all we require.

This "empty closet" is the subject of Wilde's story "The Sphinx without a Secret" (1887), in which a woman ostentatiously engages in suspicious behavior not because she has something to hide but rather because she does not. With a theatrical appearance of discretion, a lady walks to the same strange house day after day, so that her acquaintances begin to entertain suspicions. When she is followed, however, it is soon discovered that she does nothing in the house but stand quietly in the middle of an empty parlor. She desires shame, but cannot be bothered to sin. Wilde understood the performative, textual pleasures of confession, the social and even conversational construction of secrets, the reflexive trembling of the voice as we approach a revelation, the spasm of words long pent up, the virtually postcoital state of grace, and the acute sensation of shame by which our skin reddens under the hot gaze of another.

The paradox is that the sphinx is not without a secret. She has a secret, but no sin. Like the ironic confession of the masochist, the secret of the sphinx is the pure fabrication of one who has committed no crime but who nevertheless desires punishment and the aura of shame. The existence of an actual sexual transgression is immaterial. Suspicion suffices. In fact, suspicion is at the heart of the Catholic definition of scandal, which is not so much the actual commission of a sin, but its advertisement—the mere chatter about sin is an incitement to sin in others. Without the elaborate theater of suspicion, the sin is simply obvious and ugly: not an empty closet, or even a glass one, but merely the tiresome vulgarity of the brazen. Like the masochist, who is a master ironist, the sphinx even designates who are to be the righteous and who shall punish her with their shaming and suspicious gazes. Not only the secret, but the suspicion, is her invention, as is the righteous position of those who stand in judgment. The suspicious ones, whatever their own sins, are positioned as such by her; they are obliged by her to throw stones, not at a glass house, but at an empty one.

Wilde is also sometimes a sphinx without a secret. In *Dorian Gray* he writes of sins that are apparent without being certain. In broad daylight in Basil's garden, he constructs a secret, a veiled reference to homoerotic desire. He constructs a secret in a narcissistic hall of mirrors around a work of art that is the burning center of fantasy, the condensation of three homoerotic gazes: Basil at Dorian, Lord Henry at Dorian, and Dorian at Dorian. In the course of the novel, the portrait becomes a sublime object for the suspicious gaze, an effluence of the real, literally oozing with blood and decay. But like every effluence of the real, the portrait is a work of art. The portrait is a symptom, the overdetermined spectacle by which the structuration of fantasy reveals itself. It is the *point de capiton,* to use a Lacanian term. And like all such *points* of interest, it is a virtually empty space, more empty canvas than object in its own right. We would do well to heed one of Basil's remarks about his own painting: "Dorian Gray is to me simply a motive in art. You might see nothing in him. I see everything in him. He is never more present in my work than when no image of him is there. He is a suggestion, as I have said, of a new manner. I find him in the curves of certain lines, in the loveliness and subtleties of certain colours. That is all" (24). Dorian is a structural motive for Basil rather than just a thematic one. In a similar fashion, the secret of the sphinx is a structural motive, not a specific transgression. The pleasure of the sphinx Wilde, moreover, is not the pleasure of a transgressive act, homosexual or otherwise, but the purely textual pleasure of confession—or of secrecy, which is the ostentatious refusal to confess and often amounts to the same thing. Confession is a mode of pleasure for Wilde, and not just an allusion to pleasure.

In "The Sphinx without a Secret," Wilde commits the crime of giving the sphinx away, of revealing the secret that there is no crime and thereby, with a closure all too neat, eliminating her mystery and diffusing his own rhetorical seductiveness. In *Dorian Gray,* however, Wilde maintains the paradox of the empty closet. His trials, rather than revealing his secret, contributed to its propagation. More so than ever, his readers were certain that there really is something in Dorian's closet, something essentially sinful about the confessional itself, something palpable that is nevertheless not spelled out, and despite Wilde's vagueness, his circumlocution, his intentional obscurity, the novel was thought to be, no less than the stains on Wilde's sheets or the expensive cigarette cases he offered to working-class youths, sufficient evidence of very specific sexual crimes.

Edward Carson, the lawyer for the defense in the first trial, the trial for libel, was very clever in this regard. He knew that even if *Dorian Gray* was not sufficient evidence that Wilde was a sodomite, it was at least sufficient evidence that he was posing as one. Carson did not care whether the sphinx actually had a sin to keep secret. As the other trials made clear, however, there was little difference, amid a homophobic climate of suspicion and moral surveillance, between being a sodomite and posing as one. Like the Protestant lingering outside the confessional, Wilde's critics returned to the novel—indeed, they are still returning to it—with even deeper suspicion, a more intensive gaze, eager to recognize the signs of transgression. The only secret that went unrevealed, however, was the secret that there is no secret, not in the novel at any rate. The only secret is, rather, in the gaze of the curious, *curious* man, the puritan lingering outside the confessional. His fascination, his gaze, is sin itself, the scandal that goes unwhispered. That is his secret. If you tell him, he will still behave as though you did not. He will maintain the secret, even as an "open secret." As D. A. Miller has observed, "secrecy—isomorphic with its novelistic function—is not to conceal knowledge, so much as to conceal the knowledge of the knowledge."[64]

Michel Foucault is relevant in this regard when he discusses the transformation of religious confession into a *scientia sexualis* determined to reveal the truth by revealing the truth about sex. "Western man has become a confessing animal," he writes,[65] referring to all the technologies of surveillance, confession, discipline, and punishment that are disseminated throughout the institutions that govern our lives—not only the church, but also the school, the prison, and the family. As in Wilde, the confessional mode for Foucault extends well beyond the Catholic confessional. He also shares with Wilde a belief that, at least in Western tradition, different confessions presume different punishments and different pleasures.

On the pleasure of confession—the trembling, the whispering, the secret fantasies, the threat of scandal—both Wilde and Foucault are certainly eloquent. Foucault admits that he is not sure whether this pleasure amounts to an *ars erotica* or whether it is merely a bonus for obedience to superior powers. I am not sure that Wilde could make the distinction either. The insistence of the confessional mode on sincerity, penitence, and conformity has led many in Foucault's wake (however unlikely) to seek to disengage sex from the regimes of knowledge-power that determine its meaning and significance. Others have looked to Foucault's concept of the "reverse discourse," the inversion of confession by which homosexuals and other oppressed groups of people speak up in their own behalf, often in the same vocabulary by which they were disqualified. In the reverse discourse, confession is ironized as something more like coming out.

Wilde's texts suggest still another confessional strategy, one based in the irony that life imitates art, rather than art life. While for Foucault the sexual subject is determined by a vast and polyvalent discursive deployment of sexuality, Wilde propagated a romantic conception of the artist as someone who determines his sexuality and his discursive milieu through aesthetic form and style. Wilde's failure in this regard, indeed his naïveté, is evident from his trials. In his cross-examination, he countered the accusatory tone of his opponent with a confession that was in fact a subtle but insistent defense, an effort to rewrite the terms by which he was accused. He believed that homosexuality was essentially noble, and he tried to take advantage of his examiner's inarticulateness—his use of vague terms like "perverse," "unnatural," or "indecent"—to reformulate the discourse by which he was to be condemned. He would confess to being an artist or a genius, rather than a pervert, though for him all three epithets might describe much the same behavior. At his trials Wilde deployed confession as a very wily circumlocution. Obviously, he was not very successful at talking himself out of Reading Gaol. All performances require a willing audience. Justice Wills was not willing. He made no reply when, upon sentencing, Wilde could only ask, "And I? May I say nothing, my lord?"[66]

Wilde was very resourceful in the art of confessing his homosexuality. I would like to compare some of the confessions he made around the time of his imprisonment—one an admission of his love in court, another a profession of his love to Douglas, the third an acknowledgment of his guilt to the Home Secretary. During one of his trials, Wilde defined the sort of friendship that he elsewhere confessed was his ideal: "'The Love that dare not speak its name' in this century is such a great affection of an elder for a younger man as there was between David and Jonathan, such as Plato made the very basis of his philosophy, and such as you find in the sonnets of Michelangelo and Shakespeare."[67] In this comment, Wilde draws on a powerful academic apologia for homosexuality as classical friendship in order to counter accusations of his gross indecency. In another context, a letter to Douglas shortly before his sentencing, Wilde engages a more florid and biblical style. He begins by confessing his love and refers to

Douglas as a golden-haired boy with Christ's own heart. "O dearest of created things," he writes, "if someone wounded by silence and solitude comes to you, dishonoured, a laughing-stock to men, oh! you can close his wounds by touching them and restore his soul which unhappiness had for a moment smothered" (*Letters*, 398). In this letter a Christ-like conception of homosexuality is favored, presumably in order to keep a lover faithful. Wilde chose still another confessional style in his prison letters to the Home Secretary. In these letters he describes his desire for men as sexual madness, erotomania, morbid passions, obscene fancies, leprosy, malaria, and a strange disease—and he adds an appropriate reference to the criminal psychologist Cesare Lombroso (*Letters*, 402–403). In a style no less excessive than in his love letter to Douglas, Wilde here engages all the medical terminology he can think of to excite the Home Secretary's sense of mercy.

In each of these three passages, Wilde deploys a different discourse of homosexuality, no doubt with an eye to political and social effects. His confessions are a splendid artifice. Every time he opens his closet door, something new and strange pops out—usually another closet. Although the courts imprisoned him, Douglas failed him, and the Home Secretary was only mildly persuaded, we see Wilde in some of his more desperate efforts at deploying the confessional mode cynically, even subversively, for his own ends. In this way he is not unlike the character of Guido Ferranti in *The Duchess of Padua* (1883), who at the end of Act 4 says repeatedly, "I confess . . . so much I will confess . . . I confess" (632–633), even though he has not actually committed the murder to which he confesses. In Wilde's deployment of the confessional mode, there is always something of the beautiful lie.

It is in *De Profundis* that Wilde renews my faith in his contention that, even through confession, the romantic artist is the author of his own personality. If the artist does not write it, then at least he can rewrite it. Wilde's life, culminating in his spectacular trials, was recounted (even by himself) in language more appropriate to tragedy or allegory. Many have noted, however, that the interrogations of the trials brought Wilde's artfulness to a premature end and that the strains of imprisonment forced him to remove his masks. His famous prison letter is full of personal revelations and what appears to be a degree of sincerity allegedly absent from his earlier work. Jonathan

Dollimore, for example, bemoans the triumph of Victorian sexual ideology as demonstrated by the sudden solemnity and sincerity of Wilde in *De Profundis*. While his earlier comedies and fiction mark the triumph of a subversive anti-essentialist, *De Profundis* is said to renounce an earlier transgressive aesthetic in its demand for meaning. "In effect," Dollimore writes, "Wilde repositions himself as the authentic, sincere subject which before he had subverted," and he adds that Wilde's letter represents "a defeat of the marginal and the oppositional of a kind which only ideological domination can effect; a renunciation which is experienced as voluntary and self-confirming but which is in truth a self-defeat and a self-denial massively coerced through the imposition, by the dominant, of incarceration and suffering and their 'natural' medium, confession."[68]

How Dollimore, an anti-essentialist, comes upon an essential self that can "in truth" be defeated and denied is not altogether clear, nor do I understand how Wilde's letter, which is a fine example of the Foucauldian reverse discourse, could possibly be dismissed along such Foucauldian lines. I would argue, rather, that *De Profundis* represents a new deployment of the confessional mode in Wilde's writing, a mode that he had explored in different ways since his early Catholic poetry. The Victorian tendency to force the discourse of sexuality into a highly volatile and anxious confessional mode, whether the confessor be God, spouse, clergyman, physician, or barrister, was less a threat to Wilde's sexuality than an opportunity for his imagination.

At a time when Evangelicals were utterly outraged and scandalized by the presence of the Catholic confessional in the Church of England, Wilde recognized the performative and theatrical possibilities of confessional writing. As a master of the open secret, he was keenly aware of the artistry of confession, the beautiful lie that sexual revelations invariably aspire to be. The confession produces the sin by virtue of its remorse or its impenitence. It produces the priest by the solemnity of its transmission. It produces the confessional by virtue of its whisper. It produces God by its expectation of forgiveness. Furthermore, as Wilde knew, and as Foucault has proclaimed, the confessional produces sexuality by defining its interpretive frame—and talking of little else. What Wilde said of Dorian Gray's confession to Sibyl Vane might well apply to his own confession in *De Profundis:* "He covered page after page with wild words of sorrow, and wilder words of pain.

There is a luxury of self-reproach. When we blame ourselves, we feel that no one else has a right to blame us. It is the confession, not the priest, that gives us absolution" (*Dorian Gray*, 85). In Wilde's hands, the "wild words" of confession were indeed Wilde's words, and he made of his own confession a performative work of art.

With its echoing signs of self-reproach, its litany of "I confess" and "I admit" and "I blame myself," *De Profundis* is certainly a confession. But a confession of what? When Wilde writes, "A man's very highest moment is, I have no doubt at all, when he kneels in the dust, and beats his breast, and tells all the sins of his life" (502), we may feel we have cause for panic. Is this line not evidence of the ideological tyranny that Foucault ascribed to the confessional mode? On the same page, however, Wilde suggests a distaste for artless revelation when he writes, "There is no reason why a man should show his life to the world. The world does not understand things." What is clear, though, is that the poet is at work. In an especially pithy passage, Wilde reveals his peculiar understanding of confession: "I remember as I was sitting in the dock on the occasion of my last trial listening to Lockwood's appalling denunciation of me—like a thing out of Tacitus, like a passage in Dante, like one of Savonarola's indictments of the Popes at Rome—and being sickened with horror at what I heard. Suddenly it occurred to me, *'How splendid it would be, if I was saying all this about myself!'*" (502).

Splendid indeed are the sins that he recounts, and no less artful than Dante or Savonarola is his confession. He is the author of the framework through which his sins are to be interpreted, and that makes all the difference. Sins become precious works of art that decorate and sustain his own Christian tragedy: "It was like feasting with panthers. The danger was half the excitement. I used to feel as the snake-charmer must feel when he lures the cobra to stir from the painted cloth or reed-basket that holds it, and makes it spread its hood at his bidding, and sway to and fro in the air as a plant sways restfully in a stream. They were to me the brightest of gilded snakes. Their poison was part of their perfection" (492). Sin never gets much better than this, not on paper anyway, and Wilde knows it. He is a master of the paradoxical decadent passion for turning poison into perfection. He engages a homophobic discourse in a manner that transforms homosexuality into poetry. The reality of his rent boys vanishes into an exquisite cluster of similes—panthers, a cobra, a plant restfully swaying in a stream. Even his snakes are not like real snakes, but "gilded" like jewels. Throughout the letters he wrote during this period, Wilde is emphatic on the point that if homosexuality is a sin at all, it is a trivial one. "Sins of the Flesh are nothing," he writes in *De Profundis*. "They are maladies for physicians to cure, if they should be cured" (452).

Like many of his contemporaries, Wilde could idealize his homosexuality into a blameless chivalry. He even claims he eventually grew bored with the relentless indulgence that Douglas demanded—the sex, the gambling, the good wine and expensive dinners. However dull his "maladies" may have been in practice, in prose they are splendid. Wilde could never part with a conception of sin, whether it be sins of the flesh or sins of the soul. For his confession to be gilded, he needed gilded snakes. Like the sphinx without a secret, those who have no sins must invent them. Wilde's highest moment—when he kneels in the dust, beats his breast, and tells his sins—is also a moment of consummate performative pleasure in which sensual indulgences are discursively reinvented as the splendid sins of the soul. But these sins are merely symptoms of a far more exquisite indulgence, namely, the aesthetic pleasure of penitence. Paul de Man located the same phenomenon in Rousseau's *Confessions* when he noted that "shame used as excuse permits repression to function as revelation and thus to make pleasure and guilt interchangeable."[69] In "The Critic as Artist," Wilde speaks of the debt of gratitude we owe Rousseau for confessing his brilliant sins to the world rather than to a priest, and Cellini is praised in a similar tribute as the raconteur of the "story of his splendour and his shame" (1009). The rhetoric of the confessional is never exhausted by its punitive purpose. The redemptive and disciplinary intention of auricular confession is subject to a reversal, revealing the confessional to be precisely what Victorian anti-Catholic crusaders claimed it to be: a scandal.

# FIVE

# Priests and Acolytes

## Fragrant Prayers

"And if you should want me, sir" . . . the youthful acolyte possessed the power to convey the unuttered.

"If?? . . . And say a fragrant prayer for me, child," the Cardinal enjoined.                                                                                     Ronald Firbank

I have often been asked in the course of writing this book why a gay man or a lover of boys would become a priest. The motives are so numerous, however, that the real question ought to be why straight men become priests. Beyond faith, which I gather to be the primary appeal, since the priesthood would be unbearable without it, there are other motivations for men of a certain inclination: the effeminized pastoral persona, the pleasures of ritual, public trust and respect, freedom from the social pressure to marry, opportunities for intimacy with boys, passionate friendship and cohabitation with likeminded men, and a discipline for coping with sexual shame and guilt.

I can think of no better argument for the homoeroticism of the priesthood than the pederastic priest-and-acolyte narratives that proliferated in England between 1880 and about 1930. I say pederastic because there is a significant trace of the Greek in their idealized cult of devotion between man and boy, but it is a cult that the Church has promoted, despite its formal disavowals, by rendering the priesthood one of the most attractive occupations available to men who love boys.

297

Nowadays, we tend to find such priest-and-acolyte narratives construed primarily in the gothic language of child abuse case studies—in docudramas like *The Boys of Saint Vincent* or sensational pieces of journalism with irresistible titles like *A Gospel of Shame* and *Lead Us Not into Temptation*. The eighteenth and nineteenth centuries had their own version of the priestly molester, usually of a satanic or anticlerical character, but in the fin de siècle English literature produced a plethora of Catholic narratives—some of them decadent and some not—that celebrated the desire of man for boy and occasionally (as with John Gray) the desire of man for man.

The pederastic priest, whether Anglo or Roman Catholic, has always been a figure rich in paradox. Popes, saints, priests, acolytes, choirboys, curates, monks, and nuns—all were seen as privileged, if highly unstable, subject matter for writers who were contesting conventional beliefs about the relationship between sexuality and religious experience. A number of homosexual aesthetes of the 1890s were themselves priests, but homosexual clergy of all stripes figured as fictional characters as well. The range of representations was enormous. The pederastic priest, not to mention his acolyte, could be the subject of a homophobic diatribe or—a peculiarly fin de siècle genre—a "uranian" apologia. He could be debauched, guilty, pious, fraternal, sentimental, ecstatic, ritualistic, comical, or flower-like, depending on the religious and sexual motivations of the author.

In this chapter I will focus on those decadent writers who were themselves priests or who claimed to have a priestly vocation. I have taken my title from John Francis Bloxam's story "The Priest and the Acolyte" (1894), a tragic tale of a young priest, Ronald Heatherington, who falls in love with a fourteen-year-old acolyte named Wilfred. They become lovers, inspiring each other to new heights of spiritual perfection. Unfortunately, they are discovered together in a compromising situation by the rector. Ronald defends the purity and beauty of their love, but eventually, in a highly melodramatic and romantic gesture, man and boy commit suicide together in a ritual that imitates the Mass. Although not an exemplary work of decadent style, "The Priest and the Acolyte" is an interesting place to begin a discussion of decadent priests. The story was published anonymously in a highly homoerotic Oxford journal *The Chameleon,* which Bloxam edited and which also contained contributions by Oscar Wilde and

Lord Alfred Douglas. The story also gained a degree of notoriety when it was attributed to Wilde and used against him at his first trial. In addition to Bloxam's story, I will also discuss the work of a number of other decadents of an ecclesiastical persuasion—namely, John Gray, a disciple of Wilde who became a Roman Catholic priest in Edinburgh; Frederick Rolfe, also known as Baron Corvo, a self-styled priest and aesthete who never made it through the seminary; and two later writers, Montague Summers and Ronald Firbank, who revived a conception of the priest as Wildean dandy and ritualist.

In order to place "The Priest and the Acolyte" and other such stories into a historical context, we should first take a glance at various versions of priestly homoeroticism that were popular in the fin de siècle. Bloxam's story was highly original and influential in its time, in that the priest and acolyte are viewed sympathetically within an apologia for love between men and boys. It was also scandalous, no less for its apparent blasphemy than for its daring critique of Christian homophobia. Despite its originality, the story partakes of a number of clerical personae—the priest as sublimated ritualist, as celibate lover of boys, as guilty hypocrite, and as evil sodomite—that had already appeared in other contexts. The flower-like priest of Bloxam's story was indeed a hardy perennial. I have already mentioned a few Victorian priests with homoerotic and ritualistic inclinations—Frederic William Faber and Edward King, for example. We might also briefly consider two poets of the same period who were also inspired by Newman: Gerard Manley Hopkins and Digby Mackworth Dolben. It is already well known that Hopkins, a Roman Catholic convert and priest, wrote a few fine examples of homoerotic verse in the spirit of Walt Whitman. "Harry Ploughman," for example, goes on at great length about the "barrowy brawn" of a strikingly sinewy man as he works in the field, while "Epithalamion," allegedly intended as a meditation on matrimony, reads more like a tribute to the loveliness of boys, peeped at as they bathe. Hopkins also wrote a sermon that describes the beauty of Christ's person in language that might have been applied more appropriately to one of Simeon Solomon's drawings of androgynous Greeks.

Less well known is Digby Dolben, with whom it is widely assumed Hopkins was once in love. Dolben developed an effusive and highly ritualistic style, both in his poetry and his own devotional practice.

Moreover, his love poems to male friends are scarcely distinguishable from the poems he wrote to Christ or the Virgin, though he was certainly not the first man of a Tractarian disposition to find in Christianity, or even Marianism, a homoerotic cult. In the 1860s Dolben wrote a group of homoerotic poems about his Eton friend Martin Le Marchant Gosselin. He could be quite explicit in his romantic affection:

> Ah, Love, first Love, came gently through the wood,
> Under a tree he found me all alone,
> Gently, gently, he kissed me on the cheek,
> And gently took my hand within his own.[1]

The same sort of language appears in some of his devotional poems, such as "Homo Factus Est," in which Christ takes the place of his boy beloved without any diminution of eroticism:

> Jesu, my Belovéd,
> > Come to me alone;
> In Thy sweet embraces
> > Make me all Thine own.[2]

While his parents were decidedly Evangelical, Dolben became an ardent ritualist and even hoped to found his own monastic brotherhood. He also intended to become a priest. His cousin and biographer Robert Bridges suggests that Dolben was overly fond of vestments. Henry James also chimed in with his dismay, declaring that the young man's "precious and direct avidity for all the paraphernalia of a complicated ecclesiasticism" seemed to him insincere and cheaply romantic (though it might be said that the preciosity of James's own style undermines the force of his observation).[3] Anecdotes about Dolben's wearing a monk's habit while away from school or about his genuflecting shamelessly in chapel suggest that, at a very young age, he was aware of the capacity to shock other people with his ritualism. Indeed, he was thrown out of Eton in 1863 for illicitly attending a Roman Catholic service.

On a more sardonic note, Samuel Butler created a homosexual ritualist in his novel *The Way of All Flesh*, which was written between

1873 and 1885, though not published until 1903, after his death. The hero Ernest Pontifex is mystified by Pryer, a fellow curate of High Church views who is eager to initiate him into the doctrinal wisdom of the confessional and papal authority. Ernest is convinced that priests should be "absolutely sexless," but he is troubled by Pryer and his High Church circle because "certain thoughts which he had warred against as fatal to his soul, and which he had imagined he should lose once and for all on ordination, were still as troublesome to him as they had been; he also saw plainly enough that the young gentlemen who formed the circle of Pryer's friends were in much the same unhappy predicament." What are these troublesome, unhappy thoughts? Butler, who was himself apparently bisexual, is vague, but suggestive. Pryer is forever looking Ernest up and down, theorizing about the precise doctrinal definition of vice, and "wanting to approach a subject which he did not quite venture to touch upon." "As regards the clergy," Butler adds, "glimpses of a pretty large cloven hoof kept peeping out from under the saintly robe of Pryer's conversation, to the effect that so long as they were theoretically perfect, practical peccadilloes—or even peccadoccios, if there is such a word—were of less importance."[4]

In his study of what he calls "uranian" poetry, Timothy d'Arch Smith describes the careers of a great many minor poets who wrote homoerotic verse between 1880 and 1930. A number of these writers—namely, Bloxam, E. E. Bradford, Samuel Elsworth Cottam, George Gabriel Scott Gillett, Edward Cracroft Lefroy, and Edmund St. Gascoigne Mackie—were ordained as priests in the Church of England and three of them (Bloxam, Cottam, and Gillett) were associated with Anglo-Catholic churches. While Dolben and other ritualists articulated homoerotic desire through a highly sensual devotion to Christ, many of these uranian priests wrote of a classical influence, either an Apollonian comradeship that harmonized with Christian piety or a Dionysian sensuality that was characterized as demonic. Much of the poetry of these writers is so sentimental and sublimated that the sexual content is scarcely recognizable as such. Nevertheless, throughout this uranian tradition, acolytes and choirboys are peculiarly susceptible to the erotic speculations, sublimated and otherwise, of the poet. Often the cumulative effect of such poetry is one of ambivalence, the all too familiar angel-whore dilemma applied to the lovely body of a boy whose golden curls and incandescently wan complexion are at once sanctified and tempting, a ray of hope and a foretaste of death.

Edmund John's poem "The Acolyte" (1913), which was probably directly inspired by Bloxam's story, is an excellent example of the angelic boy as erotic blazon. In this poem the speaker's erotic gaze at a wan and beautiful acolyte is preceded by the solemn music of a Catholic service, even the "sensuous song of incense sighing low," a scent that virtually invokes the boy's presence through its incantatory tone. In this heady atmosphere, the Christian symbolism of the acolyte's attire is refigured as Greek, such that even his "crimson cassock and fair lace" are likened to spilled Dionysian or Lesbian wine. He even excites a Greek glance from the crucifix:

> And from the dead eyes of the Christ was flung,
> Swiftly, the live glance of Apollo.

John then describes a priest, who is apparently blanching in a moment of spiritual crisis and sexual panic under the influence of the acolyte:

> Then through the monkish hymn
> A strange note and a piercing sweetness ran;
> And a young priest, who saw thee, clutched his beads,
> And grew all pale as from the organ reeds
> Pealed once again the poignant pipes of Pan.[5]

On a similar note, Cuthbert Wright, a Church historian, seems to have the same difficulty suppressing the Greek in his devotions. In his book of verses *One Way of Love* (1915)—the title itself is a bit ambiguous—Wright dwells with much ritualistic pageantry on the "boyish beauty" of many a choirboy, or many a "surpliced faun," to use his phrase. In Wright's poem "To the Unknown," Jesus himself is seen as a lover of boys. Are the boys angels or fauns? Is the poet an angel or a faun for loving them? In poems with titles like "The Chorister" and "To a Dead Child," this pedophilic dilemma is continually reenacted but never resolved, and Wright is occasionally explicit about his ambivalence, as in these lines:

In your strange eyes shall I yet see the sin
For which I love you dear, accurséd child?[6]

Less ambivalent are the acolyte poems of E. E. Bradford, in which Greek and Christian find a common Paterian ground in a discourse of chivalry. Throughout *"The New Chivalry" and Other Poems* (1918), Bradford seeks to reclaim pederastic love as a romantic Christian ideal:

Is Boy-Love Greek? For across the seas
The warm desire of Southern men may be:
But passion freshened by a Northern breeze
Gains in male vigour and in purity.
Our yearning tenderness for boys like these
Has more in it of Christ than Socrates.[7]

Although his notion of pure love between man and boy is highly sublimated, Bradford is not averse to "touch, embrace and kiss" ("Excelsius," 67), and in "Corpus Sanum" he exclaims:

The mere word "carnal" shall not me affright;
Nor will I cease, in Puritans' despite,
To love the boyish body with the sprite,
       And hymn it too. (74)

In his pious homoeroticism, which he often construes after the fashion of *Parsifal* as a flight from the temptress Eve, Bradford happens upon some unlikely bedfellows, as in the poem "The Story of the Fall":

Most follow Woman, since the Fall,
    But as for me I'll follow Paul! (105)

Most curious, however, are the reviews for Bradford's poetry, many of which describe his work as cheery, wholesome, and virile. Apparently, the priest-and-acolyte genre could hide homoeroticism in plain sight.

Alongside this sublimated figure, however, was its evil twin, the figure of the priest as sodomite and corrupter of children—a decadent elaboration of the Catholic horror all too present in the libertine, anticlerical, and gothic literature of an earlier generation. Matthew G. Lewis, Ann Radcliffe, and Charles Maturin may have been expert at eroticizing Catholicism for English readers, even representing it as a paranoid and insidious social force, but the literary phenomenon of a priest who buggers boys against their will was decidedly French. I have already spoken of Canon Docre and his lascivious acolytes in Huysmans' *Là-Bas*, though that was, after all, the black mass. Usually, in French literature from the Marquis de Sade on, the sodomitical priest was a favorite villain of anticlerical diatribes. Octave Mirbeau's novel *Sébastien Roch* (1890) is a fine fin de siècle example. Although, like Nietzsche, Mirbeau railed against decadent writing and the Church as degenerate, his own style and eroticism place him squarely in the decadent tradition. In this particular novel, little Sébastien is left to the tyrannical and medieval wiles of a Jesuit school for the sons of gentlemen. His life there is one humiliation after another, especially when he comes under the sway of his salacious confessor, Father de Kern. However disdainfully, Mirbeau evokes the fragrant essence of decadent Catholicism: "Father de Kern had a tendency to tender melancholy, ecstatic penitence, ethereal embraces, hopeless mysticisms, where the idea of love seeks company in the idea of death, everything that was both carnal and immaterial, everything that corresponded with whatever was vague, generous, and bewildered in Sébastien's soul, a childlike soul too fragile, too delicate to bear unharmed the lightning shock of such clouds, and the corrupting fume of such poisons."[8] Huysmans could not have put it more deliciously, nor could he have written a more tortuous sentence. It may be difficult to say why intangible embraces and hopeless mysticisms should be insidious in a priest, so typical are they of an innocuous and orthodox devotional practice in the Church. Nevertheless, the sensual devotions of the priest set the stage for a far more libertine performance. He rapes the boy, then further betrays him by publicly and falsely accusing him of a homosexual dalliance with the son of a doctor. Sébastien is sent home in disgrace.

Homosexual priests of the fin de siècle, not to mention their representation in literature, ranged from the saintly to the sordid—from the sublimated endearments of Bishop King to the satanic orgies of the Abbé Boullan—and decadent literature embraced both ends of the spectrum. In "The Priest and the Acolyte," Bloxam's young clergyman, Ronald Heatherington, seems to have taken upon himself, as though through some literary act of mystical substitution, many of the virtues and sins that attracted the decadents to the figure of the pederastic priest. He is a paradox, by turns pious and blasphemous, righteous and ashamed, soulful and sensual, relentless in his sublimation and distracted by his desire.

Bloxam's story is, furthermore, an odd and not wholly successful aggregate of decadent romance and uranian polemic. This jarring generic flaw, a love story given to didacticism, might explain why Oscar Wilde claimed to be unimpressed by it. When, at his libel trial, Wilde was asked if he thought "The Priest and the Acolyte" was not immoral, he responded, "It was worse. It was badly written." When pressed for a moral opinion, he stood firmly on aesthetic grounds, calling the story "disgusting" and "perfect twaddle."[9] He was hardly in a position to say otherwise. When he was not being cross-examined in the dock, however, Wilde spoke of Bloxam as "an undergraduate of strange beauty" and regarded the young man's prose with a somewhat kindlier eye: "The story is, to my ears, too direct: there is no nuance: it profanes a little by revelation: God and other artists are always a little obscure. Still, it has interesting qualities, and is at moments poisonous: which is something."[10] Bloxam certainly lacks Wilde's subtlety, not to mention his genius for artful secrets and poisonous revelations. Nevertheless, the story has so many Wildean touches that it was sometimes attributed to him, and it was included in the first edition of his collected works. Even little Wilfred pays an ecclesiastical tribute to the divine Oscar in the peculiarity of his name, which is an anagram for "Fr. Wilde." In the story's paradoxes, its ritualism, its defense of homosexuality, its attack on "convention," Bloxam seems to be playing disciple and recounting a few lessons of the master.

"What is that story?" Edward Carson asked, addressing Wilde's jury on the meaning of "The Priest and the Acolyte." We soon discover that Carson intended the question to be a rhetorical one:

It is a story of the love of a priest for the acolyte who attended him at Mass. Exactly the same idea that runs through the two letters to Lord Alfred Douglas runs through that story, and also through *The Picture of Dorian Gray.* When the boy was discovered in the priest's bed, the priest made exactly the same defence as Mr. Wilde has made—that the world does not understand the beauty of this love.

The same idea runs through these two letters which Mr. Wilde has called beautiful, but which I call an abominable piece of disgusting immorality.[11]

Good call! Or, at any rate, the jury seemed to think so. But the comparison with *Dorian Gray* raises still other questions about Bloxam's story beyond its status as a piece of disgusting immorality or, for that matter, a piece of disgusting twaddle. As Carson observes, there is great similarity between Ronald Heatherington's confession to his rector, Basil Hallward's confession of his love for Dorian, and Wilde's "David and Jonathan" apologia, so eloquently expressed at his trial. I would add that, like Wilde, Bloxam sought to explore the peculiar eroticism of Roman Catholic discourse, even for the faithful. Although his ironic treatment of the confessional and ritual is not as skillful as Wilde's, Bloxam sought to anatomize in relatively explicit terms the homoerotic appeal of the Church, even for its priests. As in Wilde's trials, Bloxam is engaging in a hermeneutic, almost legalistic, battle over interpretations of sexual as well as religious language.

The story begins with the French adage "Honi soit qui mal y pense"—shameful is he who thinks evil.[12] In the context of the story, the saying acquires a certain irony, not the least because Bloxam, like most of his decadent compatriots, calls upon the French language to express an opinion about evil. Even a biblical passage could evoke a suspicious fragrance when an English writer quoted it in French. Indeed, the story is no less about suspicion and scandal than about boy-love and the clergy. Bloxam is following Wilde in his depiction of auricular confession as a reverse discourse. The confessional, traditionally a site of penitence and religious discipline, ironically becomes the site of sin—of seduction, suspicion, and scandal. It is also, for Bloxam, the site for a challenge to homophobic Church authority in its own terms.

After the adage about thinking evil, we hear a confession. It is a disembodied voice at first, a free-floating admission of sin and guilt that stands curiously by itself without reference to a particular speaker or audience, nor even a particular scene of enunciation. The nameless priest who listens is introduced in the next paragraph, but still the voice is disembodied, attributable to everyone and no one until the third paragraph, when the priest finally recognizes the voice of his as yet unnamed acolyte. It is a few pages before we learn the names of either character—a suggestion of Bloxam's resistance to particularity. The language of confession is immediately recognizable and powerfully suggestive of the Catholic penitential pose, but it is a discourse already at play. Even the priest's mind is wandering, fading with ennui at the usual list of "boyish sins," and he wishes that, if sin they must, his parishoners would at least be a little more original. The repetitions of confessional language are all too familiar, boring, dreary, a currency worn smooth of its meaning. But when he sees the "flower-like face" of the acolyte and meets his blue-eyed gaze, he feels he has come in contact with something beautiful and true. Auricular confession, the ritual par excellence for the naming of homosexuality as sin, becomes an ironic site for the performance, even the celebration, of the desire it seeks to contain.

As in Wilde, Bloxam abstracts the Catholic confessional into a rhetorical confessional mode that mediates virtually every articulation of the priest's desire. We begin to wonder whether the desire seeks confession or confession seeks the desire. As many an Evangelical feared, and as Foucault has proclaimed, auricular confession appears literally to produce homoeroticism, to incite it, to define the terms of its articulation, even as it seeks to invalidate it. The confessional in this story does not call for the repression of homosexual desire but rather for its re-enactment. Furthermore, the very status of confession as discourse, as free-floating signifier, renders it an uncertain avatar of homophobic authority and discipline. Kneeling before the altar the next morning, the as yet unnamed priest turns reverently toward his acolyte to "say the words of confession"; but these words are displaced in the text by the bowing gesture of the priest, his hair touching the golden halo surrounding the boy's face, and he feels "his veins burn and tingle with a strange new fascination" (30). The words of confession suffer a discursive slippage and become indistinguishable from the Wildean "fascination" that they permit, the fascination not only of desire but of Catholicism itself.

Ronald Heatherington, finally given a name, defends his love for little Wilfred in a long apologia addressed to the rector. Even this apologia is regarded by Bloxam as an auricular confession. Through a clever inversion, however, Bloxam seeks to reassign the shame, lifting the burden of sin from the penitent and placing it on the shoulders of the confessor. The angry rector insists upon the appropriate confessional pose, demanding, "Where is your penitence, your shame? have you no sense of the horror of your sin?" (39). A well-placed remark about Christian mercy quiets the rage of the rector, and the priest begins his uranian apologia.

"The rector sat down," Bloxam writes, "while his curate told him the story of his life, sitting by the empty grate with his chin resting on his clasped hands" (41). What is this mysterious grate? The only grate we have read of thus far is in the opening scene, the "grating" through which the priest first meets the blue eyes of his penitent acolyte. The apologia is refigured as a confession, but the priest has no sin to admit. He has already claimed that his love is perfect. In fact, we see him do very little with the boy apart from kissing him passionately, embracing him, and saying mass. "There is no sin for which I should feel shame," he says, adding, "God gave me my love for him, and He gave him also his love for me." The priest's confession is the admission of not his own sin, but rather the sin of his confessor. The sin is not sodomy or scandal, but rather the unjust "convention" of homophobia. "I have committed no moral offence in this matter," he insists; "in the sight of God my soul is blameless; but to you and to the world I am guilty of an abominable crime—abominable because it is a sin against convention, forsooth!" Bloxam's representation of the priest as he stands alone, *contra mundum,* resonates well with the spirit of Anglo-Catholicism itself, a rebellious Church within the Church, regarded with suspicion from all sides. It also resonates with Christ's suffering, thus justifying the priest's exclamation, "In God's eyes we are martyrs, and we shall not shrink even from death in the struggle against the idolatrous worship of convention." The priest deploys the Church's narratives against its own tendency to homophobia.

Ritual, no less than confession, is reappropriated by the priest for a pious and solemn celebration of his peculiar "fascination." Like his Tractarian and decadent forebears, Ronald Heatherington is an ardent ritualist and a bit of a dandy, and the sexual motivation of his ritualism is unusually explicit. In the account of his life that he offers to his rector, the priest explains the aesthetic and erotic motivations involved in his vocation. His choice of the priesthood is almost accidental. He says, "I had to choose a profession. I became a priest." But then he adds, "The whole aesthetic tendency of my soul was intensely attracted by the wonderful mysteries of Christianity, the artistic beauty of our services" (41) His search for beauty and a perfect love in particular people failed, and so he turned to the mystical idealism and rituals of the Church. Catholicism is seen as a kind of snare, appealing to what is most noble—and most vulnerable—in the sexual and aesthetic disposition of a lover of boys. His ordination was followed by "five years fierce battling with those terrible passions he had fostered in his boyhood" (32)—more of those tired boyish sins, I gather. Bloxam further adds that "all the intensity of his nature had been concentrated, completely absorbed, in the beautiful mysteries of his religion." Despite this vivid portrait of sublimation, the priest seems to regard ritualism and sex as different modes of the same tendency to perfection. Ritualism offers an almost perilous pleasure:

"I have found, and still find, an exquisite delight in religion: not in the regular duties of a religious life, not in the ordinary round of parish organisations;—against these I chafe incessantly;—no, my delight is in the aesthetic beauty of the services, the ecstasy of devotion, the passionate fervour that come with long fasting and meditation."

"Have you found no comfort in prayer?" asked the rector.

"Comfort?—no. But I have found in prayer pleasure, excitement, almost the fierce delight of sin." (42)

Bloxam also offers us the virtuous version of homoerotic ritualism: the priest inspired by his love for the acolyte. As he says the mass with renewed fervor, he is regarded as a "saint indeed" and the child an "angel." The priest's love is expressed in religious terms as "reverence" or "humility" before the beloved boy. Curiously, the idealized love in all these priest-and-acolyte narratives depends for its success on a typically Christian paradox. Sex must be elided but strongly hinted, invisible but unmistakable. We must always look for it, think about it, speculate about it, but never find it in the text. The threat of scandal evokes the sexual acts that Bloxam then tiptoes around—and around and around. Sexual desire is not repressed, but rather incited, through discretion. As in virtually every other Christian genre, sex is evoked as temptation for the performative pleasure of resistance. Sanctity and purity are no doubt pleasures in their own right. But in Bloxam's story they also become an open secret, a bad disguise, a peculiar summoning of desire by which all the idealized pleasures of mystical devotion—the passionate kisses, extravagant endearments, and flame-like sensations—call to mind precisely those sexual acts that they ostensibly disavow.

The final scene, regarded as blasphemous by Edward Carson for its use of "the sacrament of the Church of England" as a suicide ritual, is a further aggravation of the dialectical relation between sexual desire and Christian grace in the story. Although the choice of suicide and the misuse of the ritual is indeed blasphemous, Bloxam's tone is not mocking, but solemn, sincere, and pious: "They knelt before the altar in the silent night, the glimmer of the tapers lighting up the features of the crucifix with strange distinctness. Never had the priest's voice trembled with such wonderful earnestness, never had the acolyte responded with such devotion, as at this midnight mass for the peace of their departing souls." The melodramatic cry of the boy, "O father let us die together," and the "beautiful gold chalice, set with precious stones," and the embroidered pillow on which the dead boy rests in his lace cotta—all the funereal gorgeousness of the final scene aspires to a decadent artificiality, a Wagnerian exquisiteness, as though priest and acolyte were performing the final act of *Tristan und Isolde*. In the glory of Church ritual, in the spectacle of Christ's Passion and his own operatic gesture of love in suffering, the desire of a man for a boy undergoes an apotheosis. Their love acquires a certain tragic dignity and meaning, though only through the beautiful sacrifice of their lives—"far better to be together in death than apart in life" (46). But it is also the homophobic deployment of Catholicism that is sacrificed, recast as Caiaphas by the logic of its own narratives, condemned though not executed by the very harshness of its own judgments.

In order to make his queer Wagnerian gesture, Bloxam permits a degree of blasphemy, perhaps even a degree of ecclesiastical camp. Nevertheless, there is little doubt about the seriousness of his own priestly vocation. He was himself ordained a priest in the Church of England not long after the publication of this story—an indication that he did not pursue his vocation with the same improbable naïveté as Ronald Heatherington. Bloxam became a dedicated servant of the faith. He was associated with a number of Anglo-Catholic churches, and one of them, Saint Saviour, Hoxton, "was so 'Romanised' that its priests used the Latin Missal and followed all Roman devotions."

Upon his death Bloxam was eulogized not only for his "pastoral genius," but also for his "passionate love of beauty."[13]

## Father Silverpoints

> The procession formed. Park, with his restless, distracted habit, had begun noticing the types, the linen, the vestments, the processional cross, the candlestick he himself carried; until, moved with contrition, he said to himself:
> There is nothing more beautiful nor more terrible than the mass; and, with eyes downcast, he went about his business as an acolyte.
>
> John Gray

Among the more pious of Oscar Wilde's coterie, John Gray best exemplifies the transformation of decadent poet into Roman Catholic priest. His conversion may not have been as dramatic or as well documented as the conversions of Verlaine or Huysmans, but his dedication to the Church was so impressive that, upon his death in 1934, Canon Gray's obituary contained no reference to his early notoriety as a disciple of Wilde. Indeed, John Gray is often singled out as a homosexual decadent who, like Lord Alfred Douglas, turned to the Church as a way of escaping the reputation of his youth. Gray broke with Wilde, burned letters, took to writing Catholic poetry, and rued the hour that his quintessentially decadent volume *Silverpoints* (1893) saw light of day. Surely, we could regard his act of radical self-transformation into a priest as a classic tale of redemption, thus underscoring the tired critical narrative that regards Catholicism as an antidote to decadence rather than one of its peculiar manifestations. Nevertheless, what I find extraordinary about Gray is the way in which he integrated his homosexuality, his decadent style, even his dandyism, into a virtually seamless performance as priest. Katherine Bradley, the Michael half of Michael Field, must surely have recognized the continuity between the young John Gray and the older Canon Gray when she referred to him as "Father Silverpoints."

The passage I quoted above is taken from Gray's 1932 novel *Park*, and it is a striking instance of the way decadent Catholicism, with its characteristic gesture of submission before the religious sublime, not to mention its preoccupation with the ritual and ornamentation of the Church, left its traces on Gray's writing and devotional practice even to the end of his days. Park, who is Gray's fictional alter ego, experiences a sensual restlessness, a pious appreciation of beauty, and a dutiful contrition, during mass. The aestheticism of the poet and the downcast eyes of the acolyte are virtually indistinguishable gestures, typical of the decadent inclination to discover the pleasures of art and the pleasures of religious submission in the same ritual moment. Gray's transformation from decadent poet to Catholic poet, from *Silverpoints* to *Spiritual Poems* (1896), which he began writing the same year, was less a shift in sensibility than a shift in subject matter. In a way, Gray is a less violent and much less neurotic version of Huysmans: the hothouse erotics of his earlier work gives way to prayers no less fragrant, saintly effusions of divine love, a connoisseur's passion for symbol and ritual, and the ambiguous sexuality that the dandy has always shared with the priest. Canon Gray is what Dorian Gray might have become had he succeeded in his efforts at conversion.

This elision of John Gray with Dorian Gray is by no means accidental. The young poet was widely presumed to be the model for Dorian Gray and, since he met Wilde in 1889, the timing was certainly right. Although he was from a working-class background, John resembled Dorian in a number of ways—in particular, his dandyism, his youth and handsomeness, and his long nights in lowly haunts. More important, as his biographer Jerusha Hull McCormack has noted, John Gray was a fine example of Wilde's dictum that life imitates art. After the publication of *The Picture of Dorian Gray,* John Gray permitted himself to be addressed as Dorian, and he even signed a letter with that name. He willingly played the role of Dorian to Wilde's Lord Henry. Although the evidence for a sexual relationship is slight, both G. B. Shaw and the homosexual decadent John Barlas believed that Gray was at one time Wilde's lover. Gray also resembled Dorian in his attraction to the Church. He converted to Catholicism in 1890, a few years before *Silverpoints* established his reputation. His conversion was, however, a highly self-conscious and impulsive one, and he immediately set upon what, in retrospect, he called "a course of sin compared with which my previous life was innocence."[14] What this course of sin entailed exactly is difficult to say, but his sins no less than his conversion had a singularly artificial and premeditated perfection about them that recalls the well-wrought sins and shames of Wilde.

Like his mentor, Gray's reputation was, for a short time between 1889 and 1893, both sustained and imperiled by a careful courting of scandal.

*Silverpoints* itself is a masterpiece of decadent art, though it is still admired as much for its exquisite printing and binding as for the poetry itself. The book is long and narrow, bound in vellum or green cloth stamped with gold, and the cover, embossed with flame-like leaves on a wavy latticework, was designed by Charles Ricketts, another homosexual aesthete and friend of Wilde. The text itself was printed in virtually indecipherable italics with wide margins on expensive handmade paper, such that Ada Leverson, upon reading it, exclaimed that Wilde's next book should take the *Silverpoints* design to a further extreme—it should be "*all* margin, full of beautiful unwritten thoughts."[15] The design is appropriate to the preciosity of the poems, which are highly euphuistic and artificial in style. A number of the trademarks of decadent style are readily obvious: bizarre nightmares, sexual violence and perversity, the femme fatale, flowers, cosmetics, and "gems whose hot harsh names are never said."[16]

A few poems in this volume are on Roman Catholic themes, though none of these are original works by Gray. They are all imitations or translations of Mallarmé, Baudelaire, and especially Verlaine. Nevertheless, such borrowings—not only from the French decadents but, in his later volumes, from medieval saints—are a hallmark of Gray's style. The gesture is peculiarly decadent in the sense that he viewed himself as an aesthetic *bricoleur*, refiguring beautiful fragments in his own languid style and reassembling them in a new context, a new configuration, that reflected his own sensibility. In *Silverpoints* Gray was also introducing London literati to the pleasures of the French symbolists, and so his translations in this particular volume are among his most faithful. Beyond this literary historical significance, however, it is also important that Gray chose mostly religious verses from his French contemporaries. For example, in "Fleurs," in imitation of Mallarmé, the breathless and erotic praise of flowers is also a hymn of praise for the Madonna:

> Thou mad'st the lilies' pallor, nigh to swoon,
> Which, rolling billows of deep sighs upon,
> Through the blue incense of horizons wan,
> Creeps dreamily towards the weeping moon.

Praise in the censers, praise upon the gong,
Madone! from the garden of our woes:
On eves celestial throb the echo long!
Ecstatic visions! radiance of haloes! (35)

Through the image of the lilies, at once pious and voluptuous, the
swoon and sigh of sexual desire is effortlessly transfigured into the
throb and visions excited in the poet by the Madonna. The genius of
the imagery and the structure may be Mallarmé, but in lines like
"rolling billows of deep sighs" and "weeping moon," we find the
limpid preciosity that appealed to Gray. In poems like "Fleurs," Gray
imports an already perfect Catholic decadence from France, revising
it to his own tastes, and juxtaposing it almost seamlessly with his own
work. The art is not only in the translation, but in the selection.

Other borrowings from his French contemporaries demonstrate
Gray's penchant for all things Catholic. He returns to the theme of the
Blessed Virgin as femme fatale in his translation of Baudelaire's "A
une Madone" and Verlaine's "Parsifal." Even a poem like "Mon Dieu
m'a Dit," from Verlaine's *Sagesse,* a poem of simple piety, stripped as
it is of decadent ornamentation, is given pride of place in *Silverpoints,*
where its intensity of feeling is rendered artificial, oddly gem-like, if
only by virtue of its new context. Gray's imitation is a mere fragment
of the original sonnet sequence, and he breaks up Verlaine's heavy and
meditative lines. We may find a hint of the decadent in the "rays
refulgent" or the brutality and histrionics of Christ's Passion:

> Oh see
> My broken side, my heart,
>         its rays refulgent shine;
> My feet, insulted, stabbed;
>         that Mary bathes with brine
> Of bitter tears; my sad arms,
>         helpless, son, for thee. (34)

It is not so much Verlaine's approach nor Gray's imitation that is
startling, but rather the mere selection of this poem for a racy volume
of decadent verse. By appropriating a few lines out of context from

the relentlessly pious *Sagesse,* Gray captures some of the jarring shifts from naughtiness to piety and back again that characterize Verlaine's later work.

*Silverpoints* is also notable for its homoerotic themes, though in this early work they scarcely overlap with the more overtly Catholic poems. Gray wrote of desire between men, not to mention homophobia, in a manner similar to that of early Lord Alfred Douglas. Although he did translate Baudelaire's notoriously lesbian "Femmes Damnées," much of his interest in homosexuality focuses on romantic friendships between men and the societal disdain such friendships attract. In "Did We Not, Darling," Gray was remarkably candid about homosexuality—though, oddly enough, nowhere in the critical literature on his work have I found any acknowledgment that this poem is indeed about love between two men. The melancholic poem begins with a quotation from Jules Laforgue, a weepy line spoken by Pierrot. In the main text of the poem, however, we overhear the sad but peaceful murmurings of a man to his male lover as they lie together in the grave:

> Did we not, Darling, you and I,
> Walk on the earth like other men?
> Did we not walk and wonder why
> They spat upon us so. And then
>
> We lay us down among fresh earth,
> Sweet flowers breaking overhead,
> Sore needed rest for our frail girth,
> For our frail hearts; a well-sought bed.

In a striking evocation of Victorian homophobia, two men, apparently convinced of the beauty of their affection for each other, wonder at the people who spit on them. Finding no haven above ground, they retire to the grave, a respite from the world's pain, their "frail girth" and "frail hearts" suggesting not only a decadent weariness but also the slim-gilt soul of the aesthete.

In the grave the lovers are finally left to themselves but, ironically, they are no longer able to touch each other. With the decay of their flesh, they no longer have bodies to touch:

Deep in the dear dust, Dear, we dream
Our melancholy is a thing
At last our own; and none esteem
How our black lips are blackening.

And none note how our poor eyes fall,
Nor how our cheeks are sunk and sere . . .
Dear, when you waken, will you call? . . .
Alas! we are not very near. (28)

The poem is a brilliant though sad depiction of the sexual dilemma in which many homosexuals found themselves. Confronted with the self-righteous indignation of others, the lovers choose suicide. Or, on a more figurative level, they submit to a chilling, death-in-life rigidity in which they lie side-by-side, though not very near. They are conscious, sensible, dreaming perhaps, but unable to touch each other, unable perhaps to hear each other. The blackening and rotting away of the flesh becomes a metaphor for the repression that was all too often the fate of the Victorian homosexual. The elegy is reduced to the somber and solipsistic murmurings of a corpse to his unconscious lover and companion in the grave in the somber line "Dear, when you waken, will you call?"

In "Passing the Love of Women," an early poem that was not included in *Silverpoints*, Gray returns again to the theme of homophobia. There has been some doubt about its authorship since, late in life, Gray claimed never to have written a poem by that name. Nevertheless, according to McCormack, the manuscript is in Gray's handwriting. Certainly, the flower and honey imagery, as well as the tortuous phrasing, should be familiar to us from *Silverpoints*. The title is, of course, a reference to the love of David and Jonathan. Again, we overhear the words of a man speaking to his male lover, who is absent:

Priest nor ceremony
    Or of Orient or Rome
Bound to me my love, mine honey
    In the honey-comb,

Who, albeit of human
    Things the most sublime he knew,
Left me, to espouse a woman
    As the people do. (44)

The speaker, all but married to a man, finds himself abandoned in favor of a woman. As was often the case, the secret love of man for man is sacrificed to a more respectable and public marriage of man to woman.

Although his love stands outside the societal blessings of the marriage ceremony, the speaker nevertheless characterizes it as a force of nature, seemingly an emanation of the romantic natural setting from which he speaks, a "lonely meadow" carpeted with crocuses. This natural force will penetrate the artifice of his lover's heterosexual marriage as an irrepressible memory:

> Though he wind about her
>> Those dear arms were holden in mine.
> He shall only reach the outer
>> Precinct of the shrine;
>
> For, when pale stars shimmer
>> In the vault of violet,
> As far gleams of memory glimmer
>> He will not forget. (44)

The marital "shrine" recalls the priestly "ceremony" of the earlier stanza, and in the artificial "vault of violet," we may wonder whether the speaker is referring to the actual sky or to an ornamental ceiling.

The lover will always remain to some extent outside, out-of-doors, only reaching the outer precinct of the shrine. The stars in the vault of violet will always lead him back, like a glimmer of memory, a memory presumably of the real violet sky and the real stars sparkling in the twilight of the poem's opening lines:

> In the twilight darkling
>> When the sky was violet
> And the stars were faintly sparkling
>> Thus it was we met. (43)

Gray himself never sought respite from homophobia under the respectable cloak of marriage, but this scenario would certainly have been familiar to him, especially through his acquaintance with Oscar and Constance Wilde. In this poem, however, the marital artifice bears within it the traces of the desire it seeks to mask or repress, and that desire returns, seemingly must return, uncannily, as though by some inevitable process of metonymy. The star of desire glimmers through the very star-like shape of its own symbolic renunciation. In his marital dedication to his wife, the man will, in spite of himself, recall his love for the man he abandoned.

The very supposition that Gray was homosexual is based almost entirely on the violet thread of homoeroticism, by turns suggestive and coy, that coils through his work from beginning to end. Despite the steaminess of *Silverpoints*, the aura of scandal surrounding Gray was little more than guilt by association. He developed a number of romantic friendships with homosexual aesthetes—Wilde, Charles Shannon, and especially André Raffalovich—all of whom were artistic mentors or father figures in his life. He wrote to Wilde as "my beloved master my dear friend," for example, and Raffalovich referred to himself as Gray's "father & mother" and to Gray as the "dear child." McCormack makes much of these relationships, locating in them a lifelong emotional progress. She describes the bitter relationship between Gray and his real father, a laborer who had little sympathy for his son's artistic aspirations. On the death of his father, he wrote, "I am well pleased with the loss."[17] In McCormack's view, Gray sought a "series of surrogate father/mentors, whose relationship is not merely of older to younger man, teacher to pupil, but of master to disciple and finally, with Raffalovich, of parent to child." In fact, she extends this paternal metaphor to include Gray's religious vocation, which she characterizes as "a new hunger for acceptance by another, more adequate father."[18]

McCormack's reading of Gray's homoerotic friendships on the same continuum as his love of Christ is almost inevitable given the Christian terms through which both Gray and Raffalovich construed their friendship and their own experience of homosexuality. Gray spent much of his life in a close friendship with Raffalovich, who was inspired by his friend to convert to Catholicism from his native Judaism in 1896. The two men, along with Raffalovich's former nanny, Florence Gribbell (who also converted), created a family all their own in Edinburgh, where Gray was a priest. Gray's friendship with Raffalovich is necessary, I think, to an understanding of the erotic component of the religious poetry he wrote after the publication of *Silverpoints*.

There is a hint of jealousy in Raffalovich's distaste for Wilde and his concomitant affection for Wilde's disciple. Although he was an artful socialite and conversationalist, Raffalovich was not altogether successful in his attempt to impress London society. His French background, his Judaism, and his legendary ugliness were all hindrances to his success, but Wilde cut to the quick with his own appraisal of Raffalovich as social parvenu: "He came to London with the intention of opening a *salon,* and he has succeeded in opening a saloon."[19] Raffalovich wrote, in collaboration with Gray, a few tiresome and unsuccessful plays, one of which, *The Blackmailers* (1894), was vaguely homosexual in theme.[20] His talents as a poet were meager, though he published a few volumes of uranian verse, sentimental and tepid poetry about his love for young boys. The subject matter alone might have endeared him to Wilde, but the verses are so painfully trite and coy—the gender of the beloved is rarely marked—that he appears prudish alongside his decadent contemporaries, even the chaste ones.

Nevertheless, this prudishness seems to have resonated well with Gray's own doubts about his role as "Dorian." By 1892 Gray had become extremely anxious about his association with Wilde. When a newspaper, *The Star,* referred to him as a "disciple" of Wilde and a model for Dorian, Gray urged Wilde to write an open letter to the contrary, and he eventually sued the paper for libel. An element of homosexual panic is evident in this libel suit, though it appears only to have amused his acquaintances. This anxiety, coupled with his expensive and, by the standards of his day, dissipated lifestyle, led to the collapse of Gray's health late in 1892. He suffered what appears to have been a nervous breakdown, a protracted illness that, in its worst moments, brought on convulsions.

It was at this time that Gray finally broke with Wilde and began writing the sort of Catholic poetry that would appear in *Spiritual Poems* and the series of religious *Blue Calendars,* which he published between 1895 and 1898. Gray entered the Scots College in Rome in 1898 to prepare for the priesthood. His "course of sin" had ended, and his vocation had begun. Comparisons with Huysmans' 1891 conversion would seem inevitable, and Gray did in fact publish a review, not of *A Rebours* or *Là-Bas,* the most notorious novels of French decadence, but of *En Route.* In this review, entitled "The Redemption of Durtal," Gray is acutely critical of Huysmans, but one observation in particular strikes me as ironic. Gray uses the term "inverted spiritism" to describe Durtal's passage from the sodomitical demonism of *Là-Bas* to the hysterical contrition of *En Route*. With its discreet suggestion of sexual inversion and its recognition of the paradoxical role of sin in the course of redemption, Gray could have applied the term to his own embrace of the priesthood. Like Huysmans, he had passed from one spiritual extreme to another. And it was in the midst of this crisis that Gray's friendship with André Raffalovich became increasingly significant. In Raffalovich, Gray found an alternative to his more perilous association with Wilde. He found a way of reconciling the homosexual and the poet with the priest.

Raffalovich's long apologia for homosexuality, *Uranisme et Unisexualité* (1896), resonates well with Gray's Catholic poetry. In the 350 pages of this treatise, Raffalovich is tireless in his definition and defense of the proper social role of homosexuals, referred to here as "inverts" or "uranists." The book is addressed to medical professionals as well as the general reading public, though its publication through the Archives d'Anthropologie Criminelle is itself evidence of the sort of medical and criminological baggage that attended any public forum on homosexuality. Essentially, Raffalovich was making the familiar argument that inverts do not always deserve the stigma that has often been heaped upon them. He draws upon classical and Christian sources to define a type of sexual inversion that is blameless and noble. He speaks of "superior" or "sublime" inverts who are able to sublimate their sexual desires through art, religion, friendship, and other respectable pursuits. Against this definition of the invert, he posits the pervert or the sodomite, who in this account is usually an effeminate male enthusiast of anal and oral sex who sometimes entertains a vulgar infatuation with Wagner. At times Raffalovich sounds disturbingly like the homophobic diatribes he seeks to challenge. "We have arrived here at the borders of madness and crime," he writes, resigning himself to the sorry task of defining perversion; "passive sodomy is akin to madness and active sodomy to crime."[21]

The publication date of this book, which appeared shortly after the Wilde trials, is not coincidental, since it includes the author's regrettable commentary on the *affaire d'Oscar Wilde*. More than any other contemporary figure, Wilde bears the burden in this text of representing the criminal pervert. A spirit of revenge is evident in the claim that he fully deserved his imprisonment; nevertheless, the characterization of Wilde as a "corrupter of youth" follows logically from Raffalovich's presumption that *coït anal* and *coït buccal* are inherently demented. Having thus vilified most of the sexual acts by which the invert was traditionally defined, Raffalovich extols the virtues of Platonic love and what he refers to as a "sexual decentralization" (126). In an account of sexual development that reads startlingly like Freud *avant la lettre,* Raffalovich describes this libidinal decentralization as a rejection of adult genitality and a return to the sentimental friendships and polymorphous sensuality of childhood. Indeed, throughout his work, Raffalovich's erotic sensibility would be more accurately described as a mawkish boy-love rather than as homosexuality, though the distinction between the two terms is not always clear. His notion of the ideal sexual impulse is explicitly regressive, a return to "childish innocence," having noted, "With his chosen friend, conversations, tender caresses, long intimacies, all help to curb, suppress, annihilate this feverish insurrection of the flesh" (132). In short, the superior invert is defined not by sexual acts, but by his flight from them. "The loves of uranists," Raffalovich assures us, "are very frequently without sexual satisfaction" (130).

Needless to say, there is little in Raffalovich's argument that recommends itself to modern gay politics. Indeed, his book is yet another performance of the familiar melodrama of assimilation by which a tractable and inconspicuous homosexual makes an appeal for certain legal rights and protections at the expense of more ardent forms of sexual expression that pose a greater challenge to the status quo. Raffalovich is simply re-enacting with daunting earnestness the often hopeless gesture of choosing between Christian and Hellenic forms of sublimation. He is searching desperately for some respite from stigma, some way of preserving the pleasures of a pederastic disposition. Nevertheless, in his calls for chastity, however strained and punitive, we can distinguish some of the sexual dilemmas that characterized his friendship with Gray. They were both attracted to the male sex, and yet, as far as we can tell, they were both chaste. After all, as Raffalovich points out, "it is easy to be chaste if one has a friend who is chaste" (175).

By all appearances, Gray was perfectly content with this arrangement. In fact, his attitude toward sex was tinged with fin de siècle ennui. In a letter to Raffalovich about Charles Féré, a psychologist with whom his friend had had a dispute about the nature of homo-sexuality, Gray writes: "I am curious to know if Féré agrees with me about the overwhelming, superabounding-and-all-that-is-superlative importance of the first sexual act. All the passion of making the dis-covery that man is naturally chaste comes back to me."[22] Whatever his predilection for chastity, Gray was constantly on guard against sexual revelations of any kind. A visit to his house must have been an exasperating experience for strangers, given the myriad ways that he seemed to elicit comment about his life as "Dorian" Gray and at the same time suppress it. For example, he displayed all his first editions of decadent poetry from the nineties, but he turned their bindings to the wall—and he promptly removed them from the hands of the curious. The sexuality of the two men must have been readily apparent to many, but they both made a concerted effort to avoid any discussion of the subject. They were extremely fond of each other, and yet their guests were baffled by the curious formality between them and by their cautious and ceremonial avoidance of the signs of intimacy. As many have pointed out, their emphasis on ritual and social correctness seems to be motivated by a profound fear of scandal. As Gray once said, apologizing for his cool reserve, "If I were to relax for a single mo-ment, only God knows what might happen to me."[23] This anxiety seems to have had a chilling effect on the public demeanor of the two men. Peter F. Anson, an observer who knew them both well, has written in a memoir, "Of the friendship of John Gray and André Raffalovich it is difficult to write, because it was so aloof and de-tached. So far as the outside world was concerned it hardly existed. Their relationship—even after forty years—continued to be formal." He further adds, "Had a complete stranger been present, his impres-sion would have been that these two men were hardly more than acquaintances."[24]

Gray's correspondence reveals only a studied reserve. Raffalovich, however, wrote lively letters full of gossip, and in them we find that he pursued homoerotic yet chaste friendships much of his life. But even here the tone is coy. In his letters to Melville Wright, a handsome young man of his acquaintance whom he was wont to refer to as "cher Enfant," "My dear Boy," or "My dear manchild," Raffalovich muses, "And I will bask in your youth, if you will allow me still one more metaphor. Young friends stimulate one's imagination, I think." On a more flamboyant note, he writes that "Melville in khaki is very attractive, as is Melville out of khaki to his friends of whom I am an old one in all senses of the word," or he asks, "by the bye have you not what is in poetry honey-coloured hair?" Such letters are ripe with pederastic eros, and yet he could assure Melville's father, no doubt truthfully, that his interest in the Wright boys, not only Melville but also Cecil, was a purely "maternal" affection.[25]

This glass closet, by which sexual desire is paradoxically hidden in plain sight, is the very essence of the pederastic priest. Raffalovich and Gray both learned to master that slight and subtle shift of the lens by which sexual desire is re-envisioned as Christian or Platonic *agape*. Raffalovich, in fact, made no secret at all of the connection between the ardent Christian and the "sublime invert." As in Bloxam, the capacity for intense religious feeling among inverts is one of the hinge pins of his effort to sanitize, indeed to sanctify, homosexuality in *Uranisme et Unisexualité*. He goes so far as to speak of uranism as a "vocation," rendering it in terms that seem more apostolic than sexual. In a passage reminiscent of Hopkins's sermon on the beauty of Christ's body, Raffalovich describes the love of the virginal uranist for his "young God, naked and bleeding, disfigured and transfigured, wounded and wounding" (*Uranisme*, 30):

> The soul of man, affianced to Christ, has throughout the centuries expressed its desire and its adoration in poetry and in prose. Angelus Silesius, Friedrich von Spee, Saint John of the Cross, Saint Teresa, and so many other illustrious and gracious figures have languished in love on the shoulder of the Divine Lover. Hafiz has approached the "obscure night" of Saint John of the Cross. One might well read these poems and not recognize that it is the soul of man that cries out and clasps the feet, the hands, the merciful flanks, a lover of the sort that Krafft-Ebing describes in his *Psychopathia Sexualis* as suffering from sadism, masochism, and unisexuality. (31–32)

Raffalovich offers a list of mystics, all of whom are famous for their intensely erotic effusions of divine love. As Charcot and his followers had done in the previous decade, Raffalovich draws a subversive connection between the lives of the saints and the case studies of late-nineteenth-century sexology. For Charcot the argument was essentially anticlerical, but for Raffalovich it is just the opposite. He is searching for a justification for homosexuality in the erotic extremes of an already validated and respectable Christian mysticism.

Raffalovich is particularly intrigued with Saint John of the Cross, whose description of the spiritual man sounds uncannily like the frail and delicate body of the homosexual aesthete as he was immortalized by Wilde and others:

> Saint John of the Cross, one of the most admirable of sages, once said: "There are people of a frail and delicate complexion, and of a nature tender and sensible. From the time they really occupy themselves with spiritual things, their nature experiences a very great sweetness, and it is from this sweetness that these emotions come. When the spirit and the senses enjoy possession of each other, each part of the man is thereby excited to pleasure according to his particular characteristics, knowing: the spirit, or spiritual pleasure, which comes from God; and the senses, or sensible pleasure, which is born of the flesh." (32)

Raffalovich qualifies this foray into the lives of the saints with the assertion, "If one studied the mystics, the sectaries, the Church fathers, one would find for the superior invert a wisdom and an elevation and a practice altogether comparable to Plato in its self-sacrifice—and for the weak invert, a discipline" (32). He even makes some suggestions about the proper education of inverts, whose desires he felt should be acknowledged by society and submitted to much the same discipline as heterosexual ones (though marriage appears to be out of the question).

These thoughts about invert education were apparently attractive to Gray. In *Park* he describes a religious school that is exclusively for boys and girls who are beautiful and will never marry. They appear to be children of a slightly different species, called "three-blood children," whom Philip Healy, in his afterword to the 1984 edition, associates with the "third sex" theories of homosexuality that were popular around the turn of the century. The pious children of *Park* certainly fit the decadent pattern. As Gray writes, "It was one child kneeling on the step, whose face was the colour of an altar-bread, with shut eyes, and streaming black hair, with lips and tongue like a rose."[26]

As a "weak" invert who became later in life a "superior" one, Gray may well have been the source of Raffalovich's information on homoerotic desire and saintly devotion. Among Gray's *Spiritual Poems* are translations from Saint John of the Cross, Saint Teresa, and Jacopone da Todi—precisely the breed of Christian that populates *Uranisme et Unisexualité*. Gray wrote more than one poem about Saint Sebastian and, in the *Blue Calendar* of 1896, he published "The True Vine," which likens Dionysus to Christ, "the vine incarnate" (174). Although Gray translated a vast range of mystical and devotional poetry, much of it quite tame, he entertained a particular affection for the more homoerotic and sensual of Catholic writers, especially Saint John of the Cross, Blessed Jacopone, and Richard Crashaw. "I have invincible love of S. John of the Cross," he wrote to Katherine Bradley, "because, I suppose, he made a hole in the covering which I had woven about myself to hide me from God."[27]

The image of the hole in Gray's covering, rendering him vulnerable to God, is especially suggestive given that, in Gray's hands, the translation of "The Obscure Night of the Soul" reads more than ever like a decadent and homoerotic love poem:

> VI.
> Against my flowery breast,
> Kept whole for him alone to lean upon,
> The long night did he rest,
> The while I entertained him,
> And gentle swaying of the cedars fanned him.
>
> VII.
> His floating hair was fanned
> By breezes falling from the tower above.
> He, with his gentle hand,
> Smiting my neck, bereft me
> Of knowledge, so that all my senses left me.
>
> VIII.
> Fainting and all distraught;
> My drooping head was resting on my love;

> Senseless, resisting not,
> I cast off all my cares,
> Fallen among sweet lilies unawares. (124)

Decadent poetry never gets much queerer than this, though Gray's translation is relatively faithful to the original. In another context this poem might have described Dorian Gray wandering through London streets at night in search of mysterious sins, but Wilde was never quite this explicit. The saint becomes a secret lover, seeking out the man he loves under cover of darkness. Their union is a dreamy and ecstatic one, culminating in the touch of the divine lover's hand, at once gentle and smiting, that sends the saint into a swoon. The hallucinatory and ecstatic mode of mystical texts was an eternal source of fascination for fin de siècle writers, a site in which Christian and decadent literature overlap. But there are other hallmarks of decadent preciosity in this poem. Consider such phrases as "my flowery breast," "gentle swaying of the cedars fanned him," "floating hair," and "fallen among the sweet lilies unawares." Gray is speaking through the poetry of Saint John of the Cross, but the grain of the voice is entirely his own.

Even though Gray was for the most part successful in his effort to obliterate all recollection of his youthful excesses, a number of the Catholic poems and translations that he wrote after *Silverpoints* resonate with the decadent style he developed as a young man. These echoes are especially evident in *Spiritual Poems*, which is itself an early effort, and it is significant that Gray later regarded this collection of devotional poetry and translations as virtually heretical. Ernest Dowson noted that Gray's *Blue Calendar* of 1895 had a "Moyen-Age-fin-de-siècle" flavor about it, though he found his friend's mysticism to be sincere and not merely a pose.[28] Some of the poems that Gray wrote after *Silverpoints* demonstrate that the shift to a more exclusively Catholic mode was not really all that radical.

In a poem with the lapidary title "Jesus, Angelic Gem," Gray writes of divine grace as though it were a dangerous drug:

> O lord, remain, with us, remain;
> Ignite in us a flaming vane;
> Inflame the pulses of the brain
> Fulfill the world in sweet again. (57)

After the fashion of Wilde's early poetry, Gray wrote a translation of Pedro de Espinosa's poem about the Assumption that could only be described as decadent Marianism. The Virgin is surrounded with the sumptuous imagery of a rather Byzantine palace that recalls the dance of Salomé:

> In turquoise-hued and sunset-coloured cloud,
> Within the wide imperial palaces,
> Where many a white torch and candle is,
> The sovereign pages of the Emperor crowd.
> Shafts of a thousand fragrances are proud
> To mix with amaranth and lilies' fees,
> Assyrian gums and Indian incenses,
> On carpets deeply piled and furbelowed. (126)

On a more homoerotic note, there are the poems devoted to Jacopone da Todi, with whose name Gray sometimes signed himself. In one of them we read an effusive love letter of Saint Francis of Assisi to his Lord:

> For thee, for love, I languish and I burn.
> I sigh for thy embraces soon and late.
> When thou art hence, I live and die; I yearn
> And groan and whine in very piteous state
> To find thee; and my heart, at thy return,
> Fainteth with fear lest aught should separate.

Even Christ is embarrassed by his fervor, demanding of Saint Francis, "Control the love wherewith thou lovest me," but to no avail (98). Saint Francis goes on in the same vein for another page and half.

Gray translated another poem by Saint John of the Cross, "The Living Flame of Love." He rejected it from *Spiritual Poems*, though it is scarcely more violent and suggestive than his translation of "The Obscure Night of the Soul." In still another poem, Gray describes his patron saint as he was "locked within the riven Side" of Christ (101)— a maternal image reminiscent of Pater. He returns to the same image in the poem "Saint Bernard":

Save in thy wounded Side, for me
There rests no consolation. (110)


As McCormack writes, "In *Spiritual Poems,* the convert anatomizes his suppliant and longing posture toward God. In each collection, the poet consciously submerges himself in the flow of subjectivity to the point where metaphors of erotic fusion become equally those of dissolution and death."[29]

Even in Gray's devotional practice as a priest, many have noted the traces of Dorian Gray that remained. As his friend Walter Shewring writes, "His love of visible things would have scandalized Manichaeans had they not been shamed by his knowledge of the invisible."[30] Raffalovich funded the erection of Saint Peter's Church in Edinburgh, over which Gray presided the rest of his life. The church was built to Gray's specifications and was a peculiar blend of asceticism and aestheticism. Despite its austere whitewashed walls, the church boasts a carved baroque confessional and paintings after the fashion of the Pre-Raphaelites, not to mention a gray-green marble floor in the the chancel that is inlaid with brass fish. The beauty of the services at Saint Peter's is often remarked and, in January of each year, Gray offered prayers for the soul of Paul Verlaine. Apparently, traces of his dandyism also survived his vocation. The church was opened on April 22 because, Gray said, "it is a red day, and the best vestments I have chance to be of that colour."[31] On a similar note, there were rumors that he was attracted to Scots College because it had the most spectacular uniform in Rome: a purple cassock, red cincture, and black soprano. Others have spoken of the Turkish carpets in Gray's house and the black linens on his bed. In fact, Anson has noted that the house wanted only a gramophone playing Debussy or bits of Maeterlinck to complete its mysterious aura of elusive twilight.

The dandy returns to the priest, uncannily, even through the prayers, the vestments, the rituals, the very symbolic forms of his renunciation. Unlike the ill-fated lover in "Passing the Love of Women," a poem that its author was eager to disavow, Gray might well have got past the outer precinct of the shrine. He died Canon Gray, a much respected clergyman whose scandalous youth few were able to remember. Nevertheless, looking over the faint gleams of decadent style everywhere apparent in Gray's Catholic volumes, we might recall the final line of the poem: "He will not forget."

## Pio Corvo

"Yes, Prince. But you are a boy."

"Well, I think so. Also I am a sailor, like Uncle Luigi. Cannot You see that, White Father? Do you know what thing is a sailor?" He stood by the chair, leaning against Hadrian's knee, deliciously rosily maritime in white flannel.

"Oh, yes: We know many sailors"; the Pope responded.

Frederick William Rolfe ("Baron Corvo")

We could presume that Rolfe's English pope, Hadrian VII, is referring here to the fishermen of Galilee. On a less spiritual plane, these sailors of the Pope's acquaintance may be Rolfe's discreet allusion to the many Venetian gondoliers that populated his own erotic imagination, especially since Hadrian is one of his many fictional self-portraits. The Pope shares Rolfe's inclination to strip naked for a swim among the boys. Elsewhere, Hadrian recalls his favorite dream of being "invisible and stark-naked and fitted with great white feathery wings, flying with the movement of swimming among and above men, seeing and seeing and seeing, easily and enormously swooping,"[32] a curious mixture of Walt Whitman and Vatican whimsy. No less reminiscent of Whitman is Hadrian's affection for MacLeod a seminarian, whom he refers to as "this great virile virgin of nineteen" (243); the Pope finally betroths the young man in a kind of spiritual matrimony to another man who is smitten to poetic rapture primarily by MacLeod's wonderful blue eyes. This interweaving of Catholic piety and homoerotic idealism has insured Rolfe's reputation as a cult figure, especially among gay men of Anglo-Catholic tendencies. Hadrian himself is one of the more successful versions of the priest—in this case, the Pope—as pederastic aesthete.

If the formidable and conservative Pius IX was affectionately referred to as Pio Nono by his followers, Rolfe became through his various priestly incarnations a kind of Pio Corvo. Like John Gray, Rolfe was a pensive, ritualistic, celibate figure given to discoursing on

Catholic doctrine and love between men and yet withdrawn into a shell that shielded his emotional vulnerability.[33] Like Hadrian, Rolfe was a pious and priestly figure, but also a consummate aesthete and sensualist, convinced "it was the visionary ideal of Beauty which really inspired joy" (*Hadrian*, 125) and fond of reading Plato with "keen gentle fastidious rapture" (152). Although Rolfe once dismissed the decadents as "affected literary poseurs,"[34] his literary sensibility, no stranger to affectation or poses, was itself a decadent mixture of the aesthetic, the pederastic, and the Catholic. We are not surprised to discover that some of Rolfe's earliest Catholic tales—usually referred to as the Toto stories in honor of their wondrous boy-narrator—first appeared in *The Yellow Book*, a decadent journal.

Although Hadrian cultivates an interest in swimmers, sailors, and seminarians, it is this rosily maritime boy—this "princelet," as he is called—that commands his deepest affection. He is one of the many pederastic icons in Rolfe's fiction, boys with beautiful bodies and religious aspirations. They represent for Rolfe the always already transgressed boundary between erotic and spiritual love. This particular boy, Prince Filiberto, "a very pale-coloured very delicately-articulated slim and stalwart baby-boy with dark-star-like eyes and brows superbly drawn," is a master of flirtation. When the boy kisses the Pope's ring, a commonplace religious gesture of respect and obedience becomes a sign of chivalric courtship: "The full soft rose-leaf of his lips flitted from the pontifical to the episcopal ring. He lifted his bright head; and boldly looked into the Pope's eyes, with a smile disclosing the most wonderful little teeth—with a gaze which told of a pact of friendship sealed" (*Hadrian*, 186). The scene is repeated toward the end of the novel, and this time the Pope is more responsive: "Innocence put up its pretty lips. The Apostle lost one breath;—and stooped and kissed the stainless brow" (347). His attraction is not easily construed as the purely spiritual affection of the Pope for a pious follower, especially since, in a confession shortly before his election, Hadrian (then known less papally as George Rose) offers us a glimpse of his sexual predilection for boys: "I confess that two or three times in my life I have delighted in impure thoughts inspired by some lines in Cicero's Oration for M. Coelius: and, perhaps half a dozen times by a verse of John Addington Symonds in the *Artist*. I confess that I have dallied with these thoughts for an instant before dismissing them"

(44). The reference to Cicero may be suitably vague, but the remark about Symonds was clearly intended as a red flag to enthusiasts of man-boy love, especially the highly idealized variety to be found in Symonds's poetry and in Charles Kains-Jackson's periodical *The Artist and Journal of Home Culture,* both of which are classics of 1890s pederastic literature. In fact, Rolfe himself contributed two sonnets about Saint Sebastian to the *Artist* in 1891.

Hadrian's dalliance with Prince Filiberto further stimulates him to a more religious conception of his sexual desire for boys. "We have made experience of a feeling which—well, which We suppose—at any rate will pass for—Love," the Pope tenuously proclaims. He is amazed by the child's definition of love as self-renunciation, a willingness to keep his troubles to himself, and yet his pleasure in the princelet is also sexual. Hadrian is thrown into a rapture by the boy, who recalls for him the pederastic love-poetry of Meleager, an English edition of which Rolfe had published with another homosexual Catholic ritualist, C. H. C. Pirie-Gordon. The Pope quotes some fragments at length:

"Our Lady of desire brought me to thee, Theokles, me to thee;
"and delicate sandalled Love hath stripped and strewed me at thy
"feet:

"a lightning-flash of his sweet beauty!
"flames from his eyes he darteth!
"hath Love revealed a Child who fighteth with thunderbolts?"

In a familiar erotic double-talk, at which the decadents were often adept, Hadrian insistently spiritualizes the beauty of the boy along both Greek and Christian lines. We are told that the Pope's "ecstasy was admiration of the lovely little person and the noble little soul" (189).

Hadrian VII is only the most imaginative of the many autobiographical personae through whom Rolfe rewrote his life as fiction. In a posthumously published novel *Nicholas Crabbe* (1905, first published 1958), Rolfe tells the story of an eccentric writer, much like himself, who attempts a literary collaboration with a blind telegraph boy[35]—a scenario roughly analogous to his disastrous friendship with Sholto Douglas. In *The Desire and Pursuit of the Whole,* Rolfe returns as

Nicholas Crabbe, self-exiled to Venice, where he troubles over the spiritual future and physical charms of Zilda, a tomboy who is based on one of the many Venetian gondoliers of whom Rolfe was enamored. In both novels a priestly Crabbe finds himself preoccupied with a boy. The priest-and-acolyte scenario echoes throughout Rolfe's work, even the less autobiographical romances, such as the Toto stories and *Don Renato* (1909, first published 1963), making Rolfe one of the most prolific writers of pederastic or man-boy love literature in English.

The figure of the priest—celibate yet homosexual, pious yet eccentric—was Rolfe's preferred fictional persona. Like Pater, Rolfe was attracted to the Church at a young age and, despite his Broad Church background, chose an Anglo-Catholic path toward Rome. Saint Alban's, Holborn, the notoriously ritualistic church, figured in his youth, as it had for many young Victorian men of a homosexual and aesthetic persuasion. "I received a Divine Vocation," Rolfe wrote in a letter to a friend, James Walsh, "to serve God as a secular priest when I was a protestant boy of fifteen. I was very fervent about it. I went to confession (Stanton, St Alban's Holborn), said the rosary, used the Garden of the Soul for a prayer-book."[36] After a brief career as a schoolteacher, Rolfe entered the Roman Catholic seminaries at Oscott and (preceding John Gray) at Scots College in Rome. Unlike Gray, however, he did not succeed in becoming a priest, and was expelled from seminary for reasons that still remain vague. Despite the insistence of Church authorities to the contrary, Rolfe claimed till the end of his life that he had a vocation. At times he dressed as a priest, and he was known to refer to himself in print as "The Rev. Frederick William Rolfe" or, still more sly, "Fr. Rolfe," presumably with the hope he would be mistaken for a priest. He even took a twenty-year vow of celibacy—and apparently stuck to it, for the most part—to prove his sincerity. Although he sustained a pious love of the Church throughout his life, he developed an almost paranoid hatred of priests, arguing that they had wronged him and betrayed him. In fact, he shared with Oscar Wilde an admiration for the Church almost as strong as his disgust for its members, and he once expressed his opinion in a notably Wildean epigram: "Will you allow me to say that I myself am a Roman Catholick not even on speaking terms with any other Roman

Catholicks, for I find the Faith comfortable and the Faithful intolerable" (15).

Alongside the Corvine priest, we inevitably find the Corvine boy, sometimes an acolyte or little saint, sometimes a mere urchin with wings. Prince Filiberto, Toto, Eros, various youthful martyrs, and assorted gondoliers are the most notable among these boys, and they range in age from childhood to late adolescence. Rolfe's own sexual preference was for boys between the ages of sixteen and eighteen, or so he claimed in a letter to a similarly inclined correspondent, Charles Masson Fox. In this letter, one of the notorious *Venice Letters* (1909–1910) that gave him an unlikely reputation as a sexual profligate, Rolfe eschews any taste for younger boys, but his tone is highly suspect. Referring to Fox and another friend named Cocker, Rolfe speculates on boy love with a tongue-in-cheek duplicity:

> You both preferred the small, the 14—while my preference was for the 16, 17, 18 and large. I have been trying to understand your preference, to find a reason for it, and I totally fail. This is why. *There is not enough of a little person for me to enjoy all of it.* It lies naked on its back. I stretch myself on its belly, my yard in the softness of its thighs. I clip it with my legs and arms: it hugs my body: and we begin to wrestle. But, where is its face? Where are the sparkling eyes, in whose depths I may see the ripple of pleasure? Where are the hot sweet lips which I may devour with mine? Buried under my breast and half suffocated.[37]

Surely, we can presume from these vivid lines that Rolfe was perfectly able to sympathize with Fox's passion for younger boys, whatever their shortcomings. Indeed, he seems to be speaking from experience here, though in these particular letters he is also trying to titillate Fox with largely speculative pornographic prose. At any rate, the beautiful boy, conceived in both Greek and Christian terms, was not only Rolfe's sexual preference, but also the focus of his very theory of love and desire.

In one of his early Toto stories, "About the Love Which Is Desire and the Love Which Is Divine," Rolfe attempts through allegory to distinguish between sexual and spiritual love. What we find instead is a teasing pederastic allegory of sexual desire and sexual panic. The setting is presumably Venice, though vague. Speaking in the first person, Rolfe is the compiler of all the tales he hears from Toto. Throughout the book, he is a papal figure of sorts, a beneficent father—*la sua eccellenza,* as they call him. He is surrounded by other beautiful Italian boys, "violet-shadowed" Vittorio, Ercole "carved in Corinthian-bronze," Desiderio "all pale with buttercup-yellow hair," Guido "of chrusoberul eyes"—all "delicately dangled slim frail limbs in the sea from pier-steps, cooing each to other like white doves."[38] It is Toto, however, who plays Diotima to Rolfe's questions about love. Toto tells him that there are two kinds of love: the Divine Amore of Christ as he stands by the throne of the Virgin, and a certain *amorino* called Desire, which is often mistaken for Divine Love but is in fact a demon. The pure spirituality of Divine Love is undermined not only by the presence of the boys with their slim frail limbs, but also by the representation of Christ as himself a splendid fourteen-year-old boy not unlike Toto.

It is through Toto's depiction of love's origin, however, that Rolfe reveals the key sexual and spiritual conflict that reverberates through his work. According to Toto, both Divine Amore and Desire begin with a "little child" who, with apparent sweetness and innocence, insinuates himself into a man's affections. "You take in this little child, and show him kindness; and he returns your fondlings and your kisses and caresses, till you love him so that you find you cannot do without him." This paternal pose quickly collapses, however, into a more explicitly erotic desire, as symbolized by the boy's physical development: "In your heart, he grows to boyhood; and, on the sly, when you are not looking, he makes weapons,—arrows, and a bow, like an archer,—and wings bloom upon his arms, so that he may fly away, and leave you, when the moment comes: but of this you have no knowledge. And, then, at last, he gains his full strength; and he is vigorous, and terrible; and he arises in his majesty; and, with his arrow, he wounds your heart, and strikes you down, his victim and his slave."[39]

The love of a child, figured at first in the same parental terms that Rolfe reserved for the Virgin and her son, becomes a full-fledged eroticism, a sexual enslavement to a boy whose charms have burst the proper bounds of paternal affection. This recognition of erotic power in the child becomes a call to panic. Eros flies away, leaving his wounded lover helpless and yearning. This is where Toto makes the distinction between Divine Amore and Desire. If this is the arrow prick of Desire, the yearning it brings will be a selfish love. If one has been pricked by Divine Amore, however, one will feel Divine Love, the love of another for whom one gladly strives, suffers, lives, and dies—a Christian love, though Toto does not specify whether the other is a man or God. Desire is selfishness, while Divine Amore is sacrifice. Both, however, find their origins in the erotic charm of a beautiful, if somewhat untrustworthy, boy.

In his poem "A Mistake," which appeared in John Gambril Nicholson's anthology of boy-love poetry *A Garland of Ladslove* (1895), Rolfe describes a boy who arrives as a divine gift of love but soon departs, leaving desolation in his wake. The speaker prays daily for a visit from the boy, and God grants it to him as a form of punishment for doubting "His wise refusal." The poem ends on a penitential note:

> Now is my house left to me desolate,
> > And it were better, I confess to God,
> > If in my hall his feet had never trod;
> I bow to justice, for my sin was great.[40]

No doubt his sin was great and his repentance admirable, but what is this poem of Christian regret doing in a book devoted to the beauties of boy-love? As in much of Rolfe's work, it is not the tempting boy that brings him to Christian penitence, but the gesture of penitence that brings him to the tempting boy. The boy who overthrows the pious man, so prevalent in Rolfe's work, betrays in his character the ironic performativity of the masochist. This conception of the erotic child as *puer horribilis* would appear to be the pederastic version of the femme fatale tradition in decadent literature, those myriad Salomés and Venuses all transformed into naughty Cupids. Rolfe projects his own threatening and uncontrollable desire onto another, in this case a pious but eroticized boy, only to submit to the return of his desire in the form of cruelty. He also explored another version of this scenario in which the pious man is triumphant and which the boy is seized, punished, and sanctified—a Christian practice that affords no small degree of voyeuristic pleasure. Desire returns not as cruelty, but as exquisite submission, and the appeal of this displacement is still intensely masochistic.

Rolfe's terrible allegory of Eros sets the stage for the numerous representations of boy martyrs in his work: Saint Hugh, Saint Pancras, William of Norwich, Tarsicius, and even a childlike Saint Sebastian, all of whom are stripped and tortured for the Christian cause. In his novels no less than in his poems, Rolfe submitted his fictional boys to the violence of hagiography—the lives of the saints as masochistic blazon. Paradoxically, the Christian violence is not in the service of sexual repression, but rather sexual celebration. The very purifying and punishing movement of Christian asceticism becomes, in Rolfe's work, the gesture that gives pederastic desire a sublime voice. In Paterian fashion, pederastia is set free, though it scampers about in the hair shirt of Christian martyrdom.

The classic Corvine pose is for Rolfe to position himself as a paternal and clerical figure, devoted to the fatherly protection or spiritual admiration of a beautiful boy. In fact, while a seminarian at Oscott, he was known to decorate the walls of his room with paintings and designs, using virtually every boy in the school as a model for his angels and saints. There is also a photograph, taken by Rolfe, of a handsome youth named Cecil Castle, posing nude for an arras of Saint Michael that Rolfe was painting for a church. In the photograph we can still make out the faint traces of wings and a shield, sketched in by the artist himself. Rolfe also photographed another boy, Robin Burdett, whom he dressed as Saint Sebastian in a loincloth and tied to a tree.

Rolfe's poems about boy saints, whether based on historical accounts or on boys that he knew, are some of the earliest and simplest examples of this scenario. Early in his life, when he was assistant master at Winchester Modern School, he wrote a handful of highly sublimated and sentimental love poems addressed to some of the boy pupils. In "To R. C. A." (1882), one of two love poems written to a sixteen-year-old boy named Robert Clement Austin, Rolfe writes of "loving commune with his love" in "Heaven's court where saints do walk in white."[41] In the same vein is the poem "To F. W. M. at Sea from F. A. R. in England" (1882?), also written to a sixteen-year-old boy, Francis Walter Morrison. Rolfe addresses the boy as "my love" and likens him to the "sweet Saints" who walk in robes of white in the "land of the blessed Dead" (35). In "To E. S. A. from F. A. R.: My Beautiful Boy" (1882?), written to still another sixteen-year-old boy, Edward Sigurd Allen, Rolfe compares a "wondrous fair" boy with Christ himself, here figured as sad and sublime with glorious eyes:

> See the nimbus cruciform
> Round His Head, in the sunlight warm;
> This the Boy most fair to see,
> Altogether lovely He. (34)

In this poem we glimpse the theme of noble suffering that is far more apparent in some of Rolfe's other poems about historical boy-saints.

In "Tarcissus: The Boy Martyr of Rome" (1880), for example, Rolfe sings the praises of Tarsicius, an acolyte and uncanonized martyr who was stoned to death while attempting to bring the viaticum in secret to Christian martyrs in prison. Rolfe positions himself as a pious poet entertaining a group of boys about the sublime death of a martyr. The "bright and beauteous eyes" of the "boyish visage," coupled with ritualistic props like tapers, censers, and "radiant vestments," recall Wilde's early Catholic poems. A priest searches for "one both true and bold," someone with whom he can entrust the viaticum. Religious purity and sexual purity overlap in a chivalric gesture when, after the stoning, a Christian knight, Quadratus, takes the boy in his arms and "with reverent tender care" carries him back to the Church. A halo appears around the boy's "golden head," as he melodramatically lifts himself from his deathbed to proclaim his triumph:

> "Father, I have kept the Treasure
> Undefiled." (30)

We are left to wonder precisely what the "Treasure" is in this poem— the boy's own fetishized body or the viaticum, itself a symbol of pederastic desire, entrusted to the purity of the boy.

Rolfe wrote a number of these saintly boy poems, including no fewer than four on the subject of William of Norwich. In "A. M. D. G." (not dated), the boy William, "Slender and straight in form as lilies are" (47), is dragged off to the woods and tortured by fiends:

> They spring upon him with a sudden bound,
> And in an instant, stripped and gagged he lies.

Behind the pose of Christian horror lies a thinly veiled eroticism. The horror soon gives way to saintly masochism:

> His pure young beauty shines forth from the tree,
> The martyr's crown illumes his lifted head,
> Why this fixed gladsome look?

Why indeed? The very notion of spiritual purity resonates in these poems with an idealized man-boy eroticism, its lily-like paleness a commonplace of the priest-and-acolyte genre. Similarly masochistic is Rolfe's medieval pastiche, "Sestina yn Honour of Lytel Seynt Hew" (1888), a poem celebrating Saint Hugh, who was flogged to death. "On hys whyte fleyshe theyr scourge made roses bloome," the poet writes, again aestheticizing a figure of horror into an icon of pleasure (38). Rolfe returns again to Saint Hugh in his posthumously published romance *Hubert's Arthur* (1935), which he co-wrote with Pirie-Gordon. Duke Arthur, figured here as Saint Hugh, is lacerated with "shameless thorns" and "the whole back of him was cut and wealed by sacrilegious scourges: his right hand and his left foot gaped open, pierced by nefandous nails, so that my little finger probed them."[42] But it is not the blood and pain that horrifies him so much as the feeling of defilement, "the touch of infamous depraved perfidious hands, pawing and mauling every inch of his flesh" (84).

Rolfe also wrote a story, "The Princess's Shirts" (1906), in which Toto's uncle, "a nimble lad of sixteen," tells a tale of a boy slave who is killed in the service of a princess.[43] The boy is seized and taken to a ruined tower, where his abductors "stripped him naked and walled him up" (64). The noble slave freezes to death. A marble statue is carved in his honor, and the narrator marvels over "the plump proud agile voluptuous face and form, the opulent young flesh, the splendid great long plain curving contours" (65). Eventually, the statue is complemented with an arrow and thus transformed into a representation of Saint Sebastian. The boy soldier Sebastian, shot through with heathen arrows, was a favorite subject for Rolfe, and he was not above comparing himself to this classic pincushion of homoerotic art.[44] In the Toto stories Sebastian is an exquisite boy-god, naked but shameless in heaven. In Rolfe's poetry, however, this particular boy martyr is less pastoral and more radiant in his suffering:

> A Roman soldier boy, bound to a tree
>> His strong arms lifted up for sacrifice,
>> His gracious form all stripped of martial guise
> Naked, but brave as a young lion can be,
> Transfixed by arrows he gains the victory. (57)

Given Rolfe's anxiety about his sexuality, these various boy martyrs might be read as efforts to articulate his own pederastic desires and perhaps even to punish them within a purifying Christian discourse. At any rate, after the fifth or sixth image of a tortured yet deliriously happy boy, we begin to suspect a sexual pattern that is only reinforced by the hagiographic rhetoric.

Even the less holy boys of Rolfe's prose seem to bear their suffering with extraordinary eagerness. In "Amico di Sandro," a homoerotic tale of male comradeship that was posthumously published in 1951, the boy hero is thrashed seven or eight times in the first few pages, often because he was caught staring at beautiful men. Most of the Toto stories are simply pastoral sketches of the "bathing boys" genre, with lots of Christian boy saints in Greek poses. Thus, we find a naked Sansebastiano making mischief with an equally playful Sanpancrazio; or an angelic little Santagapito wearing a diadem of laurel and xanthine palm entwined with lilies; or Santamelio and Santamico, fresh from Pater's account of Amis and Amile in *The Renaissance*, performing a blood rite of friendship and likened by Rolfe to meadowsweet and topazalite.

Rolfe inserts himself into this limpid aestheticism as the priestly figure, *la sua eccellenza,* for whom Toto narrates the stories. Predictably, this priestly man wields a whip from time to time, lashing the boys for their interest in girls or for their failure to say their Ave Marias. He obliges the boys to "strip to my lilac twig," to quote his improbable phrase.[45] The act takes on a ritual significance, as when *la sua eccellenza* whips Toto for his attention to "hussies": "But the circumstances of this particular affair drew from me a flagellation as round and solemn (all anglican rites being duly observed) as to impress

Frat' Agostino, who was present on the occasion in official capacity, with the notion that we English regarded the function as possessing something of a sacramental nature—indeed, he spoke afterwards of the twig as the outward and visible vehicle of inward invisible grace!" (4).

At times, the boys seem eager to partake of this sacrament. Rolfe recalls the real Toto as having once said, "Dearest Excellency, how could I confess when you haven't yet whipped me." Rolfe himself, in life no less than art, seemed to relish the *vice anglais* when applied to boys, though he always cast it in purely penitential terms. "I found my Romans jumped at the idea of being whipped like Englishmen, when the alternative was dismissed," he wrote once in a letter. "Their yells were horrid at first performance. But the whole thing being voluntary they supported it; and, presently, they used to ask for their whipping when they had been naughty."[46]

The most striking of Rolfe's writings in this genre is *Don Renato,* a Catholic pederastic romance set in the Italian Renaissance. It is also one of Rolfe's more decadent books. Don Gheraldo, whose diurnal constitutes most of the text, shares with Hadrian a delight in ritual, gems, and boys. Furthermore, *Don Renato* is written in what Rolfe calls "deliciously real macaronicks with Italian originals." The prose is so laden with archaisms that the first edition, published posthumously in 1953, contains a glossary. The diurnal itself is presented as a beautiful found object, the book as decadent fetish with shades of Des Esseintes. With the fastidiousness of an affected bibliophile, Rolfe describes the diurnal as "a quarto of sorts, measuring thirteen inches by eleven by two and three-eighths; containing six hundred pages of thin opaque paper, with a space of half an inch in the middle for the insertion of a fascicule; bound in stout white vellum."[47] We are told the diurnal is written in "greenish-brown ink" and has "brownish-purple stains on the front cover and upper edge" (32).

The preciosity of the text is complemented by the peculiarities of its author, a palace priest whose only occupation appears to be his adoring attendance on the souls of a few boy dukes. Like Hadrian, Dom Gheraldo is a classic Corvine priest, an odd mixture of piety, chastity, sexual ambiguity, and eccentricity: "You must expect moods, quick changes, repetition, in a diurnal; and you always must think of Dom Gheraldo as a priest, remembering that a priest is neither masculine nor feminine but a combination of the two + sacerdotium, i.e. a priest" (38–39). Among the boy dukes, whom the priest refers to by the quaint term "puerice," Don Renato and his foster brother Don Eros Ardeati are the most delicious. In a wonderfully incestuous family romance, the boys delight not only in each other, but in the libidinous gazes of Dom Gheraldo and even their own father, Don Marcantonio. In yet another pederastic scene of bathing boys, father and priest watch from the shore and enumerate the aesthetic virtues of the two young dukes. Dom Gheraldo considers Don Marcantonio's rather Paterian appreciations, and in his diurnal he muses over Don Renato's "flexuous puerine form" (60): "When I had looked and meditated during the space of one paternoster, I responded saying that the head of the Little Lord blazed in that obscurity as though some vitilant nimbus clustered in crisp flamelets on his brow of ivory" (50–51).

Rolfe's sadomasochistic inclinations toward boys are apparent in scene after scene of religious flagellation, described with zest by Dom Gheraldo. The priest delights in the willingness of the palatial pages to submit to penitential whippings, but he also expresses concern. He notes that while some pages, "in veritable contrition for their surridiculous venialities, have adorned themselves with very severe corporeal dilacerations, the rest have scourged their concupiscent pulp quite leniently" (96). In either case, he places himself at their service, especially "in the lavatories, where I medicated the backs of those *xxx.* palatial pates who went out semi-nude with the Flagellants" (95–96). Dutifully, he administers salves and lotions of woodruff, oil of almonds, and wych-elm. He is especially preoccupied by Don Eros, whom he suspects of venial mulierity, and is much intrigued when the little duke begs him for a whipping. The boy removes his shirt for the priest, and "having exuded the said silken obstacule, totally impudibund yet admirably ingenuous, he tolerated a most severe flagellation without murmuration: but, with eyes perlucid and panting to recuperate his suave breath, he indued his vesture, while I indignantly stigmatized him with the odious epithet Recidivus" (265). Don Eros is decidedly the whipping boy of choice in the palace. Even Don Marcantonio, with evident erotic interest and "commotion of mind," wants to paint a picture of him as Marsyas, with Don Renato as Apollo. The father wishes to capture Marsyas precisely at the moment that Apollo "exquisitely begins to flay him" (202). Don Renato is posed as the god in "an implacable attitude of serene simplicity, acrid and erect," while his foster brother strikes an impassioned pose at his feet: "Before the flagrant candor of this vision, genuflects Don Eros Ardeati, his throat and breast pressing his foster-brother, his caesarial head thrown back, terror in his distended eyes, his agile arms embracing the loins of the inhuman divinity" (202).

The beautiful boys in Rolfe's later work choose a somewhat less arduous path to his priestly affection. Rolfe was eventually able to view his fictional boys as lovers without necessarily submitting them to torture and crucifixion. His exile in Venice clearly had a desublimating effect on his libido. He retained his spiritual aspirations, and yet his boys finally broke out of the Tarcissus mold. In *The Desire and Pursuit of the Whole*—the very title a reference to the pederastic theory of love put forth in Plato's *Symposium*—Rolfe tells the story of Nicholas Crabbe's love for a boy named Zildo, even though, anatomically speaking, the boy is a girl. Zildo, or Zilda or Gilda, short for Ermenegilda, is clearly based on one of Rolfe's favorite gondoliers, Ermenegildo Vianello, who was also a model for the Venetian versions of Toto. In what I presume to be an act of self-censorship, Rolfe depicts his handsome gondolier as a tomboy in the novel, a girl raised from birth to behave like a boy. The sexual ambiguity of the character is evident at the outset: "Surely Nature had been interrupted when She made this creature, a grand broad-chested thin-flanked waistless boy by intention but a girl by defect" (9). Indeed, Rolfe is at such great pains to turn the girl Zilda into the boy Zildo that I wonder why he bothered with the gender switch at all. "The form of a noble boy, in all but sex" (11), Rolfe writes of her, and farther along, "Treat her as one would treat a quiet strong nimble-fingered lad" (22).

Despite this quirk, *Desire and Pursuit* is a Catholic pederastic romance. Like Hadrian, Nicholas Crabbe even enacts a confession of sorts of his sexual inclinations: "He used to gaze at other men, courting, marrying, living in apparent happiness; and he would wonder whether that was the right way" (14). He accepts Zildo as his servant and is thrilled by her fidelity to him. Immediately, as though an effect of his sexual attraction to her, Crabbe (like Rolfe, a would-be priest) begins to trouble about her soul. "One thing which had been worrying him was the health of the boy's immortal soul" (90), we are told. Crabbe accepts the role of spiritual mentor: "In a church you will imitate me—both knees on the floor to the Lord God exposed—one knee on the floor to salute Him in His tabernacle when passing—and fortify our soul with the Sign, my boy . . . Give me time, then, and you shall see a flower, that transcendent flower called Amaranth—Christ's Scourge, or Love-Lies-Bleeding" (90–91). Shades of Rolfe's boy martyrs return, and we are reminded that Zildo is named for Saint Ermenegildo. Nevertheless, while Zildo is later depicted as a sailor with a "carnation of amaranth," she is never obliged to submit to the same Christian torture enjoyed by Rolfe's other boy martyrs.

*The Desire and Pursuit of the Whole* parallels Rolfe's life in a number of ways. There is no evidence that Rolfe ever quite got his arms around Ermenegildo, but he did pursue sexual relationships with other Venetian boys and was apparently harassed by the police for propositioning boys on the Lido. At the same time, there is no reason to presume that he abandoned his religious faith. In *Desire and Pursuit*, he elaborates on the "regular debauch of religious observances" that Crabbe attends (270). Rolfe's account of these services is strikingly sincere. He always maintained an admiration for the Mass and a profound appreciation for ritual. "A procession is a visible act of worship, and demands display," he once wrote. "Also, Holy Mother Church ordains liturgical hymns of splendour incomparable—unsurpassable."[48]

Indeed, his account of the Holy Week services at Saint Mark's is one of the most impressive accounts of Roman Catholic pageantry to be found anywhere in decadent literature. Suffering from acedia and craving inspiration, Nicholas Crabbe goes to Saint Mark's on the night of the exposition of great relics. The decadent Catholic style is immediately recognizable, the prose so mystical, so dense with primrose and gold and mosaic, as to be itself processional. Nicholas Crabbe's longed-for joy arrives in a dramatic moment of spiritual and ritual revelation:

> Came the liturgical moment when grief is banished by joy. The deacon intoned the first Alleluias of Easter. The Easter-candle flamed. Lanthorns and lamps and tapers and torches on all sides blossomed with light. Violet veils fell from images and pictures. Violet vestments were changed for tissues of silver and gold. Violet curtains swept aside, disclosing golden altar and pala d'oro blazing with enamels

and precious stones. And all the bells and organs in basilica and city rang and sounded at the chaunt of Gloria Angelical. Now, if ever, his soul would be summoned ad audiendum verbum, would have leave to rise with its Lord in newness of perfect joy. (192)

Devotional decadence is rarely more inspired than this. The Latin intonations, the flames, the bells, the gold and gems—a sumptuous profusion that in no way subverts the spiritual transfiguration that it enacts.

In Rolfe's *Venice Letters,* which were written about the same time as *The Desire and Pursuit of the Whole,* we have a startlingly frank account of Rolfe's sexual adventures and opinions that runs *parallèlement* to the account of the Christian Venice of Saint Mark's that he so loved. We are introduced through these letters to a sixteen-year-old boy, Amadeo Amadei, whose name alone might have endeared him to Rolfe. The boy is described as a mixture of sensuality and spirituality: "Such a lovely figure, young, muscular, splendidly strong, big black eyes, round black head, scented like an angel."[49] Clearly, this is an angel with legs: "He was just one brilliant rosy series of muscles, smooth as satin, breasts and belly and groin, and closely folded thighs with (in the midst of the black blossom of exuberant robustitude) a yard like a rose-tipped lance" (31). The phallus as rose-tipped lance is surely one of the more poetic metaphors in the history of homoerotic chivalry.

Amadeo offers Rolfe his sexual services in a long and graphic proposition, complete with striptease and pantomime. Although Rolfe clings to his vow of celibacy, it is primarily a lack of funds that restrains him from accepting Amadeo's offer. There are moments in these letters when Rolfe suggests that he has had sex with boys before, but it has evidently been a long time. Finally, in January 1910, not long before his death, Rolfe set all scruples aside: "It appeared to me that the time was come to break out of all caution and prudence. So I did, as thoroughly as you please" (50). He took a boy, Piero, to Burano, where they made love to each other. "The clutch of us both was amazing," he wrote. "I never knew that I loved and was loved so passionately with so much of me by so much of another" (51). It was one of Rolfe's few moments of real happiness.

Rolfe's role as the pederastic priest has ceased here, we might assume. But this was not quite the case. Like the Eros of Rolfe's early meditation on Desire and Divine Love, Piero fires his arrow and soon after vanishes. Rolfe regarded his embrace of Piero as a failure of prudence, and the priesthood was certainly on his mind. Ironically, a few weeks before his trip to Burano, Rolfe wrote a letter to the archbishop of Westminster to remind him of his vocation: "I should say also, that my vow of twenty years' celibacy (which I offered in proof of my Vocation) expires this year, and that I am not at all moved to avail myself of liberty, but propose to renew my vow for life at the year's end."[50] We may presume that Rolfe changed his mind. Or we may suspect that celibacy refers here only to marriage, a temptation that he was perfectly willing to resist. Even his notion of chastity, however, betrayed a heady eroticism under its cowl. Whether chaste, celibate, or thrilling to the guilty embraces of Piero, Rolfe's understanding of his vocation was never far removed from his desire for boys.

## Saint Oscar Redivivus

> To be 1890 in 1890 might be considered almost normal. To be 1890 in 1922 might be considered almost queer.
>
> Carl Van Vechten

Is it my imagination, or does the almost queer Carl Van Vechten sound curiously 1890 in this epigram? It is often supposed that decadent style dropped dead in 1895 when Wilde was sentenced to two years of hard labor. Nevertheless, despite Victorian disdain, followed by high modernist disdain, some lily-like prose and a number of Wildean dandies survived the turn of the century, malingerers perhaps, but exquisite unto the last. Nor did flamboyant homosexuality vanish from the literary scene in that year, though the Wilde trials had a sobering effect. Wilde and his martyrdom proved a veritable lightning rod in the literary construction of the gay aesthete throughout the first half of the new century. Most of the modernist stylists who are now read as camp classics—Evelyn Waugh, E. F. Benson, P. G. Wodehouse, and Ivy Compton-Burnett, to name a few—owe a considerable debt to Wilde, as do the great modern dandies—Stephen Tennant, Cecil Beaton, and Noel Coward.

I want to discuss the careers of two writers in particular who were explicit in their imitation of Wilde: Montague Summers and Ronald Firbank. Both were gay aesthetes, both were consummate dandies, and both were Roman Catholic converts. Summers was a priest, though there is no record of his ordination, and Firbank sought a position at the Vatican, though nothing came of it. They were born too late to have entered Wilde's charmed circle, and they certainly did not enjoy the same degree of success as their patron saint; nonetheless, each took the Wildean dandy as the starting point for his own public persona. They might have had little else in common—Summers was a belligerent literary scholar and Firbank a precious humorist—but they both exemplified the persistence of decadent Wildean style. They also represented a later version of the pederastic priest.

Montague Summers, even more than Firbank, still requires an introduction. If his name is familiar at all, it is usually as an eccentric but pioneering literary critic and scholar of Restoration theater and the gothic novel. He is noted especially for his edition of the works of Aphra Behn, and he was the first critic in English to write at length on the merits of Ann Radcliffe and the Marquis de Sade, among other less canonical writers. He was also the world's foremost authority on witchcraft, demonism, vampires, and the like. In fact, he is probably the only scholar of witchcraft in this century who sincerely believed that Satan really exists apart from myth. What is not remembered about Summers is the fabulous public persona he cultivated, his Wildean capacity for self-promotion, and his Corvine ease at vituperation in print. Also forgotten is his first published book, a slim volume of decadent homoerotic verse entitled *"Antinous" and Other Poems* (1907).

The Reverend Alphonsus Joseph-Mary Augustus Montague Summers, for so he styled himself with a Wildean plethora of names, was born into an Evangelical family in 1880. Actually, the Alphonsus, an allusion to his favorite saint, Alphonsus di Liguori, and the Joseph-Mary, were his own contributions to his name and were added after he became a priest. He was too young to have experienced the Oxford of Lord Alfred Douglas, never mind that of Wilde, but from the time he arrived at Trinity College in 1899, he recognized Wilde as "the Master." His father was outraged to discover a copy of "The Ballad of Reading Gaol" in the young Montie's possession. But when, in a rage, he demanded, "Is this filthy thing yours?"—he found that his son had already appropriated the unmistakable signs of the Wildean dandy. "Yeth, Father," he replied, in a lisp that he affected for his conversations with prudes, "I have all the workth of the Mathter."[51]

One of his college friends recalls that, at Trinity, Summers usually wore a *lavallière* cravat and an elaborately embroidered black silk waistcoat. Outdoors, he was never without his chamois-leather gloves and an ebony cane, "the silver handle of which was, when minutely inspected, an extremely immodest representation of Leda and the Swan" (5). Even as a candidate for holy orders at Lichfield Theological College, he was known to burn incense in his rooms and to wear purple silk socks during Lent. Later in life, as a priest, his sartorial splendor adopted a more flamboyantly Roman Catholic taste, and he was said to give dinner parties dressed in ecclesiastical vestments—purple stock, black cassock, wide black silk cincture with purple fringe, and large silver buckles on his patent leather shoes. Many have noted that although Summers was a brilliant conversationalist, he had always a thick carapace of artificiality in his demeanor, a kind of mask that recalled the studied falsity of the classic dandy, not to mention the distrustful reserve of Walter Pater and John Gray. His style was decidedly aristocratic, Continental, and decadent, with the inevitable intimation of sexual impropriety. His friend writes of him, "He would often meet me with such an expression as *Che! Che!*, accompanied by a conspiratorial smile; or he would look closely at me and murmur, 'Tell me strange things'" (6).

Although he went down from Oxford with an unimpressive fourth in theology, Summers set out immediately to realize his vocation as a priest in the Church of England. He was ordained a deacon in 1908, and a brief curacy at Bitton followed. His publication of a number of homoerotic and impious poems in *"Antinous"* the previous year seems not to have been noticed by Church authorities, nor for that matter did they trouble about his increasing preoccupation with the nature of evil. Despite the disregard for his various eccentricities, Summers's paranoid concern about ghosts and his researches into demonism, reminiscent of Barbey and Huysmans but certainly unusual for an English curate, did not bode well for his future in the Church. His curacy was finally cut short only by a sexual scandal. He and another clergyman were prosecuted on a sodomy charge, though Summers himself was acquitted. Later, in 1909, he formally converted to Roman Catholicism, but I have not been able to ascertain precisely why he converted. Nevertheless, the signs are relatively clear. Oscar Wilde, decadent poetry, homosexuality, dandyism, demonism, priesthood— we begin to recognize a pattern. That same year he was accepted as a candidate for holy orders and began a course of study at Saint John's Seminary at Wonersh. Not surprisingly, at about this time Summers can be found in an attitude of devotion in that baroque tribute to Tractarian effusiveness, the Brompton Oratory—the site of one of Oscar Wilde's early attempts at conversion.

At this point the record of Summers's life is sketchy at best, and there is considerable debate over whether he was ever formally ordained a priest in the Roman Catholic Church. He received his clerical tonsure from the bishop of Southwark, but there is no actual record of his ordination. Nevertheless, later in life, he claimed to be a Roman Catholic priest, he officiated at services in private chapels in England (including his own), and he is known to have said mass in churches on the Continent. It has been suggested that he was ordained in Belgium or Italy or perhaps by some schismatical source. In Bristol it was believed that his ordination was blocked when the news of the scandal surrounding his curacy reached the bishop's ears. According to his secretary and amanuensis Hector Stuart-Forbes,[52] Summers went abroad for two months, returned with a picture of an Italian bishop in his possession, and immediately had new stationery printed with a priest's heraldic hat in one corner. When questioned on the subject, Summers was evasive and inconsistent. Given that he had already studied for the priesthood, it is far from unthinkable that he simply assumed the title and, in a truly Wildean gesture of self-transformation, dressed the part.

Whether Summers was ordained or not, there were few inquiries about the authenticity of his orders during his lifetime, and even his biographer presumes them to be genuine. Nevertheless, like virtually every other decadent, Summers incited confusion among those who have written sketches of his character. In the same breath, Summers is praised for his piety, sincerity, or theological erudition and then is condemned for his demonism, blasphemous conversation, and ritualism. The paradoxes are scarcely examined. Take, for example, this account by one of Summers's friends at Lichfield: "Unfortunately he became immersed in the externals and in the extravagances of the Anglican advanced party to which he and I belonged . . . He had sincere piety"; and he further adds, "He was in part an Oscar Wilde, but far more religious" (9). That last line might well raise an eyebrow, but his remarks recall the old "outward trappings" argument that we have seen elsewhere. This anxiety about ritualism and symbolism, a seemingly irresolvable conflict at the very heart of Christianity, leads to a virtually inevitable—we might say paranoid—confusion of inside and outside by which the very rituals for the celebration of faith are suspected of subverting it.

Summers's homosexuality causes much the same crisis of interpretation. In Brocard Sewell's biography, a strange mélange of homophobia and homophilia, it is treated as a psychological malady, inimical to Christianity and exacerbated by prurient reading in ancient literature. Sewell offers considerable evidence, however, that Summers took part in a long tradition of articulating his homosexuality through the erotically ambiguous persona of the priest. We need only read *"Antinous" and Other Poems*, published while Summers was a candidate for Anglican holy orders, to discover the possibilities for homoeroticism within a Christian tradition. His poem "To a Dead Acolyte" places him squarely in the priest-and-acolyte tradition and is a good sign that he was familiar with Bloxam's tale. Like other "dead acolyte" writings (John, Wright, Rolfe), homoerotic chivalry is spoken in the language of mourning. "To a Dead Acolyte" is an excellent example of the pederastic sentimentality and high aesthetic preciosity of the acolyte genre. The speaker addresses the body of a dead acolyte at the funeral, praising his innocence and beauty and offering him a sheath of lilies. Although neither the sex nor the profession of the speaker is revealed, we might safely presume, as in Bloxam, that he is a priest, especially since he recalls the accent of the boy's voice as he answered at mass.

The priest appears to be in the throes of doubt, his faith challenged not only by the mystery of death but also by regret and the enigma of suffering. He praises precisely those virtues of the boy that are lost to him, namely, the innocence of youth and the wisdom of the dead:

> The radiance of thine wondrous eyes
> No more shall flame with earthly bliss.

For thou hast seen beyond the veil
The mysteries of God, whilst we
With many a doubt and mad surmise
Peer wonderingly.

The speaker closes with a paean to the boy's innocence—a gesture that permits him an even greater extravagance of affection:

Dear, let me look once more
Upon thine innocence,
With joy let me adore,
Since unstained love and trust were thine,
That thou hast never known the pain
The vague regret when boyish dreams
Dissolve, and all is vain.[53]

The eroticism of the poem, the devotion of a man for a boy, is by no means camouflaged by the priestly attitude of a soul in distress, further troubled by mourning. The poem does not cloak desire, but transfigures it or, at any rate, complicates its interpretation. The references to innocence and unstained love add a tone of sublimation that is, at the same time, undercut by the priest's ardor and the boy's beauty. As in Pater, mourning becomes a highly suggestive and yet chivalric romance between man and youth. Death offers an "icy kiss," the lilies "swoon," God is referred to as "Thy Lover," and the priest recalls how the boy's wondrous eyes once flamed with "earthly bliss." The funeral is given the vague but suggestive atmosphere of a lover's tryst. Furthermore, Summers relies on such Wildean phrases as "thy gilded hair" and "thy gentle flower-like feet" to ensure an intertextual relation to the homoerotic tradition of nineties aestheticism.

The argument of the poem "Antinous" is also a familiar one since, like Pater, Wilde, and Rolfe, Summers seeks to attribute a Greek homoerotic motive to Christian love among men. In the poem, Hadrian's love for Antinous and the obsessive idealization of his mourning are a gesture toward immortality, a desire to "spell the riddling secrets of the tomb." By "spell" the poet means both to "spell out" in some sort of mystical language and also to "dispel," to banish confusion presumably through faith. Through the nods of his lover, the drowned slave is rendered "pandivine," a constellation whose fierce flame is compared to the star that guided the wise men to Bethlehem:

> They could not think thee dead, nor wast thou so,
> For thou hadst newly mounted to a throne
> Gemmed with divinity. (11)

Having sung the charms of Antinous, whose "beauty wins its own apotheosis," Summers goes on to describe the slave's reincarnation in various religious contexts. Predictably, Christianity offers Antinous the chilliest reception, though Summers observes that this is a theological error:

> Did the malign fanatics, who thus wise
> Mismaking god blaspheme His holiest name,
> Thrust thee into dour darkness as a shame
> Anathema mistrustful to their eyes? (14)

Christ is then revealed to be a fellow traveler of the pagan Antinous:

> That radiant love
> Most soothly found the world right fair alway,
> Whether it was the flowers He looked upon,
> Accounting them above a monarch's worth,
> Or the Immaculate Who gave Him birth,
> Or the dear face of His beloved John. (15)

Antinous is a Christian saint, pale, pure, and virginal, as on a fresco. He is also Saint Sebastian—Guido Reni's version, of course—crowned for his naked beauty rather than his martyrdom. He is also Saint Aloysius, before whose downcast eyes the poet, with incense and votive prayer, strews fleckless lilies, pale and wan. His name is "Amor Mysticus, great mystery!" Although saintly, Antinous retains a smile on his voluptuous lips, divine love with a beautiful body. Summers further writes that, far from being a stimulus to lust, Antinous keeps our hearts from turning cold and keeps lust from sitting "usurper in the room of love" (19). He "raisest us from out the banal dust" through a Christian act of redemption through love. Through the beauty of his body and the poetic immortality granted him by Hadrian's love, Antinous has undergone a resurrection of sorts. Summers closes the poem with some enigmatic lines regarding his adoration:


For evermore
We kiss thy feet, we worship and adore,
Proceeding from desire unto desire. (20)


Redemption comes not through the repression of desire, but through the perfection of its form. The word "desire" is spoken as though it were a divine and eternal promise, the "strange sway" that prevails, even while "New gods arise, and antique altars fall" (20). Desire is part of a Paterian historical flux, an inevitable but unstable movement from perfect form to perfect form.

This highly aesthetic conception of desire is not only decadent but also rather Freudian. Summers was well read in the psychology of sex, and he was a member, along with other theorists of homosexuality such as Havelock Ellis and Edward Carpenter, of the British Society for the Study of Sex Psychology. Like Huysmans, one of his favorite writers, Summers was well aware of the sexual component of religious experience. In an essay that he wrote for the society, he observed that, like the Marquis de Sade, great moral theologians such as Sa and Sanchez and Tamburini sought ultimate knowledge through a philosophical examination of sex. As Foucault observed, truth becomes the truth about sex. "According to de Sade it is only through the sexual that the world can be grasped and understood," Summers writes. "Nor can there be a profounder truth; for the sexual, rightly comprehended is deep down at the living heart of all humanity, all philosophy, wisdom, and religion."[54]

In this light we can recognize Summers's sanctification of desire in the "Antinous" volume as an early poetic effort to define a connection between sexual and religious experience. The devotional verses to Saint Catherine and Saint Anthony, though less homoerotic than the acolyte or Antinous poems, still rely on the sensual language of sexual union. In "St. Catherine of Siena," for example, Summers writes:

Wan lily of Siena! God above,
      Himself a wooer, winning pressed on thee,
Rapt in some spasm of immortal love,
      His five red wounds for bridal jewelry. (55)

"Al 'Santo,'" written in Padua, is similar in tone and even repeats the increasingly conspicuous reference to lilies:

Antonio, upon whose holy days
Brown sons of Francis hallow vestal sprays
Of silver-sandalled lilies, heart of fire,
Give me the uttermost of my desire. (86)

The Blessed Virgin is also the subject of what is essentially a love poem of God to his bride, replete with references to calamus and cinnamon, turtledoves and incense.

    Had his fellow seminarians got hold of this volume, they would have been shocked no less by his Marianism than by his homoeroticism. Mysticism, even the cult of suffering, becomes a form of love inseparable from sexual desire. In *Essays in Petto,* the same volume in which the essay on the Marquis de Sade appears, Summers includes a treatise on mystical substitution. The extremes of love and faith implied by this extraordinary capacity to take on the sins, temptations, and suffering of others was no less fascinating to him than it was to Huysmans, whom he quotes at length. He also includes essays on Saint Catherine and Saint Anthony, who represent for him this utter devotion to another person. "Love, warm human love," he writes, is Catherine's secret.[55] Regarding Anthony, "the Lily of Padua," Summers waxes more decadent: "His shrine is splendid beyond all description with coloured marbles and glistening alabaster; it is adorned with bronzes and richest silver-work, aglow with gems and precious stones; before it burn innumerable lamps of gold, and in giant candelabra tall tapers of virgin wax are lighted unceasingly. An endless train of suppliants, each, as the custom is, laying one hand upon the cold malachite and porphyry of the tomb, beseeches the help and patronage of the Saint."[56] Extravagant adoration calls for extravagant prose. In the image of the dead saint's body, transposed into the cold malachite and porphyry of his tomb, Summers captures the chilling sensuality that the decadents found in the Christian mystics.

However bold some of his sexual and doctrinal opinions, Summers lived a quiet academic life, widely accepted by the Roman Catholic community as a good priest and an excellent, if sharp-tongued, critic. And upon his death he was buried in Richmond, dressed in amice, girdle, and violet vestments, and along with him were buried his ivory and ebony crucifix, his breviary, his rosary, and the coat belonging to his dog Tango.

Ronald Firbank is now regarded as canonical, but he has always had a cult following as a perpetrator of high camp. So original and witty is his prose, so dense with irony and suggestion, that he should be counted as one of the great stylists of English literature, though few of his critics are willing to admit it. In his work Christianity is seen as not only the special provenance of homosexuals but also their most prized victim. The failure of Christians, especially pederastic priests and lesbian nuns, to restrain the sensuality of their religious devotions is a recurrent source of humor in every one of his many short novels. All the preoccupations of decadent Catholicism are exaggerated to the point of parody in a shimmering, cynical, languid, epigrammatic style even more disarming and absurd than the paradoxical wit of Wilde's comedies. Indeed, Firbank makes Wilde seem uptight. Overzealous flagellants flaunt their masochism, and lesbian nuns affectionately agree to exchange whippings. Priests and cardinals become the focal point of high society and haute couture. Sainthood is reserved only for the most exquisite. In *The Flower beneath the Foot* (1923), the cathedral is a hub of fashionable society known as the "Blue Jesus" because of its turquoise-tinted tiles.

Like many aesthetes of the previous generation, Firbank was a convert to Roman Catholicism, and his precious mockery masks an ongoing affection for its sumptuousness and its miracles. Ecclesiastical camp would never survive apart from the moral and aesthetic authority of the Church. Firbank is camp, to be sure, but I am always hesitant in applying that term to a writer who is truly brilliant, not the least because it is most often used, even by gay critics, to denigrate the work of gay men as frivolous and therefore worthless. Camp is to my mind extremely valuable as a specifically queer mode of expression, a potentially subversive mode of humor but also a backhanded mode of worship. Camp is not the same as parody. Even Susan Sontag, in her famous essay on the subject, recognized in camp a paradoxically genuine devotion for the institution that is ostensibly ridiculed. Just as drag queens adore the tragic divas that they travesty, so ecclesiastical camp springs to the defense of the one true Church.[57]

For Firbank, the Church was decidedly an aristocracy in its decadence, an ideology in a wondrous state of decay, and he delights in its lovely gestures, its perverse sensuality, its wan-faced obsessions. Like Pater, he approved of a Church with scaffolding, a faith in a terminal state of disrepair. In *Vainglory* (1915), his first published novel, the cathedral at Ashringford is never without a little scaffolding, and Lady Anne remarks that she "couldn't bear the Cathedral without a few sticks and props."[58] In the last novel Firbank wrote, *Concerning the Eccentricities of Cardinal Pirelli* (1926), the Cardinal sums up an essentially decadent or, more precisely, Paterian observation that Christianity is part of a long history of religions interminably in a tragic state of flux, but to Pater's melancholy attitude of appreciation, Firbank adds a certain comic relief:

> The forsaken splendour of the vast closed cloisters seemed almost to augur the waning of a cult. Likewise the decline of Apollo, Diana, Isis, with the gradual downfall of their temples, had been heralded, in past times, by the dispersal of their priests. It looked as though Mother Church, like Venus or Diana, was making way in due turn for the beliefs that should follow: "and we shall begin again with intolerance, martyrdom and converts," the Cardinal ruminated, pausing before an ancient fresco depicting the eleven thousand virgins, or as many as there was room for.[59]

Firbank never fails to undercut his more serious insights with a jab of outrageous wit. This passage is followed by the appearance of the Cardinal's greatest temptation, the acolyte known as Chicklet, disrespectfully bouncing a ball against the fresco.

Firbank shared with Montague Summers not only an interest in priests and acolytes, but also a nostalgia for the nineties and Oscar Wilde. In fact, Firbank is perhaps the most decadent writer of his time. Admirers like Evelyn Waugh and Edmund Wilson, recognizing his genius, sought to make a proper modernist out of him, praising his work for its originality, economy, and elliptical suggestiveness. Nevertheless, the constant refrain of Firbank criticism is that he simply disinterred the decadent style of Wilde and Beardsley, not only in his fiction but in his personal demeanor. Nancy Cunard thought him a Max Beerbohm caricature of himself, E. M. Forster compared him to Beardsley, Wyndham Lewis to Wilde, and Carl Van Vechten exclaimed that he was Félicien Rops on a merry-go-round, Beardsley in a Rolls-Royce, and *A Rebours* à la mode. Firbank went up to Cambridge in 1906, shortly after Montague Summers went down from Oxford, and he perfected much the same Wildean style of dandyism there. He decorated his rooms sumptuously and had a taste for statuettes on pagan and Christian themes. Osbert Sitwell thought that Firbank was ecclesiastical in his appearance, and Firbank himself claimed he looked so much like a priest that Jesuits once accidentally mistook him for one of their own and tried to kidnap him. This account of his priestly aura may or may not be contradicted by his dandyism, his dark and flawless lounge suit, his gloves and cane and fashionable neckties, his long and well-manicured fingernails stained a deep carmine.

Firbank never completed his degree at Cambridge, nor did he ever sit for an exam. His education seems to have consisted of avid readings in decadent literature—Baudelaire, Verlaine, Maeterlinck, Huysmans, Wilde, Beardsley—and conversations with Monsignor Barnes, the Roman Catholic chaplain. His ritualism and his interest in mysticism are both in perfect imitation of Wilde. In 1908 he converted, and when he died in Italy in 1926, he was buried in the Catholic cemetery (after he was exhumed from the Protestant one, where he had been mistakenly laid). In between these two moments were some halfhearted plans to live a religious life, coupled with an indulgence in the mild and comical heresies of his novels. He was fascinated by evil, if only to add color to life; he contemplated going into retreat in preparation for a papal preferment but noted cleverly that it was as much for his looks as the welfare of his soul. He apparently applied for a post at the Vatican, but nothing came of it. The failure to get a position may have been the reason for his comment, "The Church of Rome wouldn't have me and so I laugh at her."[60] The line is otherwise enigmatic, for the Church of Rome did have him, and a great many others like him.

Like many decadents, Firbank was an antiquarian. The holy relics he collected all pertained to the life of his patron saint, Oscar Wilde.

Brigid Brophy makes much of this insatiable pursuit of Oscariana in her overly speculative biography of Firbank, but his collection was certainly impressive. He had a sizable cache of rare books and other similar items, especially presentation copies of works by Wilde and Beerbohm. Each new addition was cause for elation. Not only did he collect objects, he also collected people. Even before he arrived at Cambridge, he located one of Wilde's publishers, Elkin Mathews, and persuaded him to publish a thin volume of stories not unlike Wilde's fairy tales. At Trinity he befriended Wilde's son, Vyvyan Holland, and at a birthday party given by Robert Ross for Holland, he met a great many other survivors of the master's entourage, including Vyvyan's brother Cyril, Charles Ricketts and Charles Shannon, William Rothenstein, and More Adey. He also pursued an acquaintance with Lord Alfred Douglas and Ada Leverson. He once met Reginald Turner on a street in Florence and showered him from head to foot with lilies. While in Edinburgh, he met with John Gray, whom he thought the nicest of priests.

Firbank's fictions, no less than his social occasions, are dotted with tributes to Wilde. In his play *The Princess Zoubaroff* (1920), a queer version of Lysistrata, Wilde and Douglas appear as Lord Orkish and Reggie Quintus, an inseparable pair of dandies whose principal role is to make tart remarks about the other characters. His posthumously published novel *The Artificial Princess* (1934) is a revision of Wilde's *Salomé* as though it were written by Beardsley rather than simply illustrated by him. "Alas!" the Princess exclaims at one point, "Why are present-day sins so conventional—so anaemic? A mild, spectacled priest could trample them out with a large pair of boots. I prefer a Prophet who will insult me! It is then a pleasure to retaliate. I have always suspected mine to be a Salomesque temperament."[61]

His devotion to Wilde also colored his portraits of priests and acolytes. In *The Flower beneath the Foot,* pederastic priests, far from being a cause for scandal, are obliged to preside over the fashionable gatherings of aristocratic ladies given to theosophic attitudes. As his heroine, Laura de Nazianzi, is introduced to these women and their priests, Firbank describes the gatherings in terms more appropriate to the aesthetic circles of Wilde and Ada Leverson:

> The Ecclesiastical set at Court, composed of some six, or so, ex-
> Circes, under the command of the Countess Yvorra, were only too

ready to welcome her, and invitations to meet Monsignor this or "Father" that, who constantly were being *coaxed* from their musty sacristies and wan-faced acolytes in the capital, in order that they might officiate at Masses, Confessions and Breakfast-parties *à la fourchette*, were lavished daily upon the bewildered girl.[62]

Firbank might also have been describing Montague Summers, a popular enough figure by 1923, especially with the quotation marks around "Father," suggesting, I suppose, an elided defrocking or imposture. No less dense with innuendo is the italicized *"coaxed,"* especially in juxtaposition with the wan-faced acolytes. In this passage masses and confessions are likened to breakfast parties in the brilliant social whirl that surrounds the "Blue Jesus."

One of Firbank's most ingenious tributes to Wilde is the chapter in which Olga Blumenghast and the Countess of Tolga bring gifts to the exiled Count Cabinet and his choirboy-in-residence, Peter Passer. We might suppose that the fallen statesman is a parody of Napoléon, since he has been exiled to the Island of Saint Helena, but Firbank offers a few details that point to Wilde, exiled to Paris, as a likelier historical source. Besides a pannier of pears, the Countess sails to the island with a volume of pederastic poetry in hand—"Erotic Poems, bound in half calf with tasteful tooling, of a Schoolboy Poet, cherishable chiefly perhaps for the vignette frontispiece of the author" (64). These poems, with titles like "To a Faithless Friend," "To V. O. I. and S. C. P.," "For Stephen," and "When the Dormitory Lamp Burns Low," could have been lifted straight from Baron Corvo. Furthermore, "knowing how susceptible the exile was to clothes" (64–65), the Countess arrays herself in an exhaustively described winter gown of kingfisher-tinted silk with a voluminous violet veil.

Unfortunately, the two women are hopelessly becalmed and never arrive at the island. Instead, Firbank permits a brief glance at the Count, who is fishing, and his companion, who hovers nearby, "adjusting a demure-looking fly, of indeterminate sex, to his line." Clearly, the women are not welcome, as Peter Passer exclaims "in insidious, lisping tones he preferred as a rule to employ: 'oh, sir, here comes that old piece of rubbish again with a fresh pack of tracts'" (68). Peter Passer—his name alone stimulates the imagination—is not an altogether pious lad and, not insignificantly, his retirement from his position at the Blue Jesus and his escape to the island occurred at the moment when the authorities of Pisuerga were making minute inquiries into the disappearance of sundry articles from the cathedral treasury. Firbank enumerates these articles in a helpful footnote: five chasubles; a relic-casket in lapis and diamonds, containing the Tongue of Saint Thelma; and 4¾ yards of black lace, said to have "belonged to" the Madonna. As the Count looks on appreciatively, Peter betakes himself of a swim and a few hymns:

> When not boating or reading or feeding his swans, to watch Peter's fancy-diving off the terrace end was perhaps the favourite pastime of the veteran *viveur:* to behold the lad trip along the riven breakwater, as naked as a statue, shoot out his arms and spring, the *Flying-head-leap* or the *Backsadilla,* was a beautiful sight, looking up now and again—but more often now—from a volume of old Greek verse; while to hear him warbling in the water with his clear alto voice—of Kyries and Anthems he knew no end—would often stir the old man to the point of tears. (68)

Meanwhile, Olga and the Countess, despairing of a wind, have given themselves over to unspecified lesbian activities in their sailboat, over which the Count later muses through his telescope.

In Firbank's world, relations between the sexes have utterly degenerated, and even homoeroticism resolves itself into a voyeuristic prurience. Sex takes place in naughty books and idle conversations, a matter of poses, rumors, glimpses, and oblique confessions. Eroticism collapses into aestheticism, and so for that matter does religion. But the relentlessness, not only of Firbank's perversity, but also of his Catholicism, renders the prospect of desire between priests and acolytes in his books a function less of convenience or opportunism than of sheer fate. In *Concerning the Eccentricities of Cardinal Pirelli,* Firbank offers us his most brilliant characterization, that of Don Alvaro Narciso Hernando Pirelli, Cardinal-Archbishop of Clemenza, who seems to have resigned himself to the chaos around him, even as it subverts the power of Catholic dogma to say what it means and to mean what it says. In this novel, as throughout Firbank's work, Catholicism has become a ridiculous set of gestures, endlessly misappropriated. Aesthetic and erotic pleasure have staged a mutiny, such that even the Pope, absurdly named Tertius II, must ask himself why no one will simply behave—even as he glances through a half-open door at the leg of a priest in a violet stocking. Popping up at odd times is the erotic focal point of this novel of spying and illicit glances, the acolyte Chicklet, playfully coaxing the aging clergyman into further lapses.

The novel opens with the christening not of a child, but of the Duquesa's week-old police dog. All the fashionable people of Clemenza arrive to witness the performance, as Cardinal Pirelli, at great peril to his future career in the Church, christens him with white menthe. Pandemonium ensues as the Duquesa ducks into a confessional to replace the rouge the dog has licked off, and the dog himself, much to the distress of Cardinal Pirelli and Monsignor Silex, is mounted by his own father. The choirboys are evoked in conjunction with the "esoteric antics" of the dogs when, from the choir loft above, where at least one voice has been evoking heaven, one of the boys lets fall a little white spit. "Dear child, as though *that* would part them!" Firbank writes, straining to miss the point (291). Clearly, the choirboy knows precisely what is required to facilitate intercourse between father and son, even when they are dogs. The choirboys and acolytes in this novel are nothing less than rent boys; in fact, one of them has been rewarded with a cigarette case for singing at a wedding—a reference, I presume, to the silver cigarette cases that Wilde gave as gifts to his favorite boys.

The cathedral is distinguished by its troop of dancing acolytes, who compete amongst themselves for attention. Regarding Christobal, who has peach-textured cheeks, we learn, "Indeed, it was a matter of scandal already, how he was attempting to attract attention, in influential places, by the unnecessary undulation of his loins, and by affecting strong scents and attars, such as Egyptian Tahetant, or Long flirt through the violet Hours" (299). We also overhear by chance the treble voice of Tiny, talking all alone about the Father who kissed him in the dark like a lion, a remark that is greeted by an explosion of coughs. Chicklet himself, despite his power "to convey the unuttered," is not one to mince words with the Cardinal, though the old man himself is a bit slow:

"You'd do the handsome by me, sir; you'd not be mean?"
"Eh? . . ."

"The Fathers only give us texts; you'd be surprised, your Greatness, at the stinginess of some!"

". . .?"

"You'd run to something better, sir; you'd give me something more substantial?" (340)

These are not the wan, angelic acolytes of an earlier generation of uranians. Here they mean business.

Although at first he only instructs Chicklet to say some fragrant prayers for him, the Cardinal is not angelic either. Even beyond his practice of baptizing dogs, he is at best baffled by his own vocation. He grants absolution and a handsome indulgence to a bigamist. He has had a mistress. He goes out on the town dressed as a cabellero or a matron—"disliking to forgo altogether the militant bravoura of a skirt" (294). The Pope has even sent a washerwoman, Madame Poco, to spy on him and gather evidence that will finally cost him his miter. And yet, even if we fail to forgive him his foibles (which is unlikely), the Cardinal is an oddly affecting and tragic figure. He is an absurd hero, muttering vaguely to himself much of the time, lost in a hazy world of preoccupation and distraction—a popular man, it seems, but wholly ineffectual as a clergyman. He is, like the rest of Clemenza, incapable of rigid discipline and self-denial, but his languidness, the failure of all his religious gestures, the non sequitur that is his entire existence, points to the essential frivolity of language itself, especially as it is deployed by Firbank.

This frivolity is the peril for which Pirelli is virtually an anagram. "With priests like Pirelli, the Church is in peril!" Cardinal Robin exclaims to the Pope with a short, abysmal laugh. Religious discourse, here in its decadence, invariably fails to mean. It fails to do anything. Indeed, the dog baptism reads like one of J. L. Austin's examples of performative speech acts that are absurdly infelicitous, as in the case of marriage with a monkey or the saint who baptized the penguins. Dogma degenerates into farce, unable to bear the weight of its own significance, neither simple nor transparent nor coherent in itself. It is neither prophecy nor revelation. The effect is paradoxical and sometimes disturbing.

Camp, for Firbank, was not without its traces of pathos. When Cardinal Pirelli has a vision of his own, when he speaks face-to-face at long last with Saint Teresa herself, it is only through a daze of loneliness and too many bumpers of beer. She stands in his window with the manuscript of *The Way of Perfection* and a knot of whitish heliotropes. The figure is absurd, and yet the seductive religious promise of pure meaning is not one that Pirelli can ignore. Firbank waxes sentimental, in his way:

> "Mother?"
> Saint John of the Cross would scarcely have pronounced the name with more wistful ecstasy.
> Worn and ill, though sublime in laughter, exquisite in tenderness she came towards him.
> ". . . Child?"
> "Teach me, oh, teach me, dear Mother, the Way of Perfection."
> (328)

So the chapter ends, but Pirelli does not learn anything. The saint's appearance makes no sense, and her gestures are gratuitous. She has no epiphany to deliver. Luminescent but enigmatic, ardent but camp, this Teresa is like the many stained-glass saints of the decadents: a beautiful work of art but ineffectual apart from her exquisiteness.

The final scene of the novel, however light its touch, also bears this same note of tragedy. Madame Poco, hidden in a confessional, secretly observes the Cardinal as he chases the flirtatious Chicklet through the cathedral. The end is certainly near. Firbank is undoubtedly comical in his usual way, and yet there is an undertone of pathos, a trace of King Lear bereft of his kingdom or Herod undone by his own desire, as the old Cardinal dashes about the cathedral like a foolish bull to Chicklet's ironic cry "Olé, your Purpleship!" The old man's heart is painfully giving way under the exertion. He is loosing his wits, it seems, as he mutters inconsequential phrases to himself and invents endless Corvine pet-names for the boy—Don Wilful, Don Bright-eyes, Don Sunny-locks, Don Temptation, Don Endymion. He is certainly losing his mantle, which slips away unawares. Finally, he is left with nothing but a miter like a mustard pot on his head, absurd as Lear bellowing on the heath:

> Dispossessed of everything but his fabulous mitre, the Primate was nude and elementary now as Adam himself.

"As you can perfectly see, I have nothing but myself to declare,"
he addressed some phantom image in the air. (341)

The line is, of course, a reference to Wilde's famous quip at the American customs that he had nothing to declare but his genius. "I suppose,
as you cross the border, they'll want to know what you have to
declare," Chicklet has asked the Cardinal only moments before. "I
have nothing, child, but myself," he replies, an ironic reference not
only to his earthly loneliness but to his spiritual loneliness as well
(340).

Although the darkened cathedral is full of religious pictures of the
Annunciation, the Conception, the Nativity, and so on, the saints
strike attitudes without a spiritual reference. Despite the weight of
Church history and theology, they are simply a beautiful backdrop,
decadent spectacles with nothing to say, nothing to declare but themselves. The Cardinal falls back not on Wildean genius so much as the
Wildean self—and nothing else. Wilde's romantic gesture by which the
self proclaims its own apotheosis is here revealed in all its comedy and
all its loneliness. As Chicklet leaves the cathedral, the Cardinal expires
before a picture of Christ's martyrdom, muttering, "Only myself." I
am reminded of Wilde's call for a ritual with empty chalice and unconsecrated host precisely for those who are unable to believe. Doubt,
the failure of the religious gesture, makes martyrs of its own. "May
God show His pity on you, Don Alvaro of my heart," Madame Poco
says, as she stands for a moment "lost in mingled conjecture" (341).

Firbank is uncharacteristically sentimental in the final passages. He
says of the Cardinal, "Now that the ache of life, with its fevers,
passions, doubts, its routine, vulgarity, and boredom, was over, his
serene, unclouded face was a marvelment to behold. Very great distinction and sweetness was visible there, together with much nobility,
and love, all magnified and commingled" (342). The Cardinal is redeemed through sheer pity. Firbank ends on a note of hope, however
desolate in its indication that only death brings freedom from the
maladies of desire and language. Windblown banners stir in the nave,
and through the "triple windows of the chancel the sky was clear
and blue—a blue like the blue of lupins," a blue, perhaps, like the
Madonna's sash, or like the blue hyacinths that appear as a symbol
of hope at the end of Pater's "Apollo in Picardy." It is hope against

all hope, just as Wilde asserted that true faith is faith in the improbable.

But lest we should find these gestures of faith too weighty for Firbank, we might consider his own tendency to subvert them with a clever remark. As he writes on the first page of *Vainglory,* "On such a languid afternoon how hard it seemed to bear a cross!"

# Conclusion

All things are in motion and nothing is at rest.            Heraclitus

To regard all things and principles of things as inconstant modes and fashions has more and more become the tendency of postmodern thought. We might begin with that which is held to be most transcendent—religious experience. Fix upon it in any of its more exquisite intervals and we detect in them a perpetual motion of historical change, an irrepressible shift of context, and the undecidability of the signifier itself. Such an object dissipates under the play of reflection; the cohesive force of language is suspended like some trick of magic; the object is loosened into a group of impressions, a cache of symbols—color, odor, flavor, music, texture—in the mind of the observer. And if we continue to dwell in language on the nature of God, we find not a transcendent signifier but an uncertain one, flickering, inconsistent, that burns and is extinguished with its articulation. The symbolic recognition of God may well be the founding moment of culture, but it is a moment that is produced only as a memory, a moment about which we might better say it has ceased to be than that it is.

In every postmodern discussion of the Christian God, I hear the echoes of decadent Catholicism. This God is certainly not the Father promised us by theologians. Nor is it the God of modernism, that religion of high seriousness that intervenes between the languorous decadent and the playful postmodern such that we can scarcely recognize ourselves in Oscar Wilde. What came to pass when the moment of decadent Catholicism passed? Was not modernism also a literary movement that could claim a great many converts to the Church? Were they not also intrigued by the aesthetics and erotics of religion?

365

In these final few pages, I can offer only a brief sketch of the direction that Christian thought took in English literature in the new century, though the topic could occupy a very long book. Modernist Christianity, especially as it was espoused by T. S. Eliot, may be seen paradoxically as both a rejection and an elaboration of the work of the aesthetes and decadents of the fin de siècle. By the beginning of this century, Christianity had become increasingly irrelevant in the domain of culture, and yet Anglo-Catholicism had become increasingly popular, even fashionable, and was in fact enjoying its heyday. A remarkable number of the most reputable writers of the period were converts either to Rome or to a distinctly High Church Anglicanism—not only Eliot, but also Evelyn Waugh, W. H. Auden, Graham Greene, Ronald Firbank, E. F. Benson, Radclyffe Hall, and C. S. Lewis, to name a few. In the era of modernism we may indeed find the last great efflorescence of Christianity in English literature, despite a concomitant modernist trend toward atheism.

As with the decadents, there were considerable distinctions between the individual religious sensibilities of the writers I have named. Some, like Eliot, sought to make a radical break with the Catholic aesthetes of the previous generation, while others, especially Firbank, sought to elaborate on the aesthetic manner of Oscar Wilde. Modernism most distinguishes itself in this regard by its trend toward high seriousness in religious writing, a degree of earnestness that the decadents were wont to find suspect. This seriousness at times masks a certain anxiety about the role of the artist with respect to culture: if the artist should fail to maintain a solemn countenance, a philosophical gravity, and a voice of moral authority, surely art would cease to fulfill its prophetic cultural duty and lapse wholly into frivolity.

While the decadents tended to find in Catholicism a romantic cult of the imagination and a spiritualization of eros, high modernists eschewed sentiment in their relentlessly cerebral and admirably civic embrace of the Church and its traditions. Where decadent Catholicism was by turns mystical and witty, the faith of the modernists was for the most part doctrinal and dour. For example, Graham Greene's writings on his conversion are characterized less by joy than by apprehension, and any passion he demonstrated for the faith was dampened by his sober concern for the "sentimental emotionalism" and "limited intellect" of the Christians he met. Evelyn Waugh's conversion was remarkably chilly in its intellectual detachment. An intelligible and authoritative explanation of the Church's doctrines was all he required for a leap of faith. As various biographers have noted, W. H. Auden's return to the Anglo-Catholic faith of his childhood was an exclusively intellectual process rather than a spiritual journey. "I am not mystical," he once said to a friend, no doubt eager to distinguish himself from the homosexual Catholic aesthetes of an earlier decade.

T. S. Eliot offers the most dramatic evidence of this distinction between decadent and modernist Catholicism. His essay on Walter Pater, a highly idiosyncratic and unjust reading, reveals through its shortcomings Eliot's distaste for Catholic aestheticism and its proponents. He maintains that Pater is sentimental, incapable of reasoned thought, incapable of distinguishing between art and religion, and irrelevant to the orthodox tradition of Christianity. As I hope I have demonstrated, Pater was remarkably wise and eloquent on the subject of Christianity. Ironically, he is also very modern—so modern, indeed, that by comparison Eliot seems oddly Victorian. In his most important statements on Christianity and culture, *The Idea of a Christian Society* and *Notes towards the Definition of Culture,* Eliot insists that religion is necessary to culture, and he espouses a politics and aesthetic of uniformity, continuity, and coherence, with Christianity as its moral foundation. Such longing for fixed principles, such grave concern for religious doctrine—in short, such philosophical orthodoxy—is a far cry from the mystical faith of the decadents, what Wilde called his "antinomian" Christianity. If Eliot looked back to the Victorians at all, it was to Newman and Arnold, not Pater and Wilde.

At the same time, I find that even Eliot is in some ways carrying on a religious tradition in literature that was previously articulated by the decadents. In fact, he is sometimes compared to Huysmans, for whom he himself expressed a distaste. In his espousal of cultural elitism, as he called it, Eliot certainly adopts something like the *contra mundum* pose of Anglo-Catholicism, an attitude of moral, not to mention social and intellectual, superiority to the general populace. The aesthetes of the 1890s also found in the Church an aristocratic attitude, an embrace of tradition and the past, a way of distinguishing themselves from the crowd and launching a critique of the bourgeoisie. If we turn to Eliot's poetry, we also find a degree of exhaustion and weariness in his faith. The Magi of "Journey of the Magi" are jaded travelers in the decadence of the antique world, and they look upon the Nativity as a strange confusion of birth and death. In "A Song for Simeon," Eliot writes:

> I am tired with my own life and the lives of those after me,
> I am dying my own death and the death of those after me.
> Let thy servant depart,
> Having seen thy salvation.[1]

Eliot lived in the shadow of doubt, a lingering belief that his idea of a Christian society was either impossible or ignored in the modern world. His repeated prayer in "The Hollow Men," *"For Thine is the Kingdom"* (90) comes as an apocalyptic whimper, a stutter, incapable of full articulation. He is convinced that Western culture is going to hell in a handbag, though of course it is not a hilarious, high-literary handbag of the Miss Prism sort. Like Huysmans in his later years, Eliot writes of a crisis of meaning concomitant with the crisis of faith, a fear that his wings, as he describes them in "Ash-Wednesday," are no longer wings to fly but "merely vans to beat the air" (94). Over and over again, like the "tragic generation" that preceded him, Eliot discovers the melancholy pleasure, the exquisite ennui, of preaching an archaic dogma to an empty room. He also seeks, as did Pater and Huysmans, to aestheticize spiritual perception and to spiritualize the aesthetic sensibility, though he is quick to claim that this interpenetration of the aesthetic and the religious permits him to condemn what he calls decadence, diabolism, or nihilism in art.

Catholicism continued to excite the religious and artistic sensibilities of homosexuals in particular. As I point out in my preface, the association of Anglo-Catholicism with homosexuality had, by the 1920s, passed from a running joke to a historical fact. I mentioned the Anglo-Catholic sodomites whose company Charles Ryder is advised to forego in *Brideshead Revisited;* and yet it is interesting to examine Waugh's conversion to Rome in light of his own anxious fascination with homosexuality. Indeed, his novel may be seen as a modernist classic of decadent Catholicism, with its homoerotic saga of a decaying aristocratic family given to Catholic guilt, fashionable poses, and sexual self-indulgence. In *The Well of Loneliness,* Radclyffe Hall looks to Christian suffering as a lesbian pastime and Christian pity as an antidote to homophobia. She populates her novel with sad queer artists, *femmes damnées,* not to mention a few accursed *hommes,* all bemoaning the mark of Cain upon their desires. Djuna Barnes is no less vampiric in *Nightwood,* though she eschews Christian sentimentality in favor of a Roman Catholic fetishism that culminates in a resoundingly decadent remark by Matthew O'Connor, the perverse hero of the novel, who says, "Corruption is the Age of Time. It is the body and the blood of ecstasy, religion and love."[2] Even Auden, despite his cerebral detachment, figures importantly in this tradition, since he was an ardent ritualist who regarded Christianity as a religion of love. "We must love one another or die" is one of his most quoted lines, and he made its religious and homoerotic nuance abundantly clear when he wrote to his lover, Chester Kallman, "It is through you that God has chosen to show me my beatitude."[3]

With the death of T. S. Eliot the moment of Catholic modernism also passed. I would speak about Catholic postmodernism but, as far as literature is concerned, it can scarcely be said to exist. Roman Catholicism is no longer a shaping force in any of the great aesthetic movements of our own time, except perhaps as a hindrance to be overcome. There are, however, innovative artistic uses of Catholicism. Pier Paolo Pasolini and Derek Jarman spring most readily to my mind, if only because they suggested a link between radical politics, gay sexuality, and the personality of Christ. Postmodern culture, even if we look at its more traditional genres, such as painting, film, or literature, is not without its hysterical visionaries, lesbian nuns, monastic poets, screaming popes, gay Christs, and pederastic priests, though they are not usually pious in their intentions. These various Christian personae beg the question, what is the meaning of Catholicism in a postmodern context?

Oscar Wilde once remarked that science is the record of dead religions. We might add that postmodernism is the record of dead sciences. Theology is one such science. It has come increasingly to resemble the dead religions it seeks to define. In an effort to rescue it from absurdity, it has been taken over by historians and philosophers whose primary claim to expertise in the field is their failure to believe in God. I was much taken with a recent issue of the intellectual journal *Critical Inquiry* that included a collection of articles on postmodern theology. The essays themselves were suitably academic and unreadable, but it was the cover illustration that most delighted me. It was a reprint of Adam and God from the Sistine Chapel, but between their fingers, languidly extended in each other's general direction, someone had interposed a bar code. In the computer hieroglyph of the bar code, we recognize the displacement of God's grandeur by the technological sublime, the vast and polished networks of a fashionably late capitalism.

The Church has become a multinational corporate behemoth. Wilde once referred to Catholicism as the most romantic college in the great university of the world's religions, but that university has become something more like a suburban shopping mall. The mix-and-match sensibility by which we may choose a house of worship these days is, at bottom, a form of spiritual consumerism, and I might add that Roman Catholicism is doing remarkably well on the international market for converts. Even as I write, the pope is addressing a crowd of four million people in the Philippines, and he has already waded through much of the Third World, basking in adoration and beatifying martyrs of color. From a postcolonial perspective, the Church's role in the recent world population conference in Cairo was most edifying, especially when the Vatican claimed, without a trace of irony, that North America and Europe are trying to impose a "decadent" sexual ethic on the rest of the world. When radical Western academics declare that God is dead, they do so at their peril.

We might also ask precisely what is decadent about postmodern Catholicism? The Church remains to this day, as it was a century ago, a sprawling empire that is forever bemoaning the fate of itself and the world in apocalyptic terms, shuddering under the gaze of scientific rationalism, nostalgic in its imperial pomp, and alluring in its enthusiasms. Its rhetoric is improbable and archaic to postmodern ears, and papal encyclicals may now be seen as the very model for the Derridean letter that never seems to arrive at its proper destination, that disseminates endlessly among a vast array of cultures fated to misread it after their own fashion. Postmodern Catholicism is marked by a discursive heterogeneity, an impurity and polyvalence, that we might also call decadent. In the fin de siècle fascination with fragments, with unruly juxtapositions and self-contradictions, and above all, in the decadent cult of paradox, we discover a virtually postmodern belief that nothing born of language can be perfect and pure. Through poststructural theories of the sign, we might regard religion as part of the great web of discursive practices, a network of illusory patterns made up of the accumulated forms of centuries of belief, shot through with desire, politics, economics, and cultural difference. It is not unlike the web of Pater's conclusion to *The Renaissance*—a dream of design made up of various threads that disseminate and disappear beyond the grasp of consciousness. This dissemination, the play of the signifier, also leads us to question the transcendent certainty of religious language, not to mention its pretensions to immutability. Christ is only brought to life again in our interpretations of him, notwithstanding the ideological efforts of the Church to assure his resurrection.

The decadent conception of fragments, of scholarly quotation and artistic criticism, is also akin to the postmodern conception of appropriation and pastiche. The decadents were notorious for their appropriation of Christian traditions, especially the literary genres of the Church, such as mystical language, the conversion narrative, and the hagiography. In our own time I think it valuable to recognize the fact that Christianity has no necessary content, no essential politics, no inherent meanings, apart from the practices of individuals. It is no doubt true that the Church has become the bulwark of reactionary politics throughout the world, and that its tenets are deployed with the utmost cruelty as well as for noble ends. Nevertheless, as the decadents made evident, the language of the Church is easily loosened from its more conventional political moorings. The popularity of Christian socialism at the turn of the century—or, in our own day, the popularity of "liberation theology" or the work of Cornel West—is sufficient to suggest that Christianity, at various moments in its history, has exhibited a progressive political edge.

The Church's vulnerability to the appropriation of its traditions is especially important with respect to sexual politics, an arena in which Vatican pronouncements of late have been especially dreary. This book is a work of gay criticism primarily because homosexuality ought to be important to any discussion of decadent literature or Christian erotics. In addition to the historical argument, however, there is another political concern: the profound rift that is popularly assumed to exist between Christians and homosexuals. Those who are recognized as authorities on either side of the rift clearly hate each other. The Vatican has turned an archaic notion of sexuality into a political battle-cry. Lesbians and gay men are now harassed with impunity by Catholics who say, with great smugness, that they love homosexual people but hate homosexual acts, as though it were easy, or even desirable, to tell the dancer from the dance. At the same time, since Stonewall, the movement for lesbian and gay rights has all but abandoned Christian spirituality as a valid category of experience. In much queer rhetoric, as in much poststructural theory, the spiritual, not to mention the aesthetic, is dissolved entirely into the psychological and the political and permitted virtually no specificity of its own. The Roman Catholic Church in particular is construed primarily as the key site of homophobic power and sexual repression. Nevertheless, when I peruse the history of the Church and the history of homosexuality, I see a great deal of felicitous cohabitation. I would have to admit that the turbines of Christianity have traditionally spun with an extraordinary quantity of queer steam.

The lesbian-and-gay movement is eager to forget the number of Christians among its ranks, despite the fact that one of the largest and wealthiest gay organizations in the world is the Metropolitan Community Church. Poststructural theory and queer theory have both singled out Christianity as emblematic of a naive and dangerous belief in transcendence, though the radical practice of making sexual identity the basis for political action often requires a similar leap of faith. Aestheticism, once the hallmark of a certain gay sensibility, has suffered a similar decline in prestige. Beauty, belief, and sexual pleasure, insofar as they are distinct from the political, now appear simply quaint to those of a critical disposition. In academic circles all three have lapsed into a terminal decadence, old philosophical empires now in decay. The aesthetic pleasures of sex have given way to the critical pleasures of sexual politics, the temptations of art are renounced in favor of a political demystification of art, and religion is simply held in contempt as an opiate of the masses.

Walter Benjamin, whose essay "The Work of Art in the Age of Mechanical Reproduction" is now canonical among literary theorists, is an interesting case in point. Benjamin attacks the religious dimension of art by describing what he sees as the decline of its "aura" in the age of mechanical reproduction. Photography, for example, makes the image more available and erases the ritualized distance between a work of art and its audience. Nevertheless, I am left to wonder about the feeling of awe I still experience in the presence of something I find beautiful, whether it be a painting, a photograph, or a landscape, an object from the hand of man or from one of his machines. The rhetoric of aestheticism, and even the rhetoric of religion, does justice to the sensation in a way that a mere political analysis does not.

Benjamin further associates aestheticism with fascism, in particular the tendency to regard war as beautiful. The extreme form of self-alienation, in which art is merely a beautification of the modern will to mass self-destruction, "is evidently the consummation of *'l'art pour l'art.'*" In his conclusion to the essay, he writes, "This is the situation of politics which Fascism is rendering aesthetic. Communism responds by politicizing art."[4] Nevertheless, the only kind thing I have to say about this assertion is that, well, it is nicely written. From the point of view of history, however, it strikes me as absurd. First of all, in the literary tradition of *"l'art pour l'art"* the aesthetic sense did not generally incapacitate moral or political consciousness, as I hope I have demonstrated. But there is also the problem that fascists did not aestheticize politics any more than did any other social movement, conservative or progressive. Every government has its splendid architecture. The fascists did, however, politicize art. This much they had in common with communists, as many an exhibition of Nazi and Soviet kitsch has rendered all too clear. Had Benjamin written about Stalin rather than about fascists, the problems in his formulation would have been more evident. The Nazi diatribes against "decadent" art—that is to say, much of the art we call modernist and still find beautiful— should in themselves tip us off to the regrettable consequences of politicizing aesthetics. At present in the United States, the battle over "political correctness," waged between progressives and conservatives of a much tamer stripe than the ones who ravaged half the world not long ago, is evidence of the same critical impasse of blaming aesthetics for the shortcomings of politics. Beauty has no allegiances, no necessary ideology. Aestheticism is incapable of political dogma. It is therefore the villain of a great many villains.

I read an article in *The New Yorker* not long ago about the late Harold Acton, a gay man whose life as a Catholic and a renowned aesthete owed a great deal of its charm to Wilde and his entourage. I would not make any grand claims for Acton as an artistic or critical genius, but this article was essentially a character assassination written by a much younger gay man—a portrait of a decaying old queer all alone with his servants and his art collection in his decaying old Florentine mansion. It has become an unfortunate post-Stonewall cliché: the gay aesthete—sad, outmoded, and ineffectual. The writer believes that Acton tried to escape the anxieties of homosexuality by retreating into Wildean aestheticism. Surely, it would have been an unlikely place to hide! The great irony, of course, is that the author himself strikes a more recent vintage of the Wildean pose that Acton favored. He is chattering about a great aesthete in the pages of *The New Yorker,* after all. Subscribers to that magazine are likely to read the article only because Acton himself, like Wilde, knew everyone who was anyone and lived a fascinating life, filled with art, sexual intrigue, and clever conversations. There was also the stunning full-color photo spread of the mansion, which upstaged the article and sent gay men all over the city into a swoon.

I see nothing essential to being postmodern or being gay that should preclude a devotion to great art—or, for that matter, a devotion to God. In fact, I find that the gay aesthete, Catholic and otherwise, is alive and well in a postmodern context. This persona, popularized by Wilde and now more than ever in disrepute, is everywhere evident among gay men who have made high culture, including the high culture of attacking high culture, their peculiar domain. These are the gay men who overpopulate the environs of academia and the avant-garde, who spend enormous amounts of money on travel, theater, books, and restaurants, who may to this day be seen in the throes of prayer in virtually every church or synagogue I have ever visited, and who have a vast and ingenious vocabulary for articulating their sexual desires. Progressive sexual politics is clearly not the only reason Wilde is a central figure of gay studies.

My discussion is Foucauldian after a fashion, since I regard the religious, the aesthetic, and the erotic as discursive modes of multiplying, organizing, disciplining, and interpreting pleasures. At present, the religious is perhaps the most beleaguered of these categories, though I think all three, whatever their impurities, are invaluable to a more subtle and complicated apprehension of experience. For religion, no less than art and sexuality, comes to us proposing, in its own peculiar language, to give nothing but the highest quality to our moments as they pass, and simply for those moments' sake. Religion has the potential to be what Walter Pater called a *passion,* because it gives us a quickened sense of life, of ecstasy, sorrow, and love. Passion exceeds all facile orthodoxies with a flame-like abundance of possibilities. "Only be sure it is passion," Pater reminds us—"that it does yield you this fruit of a quickened, multiplied consciousness."[5]

# NOTES

## Introduction

1. Richard Gilman, *Decadence: The Strange Life of an Epithet* (New York: Farrar, Straus and Giroux, 1979), p. 158.

2. One might begin with Ruth Z. Temple's admirable effort at clarification in her essay "Truth in Labelling: Pre-Raphaelitism, Aestheticism, Decadence, Fin de Siècle," *ELT* 17, no. 4 (1974): 201–222. Other recent critical efforts that have influenced the definition of decadence I present here include John R. Reed's *Decadent Style* (Athens: Ohio University Press, 1985), Linda Dowling's *Language and Decadence in the Victorian Fin de Siècle* (Princeton: Princeton University Press, 1986), and Elaine Showalter's *Sexual Anarchy* (New York: Viking, 1990). My understanding of decadent paradox is similar to Reed's assertion that, in decadent style, there is often a juxtaposition of disruptive elements that requires an act of intellection on the part of the reader to make conceptual connections that might otherwise appear occult. I do not, however, share his belief that the category of "decadence" ought to be construed in purely stylistic, rather than thematic, terms. Dowling has demonstrated that decadent thematics, the fascination with perversity and cultural degeneration, is a symptom of its style and the romantic philological belief, prevalent at the time, that language itself was subject to decay. Showalter has sharpened my understanding of the sexual politics of decadent literature and the anxious fin de siècle belief that gender itself was in decay, especially with respect to the homosexual and the New Woman.

3. Charles Baudelaire, "Notes Nouvelles sur Edgar Poe" (1857), in *Oeuvres Complètes* (Paris: Gallimard, 1976), vol. 2, pp. 319–320. Translations mine.

4. Arthur Symons, *The Symbolist Movement in Literature* (1899) (London: Constable, 1908), pp. 4, 40, 98.

5. T. S. Eliot, "Baudelaire," in *Selected Essays, 1917–1932* (New York: Harcourt Brace, 1932), p. 342.

6. Friedrich Nietzsche, *The Antichrist* (1888), translated by Anthony M. Ludovici (New York: Russell and Russell, 1964), p. 222.

7. Octave Mirbeau, *L'Abbé Jules* (1888) (Paris: Union Générale, 1977), p. 128. Translations mine.

8. Emile Zola, *Rome* (1896), translated by Ernest Alfred Vizetelly (New York: Macmillan, 1897), vol. 1, p. 311.

9. Symons, *Symbolist Movement*, p. 147.

10. Jean Pierrot, *The Decadent Imagination, 1880–1900* (Chicago: University of Chicago Press, 1981), pp. 96–97.

11. Saint Augustine, *On Christian Doctrine*, translated by D. W. Robertson, Jr. (Indianapolis: Library of the Liberal Arts, 1958), pp. 37, 67.

12. Kenneth Burke, *The Rhetoric of Religion* (1961) (Berkeley: University of California Press, 1970), p. 7.

13. Eve Kosofsky Sedgwick, *Epistemology of the Closet* (Berkeley: University of California Press, 1990), p. 140.

14. Radclyffe Hall, *The Well of Loneliness* (1928) (New York: Doubleday, 1990), p. 405.

15. For a survey of statistics on gay priests, see A. W. Richard Sipe, *Sex, Priests, and Power* (New York: Brunner/Mazel, 1995), pp. 136–137.

## 1. The Dialectic of Shame and Grace

1. John R. Reed, *Decadent Style* (Athens: Ohio University Press, 1985), p. 206.

2. Friedrich Nietzsche, *The Case of Wagner* (1888), translated by Anthony M. Ludovici, in *The Complete Works of Friedrich Nietzsche* (New York: Russell and Russell, 1964), vol. 8, p. 13. Nietzsche's essay is quoted from this edition throughout.

3. Charles Baudelaire, *Oeuvres Complètes* (Paris: Gallimard, 1976), vol. 1, p. 11. Translations mine. All works are quoted from this edition.

4. Max Nordau, *Degeneration* (1892; first English translation, 1895) (New York: Howard Fertig, 1968), p. 213. Nordau's observations are quoted from this edition throughout.

5. Rachilde, *Monsieur Vénus*, translated by Madeline Boyd (New York: Covici, Friede, 1929), pp. 46–47.

6. Aubrey Beardsley, *Under the Hill* (1904) (New York: Grove Press, 1959), p. 58.

7. George Moore, *Evelyn Innes* (1898), in *The Collected Works of George Moore* (New York: Boni and Liveright, 1922–1924), vol. 6, p. 80.

8. Edmund Gurney, "Wagner and Wagnerism," *Nineteenth Century* 13 (March 1883): 444.

9. Friedrich Nietzsche, "Nietzsche *contra* Wagner" (1888), in Nietzsche, *Complete Works*, vol. 8, p. 70.

10. J.-K. Huysmans, "L'Ouverture de Tannhaeuser," in *Croquis Parisiens* (1886) (Paris: Plon, 1908), p. 155. Huysmans' essay is quoted from this edition throughout. All translations mine.

11. J.-K. Huysmans, *A Rebours* (1884), in *Oeuvres Complètes de J.-K. Huysmans* (Paris: Crés, 1928–1934), vol. 7, p. 240. Excerpts from *A Rebours* are quoted from this edition throughout. All translations mine.

12. Letter of 3 January 1865, quoted in Claude Pichois, *Baudelaire*, translated by Graham Robb (London: Hamish Hamilton, 1989), p. 324.

13. Jean-Paul Sartre, *Baudelaire*, translated by Martin Turnell (New York: New Directions, 1950), p. 73. Sartre's observations are quoted from this edition throughout.

14. Paul Verlaine, *Oeuvres Poétiques Complètes*, edited by Jacques Borel, (Paris: Gallimard, 1962), p. 215. Verlaine's poetry is quoted from this edition throughout. All translations mine.

15. Stefan Zweig, *Paul Verlaine*, translated by O. F. Theis (Boston: Luce, 1913), pp. 54–55.

16. Quoted in Joanna Richardson, *Verlaine* (New York: Viking Press, 1971), p. 83.

17. Zweig, *Paul Verlaine*, p. 26.

18. Paul Verlaine, from his article about himself entitled "Pauvre Lelian" (a witty anagram for his own name), originally published in *Les Poètes Maudits* (1884); in *Oeuvres en Prose Complètes*, edited by Jacques Borel (Paris: Gallimard, 1972), p. 689. Unless otherwise indicated, Verlaine's prose is quoted from this edition. All translations mine.

19. Letter to Jules Claretie, 8 January 1881, in *Correspondance de Paul Verlaine*, vol. 3 (Paris: Messein, 1929), p. 86. Translation mine.

20. Edmond Lepelletier, *Paul Verlaine: His Life—His Work*, translated by E. M. Lang (London: T. Werner Laurie, n.d.), p. 348.

21. Harold Nicholson, *Paul Verlaine* (London: Constable, 1921), p. 121.

22. Ernest Raynaud, *La Melée Symboliste (1870–1890)* (Paris: La Renaissance du Livre, 1918), p. 63. Translation mine.

23. Quoted in Richardson, *Verlaine*, p. 140.

24. W. G. C. Byvanck, *Un Hollandais à Paris en 1891* (Paris: Perrin, 1892), pp. 132–133. Translation mine.

25. Zweig, *Paul Verlaine*, p. 59.

26. A. E. Carter, *Verlaine: A Study in Parallels* (Toronto: University of Toronto Press, 1969), p. 170.

27. George Moore, *Conversations in Ebury Street* (1924), in Moore, *Collected Works*, vol. 20, pp. 187–189.

28. Eve Kosofsky Sedgwick, "Queer Performativity: Henry James's *Art of the Novel*," *GLQ* 1, no. 1 (1993): 14.

29. Lionel Johnson, "The Dark Angel," in *The Complete Poems of Lionel*

*Johnson,* edited by Iain Fletcher (London: Unicorn Press, 1953), p. 65. Johnson's poetry is quoted from this edition throughout.

30. Lord Alfred Douglas, *Poems* (Paris: Mercure de France, 1896), p. 108. Douglas's poetry is quoted from this edition throughout.

31. Oscar Wilde, *The Picture of Dorian Gray* (1891), in *The Complete Works of Oscar Wilde* (New York: Harper and Row, 1989), p. 29. Unless otherwise indicated, Wilde's works are quoted from this edition.

32. Richard Ellmann, *Oscar Wilde* (New York: Knopf, 1988), p. 139.

33. Oscar Wilde, *De Profundis* (letter to Lord Alfred Douglas, 1897), in *The Letters of Oscar Wilde,* edited by Rupert Hart-Davis (New York: Harcourt, Brace, and World, 1962), p. 486. All excerpts from *De Profundis* are quoted from this edition, which is hereafter cited in the text as *Letters.*

34. Hugh Walker, "The Birth of a Soul," *The Hibbert Journal* 3 (1905): 765. Others, however, were outraged, not only by Wilde, but also by Walker. In response to Walker, see William Valentine Kelley's gloriously alliterative diatribe in the Max Nordau style, "The Consummate Flower of Aestheticism": "That Oscar Wilde is the typical aesthete is confirmed to us by the fact that he is a preposterous megalomaniac, suffering with a tympanitic tumefaction of the organ of self-esteem" (*Methodist Review* 89 [1907]: 455; for round two, see Kelley's essay "A Romantic Christ," ibid., pp. 788–801).

35. A description of Winsome Brookes in Ronald Firbank's *Vainglory* (1915), in *3 More Novels* (New York: New Directions, 1986), p. 16.

36. See also Lord Alfred Douglas's letter to W. T. Stead at the time of Wilde's trials: "Certain it is that persecution will no more kill this instinct in a man who has it, than it killed the faith of Christian martyrs" (quoted in H. Montgomery Hyde, ed., *The Trials of Oscar Wilde* [London: William Hodge, 1948], p. 361).

## 2. Huysmans Mystérique

1. This is not at all unusual, even though Huysmans lived until 1907—after the publication in German of Freud's *Interpretation of Dreams* and the Dora case. Freud was not translated into French until much later, and his influence spread much more quickly in England and America than in France. See Martha Noel Evans, *Fits and Starts: A Genealogy of Hysteria in Modern France* (Ithaca: Cornell University Press, 1991), p. 90.

2. From the "Préface" to *A Rebours,* written twenty years after the novel; in J.-K. Huysmans, *Oeuvres Complètes de J.-K. Huysmans* (Paris: Crés, 1928–1934), vol. 7, p. xxv. Unless otherwise indicated, Huysmans' works are quoted from this edition. All translations mine.

3. All the quotations in this paragraph are drawn from Huysmans' letter to Léon Leclaire, 29 April 1904, quoted in Robert Baldick, *The Life of J.-K. Huysmans* (Oxford: Clarendon Press, 1955), p. 330.

4. Georges Bataille, himself a master of the fragmented and erotic text, is especially interesting as a Freudian descendent of Huysmans; in fact, like Durtal, he wrote a book on Gilles de Rais. Regarding morose delectation and Saint Teresa, see Bataille's chapter "Mysticism and Sensuality" in *Erotism* (1957), translated by Mary Dalwood (San Francisco: City Lights, 1986), pp. 221–251. See also Jacques Lacan's commentary on Saint Teresa from his book *Encore* (1975), in *Feminine Sexuality: Jacques Lacan and the "Ecole Freudienne,"* translated by Jacqueline Rose (New York: Norton, 1986), pp. 138–148, and Julia Kristeva's chapter on sublime Eros and "holy madness" in *Tales of Love* (1983), translated by Leon S. Roudiez (New York: Columbia University Press, 1987), pp. 57–100.

5. Alexandre Axenfeld, *Traité des Névroses,* second edition (Paris: Baillière, 1883), p. 1068; my translation. On Axenfeld and Bouchut, see Huysmans' letter to Zola of 25 May 1884 in J.-K. Huysmans, *Lettres Inédites à Emile Zola,* edited by Pierre Lambert (Geneva: Droz, 1953), p. 103.

6. Jan Goldstein, "The Uses of Male Hysteria: Medical and Literary Discourse in Nineteenth-Century France," *Representations* 34 (1991): 134–165.

7. Letters of 15 January and 5 February 1866, quoted in Claude Pichois, *Baudelaire,* translated by Graham Robb (London: Hamish Hamilton, 1989), pp. 341–342.

8. Rémy de Gourmont, *Selected Writings,* edited and translated by Glenn S. Burne (Ann Arbor: University of Michigan Press, 1966), p. 147.

9. J.-K. Huysmans, *Lettres Inédites à Arij Prins,* edited by Louis Gillet (Geneva: Droz, 1977), p. 222. Huysmans' letters to Prins are quoted from this edition throughout. All translations mine.

10. Friedrich Nietzsche, *The Antichrist* (1888), translated by Anthony M. Ludovici (New York: Russell and Russell, 1964), pp. 202–203.

11. Max Nordau, *Degeneration* (1892; first English translation, 1895) (New York: Howard Fertig, 1968), p. 43.

12. Jan Goldstein, "The Hysteria Diagnosis and the Politics of Anticlericalism in Late Nineteenth-Century France," *Journal of Modern History* 54 (1982): 238.

13. D.-M. Bourneville's preface to *La Possession de Jeanne Fery* (1886), quoted in Goldstein, "Hysteria Diagnosis," p. 236.

14. R. P. G. Hahn, "Les Phénomènes Hystériques et les Révélations de Sainte Thérèse," *Revue des Questions Scientifiques* 14 (1883): 77, 82. Translations mine.

15.  Rae Beth Gordon, *Ornament, Fantasy, and Desire in Nineteenth-Century French Literature* (Princeton: Princeton University Press, 1992), p. 223.

16.  Ibid., pp. 216, 221.

17.  Letter to Jean Lorrain, 15 April 1891, in J.-K. Huysmans, *The Road from Decadence* [a selection of Huysmans' letters], edited and translated by Barbara Beaumont (Columbus: Ohio State University Press, 1989), p. 109.

18.  Letter to Theodore Hannon, March-April 1883, in *Lettres à Théodore Hannon* (Paris: Pirot, 1985), p. 271; and letter to Emile Zola, 25 May 1884, in Huysmans, *Zola,* p. 103. Translations mine.

19.  Letter to Dr. Paul Sérieux, 15 May 1893, in Huysmans, *Road from Decadence,* p. 131.

20.  Quoted in Antony Copley, *Sexual Moralities in France, 1780–1980* (London: Routledge, 1989), p. 140.

21.  On "pearls," see letters to Arij Prins, 26 November 1889 and 19 February 1890, pp. 180, 184.

22.  Note also that Huysmans is wont to mention Hercules and circus strongmen (Miss Urania is a circus trapeze artist) in his accounts of modern-day sodomy; see, for example, his letter to Arij Prins, 21 September 1890, p. 204. See also his 1896 letter to André Raffalovich, in Huysmans, *The Road from Decadence,* pp. 157–158.

23.  Letter to Arij Prins, 6 February 1890, p. 182.

24.  In his confession in *En Route,* Durtal mentions this incident, admitting that "he had defiled a host which that woman, saturated with satanism, concealed about her" (92).

25.  Letter to Arij Prins, 19 February 1890, p. 184. Huysmans describes his researches into the "world of sodomy" again in the 1896 letter to André Raffalovich cited in n. 22.

26.  Letter to Arij Prins, 26 November 1889, p. 180.

27.  Letters to Arij Prins, 15 June, 21 July, and 19 February 1890, pp. 184, 195–196.

28.  Letter to Arij Prins, 30 September 1891, p. 231.

29.  Georges Bataille, *The Trial of Gilles de Rais* (1965), translated by Richard Robinson (Los Angeles: Amok, 1991), p. 13.

30.  Charles Baudelaire, "La Chambre Double" (1862), in *Oeuvres Complètes* (Paris: Gallimard, 1961), pp. 233–235. Translations mine.

31.  It should also be noted that Huysmans explicitly identified with Lydwina during his final bouts with cancer of the jaw; he suffered excruciating pain, his mouth literally collapsed, and he underwent surgery that can only be described as macabre. "And basically nothing is more dangerous than rejoicing in pain," he wrote in a letter to Myriam Harry a few months before his death, "and I am paying for, with no regrets, the pages of *St Lydwine*

and *Les Foules de Lourdes*" (Huysmans, *Road from Decadence*, pp. 232–233).

## 3. Pater Dolorosa

1. Lionel Johnson, "Walter Pater" (1902), *The Complete Poems of Lionel Johnson* (London: Unicorn Press, 1953), p. 269.

2. Walter Pater, *The Renaissance* (1873) (London: Macmillan, 1910), p. 235. Excerpts from *The Renaissance* throughout are quoted from this edition, whose text follows that of the third; hereafter cited in my text as *Renaissance*.

3. Paul Elmer More, "Walter Pater," in *The Drift of Romanticism* (New York: Houghton Mifflin, 1913), p. 108; T. S. Eliot, "Arnold and Pater," in *Selected Essays* (London: Faber and Faber, 1932), pp. 354, 356.

4. See R. M. Seiler, ed., *Walter Pater: The Critical Heritage* (London: Routledge and Kegan Paul, 1980), p. 92.

5. Oscar Wilde, review of *Appreciations* (1890), reprinted in R. M. Seiler, ed., *Walter Pater: A Life Remembered* (Calgary: University of Calgary Press, 1987), p. 56; George Moore, *Confessions of a Young Man* (1889) (Montreal: McGill–Queen's University Press, 1972), p. 166.

6. Reprinted in Seiler, *A Life Remembered*, p. 176.

7. Walter Pater, "Anteros," in "Walter Pater's Portrait of Marguerite of Valois, Queen of Navarre: The Hitherto Unpublished Chapters IX and X of *Gaston de Latour*," edited by Gerald Monsman, *Victorians Institute Journal* (Fall 1992): 288.

8. See Michael Levey, *The Case of Walter Pater* (London: Thames and Hudson, 1978), p. 99, and Richard Dellamora, *Masculine Desire* (Chapel Hill: University of North Carolina Press, 1990), p. 277.

9. Quoted in Levey, *Case of Walter Pater*, p. 63. Levey also finds in Pater's affection for Joseph Haydock traces of Marius's friendship with Flavian and Emerald Uthwart's friendship with James. See also Thomas Wright, *The Life of Walter Pater* (1907) (New York: Haskell House, 1969), vol. 1, pp. 96–97.

10. Quoted in Wright, *Life of Walter Pater*, vol. 2, p. 22. No correspondence between Jackson and Pater has survived, and Levey makes a vague claim that "many of the anecdotes reported by Wright have a dubious air" (Levey, *Case of Walter Pater*, p. 220).

11. Quoted in Billie Andrew Inman, "Estrangement and Connection: Walter Pater, Benjamin Jowett, and William M. Hardinge," in Laurel Brake and Ian Small, eds., *Pater in the 1990s* (Greensboro, N.C.: ELT Press, 1991), pp. 7–8.

12. W. H. Mallock, *The New Republic* (New York: Scribner, Welford, and Armstrong, 1878), pp. 271–272.

13. Graham Hough, *The Last Romantics* (London: Duckworth, 1949), pp. 169, 170.

14. Wright, *Life of Walter Pater,* vol. 2, p. 28.

15. A. C. Benson, *Walter Pater* (London: Macmillan, 1906), p. 111.

16. Walter Pater, "Dante Gabriel Rossetti" (1883), in *Appreciations* (1889) (London: Macmillan, 1910), pp. 220–221.

17. Charles Baudelaire, *La Fanfarlo* (1847), in *Oeuvres Complètes* (Paris: Gallimard, 1961), p. 509. Translation mine.

18. U. C. Knoepflmacher, *Religious Humanism and the Victorian Novel* (Princeton: Princeton University Press, 1965).

19. Hilary Fraser, *Beauty and Belief* (Cambridge: Cambridge University Press, 1986), p. 213. Unfortunately, Fraser later undermines her own argument by reasserting a notion of "normative" Christianity and claiming that Pater and Wilde's "versions of Christ have little to do with historical Christianity and are decidedly heterodox" (226), though she does not point out whose "historical Christianity" she is referring to or what this "heterodox" quality entails.

20. Reprinted in Seiler, *A Life Remembered,* p. 197.

21. Wright, *Life of Walter Pater,* vol. 1, p. 244.

22. David Hilliard, "Unenglish and Unmanly: Anglo-Catholicism and Homosexuality," *Victorian Studies* 25 (1982): 184.

23. Mallock, *New Republic,* p. 273.

24. Reprinted in Seiler, *A Life Remembered,* p. 192.

25. Walter Pater, "Prosper Mérimée" (1890), in *Miscellaneous Studies* (1895) (New York: Macmillan, 1900), p. 4.

26. Walter Pater, "Robert Elsmere" (1888), in *Essays from "The Guardian"* (1901) (London: Macmillan, 1910), p. 68.

27. Quoted in Wright, *Life of Walter Pater,* vol. 1, p. 183.

28. John Addington Symonds, *The Letters of John Addington Symonds,* edited by Herbert M. Schueller and Robert L. Peters (Detroit: Wayne State University Press, 1968), vol. 2, p. 273.

29. Frederick George Stephens, review in *Athenaeum,* 23 June 1873, reprinted in Seiler, *Critical Heritage,* p. 85.

30. Walter Pater, *Imaginary Portraits* (1887) (London: Macmillan, 1910), p. 136.

31. Walter Pater, *Greek Studies* (1895) (London: Macmillan, 1910), p. 272; *Renaissance,* p. 209.

32. Lesbianism and female friendship are notably absent from this scenario. In fact, Pater was explicit about his distaste for the Amazon, whom he

referred to dismissively as a "survival from a half-animal world," even though he admired the "half-animal" quality in his male undergraduates. See Walter Pater, *Plato and Platonism* (London: Macmillan, 1893), p. 233.

33. Jonathan Loesberg, *Aestheticism and Deconstruction: Pater, Derrida, and De Man* (Princeton: Princeton University Press, 1991), p. 187.

34. Dellamora, *Masculine Desire,* p. 140.

35. See also Sigmund Freud, *Leonardo da Vinci and a Memory of His Childhood* (1910), translated by Alan Tyson (New York: W. W. Norton, 1964), p. 60.

36. Plato, *The Symposium,* translated by William S. Cobb (Albany: State University of New York Press, 1993), p. 47.

37. Walter Pater, *Marius the Epicurean* (1885) (Oxford: Oxford University Press, 1986), p. 212. Excerpts from *Marius the Epicurean* are quoted from this edition throughout; hereafter cited in the text as *Marius.*

38. An important exception is Michael Ryan's psychoanalytic reading "Narcissus Autobiographer: *Marius the Epicurean,*" *ELH* 43 (1976): 184–208. Ryan emphasizes, as I do, the importance of Marius's mother and the concept of home.

39. The white bird also recalls the wings of the dove that open *The Renaissance,* Pater's first fruit—not to mention the bird trapped in a church, Pater's metaphor for sterile Christian dogma in his portrait of Watteau: "The bird taken captive by the ill-luck of a moment, retracing its issueless circle till it expires within the close vaulting of that great stone church" (Pater, *Imaginary Portraits,* p. 14). The word "issueless" is especially resonant in the context of Pater's work, given the frequency of maternal metaphors in his writing on Christianity.

40. Walter Pater, "Notre-Dame d'Amiens," in Pater, *Miscellaneous Studies,* p. 92.

41. This passage is also autobiographical, since Pater slighted his mother the last time he saw her before she died.

42. Charles Kains-Jackson, "The New Chivalry" (1894), reprinted in Brian Reade, comp., *Sexual Heretics* (London: Routledge and Kegan Paul, 1970), pp. 40–46. See also Dellamora, *Masculine Desire,* pp. 157–158.

43. Walter Pater, *Gaston de Latour* (1896) (London: Macmillan, 1910), p. 62.

44. Walter Pater, "Denys l'Auxerrois" (1886), in Pater, *Imaginary Portraits,* p. 58.

45. Walter Pater, "Apollo in Picardy" (1893), in Pater, *Miscellaneous Studies,* p. 122; hereafter cited in the text as "Apollo."

46. Dellamora, *Masculine Desire,* p. 190.

## 4. *The Temptation of Saint Oscar*

1. Oscar Wilde, "The Rise of Historical Criticism" (1908), in *The Complete Works of Oscar Wilde* (New York: Harper and Row, 1989), p. 1109. Unless otherwise indicated, Wilde's works are quoted from this edition.

2. Oscar Wilde, *De Profundis,* in *The Letters of Oscar Wilde,* edited by Rupert Hart-Davis (New York: Harcourt, Brace, and World, 1962), p. 468. All excerpts from *De Profundis* are quoted from this edition, which is hereafter cited in the text as *Letters.*

3. Published in Ian Small, *Oscar Wilde Revalued* (Greensboro, N.C.: ELT Press, 1993), p. 131; see also a similar phrasing in *The Picture of Dorian Gray,* p. 161.

4. As quoted by Percival W. H. Almy in Oscar Wilde, *Oscar Wilde: Interviews and Recollections,* edited by E. H. Mikhail (New York: Barnes and Noble, 1979), vol. 1, p. 231.

5. See also his letter to Mrs. R. B. Cunninghame Graham, 30 June 1889: "I want to stand apart, and look on, but being neither for God nor for his enemies" (Oscar Wilde, *More Letters of Oscar Wilde,* edited by Rupert Hart-Davis [New York: Vanguard Press, 1985], p. 83).

6. Reprinted in Karl Beckson, ed., *Oscar Wilde: The Critical Heritage* (New York: Barnes & Noble, 1970), p. 314.

7. R. B. Cunninghame Graham, reprinted ibid., p. 257.

8. In my view, the most sophisticated reading of Wilde's religious opinions—and the least read—is Hilary Fraser's chapter on Pater and Wilde in *Beauty and Belief* (Cambridge: Cambridge University Press, 1986), pp. 183–228. Fraser analyzes Wilde's beliefs, rather than dismissing them, and positions him within the Victorian tradition of religious aesthetics from the Oxford movement on. Both she and George Woodcock, in *Oscar Wilde: The Double Image* (1949) (Montreal: Black Rose Books, 1989), argue for Wilde's sincerity, though they tend to see his wit and his sexuality as incommensurate with faith. Guy Willoughby has written an entire book on the religious allusions in Wilde's texts, with especially insightful readings of *Salomé* and "The Ballad of Reading Gaol," but the book is remarkable for its refusal to discuss sex, history, or Wilde's life; see Guy Willoughby, *Art and Christhood: The Aesthetics of Oscar Wilde* (Rutherford, N.J.: Fairleigh Dickinson University Press, 1993). Other essays and books that deal specifically with Wilde's religious opinions (Knight, Nassaar, Gordon, Clark, Albert, Gray, Quintus, and Paterson, to name a few) are, by comparison, sketchy.

9. Quoted by Max Beerbohm in his *Letters to Reggie Turner,* edited by Rupert Hart-Davis (London: Rupert Hart-Davis, 1964), p. 36.

10. Oscar Wilde, "The Critic as Artist," pp. 1047, 1052; "Phrases and Philosophies for the Use of the Young," p. 1205.

11. "The artistic critic, like the mystic, is an antinomian always" (Wilde, "Critic as Artist, p. 1052). See also *The Picture of Dorian Gray,* p. 106: "Mysticism, with its marvellous power of making common things strange to us, and the subtle antinomianism that always seems to accompany it, moved him for a season"; and *De Profundis:* "I am a born antinomian. I am one of those who are made for exceptions, not for laws" in *Letters,* p. 468.

12. Wilde, *Oscar Wilde,* vol. 1, p. 13.

13. André Gide, *Oscar Wilde: In Memoriam (Reminiscences)* (1901, 1905), translated by Bernard Frechtman (New York: Philosophical Library, 1949), p. 7.

14. Wilde, *Oscar Wilde,* vol. 2, p. 237.

15. Beerbohm, *Letters to Reggie Turner,* p. 32.

16. As quoted by Robert Sherard in Wilde, *Oscar Wilde,* vol. 2, p. 337.

17. Coulson Kernahan, *In Good Company* (1917), reprinted ibid., p. 316.

18. Ibid.

19. Reprinted in Wilde, *Oscar Wilde,* vol. 2, p. 336.

20. Richard Ellmann, *Oscar Wilde* (New York: Knopf, 1988), p. 76.

21. As quoted by Robert Sherard in Oscar Wilde, *Oscar Wilde,* vol. 2, p. 337.

22. Oscar Wilde, *Wilde's Oxford Notebooks,* edited by Philip E. Smith II and Michael S. Helfand (Oxford: Oxford University Press, 1989), p. 102.

23. Wilde, *Oxford Notebooks,* p. 102.

24. Quoted in Ellmann, *Oscar Wilde,* p. 583.

25. W. S. Gilbert, *Patience; or Bunthorne's Bride* (1881) (New York: Doubleday, Page, 1902), pp. 24, 26.

26. G. S. Street, *The Autobiography of a Boy* (London: Elkin Mathews, 1894), p. 53–54.

27. [Robert Hichens], *The Green Carnation* (New York: D. Appleton, 1894), pp. 89, 122, 207; hereafter cited in the text as Hichens.

28. Walter Bagehot, "Edward Gibbon" (1856), in *The Collected Works of Walter Bagehot,* edited by Norman St. John-Stevas, vol. 1 (Cambridge: Harvard University Press, 1965), pp. 362–363. He adds, furthermore, that "every sound mind would prefer a beloved child to produce a tail, a hide of hair, and a taste for nuts, in comparison with transubstantiation, wax-candles, and a belief in the glories of Mary."

29. Quoted in Ellen Moers, *The Dandy: Brummell to Beerbohm* (London: Secker and Warburg, 1960), p. 270.

30. Ibid., p. 265.

31. J. Barbey d'Aurevilly, *Une Histoire sans Nom* (Paris: Lemerre, 1889), pp. 63–64. Translation mine.

32. Wilde, *Oscar Wilde*, vol. 1, p. 231.

33. Ibid., p. 224.

34. E. R. Norman, *Anti-Catholicism in Victorian England* (New York: Barnes and Nobel, 1968), p. 15.

35. Quoted in Robert J. Klaus, *The Pope, the Protestants, and the Irish: Papal Aggression and Anti-Catholicism in Mid-Nineteenth Century England* (New York: Garland, 1987), pp. 284–285.

36. From his essay *Vaticanism* (1875), reprinted in Norman, *Anti-Catholicism*, p. 102.

37. Klaus, *Pope*, pp. 131, 228.

38. Quoted in Ian Ker, *John Henry Newman* (Oxford: Clarendon Press, 1988), pp. 255, 363.

39. Reprinted in Norman, *Anti-Catholicism*, p. 194.

40. Charles Kingsley, *Charles Kingsley: His Letters and Memories of His Life*, edited by Frances Kingsley (London: Kegan Paul, 1881), vol. 1, p. 201.

41. "Parsons in Petticoats," *Punch* 48 (10 June 1865): 239.

42. David Hilliard, "Unenglish and Unmanly: Anglo-Catholicism and Homosexuality," *Victorian Studies* 25 (1982): 181–210.

43. Quotations from Faber are taken from Ronald Chapman, *Father Faber* (London: Burns and Oates, 1961), p. 48.

44. On King, see Norman, *Anti-Catholicism*, pp. 109–118, and G. W. E. Russell, *Edward King, the Sixtieth Bishop of Lincoln* (London, 1912), p. 27. On his homosexuality, see especially Lord Elton, *Edward King and Our Times* (London: Geoffrey Bles, 1958), pp. 52–56.

45. Wilde, *Oscar Wilde*, vol. 1, pp. 6–8.

46. From a "No Popery" sermon by William Bennett reprinted in Norman, *Anti-Catholicism*, p. 173.

47. Richard Hofstadter, *"The Paranoid Style in American Politics" and Other Essays* (1965) (Chicago: University of Chicago Press, 1979), p. 21.

48. For Chesterton's anatomy of conversion, see his book *The Catholic Church and Conversion* (London: Burns, Oates, 1926), especially pp. 57–64.

49. Reprinted in Norman, *Anti-Catholicism*, pp. 171, 174.

50. Patrick Murphy, *Popery in Ireland; or Confessionals, Abductions, Nunneries, Fenians, and Orangemen* (London: Jarrold, n.d.), pp. 73–75, 225–226.

51. Reprinted in Wilde, *Oscar Wilde*, vol. 1, p. 13.

52. Quoted in Ellmann, *Oscar Wilde*, p. 65.

53. Wilde, *Oscar Wilde*, vol. 2, pp. 337, 381.

54. *Teleny* [attributed to "Oscar Wilde and Others"], edited by John McRae (London: GMP, 1986), p. 140.

55. Michel Foucault, *The History of Sexuality,* vol. 1 (1976), translated by Robert Hurley (New York: Vintage, 1990), p. 104.

56. *Teleny,* p. 140.

57. Wilde, *Oscar Wilde,* vol. 1, p. 193.

58. William Hogan, quoted in *The Confessional Unmasked* (Protestant Evangelical Mission and Electoral Union, 1867), p. 37.

59. See Walter Arnstein, *Protestant versus Catholic in Mid-Victorian England: Mr. Newdegate and the Nuns* (Columbia: University of Missouri Press, 1982), p. 89.

60. Quoted in James Bentley, *Ritualism and Politics in Victorian Britain: The Attempt to Legislate for Belief* (Oxford: Oxford University Press, 1978), pp. 30–33.

61. Quoted in *The Priest in Absolution: A Criticism and Denunciation* (anonymous pamphlet originally published in England; New York: Peter Eckler, n.d.), p. 35.

62. Quoted in Walter Walsh, *The Secret History of the Oxford Movement* (London: Church Association, 1899), p. 98

63. Eve Kosofsky Sedgwick, *Epistemology of the Closet* (Berkeley: University of California Press, 1990), pp. 163–167. In her discussions of binarisms such as paranoia/cognition, secrecy/disclosure, and abstraction/figuration, Sedgwick touches on the dialectical relationship between secrecy and confession. On the "open secret," she draws on D. A. Miller's chapter "Secret Subjects, Open Secrets" in *The Novel and the Police* (Berkeley: University of California Press, 1988): "And the phenomenon of the 'open secret' does not, as one might think, bring about the collapse of those binarisms and their ideological effects, but rather attests to their fantasmatic recovery" (207). Miller makes passing reference to Wilde's remark in *Dorian Gray* that the commonest thing is delightful if one only hides it (195). I would add to Miller's discussion, however, an analysis of the way empty secrets may be deployed with conscious irony, as they sometimes seem to be in Wilde's fiction.

64. Miller, "Secret Subjects," p. 206.

65. Foucault, *Sexuality,* p. 59.

66. Quoted in H. Montgomery Hyde, ed., *The Trials of Oscar Wilde* (London: William Hodge, 1948), p. 339.

67. Quoted in Ellmann, *Oscar Wilde,* p. 463.

68. Jonathan Dollimore, "Different Desires: Subjectivity and Transgression in Wilde and Gide," *Textual Practice* 1 (1987): 65–66. To Dollimore's

belief that Wilde is more "sincere" or more "natural" in the prison letter, I would have to say, as does Lord Henry, that being natural is simply a pose.

69. Paul de Man, *Allegories of Reading* (New Haven: Yale University Press, 1979), p. 286.

## 5. Priests and Acolytes

1. Quoted in Robert Bernard Martin, *Gerard Manley Hopkins: A Very Private Life* (New York: Putnam, 1991), p. 88.

2. Digby Mackworth Dolben, *The Poems of Digby Mackworth Dolben,* edited by Robert Bridges (London: Oxford University Press, 1911), p. 3.

3. Quoted in Martin, *Gerald Manley Hopkins,* p. 84.

4. Samuel Butler, *The Way of All Flesh* (1903) (Baltimore: Penguin, 1966), pp. 256, 260, 287.

5. Edmund John, "The Acolyte," in *The Flute of Sardonyx: Poems* (London: H. Jenkins, 1913), pp. 25–29.

6. Cuthbert Wright, *One Way of Love* (London: Elkin Mathews, 1915), p. 53. Incidentally, this volume also contains a homoerotic poem on *Parsifal* (in imitation of Verlaine).

7. Rev. E. E. Bradford, "Boy-Love," in *"The New Chivalry" and Other Poems* (London: Kegan Paul, Trench, Trubner, 1918), p. 31.

8. Octave Mirbeau, *Sébastien Roch* (1890) (Paris: Charpentier et Fasquelle, 1906), p.157. Translation mine.

9. H. Montgomery Hyde, ed., *The Trials of Oscar Wilde* (London: William Hodge, 1948), pp. 121–122.

10. Letter to Ada Leverson, December 1894, in Oscar Wilde, *The Letters of Oscar Wilde,* edited by Rupert Hart-Davis (New York: Harcourt, Brace, and World, 1962), p. 379.

11. Hyde, *Trials,* pp. 166–167.

12. [John Francis Bloxam], "The Priest and the Acolyte," *The Chameleon* (1894), p. 29.

13. See J. Z. Eglinton, "The Later Career of John Francis Bloxam," *International Journal of Greek Love* 1, no. 2 (1966): 40–42, and David Hilliard, "Unenglish and Unmanly: Anglo-Catholicism and Homosexuality," *Victorian Studies* 25 (1982): 198.

14. Letter to André Raffalovich, 10 February 1899, in Peter J. Vernon, "The Letters of John Gray" (doctoral thesis, University of London, 1976), p. 175.

15. Quoted in Violet Wyndham, *The Sphinx and Her Circle: A Biographical Sketch of Ada Leverson, 1862–1933* (London: André Deutsch, 1963), p. 105.

16. John Gray, "The Barber," in *The Poems of John Gray,* edited by Ian Fletcher (Greensboro, N.C.: ELT Press, 1988), p. 25. Gray's poetry is quoted from this edition throughout.

17. Letter to Pierre Louÿs (originally in French), 24 November 1892, in Peter J. Vernon, "John Gray's Letters to Pierre Louÿs," *Revue de Littérature Comparée* 53 (1979): 97. Vernon's translation.

18. Jerusha Hull McCormack, *John Gray: Poet, Dandy, and Priest* ([Waltham, Mass.]: Brandeis University Press, 1991), pp. 51, 97.

19. Wilde, *Letters,* p. 173n4.

20. For a discussion of homosexuality in *The Blackmailers,* see Laurence Senelick, "The Homosexual as Villain and Victim in Fin-de-Siècle Drama," *Journal of the History of Sexuality* 4, no. 2 (1993): 207–212.

21. Marc-André Raffalovich, *Uranisme et Unisexualité* (Paris: Masson, 1896), p. 138. Hereafter cited in the text as *Uranisme;* all translations mine.

22. Letter to Raffalovich, 5 March 1900, in Vernon, "Letters of John Gray," p. 185.

23. Quoted in Edwin Essex, "The Canon in Residence," in Brocard Sewell, ed., *Two Friends* (Aylesford, England: Saint Albert's Press, 1963), p. 160.

24. Peter F. Anson, "Random Reminiscences of John Gray and André Raffalovich," in Sewell, *Two Friends,* pp. 139, 140.

25. Unpublished letters from André Raffalovich to Melville Wright, 15 July, 24 August, 1 October 1915 and 3 February, 7 July, 13 December 1916; and to Francis H. Wright, dated only "Good Friday." National Library of Scotland, Edinburgh.

26. John Gray, *Park* (1932), in *The Selected Prose of John Gray,* edited by Jerusha Hull McCormack (Greensboro, N.C.: ELT Press, 1992), p. 275.

27. Letter to Katherine Bradley, 24 November 1908, in Vernon, "Letters of John Gray," p. 285. McCormack adds that Gray had written another letter to Bradley a month earlier in which he said of his favorite saint, "I love him very much with a firm persuasion that I should now be in hell but for him" (McCormack, *John Gray,* p. 169).

28. Ernest Dowson, *The Letters of Ernest Dowson,* edited by Desmond Flower and Henry Maas (London: Cassell, 1967), pp. 337, 372.

29. McCormack, *John Gray,* p. 158.

30. Walter Shewring, "Two Friends," in Sewell, *Two Friends,* p. 149.

31. Letter to Michael Field, 2 February 1907, in Vernon, "Letters of John Gray," p. 29.

32. Frederick William Rolfe ("Baron Corvo"), *Hadrian the Seventh* (1904) (New York: Dover, 1969), p. 232; hereafter cited in the text as *Hadrian.*

33. He identified with the crab, especially in his fictional incarnation as Nicholas Crabbe, a paradox of self-righteous vituperation on the outside,

sentimentality on the inside: "Crab-like, he instantly shut himself up in his shell, throwing up ramparts and earthworks to conceal and protect his individuality" (Frederick William Rolfe, *The Desire and Pursuit of the Whole* [1909, first published 1953] [New York: Da Capo, 1986], p. 118; excerpts from this novel throughout are quoted from this edition).

34. Frederick William Rolfe, *A History of the Borgias* (New York: Random House, 1931), p. 32.

35. Presumably a wry reference to the Cleveland Street scandal, in which the historical connection between telegraph boys and a certain male brothel became legendary. Telegraph boys pop up in a number of homoerotic texts from the period. See, for example, "On the Appreciation of Trifles," an anonymous essay that follows closely upon the heels of "The Priest and the Acolyte" in *The Chameleon:* "I am sure that we must all constantly feel that we are under the deepest obligations to certain companies, and strangely enough, to the Government officials connected with the Post Office, for filling our streets with the graceful, neatly uniformed figures of those that bear our messages and our telegrams" (58).

36. Frederick William Rolfe, *Letters to James Walsh* (London: Bertram Rota, 1972), p. 9.

37. Frederick William Rolfe, *The Venice Letters* (written 1909–1910), edited by Cecil Woolf (London: Cecil and Amelia Woolf, 1974), p. 46.

38. Frederick William Rolfe, "About Some Friends," in *Stories Toto Told Me* (London: Collins, 1969), p. 215.

39. Frederick William Rolfe, "About the Love Which Is Desire and the Love Which Is Divine," in Rolfe, *Stories Toto Told Me,* p. 235.

40. Frederick William Rolfe, "A Mistake," reprinted in *Frederick Rolfe and Others* (Aylesford: St. Albert's Press, 1961), p. 6.

41. Frederick William Rolfe, "To R. C. A.," in *Collected Poems,* edited by Cecil Woolf (London: Cecil and Amelia Woolf, 1974), p. 32. Rolfe's poetry is quoted from this edition unless otherwise indicated.

42. Frederick William Rolfe and C. H. C. Pirie-Gordon [Prospero and Caliban, pseud.], *Hubert's Arthur* (London: Cassell, 1935), pp. 83–84.

43. Frederick William Rolfe, "The Princess's Shirts" (1906), reprinted in *The Cardinal Prefect of Propaganda* (London: Nicholas Vine, 1957), p. 64. For an earlier, posthumously published version of this story, see "Toto" (n.d.) in *"The Armed Hands" and Other Stories and Pieces,* edited by Cecil Woolf (London: Cecil and Amelia Woolf, 1974), pp. 54–58. In this version the boy is found frozen to death with a half-smile on his face: "They brought him in his naked beauty and laid him like a lily in his mother's arms" (58).

44. See, for example, his poem "Sonnet: A Victim" (1897) in Rolfe, *Col-*

*lected Poems,* or his intention to write another autobiographical fiction entitled *Sebastian Archer,* referred to in Rolfe, *Desire and Pursuit.*

45. Frederick William Rolfe, "Amico di Sandro," in *In His Own Image* (London: John Lane, 1901), p. 156.

46. Letter of 16 March 1908, in Frederick William Rolfe, *Letters to R. M. Dawkins,* edited by Cecil Woolf (London: Nicholas Vane, 1962), p. 119.

47. Frederick William Rolfe, *Don Renato* (written 1909), edited by Cecil Woolf (London: Chatto and Windus, 1963), p. 32.

48. Rolfe, *In His Own Image,* p. 148.

49. Rolfe, *Venice Letters,* p. 31.

50. Quoted in Cecil Woolf, introduction to Rolfe, *Venice Letters,* p. 11.

51. From an unpublished memoir by Montague Summers's friend, John Redwood-Anderson, quoted in Brocard Sewell [Jerome Joseph, pseud.], *Montague Summers: A Memoir* (London: Cecil and Amelia Woolf, 1965), p. 88.

52. This curious title, "secretary and amanuensis," is not my phrase, but Brocard Sewell's (ibid., p. 70). He has evidently lifted it from Ronald Firbank's novel *The Flower beneath the Foot,* where it is applied to the homosexual choirboy Peter Passer, who is clearly being kept by the exiled Count Cabinet. Sewell, a monk who has made a career of writing with quaint circumlocution about a number of homosexual aesthetes, may be trying to indicate here that he knows a certain something that he does not care to tell us. Given that Stuart-Forbes lived with Summers, cared for him, cooked for him, accepted the dedication of one of his books, and spent a lot of time tinkling on the pianoforte, we might well hazard a guess what that certain something might be.

53. Montague Summers, "To a Dead Acolyte," in *"Antinous" and Other Poems* (London: Sisley, 1907), pp. 57–59. Summers's poetry is quoted from this edition throughout.

54. Montague Summers, "The Marquis de Sade," in *Essays in Petto* (London: Fortune Press, 1928), p. 99.

55. Montague Summers, "S. Catherine of Siena," in Summers, *Essays,* p. 174.

56. Montague Summers, "S. Antony of Padua," in Summers, *Essays,* p. 182.

57. This sense of genuine devotion is all that is missing from Paul Davies's wonderful essay "'The Power to Convey the Unuttered': Style and Sexuality in the Work of Ronald Firbank," in Mark Lily, ed., *Lesbian and Gay Writing* (London: Macmillan, 1990), pp. 199–214.

58. Ronald Firbank, *Vainglory* (1915), in *3 More Novels* (New York: New Directions, 1986), p. 92; see also ibid., p. 68.

59. Ronald Firbank, *Concerning the Eccentricities of Cardinal Pirelli* (1926), in *Five Novels* (New York: New Directions, 1981), p. 323; excerpts from this novel throughout are quoted from this edition.

60. Quoted by his friend Lord Berners. See Mervyn Horder, ed., *Ronald Firbank: Memoirs and Critiques* (London: Duckworth, 1977), p. 85.

61. Ronald Firbank, *The Artificial Princess* (1934), in Firbank, *Five Novels,* p. 250.

62. Ronald Firbank, *The Flower beneath the Foot* (1923), in Firbank, *Five Novels,* p. 55.

## Conclusion

1. T. S. Eliot, "A Song for Simeon," in *Collected Poems, 1909–1935* (London: Faber and Faber, 1936), p. 110. Eliot's poetry is quoted from this edition throughout.

2. Djuna Barnes, *Nightwood* (1937) (New York: New Directions, 1961), p. 118.

3. On W. H. Auden's conversion, see Humphrey Carpenter, *W. H. Auden* (London: George Allen and Unwin, 1981), pp. 273–302.

4. Walter Benjamin, "The Work of Art in the Age of Mechanical Reproduction," in *Illuminations,* translated by Harry Zohn (New York: Schocken Books, 1969), p. 242.

5. Walter Pater, *The Renaissance* (1873) (Oxford: Oxford University Press, 1986), p. 153.

# INDEX

Katherine of Sienna
MS